LICENSED TO LIE

LICENSED
TO LIE

Exposing Corruption in the
Department of Justice

Sidney Powell

Licensed to Lie:
Exposing Corruption in the Department of Justice

Hardcover ISBN 978-1-7327676-1-4
Paperback ISBN 978-1-7327676-0-7
LCCN: On file with the Library of Congress

Printed in the United States
10 9 8 7 6 5 4 3 2 1

Second Edition 2018

For more information or to contact the author, please go to
www.SidneyPowell.com

To all those who seek, hallow, and do Justice.

CONTENTS

Licensed to Lie: Exposing Corruption in the Department of Justice is a disturbing, enlightening, and superbly presented account of one of the most dramatic and chilling examples of injustice in American judicial history. Written with the skill of a novelist, the keen eye of a memoirist, and the passion of an early American pamphleteer, Powell takes readers on a journey through an institutional landscape created to protect the innocent and punish the guilty. She reveals a house of "legal" horrors characterized by sacrificing an innocent man, concealing and altering evidence, ignoring the law, and constantly displaying an ego-driven desire to win at all costs. Her message resonates throughout the book: *The greatest human ideal of Justice is only as good as the character of those who administer it, existing only if its guardians are devotees to integrity and fairness.*

Michael Adams, PhD
University Distinguished Teaching Associate Professor of English,
Interim Director, James A. Michener Center for Writers,
University of Texas–Austin

FOREWORD

We Americans are extremely proud of our criminal justice system. We believe it to be the best and fairest in the world. And in many ways it is. We guarantee every criminal defendant an impartial judge, a fair jury and a defense lawyer—at public expense for the many who can't afford one. The prosecution must prove guilt beyond a reasonable doubt, and must do so in a speedy, public trial. And we have a variety of rules governing the collection and presentation of evidence, all designed to ensure that justice is done in every case. But the system only works if the participants follow the rules.

Prosecutors have a particularly strong duty to act fairly because, as the Supreme Court has explained, they are the representatives "not of an ordinary party to a controversy, but of a sovereignty whose obligation to govern impartially is as compelling as its obligation to govern at all; and whose interest, therefore, in a criminal prosecution is not that it shall win a case, but that justice shall be done." In the words of fabled defense lawyer Brendan Sullivan, "[i]f the government is not honest, it can trump even the best efforts of those of us who work in the system."

Sullivan uttered those words in the case against former Senator Ted Stevens, who was convicted after federal prosecutors concealed evidence favorable to the defense and lied about it in court. The conviction was vacated once the government's deception was revealed, but this occurred long after Stevens had lost an election—ending a 40-year Senate career and changing the balance of power in the Senate—as a direct result of the wrongful conviction.

The Stevens case is just one of several high-profile criminal prosecutions engineered by a small cadre of high-ranking United States Department of Justice lawyers. Most of the convictions obtained by the government have been set aside, but not before wasting countless millions of taxpayer dollars and wreaking havoc on the lives and businesses of those charged with federal crimes. The venerable accounting firm of Arthur Andersen was destroyed by a prosecutorial decision to charge the firm, not merely individual partners, with criminal conduct. While the Supreme Court eventually held that the "crime" of which Andersen was convicted was no crime at all—in other words, that Andersen had acted lawfully—the exoneration came too late to save the business or the 85,000 jobs it provided in its various offices world-wide. Other defendants were exonerated after spending time behind bars for conduct that turned out to be entirely lawful.

The Center for Prosecutor Integrity lists the following as some of the most serious types of prosecutorial misconduct:

- Charging a suspect with more offenses than is warranted
- Withholding or delaying the release of exculpatory evidence
- Deliberately mishandling, mistreating, or destroying evidence
- Allowing witnesses they know or should know are not truthful to testify
- Pressuring defense witnesses not to testify
- Relying on fraudulent forensic experts
- During plea negotiations, overstating the strength of the evidence

- Making statements to the media that are designed to arouse public indignation
- Making improper or misleading statements to the jury
- Failing to report prosecutor misconduct when it is discovered.

And why do prosecutors engage in misconduct? The Center provides an answer:

Prosecutors are subjected to a variety of powerful incentives that serve to reward zealous advocacy: the gratitude of victims, favorable media coverage, career promotions, appointment to judgeships, and the allure of high political office.

Much of this behavior is illustrated in the pages of this book, and requires no elaboration. However, two items on the Center for Prosecutor Integrity's list merit a few additional words, as their significance may not be immediately apparent to readers unfamiliar with the criminal justice process.

The first is the growing practice of over-charging, particularly with crimes of dubious validity. One of the bedrock principles of our criminal law is that citizens are entitled to fair notice of what is criminal and what is legal. People can then avoid prosecution by engaging in lawful activities. The right to do what the law does not prohibit, without fear of harassment or punishment, is one of the hallmarks of a free society. One of the fundamental responsibilities of a prosecutor is to charge defendants only with conduct that is clearly criminal. And yet, time and again in these high-profile prosecutions, the United States Department of Justice charged multiple defendants with crimes that simply weren't crimes. In addition to the so-called crime that destroyed Arthur Andersen, the Supreme Court held in rapid succession that the government had obtained convictions in three other cases where the charged conduct wasn't criminal. Nevertheless, the government insisted—and the judges supinely agreed—that the defendants must start serving their time behind bars even as their challenges to their convictions upon these alleged violations were being considered on appeal.

Another important responsibility of prosecutors is to disclose to the defense any exculpatory information of which the government is aware. The Supreme Court announced this as a constitutional requirement in the 1963 case of *Brady v. Maryland*, and it has confirmed its underlying principles many times since. It may not be obvious to the lay reader why the government must provide the defendant with evidence that may undermine the prosecution, so it's worth a brief explanation. Most fundamental is the fact that the government is not an ordinary litigant whose interest lies in winning at all costs. Rather, the government's legitimate interest lies in convicting only those defendants who are proven guilty beyond a reasonable doubt. If the government has evidence that casts doubt on the defendant's guilt, it has every interest in producing that evidence for the jury to consider in reaching its decision. As the Supreme Court noted in *Brady*, "[a]n inscription on the walls of the Department of Justice states the proposition candidly for the federal domain: 'The United States wins its point whenever justice is done its citizens in the courts.'"

Beyond this theoretical justification are important practical reasons for the *Brady* rule: Government agents usually have unimpeded and exclusive access to the crime scene, so they can easily remove and conceal evidence that might contradict the prosecution's case. Police also generally talk to witnesses first and can pressure them to change their story to conform to the prosecution's theory of the case. Prosecutors can, and often do, threaten to charge witnesses as accomplices or co-conspirators if they testify favorably to the defense. As a result, potential exculpatory witnesses invoke the Fifth Amendment to avoid getting themselves into trouble. The government has virtually unhampered control over forensic evidence, as well as its analysis and presentation by experts. Too often these experts turn out to be sloppy or dishonest; many defendants have spent long years behind bars because of incompetent or corrupt forensic scientists employed by law enforcement. Many of those convictions could have been avoided if the jury had been shown the evidence casting doubt on the validity of the expert reports.

While no one openly disputes the validity of the *Brady* rule, many prosecutors see it as a thorn in their sides—an obstacle to overcome rather than a welcome responsibility to be scrupulously observed. Prosecutors want to win, for all the reasons mentioned by the Center for Prosecutor Integrity Report above, and they see *Brady* as an impediment to obtaining a conviction. While there are certainly many honest and fair-minded prosecutors, a disturbing number fail to disclose exculpatory evidence to the defense. Some prosecutors affirmatively and knowingly conceal it.

There was such knowing concealment of exculpatory evidence in the case against Senator Stevens, and his conviction was vacated and the charges against him dismissed. But Senator Stevens was doubly lucky: First, an honest FBI agent broke ranks with his colleagues and the prosecutors in the Department of Justice, and disclosed the government's willful *Brady* violations and lies to the district court. And, second, Emmet Sullivan, the district judge presiding over the case, took the matter seriously and ordered an investigation of the lawyers who had conducted the prosecution. Deeply troubled that "[a]gain and again . . . the Government was caught making false representations"—a polite term for telling bald-faced lies—Judge Sullivan bristled: "The United States Government has an obligation to pursue convictions fairly and in accordance with the Constitution, and when the Government does not meet its obligations to turn over evidence, the system falters."

But what happened in Stevens's case is vanishingly rare. *Brady* violations are extremely difficult to discover because the prosecution has complete control over the evidence gathered by its investigators. Prosecutors know that if they fail to produce exculpatory evidence, no one is likely to find out. Even when the evidence is fortuitously disclosed after the defendant is convicted, judges are very reluctant to order a new trial, so they sweep the evidence under the rug as "immaterial" or "cumulative." Sanctions against prosecutors who violate *Brady* are practically unheard-of and professional discipline is non-existent. As a consequence, there is, as I've said elsewhere, "an epidemic of *Brady* violations abroad in the land."

The author of this book is a former prosecutor turned private practitioner who represented a defendant in one of the high-profile cases discussed in the pages that follow. She was called in by the defense team after the client had been convicted. As she describes her first meeting with the client and his lawyers, they were "[t]raumatized, exhausted, wrung out, meek, and broken" as a result of what had been a brutal trial. "I seemed to have more testosterone than all of them put together," she quips. In truth, Sidney Powell has more testosterone than pretty much any roomful of lawyers, be they men or women. Writing a book like this more than proves it. Not only does she take on, by name, prosecutors and former prosecutors who continue to serve in powerful and responsible positions, she is also relentless in criticizing judges before whom she has practiced for years. Few lawyers have the stones to do this.

Some of what Powell recounts—such as the concealment of evidence and lies told to the court in the Stevens case—is in the public record and not subject to reasonable dispute. As to other matters, she draws on her own experience, the trial record and evidence later uncovered to level serious accusations of malfeasance against the lawyers and judges involved in the high-profile criminal cases she discusses. Readers can make up their own minds as to whether those accusations are supported. It is hoped that those at whom she points the finger will answer the charges. One way or another, however, this book should serve as the beginning of a serious conversation about whether our criminal justice system continues to live up to its vaunted reputation. As citizens of a free society, we all have an important stake in making sure that it does.

Alex Kozinski

– 1 –

THE ULTIMATE TOLL

Sunday, September 26, 2010, began as a typical autumn day in Washington, DC. The trees were dressing in their finery, and the air was becoming crisper by the day. It was time for apples, sweaters, sweatshirts, and football games. In a quiet, northwest corner of the city, there was a mixed neighborhood of construction from the 1950s and older, small bungalows. The bungalows were almost all refurbished now and occupied by young professionals working their way up through the gray bureaucracy we call our national government. Indeed the brick and Cape Cod gray frame cottage on 8th Street Northwest was completely unremarkable to anyone on the outside until midafternoon.

Nick was flopped on the sofa in the downstairs recreation room watching the endless football games. Actually he didn't even know what he was watching. It didn't matter anymore. Around 2:00 p.m., Nick got up and trudged to the laundry room where piles of clothes were lying on the floor. He found a loose razor blade and slashed his left wrist. Then he closed his eyes and slashed his right wrist.

He opened his eyes and watched the blood run down his hands and onto the floor. He felt faint and nauseous, but he didn't think he had cut himself deeply enough to die—at least not quickly. He bled across the basement floor as he looked around for something else to use. He found a heavy-duty power cord, made a noose, and hanged himself.

Not even that worked instantly. His neck did not snap. He was suffocating.

When his wife came downstairs, she found Nick hanging by the power cord, unconscious and bleeding. She called 911, struggled to cut him down, and feverishly administered CPR.

Police cars, a fire truck, and an ambulance arrived at the house by 2:25 p.m. Nicholas Marsh, age thirty-seven, a prosecutor who had worked in the elite Public Integrity Section of the Criminal Division of the US Department of Justice, lay on his basement floor in a pool of blood, a power cord around his neck. He was pronounced dead by the DC coroner at 2:30 p.m. He died of asphyxiation.

⁂

Six weeks earlier, in the great state of Alaska, a group of friends, several with their teenage children, boarded a red and white striped, single-engine amphibious de Havilland DHC-3 Otter airplane for a day of Alaska's finest fishing. It was August 9, 2010—the sky was gray with light rain in the morning, but the weather improved in the afternoon. At take-off, visibility was good with some clouds and patches of blue sky. The friends had enjoyed a hearty lunch at the GCI lodge on Nerka Lake and were ready for an afternoon in the amazing Alaskan outdoors. Some already had on their hip waders. The plane took off about 3:00 p.m. for a nearby fishing camp.

Former NASA Chief Sean O'Keefe and his son Kevin were on board. Young Kevin had the honor of sitting in the copilot's seat, where he went to sleep. He was already exhausted from this outdoor adventure with his dad and their friends. The prominent parents and teenagers in the cabin were busy talking about the day and their plans to bring more business to Alaska. A couple more dozed off as the plane flew beneath the clouds and above the varied terrain. Suddenly the plane banked to the left.

Around 6:00 p.m., the folks at the lodge called the camp to find out when the group planned to return for dinner. The plane had never arrived. With full knowledge that Alaska is the most dangerous state for aircraft, they alerted all rescue services immediately. Other planes and helicopters were dispatched to look for the small plane. Severe weather was coming in fast.

About 7:30 p.m., one of the volunteer searchers in a Cessna plane spotted the aircraft about fifteen minutes from the lodge. The plane had crashed onto a thirty-degree slope of a heavily forested mountainside. A nearby helicopter crew arrived and reported that the aircraft appeared mostly intact. There was no fire, but the left wing was torn off, leaving a gaping hole in the side of the fuselage that was visible from the air. The helicopter crew saw one survivor waving. The chopper landed about 1,000 feet above the accident site, dropped off a technician, and went to pick up a doctor.

Shortly thereafter, the helicopter managed to drop off a doctor and then two emergency medical technicians with medical supplies and equipment. The small rescue team hiked down the mountain in difficult conditions, carrying all they could before the Alaska night and weather closed in on them. When the rescuers reached the crash site, they found five people had died, including the pilot. Sean and Kevin O'Keefe and two others were still alive. The rescue team spent the night helping the four survivors and trying to keep them warm. It took twelve hours for more rescuers to get to the site and evacuate everyone.

The plane was equipped with a terrain awareness warning system (TAWS) that would have visually and audibly notified the pilot to pull up if he was too close to the terrain. The TAWS had been "inhibited" or disabled. There was no cockpit voice recorder or flight data recorder. Three autopsies of the pilot provided no discernable reason for the crash.

The breaking news on every channel hit Alaska and then the entire country like an 8.9 earthquake:

FORMER SENATOR TED STEVENS, BELOVED CHAMPION OF ALASKA, HAS BEEN KILLED NEAR DILLINGHAM, ALASKA, IN THE CRASH OF A PRIVATE PLANE WHILE HE WAS ON A FISHING TRIP WITH LONGTIME FRIENDS.

Ted Stevens, a decorated World War II hero, a former US attorney, and living legend in Alaska, had lost his seat of more than forty years in the US Senate after being found guilty by a jury a year earlier for failing to report alleged gifts on senate forms. It turned out that Senator Stevens was innocent, and the prosecutors from the Public Integrity Section of the Department of Justice had broken ethical rules, disregarded court orders, and violated constitutional law while they hid evidence favorable to his defense—called "*Brady* material."

The defense had caught a few of these shenanigans—enough that US District Judge Emmet Sullivan had become irate. The judge's refusal to ignore or excuse the prosecutors' misconduct dealt a whopping black eye to the Department of Justice in the media. When it became obvious that Judge Sullivan was going to dismiss the indictment against Stevens, Attorney General Eric Holder swooped in, proclaimed he would clean up the department, and moved to dismiss the indictment against Stevens. Holder's pledge, however, was too little and too late for Judge Sullivan.

Holder's proclamations notwithstanding, Judge Sullivan could no longer trust the Department of Justice. The elite prosecutors had lied to him time and time again, often with Deputy Assistant Attorney General Rita Glavin—Acting Attorney General Matthew Friedrich's eyes and ears—observing in the courtroom. Judge Sullivan took the extraordinary step of appointing a special prosecutor, DC attorney Henry Schuelke III, to investigate the prosecutors for possible charges including contempt. This was unprecedented.

Former Senator Stevens, a vigorous and powerful advocate long beloved in Alaska, had publicly pledged to advocate tirelessly for new legislation that would require the government to produce *Brady* information to a defendant in every case and to impose clear penalties for any failure to do so. Stevens didn't want what had happened to him to happen to anyone else. Remarkably the Department of Justice vehemently opposed Stevens's proposal.

The news of the senator's untimely death brought attention once again to his corrupt prosecution and dominated the news for the next several days. Editorials abounded, virtually all of which extolled former Senator Stevens's accomplishments on behalf of Alaska, and they all mentioned the injustice of his prosecution and the misconduct of his prosecutors. Stevens's defense attorneys, led by Brendan Sullivan and Rob Cary of Williams & Connolly, lauded the senator's accomplishments and mourned the toll the corrupt prosecution had taken on him, his career, and his family. "The verdict against him was based on fabricated evidence," Brendan Sullivan reminded everyone. Notably Judge Sullivan had appointed Schuelke, whose investigation into the misconduct of the prosecutors was ongoing "fallout" from the case that "devastated the reputation of the Justice Department's Public Integrity Section. . . ."

"Stevens was innocent, and insisted on fighting the charges," the partners declared. "He remained profoundly affected by the government's misconduct and its implications for others. His fervent hope was that meaningful change would be brought to the criminal justice system so that others would not be mistreated as he was by the very officials whose duty it is to represent the United States justly and fairly."

⁓

The senator's death and the tsunami of renewed publicity of prosecutorial and government misconduct was drowning Nick Marsh. He could hardly breathe. It was all he could do to get up in the mornings and go to the back office to which he had been relegated at the Department of Justice. Nick felt heavier and heavier. He was on the verge of losing his career and possibly his liberty, and he felt as if he had lost his soul. He didn't recognize himself anymore. He needed peace, but he knew it would only get worse for him.

At age thirty-five, the handsome, angular-jawed, dark-haired young prosecutor had been one of the youngest attorneys in the prestigious Public Integrity Section of the Justice Department, nicknamed "PIN." His office was in "Main Justice," the impressive building that occupies a block of expensive real estate between Pennsylvania and Constitution Avenues. He was just a couple of blocks from the White House and next door to the National Archives, which houses the Constitution and the Declaration of Independence.

In the four years Marsh had been a federal prosecutor in PIN, he had led the investigation into public corruption in Alaska. He and his team of fellow PIN prosecutor Edward Sullivan and Alaska Assistant US Attorneys Joseph W. Bottini and James A. Goeke, along with FBI agents, had begun the "Polar Pen" investigation in Alaska in 2004. They had tried and convicted seven high-profile legislators and businessmen, using much of the same evidence that they later used to indict and convict Senator Ted Stevens.

PIN attorneys were the best of the best. They were supposed to adhere to the highest standards. After all, they investigated public officials for public corruption. They had to be above reproach. At the same time, there was so much pressure to win—especially in the high-profile and political prosecutions. These were the cases that would make or break a prosecutor's career. A win in these cases was a first-class ticket to seven-figure incomes in the most prestigious national or international law firms or promotions up the ladder in the Department of Justice, the White House, or the leadership of the FBI.

The pressure had been bad enough two and one-half years ago, before Matthew Friedrich had skyrocketed from his position as an Enron Task Force prosecutor to acting assistant attorney general of the Criminal Division of the Department of Justice. Within days of the arrival of Friedrich and his deputy, Rita Glavin, they intruded heavily into the Stevens case. They began weekly—sometimes daily—meetings with PIN management—Section Chief Bill Welch and Deputy Chief Brenda Morris. Friedrich and Glavin demanded a chart of evidence and defenses, and they summoned all the prosecutors, including the two assistant US attorneys from Alaska, for a presentation to them. For unknown reasons, they rushed to indict Senator Stevens, the longest-serving Republican in the senate.

Friedrich and Glavin took control of the Stevens prosecution and micromanaged it to absurd detail. On the eve of the indictment, they demoted Marsh from first chair to third chair for Stevens's trial. After Friedrich and Glavin took over, the prosecution had nothing but problems, yet no one outside of a small circle within the department would know that until long after it all started to unravel.

Nick knew the truth. When it all fell apart, he and his fellow trial team members became the targets of both an internal department investigation and the independent Schuelke investigation ordered by Judge Sullivan. Nick just knew that the life he loved as a federal prosecutor was over. He feared that everything that went wrong in the Stevens prosecution was going to be hung around his neck. Friedrich and Glavin were way too politically connected and savvy to take the fall. The judge did not name them in his order authorizing Schuelke's investigation. There was no apparent reason to do so. They were not the trial attorneys.

Nick came to realize that being a target of a criminal investigation felt very different from running one. The Schuelke and internal investigations seemed to be taking forever. It had already been more than a year. Six weeks after Senator Stevens's plane crash and death, Nick was numb.

The gruesome suicide of one of Senator Stevens's prosecutors, who was himself under investigation for corruption, dishonesty, and misconduct, sent another shock wave of distress through the department less than two months after the senator's plane crash. Yet again, the department and the wrongful prosecution of Stevens were in the national news.

Virtually everyone who saw the breaking news and knew anything about the Stevens prosecution and the investigation of the prosecutors viewed it as a message: Nicholas Marsh was guilty of hiding evidence that would have exonerated Senator Stevens or he knew more than he had said.

Patton Boggs attorney Robert Luskin was Marsh's lawyer. Luskin spoke to reporters shortly after the news broke, calling Nick's suicide a "terrible tragedy." He spoke of how Nick "loved being a prosecutor" but was "incredibly fearful" that the investigation would end his career with the Justice Department. Luskin claimed they were "on the verge of a successful resolution." He said he expected Schuelke to "exonerate" Marsh.

Luskin's optimistic proclamation was far from the reality Nicholas Marsh had felt and that insiders knew. Maybe Nick's friends and family believed it. Maybe they had to believe it. Maybe it was the only way they could protect their own feelings for the Nick they believed him to be—the Nick they thought they knew, the Nick they had always loved. Publicly, Nick's friends, and Luskin, blamed the pressure and the length of the investigations for his suicide. Luskin added, "The whole process imposed an unbelievable burden on Nick, a burden that in the end, he couldn't bear."

The *Wall Street Journal* reported that "Joshua Berman, a former prosecutor and friend," said that Nick "was anxious that the probe had dragged on but that friends never realized the depth of his worry." Berman said that the delay exacerbated Nick's stress and belief that the result would be "something bad."

No one ever seemed to consider the stress the wrongful prosecution had put on Senator Stevens and his family—for substantially longer than eighteen months—and the continuing effects it had on the remainder of his life and on his family.

Lawyers in the defense bar saw Marsh's suicide as an admission of his own guilt. Lawyers know all too well that prosecutors are almost never punished in any way—regardless of how egregious their conduct is. It is extremely difficult for a wronged defendant to sue a prosecutor. They have immunity from lawsuits because they work on behalf of the "sovereign." They can hide evidence of a defendant's innocence with impunity. They have little concern that it will ever be discovered, and even if it is, they know they will suffer no consequences.

Judges routinely believe prosecutors when they say "we've produced all *Brady* evidence." Judges rarely push back on that assertion, no matter how much the defense complains or what suspicions are raised. Only on the rarest of occasions have prosecutors even been suspended by their bar association for hiding evidence favorable to the defense. And here, Marsh and each of his fellow prosecutors had the luxury of being represented—at the taxpayers' expense—by the best criminal defense lawyers in the country.

Ironically Schuelke's investigation was moving quickly by federal standards. Many people, especially those prosecuted by Acting Attorney General Friedrich and his colleagues when they were on the Enron Task Force, lived with the torment of investigations, criminal charges, repeated prosecutions, and imprisonment for years, even a decade. No one in the department, including Marsh, gave any thought to the toll their tactics and decisions took on others—until, perhaps, Judge Sullivan turned the tables. Being investigated was very different from being the investigator. It was as different as being on opposite ends of a high-powered rifle with a laser sight.

The news reports that afternoon of September 26 and even the headlines the next morning all said almost the same things—not much: "GOVT. PROSECUTOR IN TED STEVENS CASE COMMITS SUICIDE."

They all quoted Robert Luskin's charitable assertion that Marsh would be exonerated by the investigations. Most quoted Assistant Attorney General Lanny Breuer's expression of sympathy at the loss of "this dedicated young attorney" on behalf of the "community of the Department of Justice." Some quoted Marsh's friends. No details were provided from any office investigating the unusual death. The reports seemed canned, and the story faded quickly.

Nicholas Marsh, a brilliant, capable young man, paid the ultimate price for something that should never have happened. He was shattered—by his own choices and those imposed upon him. Either way, he, Senator Stevens, and their families were needlessly sacrificed on opposite sides of the altar of injustice because of the deplorable failure of a system that is supposed to protect all of us.

Before and after the senator's death and Marsh's suicide, Special Prosecutor Schuelke and his partner, William Shields, were working diligently to pull back the cobalt-blue curtain bearing the impressive seal of the Department of Justice. Ultimately Schuelke would reveal shocking facts with ramifications of their own.

As thorough as Schuelke was, he was barely scraping the surface. The illegal and unethical tactics that unseated Senator Stevens, changed the balance of power in the senate, and had now claimed two lives were orchestrated above Nicholas Marsh. Narcissistic and terrifying tacticians were ascending to great power on a foundation and legacy of lies, corruption, and injustice that would take years to uncover. They had long practiced to win at any cost and skillfully buried the truth deep.

– 2 –

THE DANGEROUS FUEL OF
PUBLIC OUTRAGE

By the end of 1999, Houston, Texas, was booming, and the international titan Enron Corporation was consummating more than $20 billion a year in financings on more than one hundred transactions a year. The new baseball stadium in Houston was "Enron Field," and a big "E" gleamed over every entrance. The new Enron skyscraper—rising beside the company's first glass tower—marked the heart of the business district in Houston. Working at Enron meant you were a superstar. Enron's reputation was that it hired only the best and the brightest. It could do things no other company could.

On the inside, however, in the 1990s and accelerating toward the new millennium, Enron had gone from a hard-asset pipeline company to an "energy trading" company. Led primarily by the ambitious Jeffrey Skilling, who eventually became chief executive officer, and Chief Financial Officer Andrew Fastow, Enron pushed for and adopted aggressive "mark to market" accounting methods to value assets instantly. Its financial statements seemed impenetrable. Behind the scenes, Skilling and Fastow also devised extremely creative ways of "monetizing assets"—even when they were just ideas. The world and Wall Street looked on in wonder, and Enron's stock took off.

Viewed as a financial wizard, Enron's young Chief Financial Officer Andy Fastow made the cover of *CFO* magazine in October 1999 because Enron had maintained a growth rate of 15 to 20 percent a year. Fastow received the magazine's award for excellence in capital structure management. By February 2000, Enron was the seventh largest company in the world and had its tentacles in numerous countries and in many areas of business. It bought and sold natural gas; it was constructing power plants; it owned and operated pipelines, but it went far beyond that. Enron was at the cutting edge of everything. Rumors abounded that Enron was building a broadband network. It was already providing telecommunications services and trading commodities. Everything the wonder boys at Enron touched seemed to turn to gold.

Enron Chairman Ken Lay was the most popular man in Houston. Actually he was a celebrity. He and his wife, Linda, were active in many charities, and the "BIG E" itself was funding numerous charities. Lay watched baseball games at Enron Field with past and future presidents. This "son of a preacher man" was riding the biggest wave of his life. He became the largest supporter of and a friend to the president of the United States.

Enron's billions in financings translated into many millions in fees to banks and to its accounting firm, Arthur Andersen LLP. Enron had relationships with more than 120 major financial institutions worldwide. Jeff McMahon, Enron's treasurer since April 1998, coordinated the transactions so that the banks could not cherry-pick the most lucrative deals and shun the lower-value transactions.

In reality, however, the treasurer's office was little more than a front for dealing with the banks. While McMahon might make the initial introduction of a proposed transaction to a financial institution, he did not negotiate or consummate the deals for Enron. The real decisions were made by Fastow and the various divisions, which structured their own transactions to keep Chief Executive Officer Skilling happy.

It didn't hurt any that Andy Fastow's wife, Lea, was from an extremely wealthy Houston family, and they were happily ensconced in a mansion in River Oaks. Fastow, who was close to Skilling, was by far the most "creative" when it came to structuring deals. Fastow handed out so much business that he had a death grip on all the major banks. As Fastow's power within Enron rose, and as its stock price rose with his creativity, he put extraordinary pressure on the banks Enron dealt with to "lend their balance sheets" to help Enron complete deals.

The outside world didn't know it, and even many at Enron were clueless in their cubicles, but McMahon and Fastow were on a collision course. They butted heads regularly over policies and deals and came to loathe each other. Skilling sided with Fastow. Although Skilling was armed with a Harvard business degree and consulting experience with the highly regarded McKinsey think tank, and he undisputedly loved Enron, sound business judgment was not his forte. Painfully narcissistic, Skilling and Fastow enjoyed exaggerated opinions of their omniscience and their omnipotence. They understood neither reasonable limits nor morality. They fed each other's weaknesses in a sick symbiosis.

Fastow was on a roll. He had secretly created what he called the "Raptors," special entities to hide much of Enron's debt—even from many others at Enron. Then he successfully created a separate private equity fund, LJM, which would do business alongside Enron. LJM, named after Fastow's wife and children, appeared to the world to be a separate and lawful entity, with its own board, lawyers, and accountants. And it could have been a lawful entity—had Fastow and his protégé, Michael Kopper, not completely corrupted it for their own gain. To Fastow, it was like having his own $100 million piggy bank. He had accomplished it so easily and successfully, why not do it again—only bigger this time? So he formed LJM2.

Remarkably Enron's board approved Fastow's dual roles as chief financial officer of Enron and as manager of the two LJM funds. The board also approved his extraordinary compensation by the LJM funds.

Merrill Lynch, although a thriving and prestigious financial institution, was not even within the top tier of banks to which Enron turned. Merrill was more conservative and careful than many of its counterparts in the financial industry. However, upon Fastow's insistence, Merrill formed a partnership as a show of support for its client Enron and encouraged its own managing directors to invest in the Merrill partnership, which, in turn, invested in LJM2, along with other major corporations, banks, and huge pension funds. Fastow represented to everyone that LJM2 would invest alongside Enron in energy transactions. That seemed like a good idea—at the time—and, from Enron's perspective, a way to hedge or reduce its own risks in its ventures ranging from pipelines and power plant construction to power trading and weather futures.

Behind the scenes within Enron, McMahon remained concerned about Fastow's dual roles and what McMahon saw as a blatant conflict of interest. In the spring of 2000, McMahon mentioned as much to Rob Furst, Merrill's relationship manager with Enron. Word of McMahon's criticism of Fastow's conflict of interest got back to Fastow, who blew a fuse. McMahon went to Skilling about the problem, thinking that Skilling would back him up. Instead, the next thing McMahon knew, Skilling removed McMahon as Enron's treasurer and reassigned him as the chief commercial officer at a start-up business within Enron, called Enron Networks. Skilling named a new treasurer of Enron, replacing the rules-oriented McMahon with the substantially younger and more "flexible" Ben Glisan, in whom Fastow had already sunk his hooks.

Enron's stock price hit $90 a share in August 2000, and it was in the $80s in early 2001. To most, Enron was an unstoppable titan that led all things innovative. It just grew bigger and bigger. The Wall Street analysts loved it. It always met or exceeded its quarterly earnings projections.

A few who were paying close attention, however, began asking questions. By February 2001, rumors were circulating that something was amiss. Hedge fund manager Jim Chanos had studied Enron's financials, saw trouble, and shorted the stock in a big way. The stock price was edging down. Any rumblings of trouble in Camelot should have been very unsettling, but most dismissed them as corporate jealousy, if not a form of corporate espionage emanating from Enron's competitors.

The word was that Chanos tipped off *Fortune* reporter Bethany McLean. In March 2001, McLean broke away and stepped in front of the pack with a prescient article in *Fortune* magazine. This was the first major news source to challenge the titan and ask the hard question: "Is ENRON OVERPRICED? It's in a bunch of complex businesses. Its financial statements are nearly impenetrable. So why is Enron trading at such a huge multiple? Of fifty-five times its earnings?!"

McLean quoted analysts who jokingly admitted in various ways that they had no clue how Enron actually made its money. They referred to its financials as "impenetrable" or a "black box." McLean reported that Chris Wolfe, the equity market strategist at J.P. Morgan's private bank, who was actually an Enron fan, described Enron as "an earnings at risk story." Prophetically he noted: "If it doesn't meet earnings, [the stock] could implode." McLean reported that in the first nine months of 2000, Enron added $3.9 billion to its debt, raising its debt-to-capital ratio to 50 percent with a total debt of $13 billion, at the same time its cash flow was dropping. No one knew it at the time, but McLean had launched a mortar that started an avalanche.

Fastow and Skilling flew into a rage. McLean had pricked their narcissistic egos. Meanwhile the pressure on them mounted daily. The fabric of fallacy they had so carefully woven was unraveling. "The Goldman Sachs of energy trading" was losing its grip on its publicity, the analysts, and its luster. One question led to another. Fastow knew how bad it really was, and he was increasingly terrified of being exposed—his lies laid bare.

Not even Ken Lay's wheeling and dealings with the Astros Major League Baseball club and friendships with past and current presidents could solve Enron's problem. Fastow had vehemently declared back in March, as reported in McLean's article, "We are not a trading company." Meanwhile the pressure of questions about performance continued to mount as Enron struggled to meet earnings under its new business model. Enron was creating a trading market in virtually anything it could imagine—not just energy related but soon excess broadband capacity and even weather derivatives.

More questions came from Wall Street. Analysts began changing their views. Then in a conference call with investors and analysts, Skilling lost it completely. He called one of them an "asshole" for questioning Enron's release of financial information. That outburst came to haunt Enron, Lay, and Skilling. Something was going on inside the black box, and it couldn't be good. Enron's stock price was dropping.

Too much just didn't add up. Veteran *Wall Street Journal* reporter John Emshwiller was determined to get to the bottom of it. In his many years of reporting, he had learned there was no substitute for doing his homework. Enron had been the darling of Wall Street and the media for several years, but no one could figure out exactly what it was that the company did anymore. It was becoming increasingly clear that its chief financial officer was also heading up a number of related entities that were doing business with Enron. Enron's board had approved Fastow's dual roles, despite what seemed an obvious conflict of interest. Enron's stock price had fallen by half since January—just in the last six months or so.

Then on Tuesday, August 14, 2001, the first bombshell exploded. Skilling, who had been at Enron for eleven years, announced that he was leaving after only six months as chief executive officer. Lay had to step back in as chief executive officer. Analysts began wondering when the next bomb was going to drop. Lay promised that Enron would be more humble and informative than it had been under Skilling.

Emshwiller and fellow reporter Rebecca Smith had been digging. In the August 16, 2001, edition of the *Wall Street Journal*, a headline read: "ENRON'S SKILLING CITES STOCK-PRICE PLUNGE AS MAIN REASON FOR LEAVING CEO POST." Emshwiller and Smith reported that Skilling's unexpected departure from the company, ostensibly "for personal reasons," was "deeply enmeshed with feelings that he had failed in a crucial business area during his brief tenure as CEO. Calling the company's stock performance a 'kind of ultimate score card,' Mr. Skilling noted that Enron's share price had fallen by some 50% this year." Indeed it had topped $84 a share on the New York Stock Exchange (NYSE) in January, dropped to $40-ish in the last several months, and with Skilling's resignation, fell to $37 during the day, before closing back around $40.

On August 28, Emshwiller and Smith wrote again about Enron's opaque financials, Lay's reassurances, and the billions of dollars in off-balance-sheet transactions that Enron had done in the last two years with Fastow's partnerships. Fastow "quietly ended his ownership and management ties with certain limited partnerships." Lay had said that the "transactions involving Fastow had become a 'lightning rod' for criticism so 'we're better off not doing it.'" Their article concluded with a quote from UBS Warburg analyst Ron Barone that Enron was "certainly under a new kind of pressure." That was the understatement of the year.

With the unfathomable tragedy of September 11, 2001, Enron became irrelevant to the media and the country when the terrorist attacks shocked the world and knocked the United States to its knees. The face of New York City—and the very fabric of this country—were changed forever. It was beyond comprehension. Virtually everyone in New York lost friends or family that day. The trauma of what people experienced in person, or even just saw on television, was more than many could process. The world was stunned.

The NYSE closed for four days, the longest shutdown since 1933. When it reopened on September 17, everything was being sold. On the first day of trading after 9/11, the NYSE fell 684 points, a 7.1 percent decline, setting a record for the biggest loss in exchange history for one trading day. At the close of trading that Friday, September 21, the Dow Jones was down almost 1,370 points, representing a loss of more than 14 percent. Enron stock fell off a cliff.

To paraphrase Warren Buffet: the tide went out, and Enron was caught swimming naked.

The next explosion rocked the financial world just a few weeks later. Enron announced a $1.01 billion write-down on soured investments, resulting in a $618 million third-quarter loss. At least $35 million of it was tagged to the troublesome Fastow partnerships, involving the "early termination . . . of certain structured finance arrangements." That announcement thoroughly shook "the Street" and confirmed McLean's, Emshwiller and Smith's, and others' worst fears. This wasn't over yet. Fastow declined to be interviewed.

Moody's put Enron's long-term debt "on review for a possible downgrade."

Emshwiller and Smith dug into Enron's Securities and Exchange Commission filings and obtained copies of the private partnership documents, confusing as they were. They reported what they saw: Fastow was getting a management fee of 2 percent of the private funds, and as general partner he was eligible for millions more depending on the funds' performance. Lay had claimed earlier that the LJM arrangements didn't produce any conflicts of interest, but the reporters found the LJM2 offering document and reported that it stated "that the responsibilities of Mr. Fastow and other partnership officials to Enron could 'from time to time conflict with fiduciary responsibilities owed to the Partnership and its partners.'" Equally troubling was the number and nature of those companies and large pension funds that had invested heavily in Fastow's partnerships, especially LJM2.

Enron was back in the headlines every day, and all the news was bad.

Emshwiller and Smith's research disclosed that Fastow and "possibly a handful of . . . associates realized more than $7 million last year in management fees and about $4 million in capital increases on an investment" of approximately $3 million that was set up in December 1999. Enron's stock dropped 9.9 percent to $29 a share. Fastow refused to comment.

Within five days, the SEC had requested information from Enron about its dealings with Fastow's partnerships. The sharks smelled blood in the water.

With Enron stock under $20, Lay scheduled a conference call with investors and analysts, but he and Fastow refused to answer any questions concerning the Fastow partnerships. On this October 24 call, CEO Ken Lay proclaimed "we continue to have the highest faith and confidence in Andy."

Another day and the headlines read, "ENRON REPLACES FASTOW AS FINANCE CHIEF McMAHON TAKES OVER POST; MOVE FOLLOWS CONCERNS OVER PARTNERSHIP DEALS." With that, the stock of every company that did business with Enron took a beating also.

Enron tapped $3 billion from its bank lines of credit, trying to ensure its liquidity, and let everyone know it had the money to pay its debts. McMahon's move to CFO, though, was too little too late. McMahon was working day and night trying to restore confidence in the company. He was working every connection he could find to get an additional line of credit. He had not been in the position a week when Moody's downgraded Enron's debt, and the SEC moved the investigation of the company to a higher level in Washington. Although no one had voiced it yet, Enron was in a death spiral.

On November 1, 2001, the SEC announced it was making a formal investigation into the Fastow partnerships and Enron's dealings with them. It was obtaining subpoenas to force the disclosure of information from third parties who had dealt with Enron, including Enron's accounting firm, Arthur Andersen. This was serious. Enron added University of Texas School of Law Dean William Powers to its board to try to sort things out and bring in some credibility. McMahon was still working to pull out all the stops to try to save the company, seeking another billion-dollar credit line because the $3 billion he had drawn in the last week was already gone.

The November 5 *Wall Street Journal* headline was worse: "ENRON TRANSACTION RAISES NEW QUESTIONS—A COMPANY EXECUTIVE RAN ENTITY THAT RECEIVED $35 MILLION IN MARCH." That executive was none other than Michael Kopper, protégé and partner of Fastow in many of the "partnerships," including the $400 million LJM2 fund and another entity—CHEWCO—with another $383 million in debt. Kopper was also in the middle of JEDI, a limited partnership created back in 1993 between Enron and the California Public Employees' Retirement System. Fastow's partnerships appeared more and more like a billion-dollar shell game running between themselves and Enron, and Fastow and Kopper had been siphoning funds with impunity from underneath the shells.

There were talks and hopes of another company buying Enron—maybe even energy company Dynegy—but talks of a merger or buyout were mixed with antitrust worries, regulatory issues, and concerns of further unknown Enron liabilities. Frankly no one had a grip on Enron's real liabilities. McMahon found himself in new nightmares that sprang to life every day. Enron announced it would have to restate its financials from 1997 through the third quarter of 2001—decreasing income and increasing debt by hundreds of millions of dollars. Its stock slid below $7. Dynegy was under increasing pressure to walk away. Enron's stock fell to $5.01. Dynegy's stock started sliding by association.

By November 29, credit ratings agencies had downgraded Enron's bonds to junk status. Dynegy walked away, accusing Enron of "misrepresentations." Other companies stopped doing business with Enron to reduce their own risks, which dried up any cash flow. All the energy companies were in panic mode. Enron stock dived to $0.61. McMahon was still trying—"reviewing all of our options." Many of the 120 banks Enron dealt with were feeling the pain also. All the utility companies were calling. Enron assembled a war room of lawyers on its once-packed trading floor.

Plaintiffs' lawyers swarmed and filed a shareholders' suit against twenty-nine current and former Enron board members and officers. The lawyers alleged a conspiracy to conceal Enron's financial problems and the true condition of the company from other investors, while the insiders profited personally by selling their stock at an inflated price.

The thread by which Enron was hanging snapped. On December 2, 2001, within 120 days of Skilling's departure, the once $400 billion international titan declared bankruptcy, imploding in a wave of accounting scandals, mysterious partnerships, and outright thievery.

Financial devastation, human pain, rage, and anguish rolled through Houston. The city was in shock. Everyone was touched in some way by the crash of this commercial giant. Thousands lost their jobs. Countless individuals, state and teacher pension plans, and organizations across the country lost all or part of their retirement savings.

The once gleaming "E" adorning the ballpark now looked like an ugly brand burned onto the face of the city. The *Houston Chronicle* published front-page stories every day about the company, vilifying those who ran it and recounting the damage they caused. The new Enron skyscraper, still under construction, became a monstrous skeleton, casting a pall over the city. The ramifications of Enron's implosion were so far and wide that the entire US Attorney's Office for Houston had to recuse itself and not participate in any investigation.

By this time, the *New York Times* was in hot pursuit as well. Kurt Eichenwald and Richard Oppel Jr. reported that Enron had paid out $55 million in "retention bonuses" to five hundred people just before it declared bankruptcy. That just fomented the outrage.

It seemed as though everyone in the city had suffered some loss related to Enron. Houstonians ranged between livid and sick. The ripple effect was more than could have been anticipated. Every industry in Houston had benefited in some way from Enron's massive operations and philanthropic contributions. With Enron's downfall, other businesses soon collapsed: restaurants, small shops—any business that did business with Enron suffered. The public was screaming for heads to roll.

In a matter of days, by December 13, 2001, Arthur Andersen partners were testifying in congressional hearings that they had warned

Enron about "possible illegal acts" because the company was failing to provide crucial information.

President George W. Bush, with whom Enron Chief Executive Officer Ken Lay had often been photographed, vowed to ferret out and prosecute "those white-collar crooks."

Ken Lay was the leading candidate for *Texas Monthly*'s "Bum Steer of the Year" in early 2002. The publication quoted California Attorney General Bill Lockyer, who blamed Enron for the California brownouts and power failures. Lockyer said, "I would love to personally escort Lay to an eight-by-ten cell. . . ."

The *Houston Chronicle*, the eighth largest newspaper in the country, threw fuel on the already raging fire. The newspaper assigned as many as twelve reporters to Enron, and during the next three years, they generated more than four thousand negative articles, most of them extremely caustic. The local television stations piled on. Enron and those anyone deemed responsible for its downfall were denigrated and denounced publicly and profusely.

Incited by public outrage, political pressure, and cries for vindication from Enron shareholders, the Department of Justice promptly assembled the Enron Task Force—a joint effort of the department, the SEC, the FBI, and the Internal Revenue Service. Because of the Bush connection to Ken Lay, the Enron Task Force was untethered from the department. Deputy Attorney General Larry D. Thompson and his assistants in the criminal division handpicked prosecutors from across the country to staff this task force, and they gave it unlimited resources.

Assistant Attorney General Michael Chertoff, head of the criminal division, chose Leslie Caldwell to head the task force because she was extremely well-credentialed for the job and known as a "terror" as a prosecutor. A summa cum laude graduate of Penn State with a law degree from George Washington University, Caldwell was chief of the criminal division in the US Attorney's Office in San Francisco when she was selected to lead the task force. She and her handpicked team of Ivy League pit bulls set about to "send a message to Wall Street."

This prestigious team of prosecutors, IRS agents, FBI agents, and SEC agents, along with a bankruptcy examiner and endless congressional investigators and hearings, put virtually everyone who did anything with Enron under scrutiny. There were thousands of people involved with Enron, and 120 or so banks, including J.P. Morgan, Citibank, and most investment or commercial banks of any significance here or abroad.

Business professionals who had always been highly regarded and prominent in their communities were now surrounded by federal agents, walked down long dark corridors, and interviewed in barren interrogation rooms. Their offices were searched, and their documents were subpoenaed or seized. They were hauled in front of Congress and grand juries, and they were threatened with indictment and imprisonment. Most of these businesspeople had led stellar lives, done their jobs honestly, supported their churches and communities, and volunteered with charities. They had always believed in the American system of justice and confidently believed that the system would recognize their innocence.

In early January 2002, Arthur Andersen accountants testifying before Congress admitted shredding documents from Andersen's Enron files. By January 15, Andersen fired Houston partner David Duncan, who was in charge of Enron's account. Congress had Duncan in front of them the next day, and Enron fired Andersen the day after that.

Carl Levin's senate committee on investigations was issuing subpoenas for documents and testimony right and left, including to former Enron Vice Chairman Cliff Baxter, who had left Enron six months before its collapse. Baxter, along with several others, had sold the last of his Enron stock near its highs in January 2001, making about $22 million on the deals. The rumor was that Baxter, believed to be a man of integrity, had resigned because he was unhappy with the way the company was conducting its business. Some said he had objected repeatedly to Skilling about Enron's dealings with Fastow's LJM partnerships. Representatives of the senate committee badgered Baxter and had subpoenaed documents from him. Baxter, not a target himself, had finally agreed to testify.

On January 25 at 2:23 a.m., a patrol officer spotted a new Mercedes parked between two medians on the edge of a posh neighborhood in Sugarland, Texas, a quintessential suburb just outside of Houston. The officer circled back around and saw that the car was still there. The lights were on, and the engine was running. One man was inside. The officer called for backup.

Upon closer inspection, the officer saw a white male, approximately forty years old, in the driver's seat—his head slumped forward. Blood was running down the side of his face and head, and from his mouth. There appeared to be a gunshot wound to his head.

His hands were lying in blood on his lap, palms up. The black handle of a revolver rested in his open right hand, and the barrel lay across the palm of his open left hand. The barrel pointed toward the driver's door. He was barefoot.

The officers broke into the car through the passenger side rear window. They called paramedics and searched the man's pockets for identification.

They found a driver's license and an Enron ID badge.

– 3 –

THE TASK FORCE ANNIHILATES ARTHUR ANDERSEN

The body was that of former Enron executive John "Cliff" Baxter. He had just agreed to testify before Congress in the largest corporate scandal in the history of the United States. Baxter's suspicious death sent another shock wave through Houston. It was a tragic blow to his family and friends, and it was a terrifying omen to anyone who had even thought about testifying. Billions of dollars and the lives of wealthy and high-powered people were at stake. Baxter had been high up enough in Enron to see it all.

It was assumed and reported to be a suicide, but those who knew him said he had everything to live for. He had a family he loved. He was making plans for the future. He had sold his stock and left Enron before its collapse. He was not a suspect, and he had done nothing wrong. Apparently he had received threats or was afraid. A friend said that Baxter had recently wondered if he should hire a bodyguard.

Some said the death had all the hallmarks of a "hit." The police report was vague and there were significant inconsistencies. The officers couldn't even get their stories straight on who found the body and in what condition. They first said Baxter was dead when they found him, but then they had to explain why the body had been moved. So then they said that he was still alive when found, and the officer who found him had called Emergency Medical Technicians (EMT) who had tried to resuscitate him. No crime scene protocol was followed.

The body had been moved before being photographed, and the hands weren't bagged for autopsy. If the gunshot wound had been self-inflicted, it is difficult to imagine how Baxter's hands would have come to rest casually, both palms up, on his lap, with the revolver resting in them. The recoil of any gun placed against the right temple would have been significant and to the right. The "suicide" explanation seemed way too tidy.

A report came out that the coroner said the police wouldn't tell her who moved the body. Indeed the officers immediately dispatched the body straight to a funeral home. The family had to insist on an autopsy, although by law, one should have been conducted immediately.

When the autopsy report finally was released weeks later, it revealed unexplained shards of glass on the right shoulder of Baxter's shirt and abrasions at the base of the little finger on the palm of his left hand. His clothes were wet. He was barefoot, but his feet were clean. None of those facts seemed consistent with suicide. One doesn't get up out of bed at 2:00 a.m. and put on a shirt that has glass on one shoulder or clothes that are wet, or walk barefoot without getting dirt on his feet.

Why had he left his bed at 2:00 a.m. and gone outside? How could he have gotten up at all if he had taken all of the Ambien that was missing from the new prescription the doctor had recently given him to help him sleep despite all the stress? Why were his clothes wet? Where did the shards of glass and the abrasions on his left hand come from? Had someone broken something glass over his right shoulder—something that left the shards of glass and knocked him down? Had he tried to catch himself with his left hand? Was the glass from the police breaking the rear window of the car to gain access? Why were these questions not answered?

Even more bizarre was the fact that Baxter had not been shot with a bullet but rather with "rat shot"—small pellets for a pistol that are the equivalent of shotgun scatter. This is not the standard choice for someone intent on suicide, nor is it the likely ammunition kept handy in the Baxters' home in the posh suburb. There were no reports of rats or other animal problems there. That ammunition made it impossible to determine from ballistics tests what gun actually fired the shot that killed him. Where was the other ammunition like it? There was none in Baxter's house, nor was there any evidence that he had ever purchased any rat shot despite the police officers' extensive efforts to find evidence that he had.

Even more remarkable, Baxter died one day before a life insurance policy from Enron would have paid $5 million in death benefits to his family—even if he had committed suicide. Cliff Baxter was smart enough to have waited a day or two to kill himself so that his family could have the benefits of the policy—if he felt compelled to kill himself at all.

Three weeks after officers found Baxter's body in the cul-de-sac near his home, the death certificate was still unsigned. There were more questions than answers. Despite the questions and inconsistencies, the entire matter was swept under the rug very quickly. Most of the reports and all photos in the case were sealed, and efforts to obtain them to review for writing this book were promptly rebuffed.

The media seemed astonishingly unconcerned with the unanswered questions in the death of a man whose testimony would have rivaled that of John Dean's in the Watergate scandal. Imagine the difference in history if John Dean had never made it to the congressional hearing on Watergate. The only indisputable fact was that no one would ever know what Cliff Baxter would have said under oath and whom he would have implicated in what conduct.

The aftershock of Baxter's death reinvigorated the congressional hearings. Throughout February 2002, Congress was grilling Lay, Skilling, Arthur Andersen partners, and everyone it could find from Enron—before or after "the fall." Baxter's suspicious death intensified the scrutiny on those remaining and verified that something had been very wrong at Enron.

The job of the newly created Enron Task Force was to determine whether the wrongs were civil or criminal and who was legally responsible for them. Criminal charges would be met with indictments by the Enron Grand Jury. Lengthy prison time and fines would follow for those convicted. The Enron Task Force prosecutors vowed to avenge the public's losses, and it didn't take them long to start.

On March 7, within sixty days of the formation of the task force, the press room of the Department of Justice at 900 Pennsylvania Avenue was crammed with reporters and department attorneys for a major announcement. A stern and somber group walked to the stage and stood in their assigned formation. Deputy Attorney General Larry Thompson was at the podium. Behind and to his right stood Michael Chertoff, his sharp-featured, tough deputy and a former US attorney who had a prominent role in choosing the task force attorneys. To Thompson's left was Leslie Caldwell, head of the Enron Task Force, a short, no-nonsense-looking woman with closely cropped black hair. They all looked very governmental in their dark suits. The lawyers were flanked by the lead agents from the FBI and SEC.

The room was deathly quiet as Thompson began to speak: "On October 17, the Securities and Exchange Commission launched an inquiry into the financial collapse of Enron, which had been considered the nation's seventh largest corporation. The SEC's inquiry focused attention on the role of Arthur Andersen LLP, Enron's longtime auditor and one of the nation's big five accounting firms."

Oddly he said that "today we are unsealing an indictment obtained last week from a federal grand jury in Houston, Texas." The grand jury had charged the Arthur Andersen partnership with obstruction of justice "for destroying literally tons of paper documents and other electronic information related to the Enron inquiries."

Thompson explained that the indictment alleged "widespread criminal conduct by the Arthur Andersen firm, charging that the firm sought to undermine our justice system by destroying evidence relevant to the investigations." It accused Andersen personnel of the wholesale destruction of tons of paperwork at the time it "knew full well that these documents were relevant to the inquiries into Enron's collapse."

It charged that Andersen partners personally directed these efforts to destroy evidence, beginning when Andersen foresaw imminent government investigations and civil litigation and continued through the SEC's announcement that an investigation had been launched. It ended only "when the SEC officially served Andersen with a subpoena for Enron documents."

Thompson solemnly told the audience that "obstruction of justice is a grave matter and one this department takes very seriously." In words that would later prove painfully ironic, he said it was "a crime that attacks the justice system itself by impeding discovery of the truth."

When Thompson finished, the room erupted in a commotion of raised hands and rapid-fire questions. Thompson refused to answer most of the questions because "additional investigations were being conducted."

One reporter asked, "The firm's lawyers are claiming that the charges amount to the death penalty for the firm. What's your reaction to that? Do you have any sympathy for that rationale?"

Thompson's tone alone said he did not, while his words said nothing. "I'm confident that the team, the task force, as well as myself, considered all the appropriate charges in making the decision to seek the indictment that we announce today."

When asked about the maximum penalty the company faced, Thompson's speech was clipped. "The maximum penalty is a $500,000 fine and a five-year probation."

Another reporter questioned the appropriateness of the destruction of Andersen as a firm as a consequence of this indictment.

Thompson looked pissed. "We—as I said in our statement, these are serious charges, and it shouldn't be a surprise to anyone that serious charges have serious consequences." He added, "It would be unfortunate for our criminal justice system if any individual or any entity could say that he or she or it was too big or too important, so as it couldn't be indicted."

A reporter in the back had another question Thompson didn't want to answer. Referencing an older law review article by Harvey Pitt, the head of the Securities and Exchange Commission, the reporter asked if there were "some confusion in the law on when a company can destroy documents? Because Andersen stopped destroying as soon as the subpoena arrived."

Thompson had a smooth reply. "I know Mr. Pitt. He's a fine lawyer. And I haven't read the article that you're talking about, but I would direct your attention to 18 USC 1512 (e), which makes it clear that an official proceeding does not have to be pending in order for someone to come within the ambit of the obstruction-of-justice statute."

As only time would tell, Thompson and the task force were not as omniscient as they thought. Although Thompson would not acknowledge it, Andersen and everyone else knew that the indictment itself was a death sentence for the smallest of the Top Five accounting firms and the 85,000 jobs it provided around the world. Andersen counted as clients approximately 2,300 publicly traded firms. That was why the indictment had been sealed. Before the indictment was made public, the SEC had begun secret talks with the other accounting firms on ways to handle the demise of Andersen. It could have caused enormous upheaval in the public markets.

The really big news conference was a mere nine weeks later.

Enron Task Force director Leslie Caldwell stood outside the federal courthouse in Houston before a throng of reporters from all forms of media, who were hanging on her every word. Standing beside Caldwell in front of the bank of microphones was her friend and colleague, Andrew Weissmann, a narrow-faced man with a beak of a nose and large horn-rimmed glasses. Weissmann fancied himself a god among prosecutors. Armed with an undergraduate degree from Princeton and a law degree from Columbia, where he was an editor of the *Law Review,* Weissmann's original claim to fame arose from his prosecutions of Mafia bosses while he worked in the US Attorney's Office for the Eastern District of New York. He prosecuted various members of the Colombo, Gambino, and Genovese families, including their bosses—real wise guys, who were extremely dangerous and played as dirty as they come. Weissmann had developed special tactics in these prosecutions where he was convinced the end justified the means.

Weissmann became intimately involved in most of the task force's work. He was the "driving force" behind the indictment of Arthur Andersen. He quickly took on the investigations of Fastow and Enron treasurer Ben Glisan.

Then there was Sam Buell, the apparent "all-American boy." Buell served as a trial attorney on the Arthur Andersen case and coordinated the investigation of former Chief Executive Officer Jeff Skilling until early 2004. Buell had graduated magna cum laude from Brown

University and was first in his class at New York University School of Law, graduating summa cum laude.

Last but not least, Matthew Friedrich was an important part of the Andersen trial team of prosecutors. With a boyish face and an affable manner, Friedrich liked to wrap himself in the flag. After getting his undergraduate degree from the University of Virginia and his law degree with honors from the University of Texas, he served as a law clerk to US District Judge Royal Furgeson in Texas. He also served briefly in the US Attorney's Office for the Eastern District of Virginia.

The Enron Task Force proudly declared to the throng of reporters that it had achieved its first enormous victory. Within nine weeks of indictment, they had tried and convicted the venerable accounting firm of Arthur Andersen LLP of obstruction of justice. The outraged Houston jury had spoken. Andersen was guilty.

Buried with work in my federal appellate practice in Dallas and in Asheville, North Carolina, I watched the Enron train wreck approaching and knew the task force was on the march. Having been an assistant US attorney myself for a decade on hundreds of criminal cases, serving under eight US attorneys in three divisions across Texas and Virginia, I found it just as suspicious as everyone else that Andersen had chosen this particular time to resuscitate its document retention policy. I was firmly convinced Enron was rotten to its core and the task force would have plenty of people to prosecute for obvious crimes. Little did I know, as I sat in my quiet office on the edge of the Blue Ridge Parkway, finishing up a Fifth Circuit brief, that the Enron Task Force would change the next decade of my life.

The buzz of the intercom jolted me out of deep concentration. Hellen Goldfarb, my legal assistant, announced that someone from

Arthur Andersen was on the phone for me. With that phone call, I was propelled into looking into the facts and the law related to the Enron Task Force's prosecution and conviction of Arthur Andersen.

Brilliant lawyers were already writing the reply brief for Andersen. As I dived into helping them, I received an entirely new education—in more ways than one. The record on appeal was massive, but much of Andersen's evidence had been excluded from the jury's consideration. There were even more documents to review.

Andersen had requested an opportunity to make a presentation to the Enron Grand Jury before it considered the indictment, but Leslie Caldwell, Andrew Weissmann, and the rest of the task force had refused to allow Andersen to do so. The company was indicted solely on whatever evidence these prosecutors secretly presented to it. As experienced prosecutors know, that itself is not unusual, but it was extremely unusual to indict the company itself for what was done by only a few people. In fact, this was the first time it had been done. In addition, the underlying issues of the accounting practices for Enron could have been resolved as a civil matter by the SEC.

The reporter who had challenged Thompson was right. The criminal indictment took an immediate and devastating toll. Once the "gold standard" of accounting firms, Arthur Andersen was destroyed the minute it was indicted. No client could use an accounting firm under criminal charges. All the employees lost their jobs—virtually all of whom had never touched an Enron file. Hundreds of civil suits of varying natures had been filed against the firm, piling onto the criminal indictment. Only a handful of Andersen partners remained, trying to manage the litigation and wrap up the firm's affairs. Arthur Andersen LLP, the venerable eighty-nine-year-old firm that was long regarded as the benchmark of accounting ethics, had been dealt the death penalty by the new Enron Task Force.

The remaining partners at Arthur Andersen hired Maureen Mahoney, head of Latham & Watkins' appellate section in DC, to be lead counsel on appeal. I was to consult and assist as needed. As a former assistant US attorney of ten years, who served the Department of Justice and taught there frequently, I knew how prosecutors were supposed to proceed. Doing the job right required a strong sense of honor, integrity, objectivity, and fairness. A federal prosecutor has immense, unbridled power along a broad spectrum of discretion. In the hands of the wrong people, the damage that power can cause is beyond measure. A prosecutor does play God.

Having been lead counsel in more than five hundred appeals, I also knew that doing an appeal properly means going back to the beginning, with fresh eyes and as much objectivity as one can muster. I had to figure out what went wrong—if anything—to cause Andersen's conviction at trial. So I began with the indictment itself.

The first thing that hit me hard was that Caldwell and Weissmann had indicted the entire Andersen firm—the company itself. They could have and should have just indicted the individuals allegedly involved—those who actually worked on the Enron audits and transactions and who were involved in directing the destruction of documents—if they even had enough evidence against them to constitute a crime.

This unprecedented and harsh tactic alone sent a resounding message to every person and company that any failure to cooperate fully with the Enron Task Force and immediately turn over everything requested would be met with an indictment. Every company knew that an indictment was a death sentence. That knocked every business and law firm that dealt with Enron back on their heels. It put them under incredible pressure to do everything necessary to save the ship, even if it meant throwing individuals to the task force wolves and violating their constitutional rights. The Enron Task Force had destroyed Andersen in a big power play. It was a tactical flex of its own muscles, and it forced everyone else to bow to the task force or be obliterated.

The task force's exercise of its unbridled prosecutorial discretion to indict and destroy Andersen as a company had been approved by Deputy Attorney General Larry Thompson and his deputy, Michael Chertoff. They had handpicked these prosecutors because they were "terrors." That choice changed the course of history. It relegated the historically revered Arthur Andersen to the past as a criminal entity. The dismantling of the company seemed an outrageous and unnecessary toll to exact from 85,000 families and livelihoods for conduct—at worst—of those few individuals who had anything to do with the Enron account.

Then there was the matter of the obstruction of justice charge in the indictment. The indictment certainly alleged a lot of facts that sounded bad on their face. It talked about Andersen shredding tons of paper, running shredders twenty-four hours a day, and it was undisputed that they did, but where was the crime itself? What was the evidence they allegedly destroyed? The task force said that "under 18 USC §§ 1512(b)(2)," it was "a crime to "knowingly . . . corruptly persuade another person . . . with intent to . . . cause" that person to "withhold" documents from, or "alter" documents for use in an "official proceeding." That was not the "obstruction of justice" statute—although the task force described it as that to the public. Actually it was the witness-tampering statute, and the conduct they alleged did not seem to fit with the actual language in that statute. There was a separate "obstruction of justice" statute, but what they alleged as facts didn't fit with that either.

What "official proceeding" or what did "knowingly and corruptly persuade" mean? There was no formal investigation at the time

Andersen was cleaning up its files. Did it have some legal obligation to keep and produce anything the government claimed it had destroyed? Does anyone have that obligation? The company's only legal duty was to comply with a duly issued subpoena—and it did so.

Before it was issued the subpoena, Andersen had no legal duty to maintain any particular notes, drafts, duplicates, irrelevant materials, or documents. No one had asked it to do so. No law or regulation said it had to do so. Without the existence of some kind of duty or requirement that Andersen—or anyone else for that matter—actually keep something and save it for the government, how could it be convicted of a crime for destroying it? Like most companies, then and now, the firm had its own "document retention policy." That policy was lawful. Assistant Corporate Counsel Nancy Temple reminded everyone to follow that policy.

On top of that, Andersen had kept hundreds of thousands of documents either electronically or otherwise that sounded "bad" for Andersen and especially for Enron. If Andersen were really out to destroy incriminating evidence and protect itself or Enron, it had done a poor job of it.

Next there was the issue of the trial itself. Andersen asked for a speedy trial, hoping to be able to salvage something of its business and reputation. The case was assigned to Houston US District Judge Melinda Harmon. Harmon was a staunch conservative and tough on crime. She had been appointed to the bench by the first President Bush.

Andersen got speedy, but it was difficult to characterize it as much of a trial. Andersen hired Houston criminal defense attorney Rusty Hardin to lead the defense team. Hardin, an experienced and highly regarded criminal defense attorney, got nowhere fast with Judge Harmon. The task force trial team of Caldwell, Weissmann, Buell, and Friedrich got its way with the judge.

No one seemed to have noticed that Judge Harmon didn't allow the defense to introduce the hundreds of thousands of documents Andersen had retained. Andersen had saved all of its documents in one form or another and produced them to the government, but the testimony of shredders running around the clock was made to sound to the already-inflamed Houston jury that Andersen shredded everything having anything to do with Enron. The prosecutors made Andersen's in-house counsel's instruction to "follow the document retention policy" sound like a special code that really meant "destroy all documents."

Press reports during the trial were damning. To make matters worse, under threat of a lengthy prison sentence, Andersen partner David Duncan pleaded guilty and testified for the government against the firm.

Last, but certainly not least, there was the crucial jury instruction that Judge Harmon gave at the request of the task force. She took out the most important element of any crime—the intent to commit one. She told the jury that "you may find Andersen guilty" even if "Andersen honestly and sincerely believed that its conduct was lawful."

I knew as soon as I read it that the instruction was wrong. First, the very essence of a crime, as opposed to a wrong that can just get a person sued, is that criminal intent is required. Second, there had to be a close link to an "official proceeding" at the time of the destruction. There wasn't one here. Judge Harmon, however, had let the task force persuade her to remove the language from the instruction that made the case a criminal one instead of a civil one. She had removed criminal intent. This was a clear issue of law on which I was confident the Fifth US Circuit Court of Appeals should and would reverse the decision.

Though neither of us knew it at the time, Andersen's new lead counsel, Maureen Mahoney, and I had agreed on those points before we even met. The most I could tell Arthur Andersen, however, was that the instruction was clearly wrong and that the Fifth Circuit should reverse it—not that they would.

While I was busy working on the Andersen appeal, as small as my role in it was, because of my other cases, I paid no more attention to the task force's efforts. We were finishing up the Andersen reply brief and prepping for the oral argument that I was just sure Maureen would win. It had been a close case at trial. The jury had struggled for ten days. The jury instruction was indefensible. Andersen should never have been convicted.

Meanwhile the Enron Task Force was obtaining indictments, taking guilty pleas, arresting people, and generally moving right along, providing extraordinary employment opportunities for every criminal defense lawyer in Houston and then some.

Having notched their belts with the Andersen conviction so quickly and so easily, the task force, and by then, the Enron bankruptcy examiner, turned their sights to every bank that had done business with Enron. The big banks in particular, like Citibank, J.P. Morgan, and others, had done hundreds of millions of dollars in deals with Enron. Enron put its favorite banks on its Tier I list. Merrill Lynch was way down the list—not even Tier II but rather Tier III. Enron was a significant client to Merrill, but Merrill had done only a small fraction of business with Enron that Citibank and many other Tier I and II banks had done.

Nonetheless it wasn't long before Weissmann in particular turned his sights to Merrill Lynch. Having spent years in the Eastern District of New York, where Caldwell had also worked, he viewed Wall Street bankers as "wise guys on Wall Street"—no different from the mobsters, murderers, and extortionists he had prosecuted among the major crime families. He dragged countless Merrill employees in front of the Enron Grand Jury. If he didn't like their testimony, he would change their status from that of a witness to a possible target for indictment. And of course, an indictment of Merrill Lynch would have destroyed Merrill just as it had Andersen. To avoid the death sentence dealt to Andersen, Merrill consented in September 2003 to an onerous non-prosecution agreement that would later come to haunt the four executives the task force singled out for criminal indictment.

In February 2003, the SEC had filed a civil suit against Merrill Lynch, and individually against Merrill executives Daniel Bayly, Robert Furst, and several others. Merrill settled it two days later, which meant that the task force, the SEC, IRS, FBI, and Merrill had agreed to all of the government's terms before the suit was even filed. Merrill then promptly threw the individuals to the wolves. Dan Bayly, head of Merrill's Investment Banking Division and the epitome of the honorable, old-line Merrill Lynch, hired Lanny Breuer from Covington & Burling to head his defense team.

Simultaneously the task force was replenishing and beefing up its ranks. In September 2003, the task force added Kathryn Ruemmler, then a federal prosecutor in the Justice Department's Washington, DC, office. Ruemmler was a striking blonde with a well-known passion for expensive Christian Louboutin red-soled stiletto heels. She had a B.A. cum laude from the University of Washington and a law degree from Georgetown where she was editor in chief of the *Law Journal.*

John Hemann also joined the task force in September. A native of Ohio, Hemann came from the San Francisco US attorney's office where he had worked with Leslie Caldwell. Hemann had successfully prosecuted a number of securities fraud cases. Law ran in Hemann's blood. His mother was a US magistrate judge in Ohio. A graduate of George Washington University Law School, Hemann, like many of his colleagues, clerked for a federal judge for a year. Hemann's wife was also a federal prosecutor.

On September 17, 2003, the national press was abuzz again with news that the Enron Task Force and its grand jury had indicted Merrill executives Daniel Bayly, Robert Furst, and James A. Brown on criminal conspiracy charges that they had deprived Enron of "the honest services" of Andrew Fastow, in a transaction involving electrical power stations on barges. The indictment also charged Jim Brown with perjury and obstruction of justice for testifying to the Enron Grand Jury about his "personal understanding" of a telephone call in which he had not even participated. Later the task force filed a superseding indictment to add Brown's young subordinate Bill Fuhs as a defendant and two substantive wire fraud counts against each defendant.

I was paying no attention to any of the Merrill issues then, or the task force's activities for that matter. My plate was full of other cases, and the Andersen argument in the Fifth Circuit was coming up—scheduled for October 9, 2003.

Maureen Mahoney was more than ready for the Andersen argument. A brilliant advocate, she and her team at Latham & Watkins had prepared a persuasive argument, completely correct on the law and the facts. Her command of it all was masterful. The panel we had drawn I thought was a good one: Patrick Higginbotham, Fortunato "Pete" Benavides, and Thomas Reavley. They were three of my favorite judges and had excellent reputations. Reavley, a tall handsome man in his eighties, had practically raised me from a "baby lawyer" when I began arguing in the Fifth Circuit. He had been on the Texas Supreme Court and was widely regarded as a fine man who always tried to do the right thing. Everyone on the court called him "The Bishop."

Pat Higginbotham was a constitutional law scholar. He often taught constitutional law for the University of Texas School of Law. He was usually mentioned on "the short list" any time there was a Supreme Court vacancy. Pete Benavides was the newest of the three on the Fifth

Circuit, but he had served on the Texas Court of Criminal Appeals and was bright, affable, and well-regarded. I had taught with each of them at the attorney general's Advocacy Institute for the Department of Justice or at various seminars, and I had argued countless cases in front of them. I expected them to reach the correct decision based solely on the law. I thought it would be a fair panel that would take a good, hard look at the case and not be afraid of reaching the result that was clearly required by the law—even if it looked bad in the press.

The day of argument came quickly. Maureen walked to the podium first, as the appellant. She barely got a couple of words out when the judges started questioning her. They were on the wrong track. They didn't seem to be "getting it." She made every effort to direct them back to the problem of a jury instruction that eliminated any requirement of criminal intent and a pending official proceeding. She reminded them of the fundamental tenet that the law is supposed to give the citizen "fair warning" of conduct that is criminal, but her arguments seemed to be falling on deaf ears. Reavley wasn't hearing any of it. The judges seemed much more sympathetic to counsel for the government. The tone of the argument and the questions were troubling.

My official role in the *Andersen* case was over. I still thought the judges would work through their issues and come out with a correct decision reversing the conviction.

We waited and waited and waited for a decision. The longer it took, the more concerned we became. I kept telling myself that it takes longer for the court to write an opinion reversing the district court's decision than it does to affirm one, but we became more uneasy about this one. We started wondering if maybe two judges wanted to decide it one way and one judge the other—a split decision. In any event, it should not be taking so long. The Fifth Circuit usually decides cases in about three months of the oral argument.

The task force kicked off 2004 in a big way. Andrew Fastow pleaded guilty on January 14 and began cooperating with the government. A few days later, the grand jury returned a six-count criminal indictment of former Enron Chief Accounting Officer Richard Causey. The public and the press were still screaming for the heads of Ken Lay and Jeff Skilling.

Soon the task force superseded the Causey indictment to add Skilling and make it thirty-one counts. They added Lay to the indictment by July. With Weissmann's oversight, Ruemmler, Friedrich, and Hemann began preparing for the trial of the first individuals in Houston after the conviction of Andersen—the four Merrill Lynch executives and two Enron midlevel managers in what the press nicknamed the "Enron Barge" or "Nigerian Barge" case.

Suddenly, and unexpectedly to most, on March 1, 2004, just weeks after securing the indictment against Causey and Skilling, Caldwell resigned from the task force. Weissmann became the director. There was no one to rein him in at all.

The most polite description I had heard of Weissmann by any defense counsel who had dealt with him was that he was a "madman." The task force members were running amok and roughshod over anyone and everyone in their path—especially anyone with the audacity to disagree with their view of the facts or the law. No one—no judge, no supervisor in the Justice Department, no reporter—was monitoring or questioning the task force's tactics. The press was completely proprosecution (or so anti-Enron) to the point that even I and most others firmly believed they were all guilty. Most people, including many defense attorneys, thought that anyone in the task force's sights was getting whatever they deserved. The task force also indicted several

British bankers in the NatWest scheme. Meanwhile pre-trial hearings were being held involving the lower-level Enron people and Merrill executives in the Enron Barge case. According to the task force, Enron's sale of the barges to Merrill was a sham. Only a handful of bloggers, including Houston attorney Tom Kirkendall, was sounding any alarms.

Finally on June 16, 2004, the Fifth Circuit issued its first significant Enron decision. The Arthur Andersen opinion popped into our e-mail inboxes. We scurried to print and read it. *Andersen's* primary argument was that Judge Harmon's jury instructions did not require the jury to find criminal intent and the requisite interference with a "particular proceeding." The government said that to protect itself and its largest client, Andersen ordered a mass destruction of documents to keep them from the SEC, and that itself was a crime.

I saw the words "we affirm the judgment of conviction," and my heart sank.

Andersen had requested that the jury be instructed that the statutory offense of "corrupt persuasion" required an improper method of persuasion or a violation of an independent legal duty. The Fifth Circuit rejected that completely. Instead Judge Higginbotham, writing for the panel, bought Friedrich's argument from his opening statement to the jury:

"They knew that the SEC was coming. . . . Andersen was already under a form of probation with the SEC. If Andersen was found to, again, have violated securities laws, they could have their ticket pulled. . . . They could be stopped from practicing accounting in front of the SEC, and that would have meant the end of the practice. This case is all about a group of partners at Andersen who knew that the law was coming and did what they could . . . to hinder the law."

To our shock and dismay, the Fifth Circuit affirmed the conviction of Andersen and with it that horrible jury instruction that eliminated criminal intent. Removing any sign of criminal intent didn't bother these three judges at all. Once again, the task force had gotten exactly what it wanted, regardless of the law. I struggled to comprehend how Judges Higginbotham, Benavides, and Reavley had written this decision. They had just licensed—no, supercharged—Weissmann's and Friedrich's already exaggerated sense of power and their ability to terrorize all within their path.

The Andersen defense team wisely decided not to waste time seeking a rehearing with the Fifth Circuit, and instead decided to file a petition for *certiorari,* asking the United States Supreme Court to take the case. The Fifth Circuit's opinion was so wrong, it provided ample fodder. Within ninety days, Maureen and her team had written and filed the best petition for *certiorari* I had ever read. The issue boiled down to a request to grant *certiorari* on Andersen's conviction for witness tampering because the jury instructions failed to require the jury to find each of the elements of the offense. If what Andersen did was really a crime, the law at the time did not give Andersen "fair warning" of it.

Back in Houston, jury selection began in September in the Enron or Nigerian Barge case against the Merrill executives—Dan Bayly, Jim Brown, Rob Furst, Bill Fuhs, and two midlevel Enron employees. The press, especially the *Chronicle,* was having a field day. "New York bankers" were on trial there for weeks. By all reports, the task force prosecutors—Friedrich, Ruemmler, and Hemann, under Weissmann's close supervision—had the defense on the ropes. The Barge case sounded like it was going to result in easy convictions. The defense was acting like deer in headlights.

By late fall 2004, I was exhausted and looking forward to a few days off for Thanksgiving. I'd just finished filing a brief in the Fifth

Circuit in another case, and it was time for a break. I was cleaning off my desk from this months-long project when the phone rang.

The caller was a partner of Maureen Mahoney's at Latham & Watkins. After introducing himself, he said that his good friend, Jim Brown, who worked for Merrill Lynch in New York, had a serious problem. He explained that Jim was a managing director of Merrill for years and head of its Global Asset and Leasing Division on Wall Street. After a six-week trial, a federal jury in Houston had just convicted Jim and others of conspiracy, wire fraud, perjury, and obstruction of justice for a business transaction involving Enron. It was the Nigerian Barge case. Jim had been represented at trial by New York counsel from the international firm of Heller Ehrman.

I couldn't believe my ears. The pitch of my voice became noticeably higher: "New York lawyers tried this criminal case of a New York banker in Houston with a Houston jury?"

He asked me to come to New York for a meeting with Jim two days later.

I agreed, but I cautioned him that I would have to talk to Jim at length to decide if I would be able to represent him. Having been a prosecutor for ten years, I rarely took a criminal case.

I hung up the phone and ran a quick online search to pull newspaper articles on the case and the parties. Then I stayed up most of the night reading them. This case had been highly publicized. Even without knowing any of the facts, I knew that New York lawyers had no chance of winning a case like this in Houston. Despite being one of the five largest cities in the country, Houston is really a very small town and, amid Enron's rubble, a very angry one.

As I got ready to leave for New York, I seriously questioned if I should take this case. I had accepted paid representation to defend only three alleged criminals in the seventeen years I'd been in private practice. Other than the rare *pro-bono* court appointments, I didn't represent a criminal defendant unless I was convinced that he or she was innocent. That was true for each of the criminal cases I'd accepted, and I had eventually prevailed in each. I hadn't paid much attention to the Enron debacle at all, and I was clueless about Merrill's role. On the other hand, the Andersen experience had shown me that the tactics and swath of the Enron Task Force made Sherman's march through Georgia look like a Christmas parade.

Having represented the United States in 350 criminal cases, I knew that it was rare for someone to be innocent of federal criminal charges. Neither I nor any of the many US attorneys or assistant US attorneys with whom I had worked would put someone through the life-changing ordeal and anxiety of criminal charges unless we were sure they were guilty and the evidence was strong. There were more than enough cases with clear evidence of guilt of clear crimes to prosecute without looking for problems on or beyond the fringes.

I knew from the few criminal defense cases I had accepted in recent years that the government did make occasional mistakes. For some reason, the Department of Justice seemed to be making them more and more frequently. Here a special task force had been assembled to bring these charges in an emotionally charged setting under intense political and public scrutiny—with the public and press screaming for blood. It was a perfect storm for injustice to rise from the ruins of Enron.

The attorney who called me had known the Browns for years. He believed Jim Brown had been railroaded. I decided I would listen to the trial team and Mr. Brown with an open mind. If they could convince me that Jim was innocent, and if my instincts and extensive experience told me that something was wrong with the charges or the trial, I decided that I would consider accepting the case if it were offered to me. If I didn't like anything about Jim or the case, I had plenty of other things I could do.

At the same time, I was well aware of the fact that it would involve a gargantuan effort from me, primarily, but also from my assistant and my associate for a prolonged period of time. At least the first year would be intense for all of us, and it would be a huge, uphill battle. The Fifth Circuit reverses only about 10 percent of the cases it hears, and it rarely reverses without oral argument, which it grants in less than 30 percent of the cases. I'd have to make certain that Mr. Brown knew that the chances of reversal were not good. I did not want to raise false hopes.

On the short and uneventful flight to New York, I wondered what I was walking into. I hopped in a cab, and we drove toward the skyscraper on Park Avenue that housed the New York City office of the international firm of Heller Ehrman. I expected to be ushered into a sleek and elegant but contemporary large conference room. I anticipated a breathtaking view of the city, great artwork, and a room full of type-A personality "alpha" males—highly paid, tightly wound New Yorkers who were rude, overbearing, and pounding the table in rage.

To my surprise, I was ushered to a small, bare, tan-colored, bleak back-corner conference room, where I was introduced to Jim Brown, his lead trial counsel Larry Zweifach, associate Holly Kulka, and—on the telephone—Warrington Parker from their San Francisco appellate section. They all looked and sounded like they had been on the losing side of a twelve-round boxing match with the Incredible Hulk. Traumatized, exhausted, wrung out, meek, and broken, they looked pitiful. I seemed to have more testosterone than all of them put together.

There was not a discernible type-A or alpha male in the bunch. Zweifach was slender, bespectacled, and well-spoken. He too had been an assistant US attorney. Obviously intelligent, he had a clear grasp of the issues, but he didn't have the force of personality needed to represent a New York banker in a Houston courtroom—much less to stand up against a federal judge who had seemed determined to rule against the defense whenever possible.

Jim Brown was about five feet ten inches tall, medium build but a little pudgy, had brown hair and a mustache, and was casually dressed. Nothing about his appearance or his demeanor that day would create the impression that he could manage Merrill's hundreds of millions of dollars of global assets, although he was clearly bright enough to do so. Jim Brown was devastated. His entire life and that of his family had been turned upside down. Now he was facing prison time. He was in shock.

Two years earlier, he had voluntarily testified in front of the SEC, the Enron Grand Jury, and the bankruptcy examiner. He was sure that if he just told the truth, everything would be fine. Then one day, Zweifach called him and told him that he was not to go in to work that morning. He was being indicted and fired. He had voluntarily surrendered to the US Marshals, was booked, hauled in front of the press in a "perp walk," and taken before a judge to set bond. It only got worse from there—for him, his wife, Nancy, and their two teenagers, who watched in horror as the father they adored was all over the news as a major criminal.

I listened for two hours as the trial team described the nightmare of the six-week ordeal they had just endured. I had seen hundreds of indictments in my ten years with the Department of Justice. I immediately recognized that the charges in the indictment of Jim Brown and his codefendants were absurd. By the end of the first hour of our meeting, I had heard at least two serious errors that warranted reversal. Jim had been convicted of conspiracy and wire fraud for depriving Enron of the "intangible right" of the "honest services" of Andrew Fastow and falsifying Enron's books and records—allegedly by Jim's tangential involvement in a business transaction between Enron and Merrill. In the height of irony, Jim told his colleagues at Merrill not to participate in this deal for many reasons. Jim had not taken any money or any property from Enron or anyone else in the deal as must be proved in a typical wire fraud case. There were no bribes or kickbacks; and I was sure that Jim—an employee of Merrill Lynch—did not owe any duty to anyone at Enron. His only legal duties ran to his employer, Merrill Lynch. He had clearly met those. The amorphous concept of "honest services" that Congress had added years earlier to broaden the crimes of mail and wire fraud was meant to apply only to employees and people who corrupted them by bribes, kickbacks, or self-dealing in betrayal of their employer. There was none of that in this case. Without bribes, kickbacks, or self-dealing for his personal gain, I didn't believe Jim's convictions could stand.

The trial itself sounded like a farce. Jim's lawyers had filed all the appropriate motions to preserve error on all the issues that would be important in a defense on appeal. Regardless of how right the defense was on the law, the task force ran the courtroom. The judge, Ewing Werlein, ruled for the government on nearly every important issue, motion, objection, instruction, or dispute. The defense had received virtually no discovery before trial. The government claimed that it had no exculpatory material, known as *Brady* material, and Judge Werlein routinely denied the defense motions or simply ignored them. It sounded like the most prosecution-biased trial I had ever heard described.

No witnesses would talk with the defense because the task force had either indicted them, named them as unindicted coconspirators, or threatened to indict them. Counsel for Brown could not even find out what role other Merrill employees had performed on the deal after Brown left for vacation on December 23, 1999.

Even though the trial sounded horribly unfair and the indictment itself did not seem to allege a crime, still I knew it would be an enormous, uphill fight to overturn a criminal conviction by a jury. Chances for reversal were very slim. The Fifth Circuit had just affirmed the Andersen conviction even though the jury instruction did not correctly state the law. Judges are loath to overturn criminal convictions, and the fact that this was a high-profile, Enron-related case just made it worse.

I told Jim that it would take a careful and thorough review of the record and intensive and extensive research anew on the key issues. I would have to make certain the record supported the errors we discussed. Additionally we would have to get oral argument to have a prayer of getting it reversed. Basically I would have to take the case completely apart and put it back together in a different way—a way that made it clear to the Fifth Circuit what went wrong and why.

Jim noticeably perked up. "Can you get us oral argument in this case?"

That much I was sure of. "We'll get oral argument in this case. We have multiple parties, and the record is enormous. Those factors by themselves warrant oral argument. In addition, there are unusual issues, and this is an important case. It will make law. This honest services allegation is crap. You had no duty to Enron or its shareholders; you had no responsibility for Enron's books; and you told the truth in the grand jury about your personal understanding of a phone call you were not even on. Werlein should have dismissed the case before trial. We'll at least get argument, and that's the first step toward a possible reversal. They won't reverse it without granting argument."

Jim asked, and I agreed to take the case.

I asked for the trial transcript electronically and in hard copy as fast as they could get it to me with all their motions—especially any challenges to the indictment. I said I'd start immediately to read the record while they were preparing for sentencing. I would need the entire record.

Jim sighed in noticeable relief, like he had taken the first step toward turning this disaster around. At least now he had a small glimmer of hope. Very small.

As for me, I had an even smaller perspective on what I'd just stepped into.

– 4 –

WANNA BUY A BARGE?

I had been back in Asheville a few days when Hellen rang my intercom. "Federal Express is on the phone for you."

"This is Sidney Powell. OK . . . yes . . . yes . . . I'm expecting a shipment . . .What? . . . Eight hundred boxes? . . . Two trucks? . . . Well . . . bring it on. . . . Thank you."

Within an hour, two Federal Express Ground trucks backed up and unloaded eight hundred boxes of trial transcripts, documents, and files from the Enron Barge case at my two-person law office at the edge of the Blue Ridge Parkway. Our little team was replacing the New York lawyers from the international megafirm that had defended Jim Brown at trial. We had boxes piled to the ceiling along the walls of every room and down the halls. I felt on the verge of being buried alive in boxes of paper.

It took a week just to organize and sort the boxes. We found all the trial transcript volumes and piled them on and around my desk. There were multiple three-foot-high stacks. The situation looked bleak. It was a daunting task. I had to remind myself to take it one volume at a time and keep a steady pace. I started eighteen-hour days, seven days a week.

We caught a glimpse of sunlight on January 7, 2005, when we learned that the Supreme Court had just granted Maureen's petition for *certiorari* in *Andersen*. We were all elated. That was the first good news in a long time—really since the task force had been formed. Usually the Supreme Court only accepts a case to reverse it. If that held true here, the Fifth Circuit's decision would be reversed—as would the district court's. It would mean that Andersen was wrongly convicted based on a jury instruction that removed the most important element of criminal intent—just as Maureen and I had said. It would also be the first indication that any court was really paying attention to what the Enron Task Force prosecutors were doing. Even better, the Supreme Court imposed a tight briefing schedule and set argument for April 27—just a few months away.

I went back to reading trial transcript and taking handwritten notes. I'd found no substitute for doing so, but knowing that the Supreme Court was going to hear *Andersen* certainly buoyed my spirits—and they needed it. The other defendants had each hired megafirms or much larger boutique appellate firms. They each had at least five lawyers and any number of other staff working on their briefing.

Reading the record of the six-week trial of the Merrill defendants and others in the Barge case was a remarkable experience. I had read the transcripts of more than 350 criminal trials in my career at that point and consulted in countless other criminal cases. As I had done in *Andersen*, I started with the indictment. From the way it was drafted, I knew this was another Caldwell/Weissmann-crafted and Weissmann-driven prosecution.

As hard as I looked, I couldn't find a criminal offense alleged in the indictment. Sure it cited statutes, and said Jim did this, Dan Bayly did that, and Andrew Fastow was a thief, but it failed to allege anything that actually constituted a crime by the Merrill Lynch executives. Instead it cobbled together parts of different statutes to make up some kind of new crime that didn't even make sense.

The law, for all its quirks and technicalities, is generally supposed to make sense. This is especially true for criminal law. The Supreme Court has long insisted that "because of the seriousness of criminal penalties and because criminal punishment usually represents the moral condemnation of the community, legislatures and not courts should define criminal activity." The legendary Justice Oliver Wendell Holmes Jr. wrote that US citizens are entitled to "fair warning . . . in language that the common world will understand of what the law intends to do if a certain line is passed. To make the warning fair, so far as possible, the line should be clear." There was nothing clear about the alleged crime in this case. Despite studying the indictment for hours, I couldn't find one—from neither the facts nor the law alleged in it.

Since when was it illegal for an employee to seek business for his company? When did the law require someone at Merrill Lynch to be responsible for the bookkeeping at Enron or any other business? There were a lot of questions, and eight hundred boxes between us and the answers. It was going to be a challenge to "unpack" the case in those boxes in more ways than one. It was an even taller order to discern the best way to help the Fifth Circuit understand how a case this high profile—and prosecuted by an "all-star" team of prosecutors—could be so completely screwed up and how one of its brethren federal judges in Houston could let this happen.

Federal judges—especially at the district court level but even at the appellate level—want and expect to be able to believe that what the prosecutors say is true. The judges know the Supreme Court's rule of *Berger* demands that the US attorney seek justice. Federal judges at all levels are loath to reverse a criminal conviction, and they rely—rightly or wrongly—on the federal prosecutors to do the right thing.

The Barge case arose from a relatively small business transaction between Merrill Lynch and Enron at year-end 1999. At that time,

Enron was a highly respected company with revenues of $40 billion—growing to $101 billion—and profits of $957 million. Enron solicited—indeed pushed and cajoled—Merrill Lynch to invest $7 million cash to purchase a minority equity interest in a company that would profit from three electrical power barges stationed off the coast of Nigeria. Enron held the majority interest and controlled the barge project. Supposedly the US State Department had asked Enron to send the barges to Nigeria to help the war-torn country with emergency electrical power.

According to the Merrill executives, on December 23, 1999, there was a five-minute telephone conversation between Andrew Fastow (Enron's chief financial officer), Jeff McMahon (Enron's treasurer), Daniel Bayly of Merrill Lynch, and several others—but not Jim Brown. During that call, Fastow assured Merrill that Enron would use its best efforts and continue the process it had already started to remarket Merrill's interest in the barges to another party within six months. Bayly made clear to Enron that Merrill did not want to hold its equity in these barges very long. Vinson & Elkins, which represented Enron, and Winston & Strawn, which represented Merrill, finalized documents for the sale that expressly excluded any party's reliance on any prior oral conversations or representations. This was standard business and contract procedure. An agreement to use best efforts to remarket the barges was lawful, and the Enron Task Force knew that.

According to the prosecutors, the Merrill executives committed a crime because McMahon had "guaranteed" that Enron would buy back the barges, and Fastow ratified that guarantee in "code" during that five-minute telephone conversation. The linchpin of the prosecution was the prosecutors' claim that McMahon and Fastow made a guarantee to buy back the barges from Merrill, which made Enron's accounting wrong. The prosecutors said the sale of equity in the barges was a "sham"—a loan and not a sale, so Enron could not legitimately book a "gain." Therefore these Merrill executives were criminally responsible for "cooking Enron's books" and "depriving Enron of the honest services of Andrew Fastow."

The prosecutors said it didn't matter that none of the Merrill defendants personally profited from this transaction. It didn't matter that none engaged in any conduct that they thought was unlawful. With a conspiracy charge, it didn't matter that Jim Brown was not on that phone call between Bayly, Fastow, McMahon, and others where "Fastow ratified the McMahon guarantee." Likewise it didn't matter that in the grand jury, Weissmann had told Jim to share his personal understanding with the grand jury—whether it was "accurate or not"—then indicted him for perjury and obstruction of justice for his answer.

In addition, Merrill Lynch corporate counsel had approved the transaction, but the prosecutors had an excuse for that also. According to the prosecutors, the Merrill executives lied to their own lawyers and kept them in the dark about the real deal—the secret oral side deal that Enron guaranteed to buy back the barges.

So Weissmann's, Ruemmler's, Friedrich's, and Hemann's only theory of any crime rested on their ability to prove that McMahon and Fastow guaranteed that Enron would buy back the barges in that five-minute phone conversation on December 23, when everyone was trying to get out the door for the holidays. An Enron guarantee that it would buy back the barges would make Enron's accounting as a gain from its sale to Merrill wrong.

Four outstanding, well-respected, loved, and lifelong law-abiding family men and responsible Merrill Lynch executives were indicted and arrested for conspiracy and wire fraud based on having "deprived Enron of the honest services of Andrew Fastow" and the way Enron accounted for its own gain. The situation would be laughable were it not for the fact that their lives and the futures of their families hung in the balance, and they had already lived in hell daily for the past two years since the investigation began.

Long before the trial, the defense attorneys repeatedly asked for "*Brady* material"—evidence that is favorable to a defendant with respect to his guilt, sentence, or the impeachment of a witness against him. Judge Werlein either did not rule on their motions or denied them. The defense specifically asked for any statements by Merrill Lynch's lead corporate counsel Kathy Zrike, other Merrill counsel, and Fastow and McMahon at Enron—the primary participants in the transaction, and, as to McMahon and Fastow, the parties who made the guarantee on which the prosecution depended. The Supreme Court has long held that the Constitution requires the prosecutors to look for *Brady* material and to give it to the defense in time for the defense to use it at trial. The requirement is an essential underpinning of a fair trial, and all prosecutors know it. These elite and experienced task force prosecutors certainly knew it.

By September 20, 2004, the first day of trial, despite having thousands of pages of notes of witness interviews, grand jury testimony, and FBI reports called 302s, the prosecutors had produced to the defense only nineteen pages of their own "summaries" of exculpatory evidence. After Werlein ordered them to provide summaries, the prosecutors repeatedly said they had no *Brady* material. At the same time they produced the "summaries," they denied that even that information was exculpatory, and they asserted that they were exceeding their obligation by producing those summaries. Of course, nothing they provided was admissible at trial—if you can call it a trial. It would be years before anyone would uncover what they were hiding.

Throngs of reporters gathered outside the courthouse. Television reporters were taking footage and cameras were flashing on three sides. The four Merrill defendants, their attorneys, and their families had to push through the media to get inside.

Task force prosecutors Kathryn Ruemmler, Matthew Friedrich, and John Hemann were already ensconced in Ewing Werlein's courtroom. They were as at home there as if they owned the real estate. Task force chief Andrew Weissmann sat in the front row of the court gallery with his arm around *Houston Chronicle* reporter Mary Flood. There wasn't an empty seat in the large, dark-paneled courtroom. Lawyers alone took up many of them.

Werlein, a tall, handsome, gray-haired, distinguished-looking man, appeared the epitome of a judge. Central casting could not have done a better job choosing an actor who looked like everyone's mental image of the quintessential federal judge.

The stage was carefully set in the supercharged Houston atmosphere, where it was easy to instill hatred of "New York bankers," not to mention those who had anything to do with Enron. Almost all the defense lawyers, except the two for the two local Enron employees and one for Dan Bayly, were from New York. The selection of New York counsel to try a case in Houston was its own mistake. Houston can be bubba country. When they say "Don't mess with Texas," they mean it.

Weissmann and Friedrich were riding high from their conviction of accounting powerhouse Arthur Andersen in the courtroom downstairs. Friedrich was a Texas lawyer—boots and all. This Barge trial was the task force's next move toward convicting others. The Barge transaction was one of the underpinnings of the Skilling–Lay indictment. The ultimate prize for the task force would be the convictions of Ken Lay and Jeff Skilling. The prosecutors could smell the blood, along with the defendants' fear—and that of their defense attorneys. The task force prosecutors had the defense right where they wanted them—blind and defenseless with only prosecutor-crafted "summaries" of what the prosecutors knew.

Picking the jury didn't take long. One of the defense lawyers, Ike Sorkin, asked Judge Werlein "whether Your Honor is going to ask the jury whether they've read—obviously they've read about Enron?"

Without looking up, Werlein snapped, "There's always articles."

It seemed that before they could blink their eyes, Werlein had sworn in the jury.

Hemann made the opening statement for the government. Looking at each juror one by one, he pounded the government's theme straight home.

"McMahon called Merrill Lynch and he cut a deal . . . and what was the deal? . . . That was the guarantee that Merrill Lynch got from McMahon. The purpose of the handshake . . . was to confirm the deal that had been cut by Mr. McMahon."

The jurors kept their poker faces, but they were taking it all in. By the time Hemann sat down, it was already looking bad for the defense.

The defense made its opening statements, explaining, as the Merrill executives had long said, that the only agreement was that Enron would use its "best efforts" to remarket the barges to an industry buyer—a company that really wanted to own and run electrical power stations on barges floating in the harbor in Nigeria. The jurors kept their poker faces, but their eyes wandered.

Then under Weissmann's masterful tutelage and watchful eye, Ruemmler, Friedrich, and Hemann orchestrated a finely tuned symphony of government witnesses who testified about two crucial phone calls: first, an internal Merrill call, and second, "the guarantee."

Friedrich rose from his chair and commanded: "The government calls Tina Trinkle."

Trinkle, a petite woman then living in England, walked timidly to the witness stand. Jim Brown didn't even recognize her. It soon became apparent that her job was to make it appear that the Merrill executives had plotted a criminal conspiracy. Even though she was out for the Christmas holidays at the time (five years earlier) and not required to participate, she said that she had called in from her home to listen in on an internal Merrill conference call with Bayly, Brown, Furst, and several other Merrill executives. According to Trinkle, Schuyler Tilney, a Merrill executive in Houston who was pushing the deal, said that Enron would help Merrill find a third-party buyer for the barges or would buy back the barges.

According to Trinkle, either Tilney (who was not indicted) or Rob Furst (who was sitting there on trial) said "someone at Enron" had given his "strongest assurances" that Merrill would not own the barges past June 30. In response to someone's question about the possibility of getting a written guarantee that Enron would buy back the barges, Trinkle said that either Furst, Tilney, or Brown (she could not remember who) said that Enron "could not do that and get the accounting treatment it wanted."

"I knew there was something wrong with the deal," she said. "They approved the deal on the phone call."

On cross-examination, Trinkle admitted that she and her boss, Paul Wood, met at length with Brown, who hated the deal because of all the risks. She testified that Jim was "very negative on the deal, and he felt that it had a lot of risks." She said Jim opposed Merrill's participation in the Barge deal because Nigeria was too dangerous, and there were environmental issues, danger of an explosion and collateral liability, political risks, foreign currency and tax issues, performance risk, potential negative publicity if anything bad happened, and—presciently—a "headline risk" that if Enron had any financial problems, it could look like "income statement manipulation." In fact, Trinkle said that Jim "was so negative on the deal that it was striking." Trinkle admitted that the deal "probably wasn't going to go anywhere because Jim was obviously not supportive."

Nonetheless Friedrich got the crux of her testimony down to something the prosecutors could make sound really bad. "Somebody at Enron" had "told Merrill Lynch that they would help us find a third party to buy the barges . . . and if that did not happen by June 30, 2000, Enron Corporation would buy the barges back from us." Kevin Cox (not indicted) or Bayly (on trial) asked about a written guarantee. Either Furst, Tilney, or Brown said, "No, they can't do that because otherwise they won't get the right accounting treatment."

As Trinkle left the witness stand, the jury glared at the defendants. It was the first watershed moment of the trial.

Jim got a sinking feeling in his stomach, as did all of the defense counsel. They knew that no one from Enron was on that phone call, and no agreement was reached then. No one on the call could even approve the transaction, and there were three other meetings with more people after that before the deal was even authorized to proceed by Dan Bayly's superior—Tom Davis. But the way it sounded when Trinkle finished was damning.

Trinkle was the only prosecution witness from Merrill. After Trinkle's testimony focusing on this preliminary internal call, which the prosecutors referred to repeatedly as the "Trinkle call," the defense took one body blow after another—all hearsay evidence.

Prosecutor Hemann called Michael Kopper to the witness stand. Kopper, a young, slender man, who was effeminate and wore glasses, was doing his level best to give Hemann whatever he wanted. Kopper,

Fastow's protégé at Enron, had destroyed his computer to keep the government from finding evidence of his fraud. That was unequivocal obstruction of justice, but he wasn't charged with it. Kopper had stolen millions with Fastow, but he had worked out a really sweet deal with the prosecutors in exchange for his testimony. Because the task force had indicted the Merrill defendants on a conspiracy charge, it didn't matter that Kopper was not a party to the Trinkle call or the phone call on December 23 between Fastow and McMahon at Enron, and Bayly, Tilney, and others at Merrill when the alleged "McMahon guarantee" was ratified. Kopper could testify against the Merrill defendants based on what he claimed Fastow had told him in a conversation just between Fastow and Kopper after the Merrill–Enron call on December 23.

Hemann set it up well—never mind the use of an objectionable, completely leading question on direct examination. "Based on your understanding, Mr. Kopper, was this a best-efforts deal?"

Kopper said, "No, not on my understanding."

Bill Fuhs's attorney, David Spears, an excellent New York lawyer, took Kopper on cross-examination. Spears went to the crux of the defense. Spears did his best to get Kopper to admit that this was only an agreement that Enron would "do the best we can to find a third-party investor." That was a tidbit in the FBI 302—its summary of what Kopper had supposedly told the agents and prosecutors long before trial.

Kopper rebuffed that statement with his professed "understanding" that "Enron had made a 'promise' to take Merrill Lynch out."

Dan Horwitz, counsel for Furst, also made a run at trying to get Kopper to admit there was only a best-efforts deal, just as the defendants said.

Horwitz pushed. "And do you remember Mr. Fastow telling you that, what Merrill Lynch was told, was that Enron would do 'their best' to get Merrill Lynch out in six months?"

Kopper was adamant, "No. That is not what I recall."

Horwitz tried again with more specific details available from the 302. "Do you remember meeting with FBI Agent Bhatia and a representative of the SEC in October of 2002, and telling Agent Bhatia and the agent of the SEC that it was promised to Merrill Lynch that Enron 'would do their best' to get Merrill Lynch out in six months? Do you remember saying that to Agent Bhatia?"

Squirming almost imperceptibly, Kopper hedged. "I don't recall those exact words."

Horwitz showed Kopper the FBI 302 report to "refresh his recollection" and asked again in a firm, angry tone, "Did you tell the FBI agent Enron would 'do their best to get Merrill Lynch out in six months'?"

Kopper was inexorable. "This does not change my recollection of what I said."

Horwitz was furious. He knew Kopper was lying. "This does not change your recollection, sir, that you told the FBI that it was promised to Merrill Lynch that Enron would 'do their best to get Merrill Lynch out in six months'?"

Hemann jumped up and objected that the question had been "asked and answered." Werlein sustained the objection. Defense counsel could go no further into Kopper's about-face from what the FBI report said he had told the FBI.

Hemann took Kopper back on redirect, confident that Kopper would do anything the prosecutors wanted to avoid a prison term. Kopper clearly would not fare well in the prison environment. He had even negotiated the non-prosecution of his domestic partner in his plea agreement with the government. Remarkably the prosecutors allowed Kopper's partner to keep his own illegal profits from Kopper's thievery with Fastow on other transactions. Not even Fastow or Kopper had stolen any money in the Barge deal, but the prosecutors had witnesses testify that the Barge deal was just like their dirty deals.

Hemann reminded Kopper of the defense attorneys' questions about "best efforts," then asked, "Are you familiar, Mr. Kopper, with the term 'best-efforts remarketing agreement'?"

Horwitz jumped up. "Your Honor. This is definitely beyond the scope. There were objections, and the objections were sustained on this line of questioning."

Werlein jolted. "What is . . . ? All right. What is the question about?"

Hemann was confused. "The question is—what is it about?"

Werlein replied, "Yes."

Hemann responded, "It's about—I just want to clear up what this 'best efforts' term that was thrown out by Mr. Horwitz means."

Werlein had been cued. "All right. Overruled. Let's see if we can clear it up."

Hemann began again. "Are you familiar with that term?"

"Yes, I am," Kopper replied. "'Best efforts' is a term I was most familiar with from the days when I was a banker. It was a commitment that you would do all you could to make something happen." However, he acknowledged, it was not a commitment to make up for any shortfall.

Hemann could ice the cake now. "Based on your understanding of this deal, Mr. Kopper, was this a 'best-efforts' deal?"

"No, not on my understanding," Kopper said. "My understanding was that it was a promise."

The prosecutors were whispering, nodding, and practically "high fiving" each other at the counsel table. The defense was outraged.

Defense counsel Horwitz tried again on re-cross-examination. "And, again, I would ask you—is that, in fact, what you told Agent

Bhatia, that it was promised to Merrill Lynch that Enron would 'do their best' to get Merrill Lynch out in six months?"

Hemann jumped up to object. "This was asked and answered, Your Honor."

"Overruled."

Kopper seemed to equivocate. "I do not recall using those words in my interview."

Slightly encouraged, Horwitz continued, "Again, I'd like to show you the 302 that was prepared in connection with that statement and ask you if that refreshes your recollection about whether you said Enron promised it would 'do their best' to get Merrill Lynch out?"

Hemann jumped up again—more emphatic. "This was asked and answered. This is where I got confused about who was doing it yesterday, Your Honor."

Werlein didn't even look up. "Yes. That is sustained on this. This has been covered."

The government eventually called its FBI case agent, Raju Bhatia. Defense counsel Ike Sorkin, a handsome man with thick gray hair, tried to get an admission from the smarmy Bhatia that Kopper had told them Enron would just "do its best."

Bhatia slammed the door. "He did not say that, Mr. Sorkin. Those are not his words. I did not take a verbatim transcript."

The prosecution's "star witness" was former Enron Treasurer Ben Glisan. Ruemmler called him to the witness stand, fresh from his Houston holding cell—a vast improvement over his prison conditions. Glisan had originally gone to prison with no deal from the government. He had refused to "cooperate." He had just pleaded guilty and refused to testify in front of the grand jury or about anyone. When he reported to prison, the government put him straight into solitary confinement—the hole—a bug-infested cage barely big enough to stand in, with only a slit for light. Glisan euphemistically described solitary as "a shock." After weeks in solitary, he spent five months at a prison facility far more dangerous and oppressive than what he had expected. He endured this treatment until the task force brought him to the Houston grand jury to see if he was ready to be more "credible" in the view of the task force prosecutors. To no one's astonishment, he was ready to join the task force orchestra—first chair.

Glisan looked like a Boy Scout on the stand and managed to sound like one too: contrite, with no ax to grind and no deal with the government. Ruemmler was at the podium, in total control, and she led him straight down the path to righteousness with the task force. After reading an e-mail Glisan had sent regarding the barges, she asked, "Why, Mr. Glisan, in this e-mail, did you use the term 'obligated'?"

Glisan replied, "I felt that Enron was obligated to buy back the barges."

Ruemmler asked, "And when you say 'you felt,' why did you feel that way?"

Glisan replied, "Based upon Mr. McMahon's oral guarantee, which, as I understood it, was ratified by Mr. Fastow as well."

Ruemmler was more specific to rebut the defense in advance of their cross-examination. "Did the term 'best efforts' ever come up in your conversation with Mr. Furst?"

Glisan said, "No."

By the time the government rested its opening case, the jury looked hostile toward the defendants.

For the defense, Herb Washer, former attorney for Merrill Lynch, tried to testify that Fuhs told him on October 6, 2003, that "Merrill Lynch had been told by Enron that they would use their best efforts to find a third-party buyer to take out Merrill Lynch's interest."

Hemann objected, Judge Werlein sustained the government's objection, and the evidence was excluded.

The defense's best hope—indeed its only hope—was its own corporate counsel, Kathy Zrike. The task force held more than one thousand pages of Zrike's extensive testimony in front of the grand jury and the SEC, and her full FBI 302.

The defense had only the prosecutors' selective two-page "summary" of what Zrike did or knew or recalled about the deal. They could not interview her before trial because she refused to speak with any defendant. After she testified in front of the grand jury, Weissmann threatened to indict her. The prosecutors put tremendous pressure on her before and during the trial. Zrike's attorney had even told the defendants that if they called her to the witness stand, she would take the Fifth. Not even Dan Bayly, who had been her superior and a man she greatly admired, knew if she would actually testify if his attorney called her or had any idea what she would say. And the "summary" the task force provided did not even mention Jim Brown.

Counsel for Bayly did call Zrike to testify, and to everyone's surprise, she did not assert her Fifth Amendment privilege. She was terrified, however, and Weissmann—who had grilled her for hours in front of the grand jury—sat directly in front of her throughout her testimony, glaring at her and taking notes. Zrike feared indictment herself because not only had Weissmann specifically threatened her with that possibility, but he had also extracted the onerous non-prosecution agreement from Merrill that obligated her to testify consistently with the government's theory of the case. If she did not, Merrill Lynch as a company could receive Arthur Andersen's death sentence—at the total discretion of the task force.

The defense had to question her "blind"—without any of the information the government had obtained from her. They didn't know what to ask her, and the first rule of witness questioning is: Don't ask a question for which you don't know the answer.

Friedrich took her on cross examination. Zrike was fragile.

Leading questions are proper on cross-examination. Friedrich led well, and she followed him. "Your understanding was that the only agreement was a remarketing agreement, correct?"

"That's correct," Zrike confirmed.

Friedrich had her right where he wanted her. He had Zrike admit that she met with Bayly and expressed her understanding that it was simply a remarketing agreement.

"OK," Friedrich said. "When you said in front of Mr. Bayly that the only agreement was to remarket, did Mr. Bayly ever say, 'You know what? Actually I was on a phone call the other day, and the agreement is that they're going to buy it back if we can't resell it'?"

Defense counsel jumped to their feet in unison. Richard Schaeffer, a tall, handsome, impeccably dressed New York lawyer representing Bayly, leaped to his feet shouting, "Objection!"

Sorkin also objected. "There is no foundation to that."

Schaeffer argued, "No testimony to that."

Friedrich only said, "Ms. Trinkle's testimony."

Werlein clipped, "Overruled."

Friedrich turned back to glare at Zrike. "Did he ever say that?"

"No, he did not," she said as she looked down.

"Did he ever mention that he knew that there was a buyback?" Friedrich pressed.

"No, he did not," Zrike said.

"Did Mr. Bayly ever let you know that he had a different understanding besides your understanding that this was simply a remarketing agreement?" Friedrich asked.

"No, he did not."

"OK. And the meeting ends with Mr. Davis telling Mr. Bayly to make a phone call. Is that right?"

"Yes," Zrike admitted.

"OK. And, by the way, based on everything that you saw and observed, Merrill Lynch wouldn't have gone forward in this deal unless they had that remarketing agreement. Is that correct?"

"'I agree. It would—I don't believe that it would have gone forward if we didn't have at least some cooperation from the seller, Enron, to continue to pursue the transaction that it had on the table,' consistent with Enron's representation that there was an industry buyer that just wasn't ready to close the deal but would do so soon."

That was as close as Zrike came to deviating from the task force's version of the "facts." Zrike was cracking. Weissmann was glaring at her. Friedrich was pounding her. Zrike's lip was quivering. Friedrich made it sound as if Zrike had "a belief" that there was an agreement to remarket the barges only because the defendants had not told her the truth. Zrike was shattered, the defense was crushed, and the task force had played it perfectly.

The entire defense team looked and felt sick. These five and one-half weeks of trial had been a bloodbath.

– 5 –

NAILING THE COFFINS

The charge conference—the meeting of all counsel and the judge during which the judge decides how to instruct the jury—was very telling. The Fifth Circuit has a book of pattern jury instructions. These cover most offenses and issues that arise in most criminal trials. It is rare that federal district judges deviate from the pattern instruction, and there is rarely a need to do so. The pattern instructions are fair and already approved by the court of appeals.

First, at the request of Friedrich and Ruemmler, Judge Werlein expanded the already broad definition of conspiracy (which requires an "agreement") beyond all prior boundaries by adding "or understanding." This was an astonishing redefinition of the standard conspiracy instruction. No prior decision of any court supported it. Second, he disregarded the Fifth Circuit's pattern instructions and did not give the requisite instructions as to the elements that create criminal intent: "knowingly" and "willfully." Third, he refused to give an instruction that the defendants were acting in good faith in relying on their counsel. Fourth, he refused to give an instruction that would explain the best-efforts or remarketing agreement as the theory of the defense.

Just as Calswell, Weissmann, and Friedrich had persuaded Judge Harmon to do in *Andersen*, the prosecutors convinced Werlein to remove the criminal intent elements from the jury instructions. Indeed the task force prosecutors consistently maintained the extraordinary and novel position that they only needed to show that these defendants "intend to accomplish an objective. They do not have to show that the objective is illegal."

This new definition of "conspiracy" alone had no basis in law. If something is not illegal, it is not a crime to do it—much less to agree to do it—but that was a minor detail to the prosecutors and Judge Werlein. Werlein gave the jury instructions that these prosecutors requested—effectively guaranteeing the convictions. The word "understanding" had been used hundreds of times throughout the trial. Any "understanding" by any defendant was now criminal.

In addition to the conspiracy and wire fraud charges, Jim Brown was also charged with perjury and obstruction of justice based on his answers to three questions from Weissmann in the Enron Grand Jury. Defense counsel is not allowed in a grand jury room. A witness or "target" sits alone in front of the prosecutor and usually twenty-three citizens. It's not a comfortable environment.

When Jim was before the grand jury, Weissmann instructed him to share with the grand jury whatever his "personal understanding" was—whether it "was accurate or not." Months afterward, Weissmann indicted Jim for perjury and obstruction for testifying that his personal understanding was "inconsistent with" Enron's belief that it was "obligated" to get Merrill out of the deal. Jim had said that he was "aware of a discussion between Merrill Lynch and Enron on or around the time of the transaction," but he "did not think it was a promise" or any kind of binding obligation.

Jim was not on the telephone call that Weissmann had questioned him about in the grand jury, and Weissmann knew it. But Merrill had given the prosecutors an e-mail that Jim had written more than a year later in an entirely different context. In the e-mail, Jim referred to the December 23 call with Fastow and Bayly, and said, loosely, "we had Fastow get on the phone with Bayly and the lawyers and promise to pay us back no matter what. Deal was approved and all went well."

The prosecutors were able to exclude the defense evidence that provided context and explained the meaning of the e-mail and Jim's grand jury testimony. They excluded hundreds of pages of Jim's voluntary testimony to the SEC, the grand jury, and the bankruptcy examiner. Then Friedrich used the e-mail to argue that Jim did two illegal deals.

The day of closing arguments finally arrived after more than five weeks of testimony. Weissmann, Ruemmler, Friedrich, and Hemann had this jury right in their palms. Throughout the trial, the defense lawyers were blindsided at every turn. The prosecutors' tactics kept them reeling.

Kathryn Ruemmler, impeccably dressed in a suit and her signature stiletto heels, stood at the podium. She smiled first at Judge Werlein and then at the jury. Then she struck like a viper at the jugular of the defense.

"You know that Enron, through its Treasurer McMahon and Chief Financial Officer Fastow, made an oral guarantee to these Merrill Lynch defendants, that they would be taken out of the barge deal by June 30th, 2000, at a guaranteed rate of return. . . . So the key . . . was Jeff McMahon. . . . Trinkle told you . . . and Glisan told you that Jeff McMahon confirmed to him that he gave that exact guarantee. . . . It was Bayly's job . . . to get on the phone with Mr. Fastow . . . and make sure that Mr. Fastow ratified the oral guarantee that Mr. McMahon had already given to Mr. Furst."

She also said forcefully, "Remember again what Mr. Glisan told you that . . . Andy Fastow was the one who ratified the comments that had already been made by Mr. McMahon."

Then she turned to mock the defense's contention that there was only a best-efforts agreement to remarket the barges to a third party. "The written agreement between Enron and Merrill Lynch had no remarketing or best-efforts provision. . . . That there was some suggestion, made primarily through Ms. Zrike . . . that the Merrill Lynch defendants believed that all that Enron had committed to do was to remarket . . . Merrill Lynch's interest in the barges. . . . You can spend as many hours as you would like. You will nowhere in those documents ever find a reference to a remarketing agreement or a best-efforts provision. It's not there."

Ruemmler told the jury that "based on the . . . testimony of Tina Trinkle, the jury could conclude beyond a reasonable doubt, that Enron gave Merrill Lynch executives a guarantee . . . and Dan Bayly, Rob Furst, and Jim Brown knew the verbal guarantee made the deal a fraud. That alone proves their participation in this conspiracy."

Pointing to Jim in particular, Ruemmler argued that his silence on the Trinkle call was sufficient evidence to show his guilty knowledge, place him in the conspiracy, and convict him.

The defense attorneys valiantly tried to turn the jury around. Schaeffer argued, "Those witnesses—Mr. Glisan, Mr. Long, Mr. Garrett, Mr. Lawrence—none of them were on the telephone call with Mr. Fastow." Then he catalogued the "overwhelming" evidence that Merrill Lynch didn't think there was an obligation by Enron to repurchase the barges. "Mr. Brown's note clearly states 'no repurchase obligation.' Zrike's notes say, 'High probability of completion with another investor to come in. Another investor to come in. A third-party buyer, and high probability, no guarantee.' And her notes also say, 'Real equity with only agreement from Enron to remarket our equity.' It was an equity investment by Merrill Lynch. It was an agreement only to remarket to a third-party buyer."

Larry Zweifach argued for Jim Brown. He had the extra charges of perjury and obstruction of justice to answer. Zweifach tried to explain, quoting from the snippet of grand jury transcript the defense was allowed to get in the record. "So Jim is asked about the word 'assurance,' 'was this an assurance?' Again, a word that has special meaning to Mr. Brown based upon what he's trying to convey. 'Answer: No. I thought we had received comfort from Enron that we would be taken out of the transaction within six months or would get that comfort. If "assurance" is synonymous with "guarantee," that is not my understanding. If "assurance" is interpreted to be more along the lines of strong comfort or best efforts, that is my understanding.'"

So, Zweifach explained to the jury, "even with the word 'assurance,' what Mr. Brown is trying to say is that it depends what you mean. If it means something like a 'guarantee,' then no, I don't agree with that because they don't have the obligation. But if it's more like comfort, then I agree it's an assurance. And you can see, ladies and gentlemen, when Mr. Brown said, 'I wouldn't call it a promise,' he's characterizing it as his understanding of it not being a promise."

Friedrich leaped to the podium to argue rebuttal. His words were the last the jury would hear about the evidence, and he was on fire: "The Merrill Lynch defendants take the uniform approach . . . that all that was going on was just that it was a remarketing agreement. That's all it was. There was no buyback. It's just a remarketing agreement. But ask yourselves this simple question: If it's a remarketing agreement, if that's all it is, why was it not put in writing? . . . If it was a remarketing agreement, there wouldn't have been a problem with that. If that's all it was, why wasn't it put in writing?" Then he shifted the blame to the defense lawyers who talked "for hours" but had no answer to the question of why the purported remarketing agreement was not in writing.

He was making eye contact with each juror. He had their rapt attention. He pointed to Zrike's testimony as "one of the defining moments in this trial." He said, "She was about to break up into tears because she was so hurt and so bothered by the difference between what she was told at the time by the bankers and what she learned now."

Friedrich all but exploded, "This was a case, not about reliance on counsel; this was a case about defiance of counsel."

He teed up the crucial issue. "Is it just a remarketing agreement, where Enron is going to try to help Merrill sell this thing? Or is the anchor a buyback agreement and that then they're going to get a 15 percent return no matter what? That's what all the evidence tells you that the agreement was." Friedrich didn't seem to stop to breathe.

Weaving Zrike in again, he told the jury: "They never talked to her about a buyback agreement. She never knows about it. But you know that. That's what the deal was. She tells you, had she known that, the deal never would have been approved. She would not have gone through with the deal, because it would have been a parking arrangement, and it would have been wrong, and it would have been contrary to the company policy."

Just as Friedrich had argued in the Andersen case, that Andersen had done something wrong before, he argued that this hidden "parking transaction" was a repeat offense for Merrill. He told the jury that "Mr. Schaeffer said that nothing was hidden from Kathy Zrike, and that's just not true. Things were hidden from her time and time again." Friedrich was on a roll. The jury was all his. He was free to mock the defense, even more than Ruemmler had, and he did it well.

Weissmann sat on the front row, next to *Houston Chronicle* reporter Mary Flood. He smirked and nodded while Ruemmler and Friedrich repeatedly mocked the existence of a lawful remarketing agreement and implied to the jury that the defendants were lying about it.

Friedrich turned back to the crucial theme that McMahon had made a guarantee and added that Jim had lied about it: "You know from the e-mail, you know from the Tina Trinkle conversation that McMahon made a guarantee . . . that there was an agreement, there was a promise, and that Mr. Brown lied when he went into the grand jury."

In the end, Friedrich appealed directly to the jury, their own losses and those of people they doubtlessly knew, and the "public" nature of the stock market. As if it were a securities fraud case, he declared, "This is a case about the integrity of our public markets. Publicly traded companies mean that the public owns that stock. Members of the public, moms, dads, pension funds, people of all races, all creeds, all beliefs, people just like you. . . . They didn't have a guarantee like these guys had. . . . They weren't entitled to much, but they were entitled not to be lied to. They were entitled not to be cheated. And don't forget that as you deliberate," Friedrich stressed, "because the evidence supports it and because you believe it's right, find these defendants guilty on all counts of this indictment."

———

The trial had taken six weeks. The jury was out for three days. The defendants were exhausted and felt hopeless, but they still couldn't process the possibility of a guilty verdict. As the jurors filed back into the courtroom, they were solemn and looked down or glanced sideways quickly at Friedrich, Ruemmler, and Hemann.

Werlein asked the compulsory question: "Mr. Foreman, have you reached a verdict?"

"We have, Your Honor. The jury finds the defendants Bayly, Brown, Furst, and Fuhs guilty on all counts."

The prosecutors were jubilant.

The defendants were shell-shocked.

The only defendant who left the courtroom free that day was Sheila Kahanek, a midlevel Enron employee. Another Enron employee, Dan Boyle, was convicted. A sensitive soul, he seemed to have felt guilty just for working at Enron.

Sheila Kahanek was innocent, but it was clear the jury liked her attorney. She was represented by colorful Houston defense attorney Dan Cogdell—a tall, handsome, strapping Texan, with a collection of ex-wives and an avowed fondness for strippers. Cogdell had kept her defense clear and simple. He was funny, and he had flirted and charmed the jury into acquitting his client. Kahanek, like Jim Brown at Merrill, had told her people at Enron that they could not take a gain unless they sold the barge equity with no buyback. That defense worked for her.

Once I had finally read the entire record of the trial, it was easy to see why the Merrill executives had been convicted. Usually there were no more than three errors for briefing in any trial. Here there were so many clear errors of law that it was hard to know where to begin to explain it all. Add to that all of the color and prejudice; Werlein's unprecedented rulings; the task force's tactics and control of the facts, witnesses, and courtroom; and the outcome was a foregone conclusion.

While I was sorting all of the issues and beginning to formulate briefing, we all were awaiting the most dreaded day of Jim's life— his sentencing.

Jim was at home when he got a call from his trial attorney, Larry Zweifach. Zweifach's tone was terse and cold. Upon Jim's conviction, Weissmann and his task force had pressured Merrill Lynch to stop paying the legal fees for the defense of the executives. Merrill, still under the onerous non-prosecution agreement Weissmann had extracted, was forced to comply with Weissmann's demand. The task force had even installed a supervisor at Merrill, who reviewed all of the attorneys' bills and knew exactly what they were working on and how much Merrill was paying them. Zweifach informed Jim that Merrill would no longer pay for Jim's defense. Zweifach said Jim owed the firm hundreds of thousands of dollars.

Jim felt his chest tighten and a knot in his stomach. He hung up the phone and walked out to his back porch. He sat down on the stoop, his head in his hands. *How could Larry do this? After all he had been paid over these last several years? All they had been through together? Larry lost the trial—and he wanted more money or he would withdraw?* Jim couldn't believe what he had just heard, and he couldn't think or take anymore. He didn't know how his family could either.

Sentencing loomed only a few weeks away.

– 6 –

FACING THE FIRING SQUAD

Nancy Brown was busy in the kitchen, trying to fix dinner, when the phone rang. She answered it. "Jim, it's your pretrial services officer, doing the report for the judge for your sentencing."

"I'll take it in the den."

Jim returned shortly, his face ashen. "The task force is asking that I be sentenced to prison for at least twenty-seven years. According to them—and the pretrial services officer—we caused Enron a loss of $45 million."

Nancy dropped the spoon she was using to stir.

"Oh, my God. How can that be?"

In thirteen days, Jim could be sent to prison. He didn't know how long he would be in jail. He didn't know if he would be taken from the courtroom in chains. All he knew was that April 21, 2005, was bearing down on him, increasing a weight in his chest that made it harder and harder to breathe. The anxiety in the household was palpable. Jim and Nancy had hardly slept since the verdict was returned. They tossed and turned. They felt like zombies—walking in a nightmare that, to their horror, was real. Surely this was someone else's life. It could not be theirs.

The toll on them was visible. A day or two later, Nancy told Jim she was going to get groceries. She got in the car and mindlessly drove to the store. She walked in, got a cart, and walked up and down the aisles, just staring at the full shelves. She finally stopped and just stood there. Her eyes welled with tears. She had no idea what she had intended to buy. She wandered the aisles for twenty minutes. Then, on the brink of tears again, she gave up, put the empty cart back in its row, and drove back home.

Their stress increased day by day as sentencing drew closer. They both understood that the judge had the power to send Jim to prison straight from the courtroom, and the marshals could take him into custody immediately. From everything they had seen so far, they believed that if Ruemmler and Friedrich asked that he be remanded into custody immediately, Werlein might very well grant their request.

Jim felt like he was being hauled in front of a firing squad. He had no hope. He thought about running or leaving the country. He even considered—briefly—the possibility of suicide. If he did any of those things though, people would think he was guilty. He would lose his family and his friends. In fact, the lawyers had all told him that under the law, flight is evidence of guilt.

He was not guilty of anything, so for that reason alone he could not flee. He would just have to stick it out and fight. He had always believed in the justice system and in this country. He had followed the rules and relied on Merrill's legal counsel. He had steadfastly opposed the deal. It was Merrill's own in-house counsel Zrike who had taken it over his head, over Bayly's head, and all the way up to get it approved. He had to believe that the system would work. It could not fail him now. He had to believe. He was strong. He could deal with whatever he needed to deal with. His family would be OK as long as he could stay alive. He had been warned about how to act to protect himself in prison.

That pep talk to himself lasted about ten minutes, and he was back in the pits. He and Nancy had been a team for thirty years. He would miss her terribly. She had been a source of great strength and comfort to him all these years. He could not imagine life without her. Daily he faced the realization that he would not see his children graduate from high school or college. He would not be at their weddings. He would never see his grandchildren. He couldn't even stand the thought of Nancy, Chris, and Lauren seeing him behind bars.

These thoughts alone were pure torture. He might as well be dead. In fact, he sometimes believed that it would be easier for his family to handle his death than it would be to see him in prison for the rest of his life. He wasn't a coward either. He had to find a way to set a good example—to make some good come from this. His family came first, and Nancy was so strong, she would hold them all together.

———

Preparing Jim for sentencing was difficult. When a defendant appears before a federal judge for sentencing, he is supposed to acknowledge his wrongs, apologize, and be completely contrite. If he is not, the judge may very well impose a harsher sentence or deny a request for a recommendation that the defendant be placed in, for example, a minimum-security prison rather than a maximum-security prison. Supposedly only the Bureau of Prisons controls where a prisoner ultimately goes and how he is treated, but it was painfully clear from Glisan's treatment that these high-ranking prosecutors had considerable influence. Sometimes it can help to have the sentencing judge make a recommendation. The Merrill defendants were not a security risk. It would make sense that they be confined in what are called prison "camps." Those camps were by no means pleasant, but each reduction in security level meant the facility was somewhat better than the one above it, and there would be less risk of personal physical danger in a less restrictive facility. Because the Merrill executives were certainly not dangerous or any risk at all, each defendant would request that Judge Werlein recommend a "camp."

Despite these very real pressures to placate and pander to Judge Werlein, Jim could not bring himself to admit he had done anything wrong, and neither could Bayly, Furst, or Fuhs. From Jim's perspective and even Merrill's, they had donated or rebated $7 million to Enron with no expectation of return. He would be committing perjury if he stood there and said he was guilty when the truth was that he was not. So he worked on a statement that would strike a tone to express regret for the situation without assuming guilt that he did not have. He and Nancy lay awake each night until sheer exhaustion produced an hour or two of sleep.

Dan Bayly was scheduled to be sentenced the morning of April 21 and Jim Brown that afternoon. We had prepared for all contingencies.

The night of April 20, Jim, Nancy, their children, and I had what Jim felt was his "last supper" at a steak house near the Four Seasons Hotel in Houston. We ordered small steaks and salads, but none of us had an appetite.

Jim was exasperated and full of questions, and so were the kids. Their agony was visible. Jim looked ten years older than when we had met. "How can the government blame me for the downfall of Enron? What should I have done differently? I told them not to do this stupid deal. I never trusted Fastow. How can they possibly say that we caused a $45 million loss to Enron? None of this makes any sense!"

Nancy was trying to be strong. In fact, she was amazing, but she was also terribly worried—and she had every right to be. The notion that these Merrill executives somehow caused a $45 million loss was the key factor in increasing the sentencing guidelines to require a sentence ranging from thirty to thirty-five years.

Based on a recent Supreme Court decision, the Bayly appellate defense team had filed a monumental memo on the issue of the "loss to Enron" that the government claimed this deal had caused. The government's allegation of financial loss from this transaction was ludicrous. The Barge deal had actually resulted in a profit to Enron of $53 million. The barges were real. Merrill Lynch had paid Enron $7 million for its interest in the company that owned the barges, and Enron kept that money. No one in the press or the Department of Justice or anyone other than the defense team had ever seemed to notice those salient facts.

Notably this was not a securities fraud case. The task force didn't allege a securities fraud in this case because the barge deal was too small a financial transaction by comparison to Enron's earnings to meet the legal requirement for securities fraud. This transaction, unlike many of Fastow's schemes, had no relationship to Enron's stock price, and the entire concept of "loss" was legally irrelevant when the defendants had not stolen any money from Enron or anyone else. Would Werlein understand any of it? It would take a miracle.

Nancy and Jim agreed that I would go to the courthouse the next morning and observe Bayly's sentencing. I would text them the important news. Jim would go out for a walk. Nancy would pace in the room. We wished each other a "good night"—even though we all knew it would not be—and went to our rooms to try to rest.

Ewing Werlein's wood-paneled courtroom on the fourteenth floor of the federal courthouse in Houston was full by 8:30 a.m. on April 21.

The usual cast was present: Friedrich and Ruemmler for the government, along with appellate division attorney Sangita Rao. Tom

Hagemann, Richard Schaeffer, Robert Fiske, and Larry Robbins were there representing Dan Bayly, and Bayly's friends and family packed the courtroom.

A distinguished, slender, and immaculately groomed gentleman of the first order, Bayly looked ten years older also.

The press was also present: Mary Flood for the *Chronicle*, Laurel Calkins for Bloomberg, Juan Lozano for the Associated Press, and various other reporters.

The loud bang on the judge's door into the courtroom jolted everyone to their feet. Werlein, somber and clipped, ordered Schaeffer and Bayly to come stand right in front of the bench so he could look down at them from his elevated position. Hagemann, Fiske, and Robbins went also. The five of them stood penitently in a line in front of the judge's bench. The tension in the courtroom was thick. Looking very stern, Werlein recited the long list of the material that he said he had read: the presentence report and objections to it, the defendants' loss memorandum, an *amicus* (friend of the court) brief filed by the United States Chamber of Commerce in support of the defendants' position on the absence of any loss to Enron, and the many character letters filed on Bayly's behalf. Werlein quickly sustained the government's objections to the presentence report.

To no one's surprise, he denied multiple defense objections; a few, he sustained. This was already taking forever.

Then Werlein launched into a prepared soliloquy, which began sounding better than I had expected. Had he actually read and understood some of the Merrill defendants' recent briefing? The entire gallery of friends and family who had come to support the Baylys caught their breath.

That glimmer of hope was fleeting. Werlein seemed to be buying into the government's argument that the Barge deal added a penny a share to Enron's earnings. As he droned on, and we all hung on every word, he eventually rejected Ruemmler and Friedrich's argument that the Merrill defendants caused a $45 million loss to Enron shareholders.

Then it got really interesting. Werlein continued reading his script: "During these years, in the late 1990s and into 2001, it appears that at least several key executives at Enron, two of whom testified in this trial, had set upon a course of what those who testified now admit was lying, stealing, and committing various kinds of fraud upon Enron, its shareholders and its potential investors. The Nigerian Barge fraud, from the evidence received in this trial, would appear to have been one of the smaller and more benign frauds committed by these conspirators at Enron."

Werlein seemed to have finally absorbed some of the points we had stressed in our briefing. He continued, "In this instance, at least, the Nigerian barge assets were real, the negotiations with Nigeria for the sale of power generated from the barges were real, and a bona fide sale ultimately was consummated in the year 2000, producing an authentic profit for Enron in an amount of more than $50 million."

The courtroom seemed to breathe in hope again.

Werlein wasn't finished. "Because the court is satisfied that there was some loss by Enron and its shareholders, the court finds that it is reasonable to adopt the gain procured by the offender from committing the fraud as an alternative estimate of loss."

I'm sure my face showed sheer disbelief. There was "no gain procured by the offender." None of the Merrill or Enron defendants took a dime in this case. This wasn't like the British bankers in NatWest, the Southampton deal, or any of Fastow's other side deals where he, Kopper, and Glisan pocketed millions. In this case, Merrill Lynch—the company—only made $775,000 for taking the risk of the power barges, and Enron made $53 million. Enron lost nothing, and its shareholders lost nothing. There was no gain procured by Bayly at all. He was just doing his job.

Werlein, ever resourceful in his ways of ruling for the task force, had figured out a way to tag Bayly with some loss amount. He was holding Bayly responsible for the gain procured for Merrill Lynch in the amount of $775,000. He also tagged Bayly for a $700,000 fee that Enron paid Fastow's LJM2 fund.

Clearly Werlein had failed to grasp the irrefutable fact that none of the Merrill defendants had anything to do with Enron's sale of the barge investment to Fastow's LJM2 fund and could not have done anything to stop it even if they had. Only Fastow knew before the fact that LJM2 was buying the barges, and the Merrill defendants certainly had no control over him—or knowledge of what he was doing. Enron's board of directors had blessed Fastow's dual roles as Enron chief financial officer and head of LJM2.

Ironically Jim of all people never would have agreed for LJM2 to buy the barges. He and Bayly had invested relatively small amounts in a Merrill partnership with LJM2. Jim didn't want to touch the barges with the proverbial ten-foot pole. We had the trial record now. There was no evidence that any of the Merrill defendants planned or agreed to sell the barges to LJM2—much less that they knew Fastow was stealing from and manipulating LJM2 for his own gain.

To the contrary, the evidence at trial had been that Fastow had literally giggled with glee at the thought of LJM2 buying the barges from Merrill in June 2000. Fastow had just learned that a nine-barge power purchase agreement was being signed with Nigeria, and Citibank had issued a $60 million letter of credit, virtually gold-plating the barges. To Fastow, it was a sure win and a quick fee from Enron for LJM2 to swoop in and buy these—as long as Merrill did not find out about the new deal—and Fastow would look like a hero to Enron on top of it all. Of course, Fastow did not share any of these new developments with Merrill Lynch. By the end of June, Fastow wanted the barges and fast—before anyone else had an opportunity to buy them.

I wondered how long Werlein had worked on writing all of this and which law clerk had helped him come up with this novel approach.

Werlein droned on. "The actual loss to Enron and its shareholders . . . total $1,475,000 . . . and the court accepts those measures of gains of Merrill Lynch and LJM2 as the loss amount in this case."

The men standing in front of his bench for more than an hour by now were shifting, obviously tired of standing, and struggling to comprehend what they were hearing.

"Your Honor," Robbins tried to interrupt when Werlein paused.

Werlein barked, "I'm not through yet."

Robbins quickly apologized.

Werlein resumed. "The court finds that the organizers, leaders, managers, and supervisors of this criminal activity were the executives at Enron who conceived, planned, and directed the execution of this entire fraudulent Nigeria Barge transaction. . . ."

That was sounding a little better. Werlein continued, "Defendant Bayly and the other Merrill executives who acceded to the importunities of the Enron decision makers to engage Merrill in the fraudulent transaction were acting in their ordinary roles commensurate with the positions they held at Merrill Lynch. The facts of this case are therefore most unique when considering the individual role adjustments."

"No shit, Sherlock," someone in the gallery murmured. This case was completely unique—literally unprecedented. There had never been a conspiracy conviction for just doing a job when the person did not personally pocket the ill-gotten gains, and everything was documented and reported to counsel and the IRS. I had long said this was a case without a crime.

Werlein was still reading. "This entire fraud was organized and driven by certain executives at Enron. The executives at Merrill who were enlisted in the conspiracy were motivated by a desire to prove that Merrill was a friend of Enron and to ingratiate Merrill with Enron to improve chances to obtain future legitimate business."

The monologue continued. "Defendant Bayly and the other Merrill defendants were not recruiting accomplices or claiming for themselves a right to a larger share of the fruits of the crime or planning or organizing the offense. Instead the Merrill defendants, here, Defendant Bayly, while engaged in his regular job, joined Enron's criminal conspiracy to create an ostensible sale to Merrill of future revenues on the barges with an oral side deal that Enron would extricate Merrill within six months and pay an agreed rate of return to Merrill on the $7 million that it advanced. Merrill's actual decision to enter this deal was made by a more senior executive not charged in this case."

Had I heard it correctly? Werlein had just told the world that the defendants were just doing their jobs, trying to build their business, and he recognized that they did not even have the authority to make the deal happen.

The people in the gallery were squirming in their seats. Where was he going with this? It was sounding good for the defense.

Emotional and physical fatigue was setting in for Bayly, his counsel, and everyone in the courtroom who had been listening to the judge drone on for more than an hour.

Bayly and his counsel were shifting from one foot to the other. The discomfort of being forced to stand at attention for hours and look up at the judge while waiting to be sent to prison for the rest of your life was part of the torture of these defendants. Friedrich and Ruemmler, sitting comfortably at the counsel table, had been enjoying it—until now. They were whispering to each other and looking concerned.

To Bayly and his family and friends, it felt like an eternity. After his monologue, Werlein resumed ruling on objections to the presentence report. Finally he asked if he had ruled on all the objections.

"I believe you have, Judge," Hagemann responded.

Werlein then offered the defense an opportunity to speak on behalf of Bayly or for Bayly to speak to the court himself.

Hagemann asked that Robbins be allowed to speak to the loss calculation, but Werlein shut that down. "Well, I've ruled on the loss, and I've had this many briefs on the loss," he said, holding his hand horizontal to his desk at about the one-foot mark. "So you'll get a chance to speak to others on the loss, I'm sure" (meaning the court of appeals). "That brings the sentencing guidelines recommended custody range to forty-six to fifty-seven months and the fine to $10,000 to $100,000."

Robbins spoke up, ostensibly to preserve a point for the record, thereby making it harder for Werlein to shut him up. Robbins explained that if the court was going to use "gain" to punish the defendants, it would have to be gain to the defendants themselves, not gain that someone else received. The law did not allow them to be sentenced for money that was documented and paid to their employer, Merrill Lynch. Robbins was correct; I had argued that point from our very first meeting.

Robbins made a valiant effort, but Werlein quickly shot him down. "It's an alternative estimate of loss, of course."

Hagemann then spoke on Bayly's behalf. First pandering to the judge as he often did, Hagemann thanked Judge Werlein for "the amount of thought you have obviously devoted to this."

Hagemann then queried, "I'm assuming, Judge, that you have read each and every letter in the extraordinary outpouring of support for Mr. Bayly?"

Werlein said, "Yes," but his squirm and failure to make eye contact revealed that he had not read them all. In a moment, he admitted this. "I should say, perhaps, that I have read all of the—at least three score of letters that were received."

Everyone in the gallery knew that meant he had read only a fraction of them. More than one hundred letters were written about Dan Bayly, detailing examples of kindness and professionalism, providing touching testimonials of his integrity and character, and explaining how much he meant to everyone at Merrill Lynch. One would hope that before passing judgment on another human being that would alter his life forever, a federal judge would read all of the letters sent to him.

One of the most important letters was written by a woman who had suffered sexual harassment at Merrill. She felt that no one was listening to her or paying attention to her plight, complaints, or concerns. Like most women in that position, she feared she would not be believed and that she would lose her job if she reported it. She finally worked up the courage to talk to Dan Bayly. She wrote, "As I got to know Dan better, I decided to approach him on the harassment matter and discuss its effects on me. Without even blinking, Dan pursued two courses: A quiet investigation of the senior executive involved to evaluate his behavior and a review of my promotion process to determine whether it was fair and appropriate, given the possible conflict of the committee member. The conclusion of these efforts was (i) the institutional recognition that the individual in question had been a habitual harasser and that multiple women had been victims; and (ii), an apology to me and recognition that my career had been inappropriately and unfairly influenced by this individual's participation on the committee. No senior individual other than Dan Bayly had the courage or institutional fortitude to pursue an investigation into this situation."

A more senior woman executive wrote at length about how Dan Bayly had stood by her when everyone else fled, describing his calls and letters as a "lifeline." She prophesied, "Years from now, in a calmer and less heady time, when the story of Dan Bayly is recounted, it will read as a cruel tragedy. You have great power and responsibility at this time, Your Honor, since you stand as the sole actor in this drama who can put some right into it. Please let courage and compassion guide your sentencing deliberations. Consider your legacy, consider justice, consider the man. Do not send this man to prison."

Finally Werlein looked at Dan Bayly. "Do you wish to make a statement?"

Dan looked the judge in the eye and was unwavering. "Yes, Your Honor, briefly. I've always tried to live my life both personally and professionally with the greatest integrity and the greatest respect for others. This whole experience has been devastating to me in a way that I cannot adequately convey. The one thing that has gotten me through this extraordinary experience is the wonderful support that I have received from my family and friends, my colleagues, much of which you have had the opportunity to read in the letters. I hope they convey the kind of person that I really am and the kind of life that I have led for fifty-seven years and that you'll take that into account in your sentencing. Thank you."

Ruemmler rose first to speak for the government. "Mr. Bayly presents himself to you as a victim, as a victim of an overzealous prosecution, as a victim of bad executives at Enron. There is not one iota of acceptance of responsibility." Spewing self-righteous indignation and fury, she continued. "Mr. Bayly was convicted of three felony offenses because of his own actions and conduct. This was not an isolated event. This is a conspiracy that spanned a six-month period of time. And after that, Mr. Bayly met with investigators and he continued to attempt to conceal the conspiracy through his lies."

Friedrich picked up the torch. He asked the court for a greater term of imprisonment than what the guidelines recommended. He went back to the securities fraud theme that he had pounded at trial. "The $1.4 million is not the money that this case was about. This was executed as a scheme to manipulate publicly reported earnings. That's what it was about." Friedrich was fuming and snide. "There is no 'benign fraud' when it comes to playing God with the earnings of publicly reported companies."

Now the gallery was fuming. Friedrich knew that the Merrill defendants had no role in what or how Enron reported its earnings—and Friedrich damn well knew this wasn't a securities fraud case. Nonetheless Friedrich returned to the mantra that had worked so well for him at the trial. He blamed Bayly and the Merrill men for lying to their own lawyers and investors. "Bayly and his conspirators totally misled Merrill counsel Kathy Zrike about what was going on. . . . This case is about lying to investors. . . . And when the jury convicted, they had to find that Dan Bayly acted with an intent to deceive or cheat. . . . It's not about $1.4 million. It's about $383 million." Friedrich requested that the sentence "send a message to Wall Street."

Once again, Friedrich had misstated the law and the record in the case. This time, Robbins took him on, calmly reminding Judge Werlein that it was his responsibility to sentence Bayly according to the law and the recent decision of the Supreme Court. Nothing Friedrich had just argued had any basis in the law or the facts.

Judge Werlein was ready to move on. His mind was clearly made up as to whatever it was he was going to do. He came out with his script set. It didn't matter a flip what anyone said. By now, Bayly and his counsel had been standing at the bench for almost two hours. Bayly's family and friends were exhausted from sitting on the hard wooden benches and the tension of all of it.

Werlein denied Friedrich's request for a greater sentencing range. Friedrich was turning red.

Suddenly Werlein visibly softened. His tone and demeanor changed dramatically. He seemed to feel some measure of compassion, which no one in the courtroom had seen from him before. He acknowledged the detailed letters and that "Mr. Bayly has established a very, very high reputation. Certainly, over thirty years, that reputation was earned as one who was an extraordinarily honest man, the highest integrity. . . . It is that reputation that some remarked led him to be known as 'Boy Scout Bayly' or 'By the Book Bayly.' And yet as successful as he was, he's always remained a highly disciplined and modest man."

To everyone's amazement, Werlein admitted, "It may be that I've never had a defendant stand before me, probably in my years as a judge and having sentenced hundreds of people, that has had a more glowing and extraordinary record of being a good citizen than in this particular case."

Werlein unexpectedly reduced the sentencing range to thirty to thirty-seven months, finding that Bayly's behavior in this case was "aberrant."

Friedrich and Ruemmler were turning purple and looking apoplectic. They were about to explode, especially Friedrich.

Remarkably Judge Werlein then compared and contrasted the conduct of the Merrill defendants to that of Andrew Fastow, "Enron's chief financial officer, who was at the epicenter of criminal activity and fraudulent transactions at Enron, who has appropriated to himself untold millions of dollars to which Enron was entitled." Werlein pointed to the prosecutors' decision that Fastow deserved a plea deal on terms that permitted him to avoid any imprisonment beyond a statutory maximum of ten years.

Werlein was actually diverging from the government's view. He was recognizing the unfairness of the sweetheart deals the government had made with those who actually stole millions of dollars from Enron. We had hammered on those points and others he had mentioned in the brief we had filed for Jim.

Friedrich and Ruemmler cringed as Werlein noted, "The government brought in from prison Glisan, who admitted to having stolen $1 million for himself from Enron, and the government viewed him as worthy of a deal that subjected him to a maximum of five years in prison, which he is now serving. Mr. Glisan and Mr. Fastow established some benchmarks for sentencing the defendants in this case."

Now Friedrich and Ruemmler were gripping the arms of their chairs and sharing looks of rage. The gallery of friends and family was hopeful again. What was Werlein going to do? There was no way he could sentence Dan Bayly—the finest man who had ever stood before him, a man who had not taken anything from anyone—to anything approaching five years in prison. Most of us wondered how Judge Werlein could send Dan Bayly to prison at all.

Werlein was still lecturing—but this time to the government. "While the court does not condone or excuse the defendant or the other Merrill defendants, there are dramatic differences—like the differences between night and day—between the fraudulent conduct, motives, and magnitude of criminal involvement engaged in by this defendant and those for whom the government believes that a maximum five- or ten-year sentence is sufficient. The Merrill defendants stand convicted of relatively lesser offenses—with no personal gain. Fastow, Glisan, and others reaped huge personal gains."

This was encouraging. Werlein was making the very points I had made to the collective appellate team from the day of our first meeting and to the court in our motion for Jim's release on bail pending appeal. I wondered if Werlein understood the full legal impact of what he was saying.

"Now I am going to impose sentence. The defendant Dan Bayly is hereby committed to the custody of the Bureau of Prisons to be imprisoned for a term of thirty months. He must pay restitution in the amount of $492,500, and a fine of $250,000."

Ruemmler and Friedrich couldn't stand it. They leaped to their feet and objected to the reduced sentence and asked for a second calculation of the gain/loss. Friedrich, apparently not having understood the judge's words or noticed the marked change in his tone and demeanor, actually asked the judge a question.

Werlein made clear that he was taking objections—not answering questions.

Friedrich was livid over the judge's use of the plea agreements of Glisan and Fastow as benchmarks for the sentences of these defendants. He wouldn't quit.

For the first time, this really had not gone the way the prosecutors had planned. Ruemmler tried again. "Your Honor, the court repeatedly said it was a maximum of ten and five years respectively for Mr. Fastow and Mr. Glisan. In fact, Your Honor, these are minimums. In other words, those two defendants—Mr. Glisan is serving a sixty-month sentence. He will serve no less than sixty months. And the same is true with Mr. Fastow. He will serve under the terms of his agreement no less than ten years."

Werlein was finally irritated with the prosecutors. This was a first!

He pushed Ruemmler until she admitted that Fastow had been allowed to plead to an offense with a ten-year maximum. Still she steadfastly maintained that ten years is what Andrew Fastow would be required to serve. That was an affirmative misrepresentation.

When Ruemmler and Werlein concluded their exchange over the prior plea deals for those who actually stole money from Enron, defense attorney Fiske requested bail pending appeal for Bayly. Fiske also asked that Bayly be allowed to "voluntarily report" to prison as opposed to being picked up by marshals and taken in handcuffs.

Werlein agreed to two of the three key elements necessary for a convicted defendant to remain on bail pending his appeal. He found that Bayly was no danger to the community and no risk of flight. The gallery was deathly quiet. No one so much as shuffled as we awaited Werlein's decision as to whether Bayly would be hauled from the courtroom in chains.

Any sign of softness or compassion evaporated from Werlein as quickly as it had appeared. The icy Werlein said that the third element required for release pending appeal would require him to find that the case would be reversed on appeal. I knew that was not a correct statement of the legal standard, and, of course, he believed that all of his rulings were correct. He couldn't possibly have made a mistake. He self-righteously declared the bail motion denied. In the height of arrogance or blind denial, he found that there was no substantial issue for appeal, just as the government had argued, even though there was no legal precedent for these charges on any similar facts.

There was an audible gasp from the gallery.

Reignited by this favorable ruling, Friedrich exploded to his feet. This was the moment he had been waiting for. He and Ruemmler were salivating at the thought of seeing the former head of Merrill Lynch's Investment Banking Division handcuffed in front of his family, friends, colleagues, and the press, and hauled from the courtroom, straight to prison. The armed marshals around the courtroom doors were shuffling.

Predictably Friedrich said, "Under what Your Honor just found, we'd like Mr. Bayly to be detained now."

Bayly and his family froze as they waited for their ultimate and immediate fear to materialize. Would Judge Werlein—over the government's vehement opposition—let Dan Bayly go home and then drive himself to prison when he was ordered to do so?

Werlein's tone flipped again. He replied brusquely to Friedrich, "I have read your submission on that." Then he turned and looked straight at Dan Bayly. "If I let you walk out of here, are you going to report when you're expected to in three, four, or five weeks?"

Bayly stood straight and tall. He looked Werlein dead in the eyes and affirmed: "There is no question, Your Honor, that I will report as directed."

"All right. I'll permit the defendant to voluntarily surrender."

The gallery sounded like someone had just let the air out of a tire—a huge sigh in unified relief.

After two hours and eight minutes of standing at the bench, under the greatest strain of his life, Dan Bayly walked out of the courtroom with his wife, family, and friends. They all knew, though, that with a simple phone call any day, he and his wife would have to make the long drive to a federal prison where he would face the unfathomable—forced to spend the next thirty months of his life behind bars for simply doing his job. They could only hope that the Fifth Circuit would see the error in Judge Werlein's ruling denying Bayly's release on bail pending appeal.

We attorneys knew there was far more than a "substantial issue for appeal." Werlein had looked at the issue from the wrong end of the telescope. The Fifth Circuit should give these men the freedom to remain on bail pending appeal of an indictment that failed to allege a crime and a trial that was so riddled with errors it would have to be reversed. We'd already prepared a motion for release on bail pending appeal for Jim, and we knew we were correct on the law.

I texted the news of Bayly's sentence to Jim and Nancy. We were up next. They would have to be in the courtroom to stand at the bench themselves in little more than an hour and a half. Jim had been convicted of two more counts than had Bayly. We knew it was going to be worse for Jim than it had been for Dan.

The loud bang on the door from the judge's chambers into the courtroom prompted us all to stand as Werlein entered, his black robe billowing as he briskly ascended to the bench.

"Mr. Brown . . . counsel, are you ready to proceed with sentencing?"

"We are, Your Honor."

"Step forward then please."

Three of us walked up to the bench. Larry Zweifach stood meekly on the left; Jim was in the center—dead square in front of Werlein; and then there was me, in my red suit, measuring six feet tall barefoot and with my hair wet. My three-inch heels put me at about eye level with Werlein even though he was on the bench. I stood ramrod straight on Jim's right. Livid over what I had read in the trial transcript and appalled at the blatant unfairness of it all, I was "seeing red," and I decided Werlein could just see it too. I was loaded for bear, and I was happy for him to know it—not that it mattered a whit.

Jim was terrified but resolute and brave. Nancy and the kids were borderline sick, mixed with anger and fear. They sat in the gallery—on the other side of the rail that divides the courtroom.

Armed marshals hovered menacingly at various exits from the courtroom.

Werlein started the same as he had with Bayly. Friedrich, Ruemmler, and Sangita Rao from the appellate section at the Justice Department were at the counsel table for the government. They were a combination of deflated, seething, and ready to take their fury out on Jim Brown.

After dealing with numerous objections from both sides to the presentence report on which Werlein would rely to formulate the sentence, the judge continued as he had with Bayly. He had the same script, and he started reading it all again.

We stood, and we stood, and we stood. An hour passed, then an hour and a half. My back was aching. Werlein was droning on. I was listening to every word in case anything was different.

The closer we got to the actual pronouncement of sentencing, the more the marshals shuffled. I dared not look back at Nancy. I kept glaring at Werlein who was just reading on and on. It had been obvious that Werlein really liked Dan Bayly. We couldn't say the same for Brown or any of the others.

We caught our first breath of relief when Werlein surprised everyone by adopting a sentencing guideline range of forty-six to fifty-seven months of imprisonment and a fine of $10,000 to $100,000. That range was larger than Bayly's, but Jim had the additional convictions of perjury and obstruction of justice. It was far less than thirty years though.

Ruemmler and Friedrich started fuming again.

Finally the judge was ready to hear from the defendant.

Jim was somber and respectful.

"The last twenty months have been the most difficult time ever in the lives of my family and me. Since we learned I would be indicted for my involvement in this transaction, I have been branded a liar and a criminal. I can no longer earn a living in my chosen occupation. My health and well-being have significantly deteriorated. My wife and children deeply share this pain. What hurts me the most is that they should suffer due to my circumstances. Notwithstanding these tribulations, I have learned and grown a great deal, perhaps more so now than at any time during my life. Remarkably this experience has brought some positive changes. I've been blessed with a loving wife and two wonderful children. This experience has strengthened the bonds between all of us."

Jim took a deep breath and continued. "I realize we are blessed with many good and loyal friends and a wonderful, caring church and community. They have selflessly and clearly given us their strong support and fellowship during this most difficult time. More than ever before, I've learned to enjoy life at the present moment and appreciate its simple pleasures. My senses are sharper. I appreciate the daily facets of my life, and I have a feeling of peace and acceptance. With God's help and the support of our family and friends, I pray that my wife and children will be able to continue to lead happy and productive lives, always substituting love and acceptance for bitterness and anguish."

In conclusion, Jim added, "If I am imprisoned, the greatest punishment would be the separation from my family, especially at this important stage in the young adult lives of my children. However, I am confident that God will continue to provide me with the strength to accept whatever this court may impose upon me. Thank you."

I patted Jim on the shoulder behind his back when Werlein looked down.

"All right, very well." Looking at Ruemmler and Friedrich, Werlein asked, "Do you wish to make a statement for the government?"

Friedrich jumped up with a firm "Yes, Your Honor."

Friedrich immediately began with a request for a significantly higher sentence—just as he had done with Bayly. He argued for a higher sentence as a deterrent to others because the range the judge chose "does not reflect the degree of seriousness of the crime in messing with a public company's earnings."

Friedrich never cared or accepted that the task force did not indict this case as a securities fraud—a fact which rendered his earnings argument irrelevant. He and Ruemmler simply wanted these men put away for at least fourteen years, preferably thirty.

He continued to argue for "a harsh sentence . . . in earnings management and earnings manipulation cases. That is not simply our view. That is Congress's view." He claimed the true loss could not be measured in a drop in Enron's stock price because these "criminals were good. They were good at what they did, and they hid the fraud. It wasn't revealed to the market, and that's the only reason why it's not measurable. It's not that there's no loss." According to Friedrich, the guidelines would provide "for a fourteen-year sentence were there an objective measure of loss that could be arrived at."

There were two things wrong with that argument. First, there was no objective measure of loss here because there was no loss at all. Second, once again, this was not a securities fraud case, so stock value didn't even matter. How could this honors graduate of the University of Texas School of Law argue this with a straight face?

Werlein's mind was made up as to whatever the sentence was going to be, but he thought Ruemmler wanted to weigh in, and he gave her the opportunity to speak. Surprisingly she did not.

In his most serious tone, Werlein announced, "I'll state now the sentence the court intends to impose."

We steeled ourselves. The sentence itself was the first hurdle; then the questions would be whether he would let Jim voluntarily report to prison as he had let Bayly and whether he would allow Jim bail pending appeal.

"It's the judgment of the court the defendant James A. Brown is hereby committed to the custody of the Bureau of Prisons to be imprisoned for a term of forty-six months with respect to Counts One, Two, Three, Four, and Five of the Third Superseding Indictment, all such terms to run concurrent for a total term of imprisonment of forty-six months, a fine of $250,000, and restitution in the amount of $295,000 plus $147,500."

I heard Jim breathe. At least the unknown was now known. Compared to fourteen or more years in prison, he would at least get out in time to see his future grandchildren.

Friedrich was beside himself with rage. He just couldn't stand it. He said, "This is just awkward to do. I would simply ask the court whether the sentencing disparity that the government objected to this morning regarding Bayly was the part of the basis for its sentence in this case. I don't know how else I can preserve an objection. I hope you don't mind me asking that?"

Werlein had no clue what Friedrich was talking about and asking the court a question is rarely a good thing for a lawyer to do—even a federal prosecutor. Werlein didn't like it one bit. "I have considered all the requirements of Section 3553A as required by Congress. Any other objection besides those—"

Friedrich wouldn't turn it loose. He interrupted the judge. "I'm sorry?"

Werlein talked through him: "—that have already been made?"

Friedrich still wouldn't quit. "I'm sorry. I have to ask if the disparity comments that the court made—"

Ruemmler was squirming.

Now Werlein was really getting irritated. He barked, "I've given you my ruling. Is there anything else you object to?"

Finally Friedrich stopped with "No, sir."

Werlein turned to the issue of reporting to prison. "Now, what's the government's position with respect to Mr. Brown voluntarily surrendering?"

Friedrich responded, slightly cowed, "The same as we took with respect to Mr. Bayly this morning, Your Honor."

"All right. You understand, Mr. Brown, that if I permit you to voluntarily surrender, you have to report to a facility when you get the notice."

Jim replied, "Yes, Your Honor."

"And if you don't, you will have committed another crime."

"Yes, Your Honor."

Werlein looked Jim in the eyes. "I've got this whole booklet of letters of people that have written good things about you."

"I won't disappoint them," Jim volunteered.

Judge Werlein asked, "You won't make me look foolish?"

"No, Your Honor," Jim answered him.

"By failing to report when ordered?"

"I will report when ordered to do so," Jim said again.

"You will probably get that notice within a few weeks. I'll permit you to continue on terms of release as you have before. Your reporting when and where required also assists the Bureau of Prisons in considering the assignment that you should have in your case. I would recommend to the Bureau of Prisons that you be considered for a minimum-security prison based upon my belief that you will report and that you will do the things required to fulfill this time."

"I will give you my word I will report as ordered," Jim assured him.

Werlein was finally satisfied. "All right. Is there anything else?"

My turn now. "Yes, Your Honor. We also have a motion for release pending appeal before the court for a ruling."

Tersely Werlein returned to his script. "Mr. Brown is not likely to flee or pose a danger to the safety of any other person in the community. However, apart from that, the court must conclude that the appeal is not likely to result in reversal or order for new trial. I'm unable to make any of those findings and, therefore, that motion is denied. Anything else?"

Friedrich, his tail between his legs, responded, "No, thank you, Your Honor."

"All right. Thank you. That concludes this session. Court will be in recess."

I e-mailed Hellen, who filed the notice of appeal for Jim before I left the courtroom. We would ask the Fifth Circuit for bail pending appeal as quickly as we could get the papers finished and filed. We believed the Fifth Circuit would grant it. The law was clear. There was not just "a substantial issue" for appeal—there were several.

Jim, in particular, felt like he had escaped the firing squad. Our sense of relief soon faded though. Hanging over Jim's family was the reality that they had only about thirty days to get everything in order before Jim would go to a yet-undetermined prison for almost four years.

– 7 –

Supreme Reversals

O n April 21, 2005, I told Jim and Nancy good-bye in Houston, flew to Asheville, North Carolina, for a couple of nights, repacked, and headed to Washington, DC. Maureen Mahoney was arguing the *Andersen* case in the Supreme Court on April 27. The plan was to be at the courthouse early. The gallery would be packed. I wanted a personal read on how the court would respond to our arguments in this first serious challenge to the task force's terror tactics.

Lawyers who were members of "the Bar of the Court"—actually admitted to practice before it—would be standing in a separate line beginning at 7:30 a.m. for a case this important. It was basically first come, first served. Members of the public would have to stand in an even longer line, and they would be allowed to sit in the back of the Supreme Court chamber for only ten minutes of argument at a time. The arguments were scheduled from 10:00 a.m. until noon.

The majesty of the Supreme Court building and courtroom cannot be overstated. It is a solemn and awesome place. White marble and magnificent columns are everywhere. Counsel enter the court building through security at a special side door. Everything is searched, and cell phones must be left behind. Most of us just don't take them. Antique mahogany and brass elevators take counsel to the second floor.

As a member of the Supreme Court Bar, I breezed through to the shorter line, and who did I see upon my arrival in the main hall but Matthew Friedrich and Kathryn Ruemmler. Ruemmler ignored me. Friedrich came over to greet me. I nodded and gritted my teeth.

Because of my earlier albeit minor role in the *Andersen* case, Maureen extended me the privilege of being with her and her colleagues, so I was ushered into the attorneys' lounge, upstairs across from the courtroom and adjoining the office of the solicitor general of the United States.

The solicitor general, often called the "Tenth Justice" because he or she is so important to much of the court's work and so trusted, runs the office of elite attorneys privileged to argue cases for the government in the Supreme Court. The solicitor general and his or her assistants' attire for argument was still the traditional gray and black striped morning coat with tails. Assistant Solicitor General Michael Dreeben, a brilliant, tall, gangly man with glasses, was arguing this case for the United States.

When it was time for the arguments, we were ushered into the courtroom together. I sat behind Maureen at counsel table. Dreeben and a colleague were at the table to our right. Maureen was composed and confident. She had clerked for Chief Justice Rehnquist who would preside over this argument even though his health was failing rapidly. She seemed completely at home here—natural, with no pretense or arrogance—just comfortable in her ability, her knowledge of her case, the correctness of her position, and the law.

Behind the bench in the courtroom is a ceiling to floor thick, red velvet curtain. The justices walk through invisible slits in it to almost magically appear and take their high-backed leather seats behind the bench. The dark wood tables for counsel and the podium are within whisper distance of the bench. For all its majesty and the grand scale of the chamber, it's an intimate setting for counsel at the podium.

We all rose solemnly as the justices entered. After they were seated, Rehnquist called the case. Maureen stepped to the podium and began, with a slight smile, looking straight at the chief justice. Rehnquist had hands and fingers so long I thought he could span at least two octaves on a piano. It appeared that he could have reached out and almost touched her.

Maureen began by explaining that the "government concedes that the destruction of documents in anticipation of a proceeding was not a crime in the fall of 2001 based upon a statutory rule that Congress had preserved for over a century. The central question in this case is whether Congress, nevertheless, intended to make a polite request to engage in that lawful conduct a form of witness tampering punishable by ten years in prison. We ask this court to reject the government's interpretation of the statute and to hold that Arthur Andersen did not commit a crime."

Then Maureen turned to set the stage with the statute itself. Under Section 1512, "Congress did not prohibit all persuasion to destroy documents for the specific purpose of making them unavailable for use in an official proceeding. It did not simply say, 'Anyone who persuades a witness to do this has violated the statute.' It added a very important limitation, and that is the word 'corruptly'—'corruptly persuades.'"

She was holding the attention of every member of the court. It could only be a good sign for Andersen's position. Rarely does anyone argue as many minutes as she had without being interrupted by a justice with a question about something troubling.

Maureen continued in a nice, conversational but persuasive and professional style—the hallmark of a superlative advocate. "So what kinds of requests are excluded from the definition? When is it OK to persuade someone to destroy a document for use in an official proceeding? And the answer, we think, based on the traditional meaning of the term 'corruptly,' is that 'corruptly' means that you have persuaded someone in a fashion that uses improper means, such as bribery, or you've asked the witness to violate duties imposed by other law, whether that's the duties imposed by contempt or the duties imposed by a whole range of statutes that govern the obligations of people in our society."

Justice Kennedy leaned forward. He had a question. He was trying to decide where the line should be drawn. Could someone destroy documents to conceal a fraud?

Maureen had anticipated and prepared for this very question. "If this is in the course of a proceeding, then it's obviously going to be a crime, prohibited by Section 1512. If it is in advance of a proceeding—and let's assume that you know that a proceeding—"

Justice Kennedy was nodding in agreement, "Yes."

So Maureen continued, "—is likely, then the answer depends on whether you know that a crime has been committed. And if you know that a crime has been committed, then you are violating a federal statute."

Justice Kennedy was still working on it. "My question is, would that give some content to the meaning of 'corruptly,' in your view?"

At this point, I was very glad Maureen was up there arguing this case. Supreme Court arguments can be very esoteric and vague. The argument to me was as simple as if you don't have a legal duty to keep something, you can shred it, torch it, or use it to wipe the floor—whatever you want to do with it—and "corruptly" meant by bribery, threat, extortion, or a clear violation of a legal duty. None of those existed in *Andersen*.

Maureen answered Justice Kennedy and worked back around to the requirement of a duty. "Well, in that case, if the witness knows that you have committed a crime, and you are asking them to violate, they have a duty, under those circumstances, not to assist you in concealing your offense. That's a duty that's imposed by criminal law. So if you ask them to violate that, it would fall within the interpretation of the statute that Arthur Andersen is advancing here. And it fits, Your Honor, with what Congress really did for a hundred years before 2002 . . . under the *Pettibone* rule, that it is not a crime to simply destroy documents in anticipation of a proceeding. But if you know that a crime has been committed and you destroy documents, that is a crime."

That certainly made sense, I thought. *Several criminal statutes forbid helping someone who you know has committed a crime.* Justice O'Connor teed up the next question, followed soon by Justice Scalia and others. Maureen answered each question deftly. This was like watching a fascinating conversation on the law among the ten most brilliant people in the country. Finally she had the opportunity to hit a home run. According to the government, Maureen explained, "any intent to keep any kind of information away from the SEC was enough to satisfy the definition of a crime in this case."

The justices were attentive, and she continued. "And, in fact, Your Honor, the pattern instruction for the Fifth Circuit included the words 'knowingly or dishonestly to subvert the integrity of the proceeding.' The government insisted that the word 'dishonestly' not be used, that the word 'impede' be added, and they changed 'subverting the proceedings' to 'the fact-finding ability.' They did everything they could to strip this instruction of any *mens rea* or criminal intent. They went beyond that and said, 'And in addition, even if the Andersen employees had a good-faith belief that their conduct was lawful, it's still a crime.'"

Justice Ginsburg intervened with a question to sort out the effect of Andersen partner David Duncan's guilty plea on the entire matter.

Maureen explained that he had pleaded guilty, but when he testified in the *Andersen* trial, he repeatedly said that he did not believe, at the time, that he had done anything unlawful or improper. Duncan had told the *Andersen* jury that he thought his conduct was perfectly appropriate. He had pleaded guilty only because the task force "persuaded" him that it "didn't matter what he thought at the time."

The justices were hanging on Maureen's every word, and they were allowing her to continue without interruption. "Duncan's testimony at the Andersen trial was explicit. He never testified that he even thought that an SEC proceeding was probable at the time; he just thought it was possible. Nor did he say that he ever consciously tried to hide the truth or hide the facts. What he did say was that part of what was on his mind at the time that he asked for compliance with this policy was that the SEC and others might want to look at these files someday. He thought that they had better get the files in compliance with the firm's retention policy, because he knew that drafts and notes are the kinds of things that could be misused and misconstrued at some point in the future."

Maureen explained that Andersen had retained all of its work papers that were required to document its audit. The only things that were discarded were notes of drafts that were preliminary or partial, and could be misconstrued. Many companies and federal agencies routinely destroy notes and preliminary papers once a final report is complete. She specifically noted the FBI's practice of destroying notes upon completion of their 302 reports. Because she knew another question would come soon, Maureen deftly worked the answer back to her primary theme. "The government's interpretation, the instructions that were given to this jury, deprived the term 'corruptly persuade' of any of its ordinary and traditional meaning. Under the government's view, for instance, of 'corruptly,' bribery becomes irrelevant under this statute."

In perfect conversational tone, she asked the crucial question—and then answered it: "What was Congress trying to prohibit here when it lists wrongful means of interfering with witnesses? It says 'intimidate' and 'threaten' and 'use of physical force,' and it says 'corruptly persuades.' The first thing that would come to your mind is bribery. But bribery is irrelevant under the government's interpretation, and let me explain why. Because they say that, 'Well, yes, it's true, it says "corruptly persuade."' But, all that means is if you had any intent to impede the fact-finding ability of a 'proceeding,' then you're guilty, just for asking. It doesn't matter whether you used any money as a bribe to extract this behavior; you're automatically guilty."

Justice Scalia interrupted: "I assume it also would make 'intimidate,' and so forth, quite superfluous."

Maureen was just waiting for that softball. "It absolutely would, Your Honor, because it would basically cover any kind of request."

I had been reasonably certain that Justice Scalia would vote to reverse, but this question confirmed it. We could count Justice Scalia on the side of Andersen. He's the Supreme Court's textualist. He always looks to the words of the statute itself.

Justice Kennedy was still bothered. Andersen's conduct just didn't feel right. He chimed in, "There is, in the case, this lingering feeling that something's wrong out there. I know that we don't—we don't convict people on that basis; we require something more specific."

Maureen understood and was ready for any concern. "Well, and I think that this statute, reasonably read, Your Honor, tells you exactly what that specific thing is. If you intimidate them, if you mislead them, if you use physical force, if you corruptly persuade them. And that means either you've used unlawful means, like bribery, or you asked them to violate their independent legal duties. And that definition, Your Honor, is quite consistent with the traditional interpretation of the term 'corruptly.' . . . The *Pettibone* rule, for a hundred years, was that destruction and other kinds of acts of potential obstruction in advance of a proceeding were not a crime."

Justice O'Connor asked if Section 1519 was at issue here. Maureen said it was not. Indeed Section 1519 was not enacted until 2002—after Andersen's actions. Section 1505, the statute that actually applies to the destruction of documents, required that a proceeding be pending. That was why the prosecutors tried to fit this conduct under the "witness tampering" statute. All the justices seemed satisfied by the end of her argument. It was a little hard to tell about Justice Ginsburg, and maybe Justice Kennedy was still on the fence about how to write the decision, but Andersen's position had improved significantly.

Dreeben stepped to the podium and began. "Arthur Andersen's conduct in this case explains why Congress enacted a statute like Section 1512 that protects against the anticipatory destruction of documents when a proceeding is—"

He didn't get a complete sentence out before he was interrupted by Justice O'Connor. "Well Section 1519, enacted subsequently, comes closer to the mark, doesn't it, than 1512?" she asked. Dreeben's first answer effectively ensured reversal. He had to admit "Section 1519 was enacted after the events in this case to plug the loophole that Arthur Andersen has pointed out existed in Section 1512 at the time."

We could see the problem becoming increasingly clear to the court. Caldwell and Weissmann, the lead task force prosecutors here, had manipulated the witness tampering statute (§ 1512) to deal with Andersen's destruction of documents. It wouldn't work—it was the square peg/round hole problem. Andersen didn't engage in witness tampering. The statute the task force charged didn't fit the conduct that occurred. The witness tampering statute was not intended to cover shredding documents. Once the task force twisted the law to cram Andersen's conduct into the elements of the crime of witness tampering, then they also had to distort the jury instructions to convict

Andersen on that basis. Caldwell, Weissmann, Friedrich, Buell, and the Department of Justice had destroyed an eighty-nine-year-old accounting institution and eliminated 85,000 jobs by distorting the law, denying the defendants a fair trial, and taking intent out of the jury instructions—and all for what purpose?

After Andersen's conduct, Congress had enacted a law (Section 1519) to require retention of documents, but that just proved that there wasn't such a law in place at the time. The enactment of the new statute confirmed that Andersen's conduct in 2001 was not criminal under existing law, so it didn't solve the task force's problem. Instead the new law proved the task force was wrong. Prosecutors can't make up laws, piece laws together, and create new ways of criminalizing business behavior. That power is entrusted only to Congress.

Justice Scalia pounced on Dreeben, who only made it worse. Dreeben conceded that the law in 2001 "did not already do what 1519 says."

Then Justice O'Connor tried again. "Well, what about the *Pettibone* interpretation that has been outstanding for a long time?"

Dreeben was sounding frustrated with himself and the court. "*Pettibone* applied, Justice O'Connor, to a specific statute, Section 1503, and it's similarly incorporated in 1505. Those statutes protected against obstruction of pending judicial, administrative, and congressional proceedings. The innovation in Section 1512 was to reach beyond the existence of a pending proceeding and to ensure that basically the store doesn't get robbed before the proceeding starts. If Arthur Andersen is correct, then in anticipation of a grand jury investigation that is thought to occur the next day, a corporation can send out a directive to its employees and say, 'Shred all the smoking guns.' It's the corporate equivalent of seeing something that looks like a crime scene and sending somebody in to wipe away the fingerprints before the police can get the yellow tape up."

Justice Scalia was visibly perturbed. The prosecutors had been very creative here. "When can they do it? When can they do it? You didn't allege here that it was in anticipation of any particular proceeding. You say they can't do it once they know that the investigation is on the way. But your theory in this case is that they can't do it, whether they know the investigation is on the way or not. They can't destroy any evidence that might be the subject of an investigation."

Dreeben was on the ropes. "No, that's not our theory—"

Justice Scalia's blood pressure and voice were rising. His face was turning red, and he was leaning forward now. "What is your theory?"

"Our theory is that a person acts corruptly when anticipating a reasonable possibility of an investigation into a specific matter, directs another person to destroy documents that are potentially relevant."

That really set off Scalia and rightfully so. *What did that mean? "Possible investigation?" "Potentially relevant?" What kind of a standard was that?* I looked at the lawyer on my left and grinned. This was looking better by the minute.

Justice Scalia was literally mocking Dreeben now. "A reasonable possibility of an investigation?!"

"That's right," Dreeben replied.

Justice Scalia wasn't letting this one go, and his voice was rising with intensity. "And you want criminal liability to turn upon that? Whether or not there is a reasonable possibility of an investigation? You want somebody to go to jail on how a jury decides that question?"

Dreeben might as well have packed up then and gone home. He had sunk the ship. This argument was going to cost him the justices who might have gone with him at the outset.

He tried again. "It turns on whether the intent there is to subvert, undermine, or impede the proceeding. And the answer is, if it is yes, then it would be prohibited by this statute."

Justice Scalia took another swipe. "Well, it would be prohibited to tell somebody to do it?"

"That's right," Dreeben replied.

"But you could do it. The doing of it is perfectly OK. Doesn't that seem strange to you?"

Dreeben tried another tack. "It seemed strange to Congress too. And when this case threw a spotlight on that omission in the statute, Congress didn't react—"

Dreeben walked right into that one. Justice Scalia brought him up short. "I would suggest that it throws a spotlight on the fact that your theory is wrong."

As the courtroom broke out in laughter, Justice Scalia continued. "It doesn't make any sense to make unlawful the asking of somebody to do something which is, itself, not unlawful, so that the person could do it, but if you asked them to do it, you're guilty, he's not guilty. And that's—that is weird."

Laughter broke out in the gallery again. Dreeben was losing ground rapidly.

Scalia tried again. "Well, let me ask you about this precise thing. Is it Mr. Duncan? If he had, himself, shredded the documents, or destroyed them, that was perfectly OK at the time it was done."

Justice O'Connor interrupted this time. "Is that right?"

Dreeben answered. "It wasn't—prohibited by this statute."

This was such a ridiculous argument that Justice O'Connor wasn't sure she heard it correctly. "It would not have been a violation?"

Dreeben had to concede, "That's right."

Now Dreeben had lost Justice O'Connor, who was clearly appalled. "But the government got the conviction, got him to plead guilty, apparently, on the basis that if he asked somebody else to do what was perfectly lawful for him to do, it would violate the statute?"

Dreeben was going down for the count. "That's right, Justice O'Connor."

Perhaps only Dreeben did not know, but it was "game over" for the government. The only question was how many votes would be in the majority to reverse the conviction of Arthur Andersen under a statute that wasn't intended to reach the conduct alleged and upon a jury instruction that eliminated the key element of any crime—criminal intent.

Maureen had saved a few minutes for rebuttal and tied it up with a bow.

And with that, Chief Justice Rehnquist smiled, nodded, and thanked her, and court was adjourned. She was mobbed with congratulations.

After the arguments, Maureen was cautiously optimistic. CNN and its camera crew were outside the courthouse waiting for her, and the rest of us were all but cheering. Anyone who understood the Supreme Court knew the case would be reversed. The justices had cut Dreeben off at the knees. It was the first time I'd personally seen the solicitor general make a ridiculous, completely unsupportable argument. They should have confessed error. Only time would tell how many justices would vote to reverse the conviction and what they would say in doing so. It could take several months.

Meanwhile, back on the Barge case, I was hoping the Fifth Circuit would understand Jim's arguments for bail pending appeal this well. We filed our motion for Jim's release on bail within a week of Maureen's argument in *Andersen* and within ten days of Jim's sentencing.

Our bail arguments were quite straightforward. There was no dispute about two of the key issues: Jim was not a danger to the community and he was not a flight risk. Judge Werlein had found that much in Jim's favor. The only question was whether there was "a substantial issue for appeal," or the likelihood of reversible error.

Ruemmler, Friedrich, and Sangita Rao said there was no substantial issue for appeal. Werlein had agreed with them, based on his notion that it required him to find that he had committed an error during the trial. That was not the correct legal standard. We did not have to prove that the case would be reversed on appeal. Rather to get bail for Jim pending his appeal, we just needed to show that the case was "close" or "that it could very well be decided the other way by the appellate court." We need only show that if any of these issues were decided in Jim's favor, it would result in a reversal. We found several other cases where the court had granted bail pending appeal for people with the same issues or worse facts than Jim's. We were certain the Fifth Circuit would see that and grant bail for Jim.

A few weeks later, at 10:00 a.m. on May 31, only five weeks after the Supreme Court heard the arguments in *Andersen*, it unanimously reversed the Fifth Circuit's decision, and with it, Judge Harmon's damning jury instruction that eliminated criminal intent.

Finally justice. It was extremely rare to get a unanimous decision out of this Supreme Court, and to get one so quickly was significant as well. The court was more than clear in its choice of words. Chief Justice Rehnquist wrote the opinion, but all the justices joined.

The court held that the instructions allowed the jury to convict Andersen without proving that the firm knew it had broken the law or that there had been a link to any official proceeding that prohibited the destruction of documents. The court said the instructions were so vague that they "simply failed to convey the requisite consciousness of wrongdoing." Chief Justice Rehnquist wrote: "Indeed it is striking how little culpability the instructions required." His opinion also rejected the government's definition of "corrupt persuasion"—persuasion with an improper purpose even without knowing an act is unlawful. "Only persons conscious of wrongdoing can be said to 'knowingly corruptly persuade,'" he wrote. It was a grand slam.

Maureen had to be deeply gratified, and it meant even more that the chief justice for whom she had clerked years before had written the decision. In fact, it was one of the last opinions Chief Justice Rehnquist wrote before he died a few months later. In addition, the reversal of the decision in *Andersen* was a slap to the Fifth Circuit, which had been dismissive of the twisted indictment and the woefully deficient jury instructions proposed by the Enron Task Force and given by Judge Harmon.

The Supreme Court's decision that morning gave us hope that the Fifth Circuit and the district judges in Houston would begin to scrutinize the task force prosecutors' methods and "tasks." It buoyed our belief that the Fifth Circuit would grant our request for Jim to remain on bail pending appeal. After all, it was the same prosecutors—at least Weissmann and Friedrich—who had cobbled together an indictment, tortured the law, rewritten the jury instructions, and persuaded a district judge to give them in order to create a crime in *Andersen* where there was not one. They had done exactly the same thing—if not worse—in the Merrill case.

We had no more gotten our hopes up for Jim's bail to be granted than we received by e-mail an order from the Fifth Circuit denying our motion for his release—on the very same day the Supreme Court reversed *Andersen*. The judge was Carl Stewart from Shreveport, a good man with a solid reputation and widely regarded as fair. He had served on a Louisiana appellate court. I liked and respected him.

He had to have missed something. The *Andersen* decision had been released only hours earlier, so Judge Stewart didn't have the benefit of that decision. We needed to seek rehearing on that basis and identify for the panel the similarities between the two task force prosecutions. Then surely, the Fifth Circuit would realize what an injustice the task force had perpetrated here—or at least the court would realize that it should look at the case carefully before anyone went to prison.

Our research was unequivocal. We looked at cases in every circuit. Not a single case in the country had ever affirmed a criminal conviction for "honest services" fraud unless there had been bribes or kickbacks. Judge Werlein himself had acknowledged there were no bribes or kickbacks here. This prosecution was literally unprecedented. We couldn't understand how the task force could even argue there was "no substantial issue for appeal," much less find a Fifth Circuit judge who would agree. Not a single case supported denying Jim bail pending appeal on these facts. Not a single case had ever held that his conduct was criminal.

The Fifth Circuit had long been a court of legal giants—men who made law by reaching the correct result on hard facts and doing what the law required regardless of public opinion. Judges like John R. Brown, John Minor Wisdom, Al Tate, Irving Goldberg—some had even had their children threatened and crosses burned in their yards because they made the hard and unpopular decisions that defended and empowered the civil rights movement. The history of the Fifth Circuit was rich and populated with living legends. Some of its judges had been immortalized in Jack Bass's book, *Unlikely Heroes*. One of my most prized possessions is a copy autographed by most of the judges mentioned in it. I knew the Fifth Circuit would grant Jim bail pending appeal once they considered it in light of the *Andersen* reversal.

Far too much went wrong in this trial for anyone to be incarcerated while the court sorted it out—and no Merrill defendant was a danger to anyone or a risk of flight. The Fifth Circuit had allowed other high-profile criminal defendants who had been convicted of serious crimes to remain on bail pending their appeals. One example we found and cited was that of former Louisiana Governor Edwin Edwards. The Fifth Circuit let him stay out of jail while his appeal was pending, and his prosecution and convictions on multiple counts were much more clear and straightforward.

Confident that Judge Stewart had simply missed something or been too busy to pay close attention, we drafted and filed a petition for rehearing. We asked an entire panel of the Fifth Circuit—three judges—to look more carefully at the issue of granting the Merrill defendants bail pending appeal.

Meanwhile Jim and Nancy were jumping every time the phone rang, afraid it was the Bureau of Prisons with Jim's date to report to prison.

– 8 –

THE LONGEST YEAR

Less than two weeks later, a handsome young college student, about twenty-two, was driving up a winding narrow mountain road near Gunnison, Colorado. He soon found himself high up the mountain and in the fury of a massive thunderstorm. It was all he could do to see the hood ornament on his old coupe. He couldn't think straight. He couldn't study. He hadn't slept well in weeks. He felt like he was living in the twilight zone. It was all surreal. He kept losing himself in his thoughts, and the storm was beating down on him.

Suddenly he hit the rock wall of the mountain on his right, ricocheted across the oncoming lane, and crashed through the guardrail. His car became airborne and careened over the side of the mountain. The car rolled and smashed, and glass shattered as it crashed through the trees and landed upside down in a cold mountain stream. The young man was thrown halfway out of the car, which was crushed all around and on top of him. Part of the dashboard was embedded in his chest, and his face was smashed beyond recognition. He lay in the cold, rushing creek, unconscious or dead.

Waiting for Jim's reporting date was weighing heavily on me.

I arrived at the office late the morning of June 15. Hellen was opening the mail. She had a sick look on her face when I walked in.

"What's wrong?"

"We've just been informed by the Bureau of Prisons that Jim is to surrender to the United States Marshals on July 5 to begin his prison sentence."

"Oh, no, I can't believe it. Any word from the Fifth Circuit on our motion for reconsideration of bail pending appeal?"

"No, we filed it just a week ago. How can they make him go to prison like this? It's so wrong." Hellen's eyes were welling with tears.

"I know. We have to hope the Fifth Circuit panel does the right thing. I believe they will. They don't have a legal basis to do anything else."

"When are you going to tell Jim?"

"I don't know. I guess I'll have to tell him soon, but I'd like to give the court a few more days to get it right and save him this agony."

Nancy and Jim Brown were tossing and turning, trying to sleep, under the shroud of Jim's pending reporting date. Jim's thoughts were racing. This wasn't their life. Where had it gone? How in the hell had all this happened to them? And because of a deal Jim had told everyone at Merrill not to do. They couldn't make sense out of any of it. Yes, it was a stupid deal, but it wasn't illegal. He had done his job by warning his superiors of the risks. The others had decided to take the risk anyway. Basically Tom Davis, Dan Bayly's superior over the Investment Banking Division at Merrill, had decided that just this once, Merrill would risk losing the $7 million. Merrill would view it as a gift if necessary to help a client who had brought the company far more business than that. Zrike said it was OK. If Jim had only known then what he knew now. Finally sheer exhaustion overtook him, and he was asleep.

There was a noise. Something was ringing or buzzing. It wouldn't stop. He tried to rouse himself.

He took a few moments to pull himself out of what was finally a deep sleep. He struggled to comprehend the day, the time, or where he was. When he finally pulled himself awake enough, he realized the phone was ringing. Nancy was mumbling about turning off the alarm clock. Jim struggled to reach the phone. It was pitch black outside.

"Mr. Brown?"

"Yes, this is Jim Brown."

"Do you have a twenty-two-year-old son in Colorado?"

"Yes, I do. What's wrong?" By this time, Nancy was awake and terrified.

"I'm sorry to tell you, but your son has been in a very bad accident. This is Saint Mary's Hospital. Your son is here."

"Is he alive? Is he alive?" Jim asked in panic. Nancy was already getting dressed.

"Yes, but he's in surgery now. It's very serious. You should come as fast as you can."

"Please tell him we'll be there when he wakes up. We're on our way. We're leaving right now. Tell him—you must tell him. We'll be right there!"

"We will. We'll tell him. You be careful, Mr. Brown."

Jim hung up the phone. Nancy was already throwing clothes in a bag. "How bad is it?"

"They just said it was bad—a bad accident. It's very serious. He's in surgery."

Instantly nothing else mattered. They had to get to Chris. Neither of them could fathom losing him.

By the time they arrived at the hospital in Colorado, Chris had been through multiple surgeries. The kind but somber doctor told them their son had numerous broken bones—ribs, clavicle, jaw, facial bones, arm, and leg—massive internal injuries, and deep gashes in his torso.

"Mr. and Mrs. Brown," the doctor said softly, "your son's strength and youth are on his side, but we don't know if he will pull through. We're doing everything we can, but only time will tell." Jim and Nancy stood with their eyes full of tears, trying to process what they were hearing. "It's a miracle he's alive now, and each day he lives increases his chances of making it. I'm so glad you're here. He's unconscious, in intensive care, intubated, catheterized, on every monitor known to the medical profession, and unrecognizable because of the facial injuries and bandages. Brace yourselves."

"Take us to him now," Jim said. The doctor was right. They could tell that Chris was alive only by the beeping and lines on the monitors.

Later that day, Jim called to tell me they were in Colorado and the news of Chris's accident. They still didn't know if Chris would live. They had learned that the only reason Chris had even made it to the hospital was because the driver of another car saw the accident. The driver had climbed down the mountain in the pouring rain and held Chris's head out of the almost frozen creek so he could breathe until paramedics could get there. As Jim related this tragic story, my eyes welled with tears. My mother always said that God uses human hands. This was a miracle.

"Oh, Jim, I'm so sorry. You do whatever you need to do for him, you and Nancy. Please just give the hospital permission to send me the records today and keep me posted. We'll file immediately and ask for a stay of the reporting date and update the Fifth Circuit. The circuit hasn't decided the bail issue yet. We need to tell them that Chris is clinging to life by a thread."

Jim and Nancy stayed with Chris around the clock. They held his hand and talked to him. They took breaks one at a time. We obtained the medical records from the hospital and went over them in detail with my friend, Dr. Battle Haslam, who helped me explain Chris's injuries in English as I drafted motions asking Judge Werlein and the Fifth Circuit to extend the deadline by which Jim had to report to prison.

I contacted counsel for the government as is required by the rules to ask their position on the motion. I explained the situation in great detail and provided a copy of the medical information. I asked them to agree to our motion for release pending appeal. That was immediately rejected. I asked for a ninety-day extension. After consulting with the task force, Sangita Rao, the appellate attorney assigned the case now, agreed to a thirty-day extension—that was all.

I couldn't begin to imagine how Nancy Brown was even putting one foot in front of the other. Her only son was lying unconscious in intensive care, and her husband of thirty years was due to report to prison in two weeks.

Nancy and Jim held constant vigil beside Chris's bed. All the doctors could say was that he had youth and strength on his side, and only time would tell.

Nancy held Chris's hand as he fought for his life. Jim returned to the motel for a few hours of sleep. They had been at the hospital for seventy-two hours straight. Her life was shattering in front of her. She teetered on the brink of losing her son to death and her husband to years in prison. She was beyond exhausted and on the verge of collapsing herself.

Late the fourth night, Jim went to the hospital chapel. Alone in the dim light of the chapel, he dropped to his knees and prayed. "God, if you could just please let Chris live, I promise you I will go to prison with the best attitude I possibly can. I'll use the time I have to spend there to do good things and try to help everyone I meet. Please, God, please let Chris live. I'll try not to ever ask for anything else. Amen."

We filed our motion with Judge Werlein, detailing Chris's extensive injuries and precarious condition and asked for an extension of time for Jim to report to prison. We did the same with our motion pending appeal in the Fifth Circuit.

Werlein took seven days to give Jim the thirty-day extension to which the government had already agreed—thereby extending Jim's reporting date to August. We also notified the Fifth Circuit and renewed our request for bail pending appeal, updating them on Chris's condition, which remained critical.

Bayly, Furst, and Fuhs were also filing motions for reconsideration of denial of their bail pending appeal and to stay their reporting dates. All of the appellate counsel on this case, including two former assistant US attorneys, a former US attorney, a former solicitor general, and a former deputy solicitor general, all lawyers of great credibility and legal stature, were telling the Fifth Circuit clearly and repeatedly that there was a serious problem with this case, and it was wrong to send these people to prison pending their appeals. The court really needed to pay attention to this, and we all told the judges so.

Weissmann, Ruemmler, and Friedrich appeared on the government's strident opposition to our motions. They steadfastly maintained that there were "no substantial issues for appeal." The prosecutors told the Fifth Circuit that "the oral guarantee was initially provided by Enron's then-treasurer Jeff McMahon to another codefendant, Robert Furst. The conference call between Bayly and Fastow was merely a ratification of the deal to which the parties had previously agreed."

Dan Bayly—the finest man who had ever appeared in Werlein's court—was due to report to federal prison at Petersburg, Virginia, on July 14, 2005. Still the Fifth Circuit had not ruled. Finally, only two days before Bayly was to report, the Fifth Circuit denied all the defendants' requests for bail. The opinion noted only that the denial was "not a comment on the merits of the appeals." The three-judge panel of Judges Carl Stewart of Shreveport, Jacques Wiener of New Orleans, and Pete Benavides of Austin had spoken. They simply affirmed the one-sentence denial that Judge Stewart had entered on his own weeks earlier. They said nothing about the law. This was incomprehensible to all of us, a nightmare, and a disappointment beyond measure.

I had to call Nancy and Jim at the hospital to tell them that the Fifth Circuit had denied our request for rehearing and that Jim would have to report to prison in August as ordered. They both said that they had received their miracle for their lifetimes: Chris was alive, he had regained consciousness, and he would eventually recover. Jim said that knowing that Chris would live was all that he could ask for. He could and would deal with anything after that with a positive attitude. I hung up the phone—simply awestruck.

Back in Houston, Enron Task Force members Benton Campbell, Lisa Monaco, and Cliff Stricklin, under Weissmann's direction, were prosecuting the Enron Broadband case. The Broadband trial involved five of seven defendants indicted on 170 counts of conspiracy, wire and securities fraud, insider trading, and money laundering. The defendants on trial were Joe Hirko, Rex Shelby, Scott Yeager, Michael Krautz, and Kevin Howard. Kenneth Rice and Kevin Hannon, who had each served as president of the broadband division, pleaded guilty.

These men were all involved in Enron's efforts to develop a market for broadband technology—common today but at the cutting edge when they began. Hirko had been a well-liked CFO at Portland General Electric. He worked on operations for Enron Broadband Services. Shelby was in engineering and operations. Yeager was a strategic business executive. Michael Krautz and Kevin Howard were involved in financial allegations, specifically a transaction called "Braveheart" that the task force claimed was illegal. Kevin Howard was chief financial officer of Enron Broadband Services.

The trial was so infected with prosecutorial misconduct that even the pro-prosecution *Houston Chronicle* began reporting on the problems. The bloggers were all over it. Prosecutors elicited false testimony from former Enron Co-Chief Executive Officer Ken Rice. Two brave witnesses, Beth Stier and Lawrence Ciscon, testified that the task force had threatened to indict them if they testified for the defense. As was their typical tactic of intimidation, the prosecutors telephoned Ciscon three times the night before he was to testify to remind him that he was "a target." The prosecutors even showed a video that the judge had specifically ordered not be shown to the jury. They claimed it was "an accident." Houston Judge Vanessa Gilmore was irate.

Finally the armor of "the invincible" task force was chinking. The Supreme Court had just bludgeoned the task force for its handling of *Andersen* and reversed the conviction for the prosecutors' overreaching charge and the jury instruction that eliminated criminal intent. The Barge trial had gone well for them with Judge Werlein, but even he had shocked them by rejecting the lengthy prison sentences they had demanded. Now Judge Gilmore was trying to give the defendants a fair trial, and two witnesses had the audacity to tell the truth despite intense task force threats. Judge Gilmore was livid with the prosecutors.

While the Broadband jury was out deliberating, Andrew Weissmann resigned from the task force on July 18, 2005.

Two days later, the Broadband jury returned a mixed verdict of acquittals and inability to reach a verdict on the charges against Krautz, Yeager, Hirko, Howard, and Shelby. No one was convicted.

The task force was stunned. They announced that they would prosecute the Broadband defendants again. After all, they had the unlimited resources of the taxpayers behind them, and they couldn't possibly admit they were wrong.

Jim was at least able to help Nancy get Chris home from the hospital before he had to report to Fort Dix prison on August 14, 2005. It was not a "camp."

Jim and Nancy made the long drive to Fort Dix, New Jersey, together—neither able to absorb the reality they faced. Jim hugged Nancy a tearful good-bye and turned to submit himself to the horrors of the unknown before him. He heard the cold steel door clang behind him, but he had the strength and comfort that came from knowing the truth, and he had experienced the miracle that Chris would live. Jim Brown checked into prison with an amazing attitude of gratitude that his son was alive. He remembered the promise he had made in the chapel, and he intended to honor it.

While Jim began to endure the indignities, humiliations, and degradations that accompany imprisonment, Nancy made the several-hour drive back to their home alone with her thoughts racing and tears flowing. She had to pull it together fast, though. Chris was at home and needed her now more than ever. Lauren too. Jim had promised he'd be careful and take care of himself. He could get along with almost anyone, and he was determined not to let this ruin his life. They would all just have to be strong. They knew the truth. They knew he had done nothing wrong, and that knowledge, their faith, and their friends would keep them going.

Nancy made it through the first night alone in their room, finally passing out from emotional and physical exhaustion that seemed to penetrate her bones. When she got up the next morning and went to the front door to get the paper, there was a large brown box from Fort Dix. She opened it with trembling hands. Someone had thrown every piece of Jim's clothes and shoes that he had worn to prison into the box and sent them to her. She felt as though she had just been kicked hard in the stomach. She was reeling. She collapsed on the step and wept.

The various appellate teams for each of the four Merrill defendants were in high gear, trying to work on some issues together and some separately. Because we knew our clients were innocent, we wanted to file the briefs without any extensions of time and to ask for expedited oral argument scheduling. John Nields had hosted an early meeting of appellate counsel for all defendants in his dramatic offices in Washington, DC, where the movie *The Pelican Brief* had been filmed. John was a gentleman, extremely talented, and a pleasure to consult.

The large, elegantly appointed conference room was full of high-powered appellate lawyers from big law firms and their extensive entourages. I was the only one who had come alone. I knew and had worked with most of the men at the table at different times and places—some from days at the Department of Justice. Larry Robbins, lead appellate counsel for Bayly, had been in the solicitor general's office long ago. Larry was smart and funny. Seth Waxman, lead counsel for Fuhs, and at the WilmerHale firm, had been solicitor general. Seth had been on our Fifth Circuit Bar program in the past.

There were three or four women associates in the room sitting behind their partners, but I was the only woman sitting at the massive conference table. Some of the trial lawyers were there. Prominent New York attorney and former SEC Director Ike Sorkin, who represented Furst, was sitting near me with two associates. John Nields and his team would be taking over for Furst on appeal. Tom Hagemann, Bayly's trial counsel from Houston, was on the phone. At least twenty-five lawyers were participating in this conference—some by conference call. By my count, that was eight attorneys for each of the other defendants—Bayly, Furst, and Fuhs—and one—me—for Brown.

Larry Robbins took over the meeting, as if everyone knew that's what he was supposed to do. He outlined all the winning arguments that he had decided we would be making. Apparently I had missed the memo or the meeting before the meeting. I knew Larry was very bright, so I listened supportively and encouragingly for over an hour. Then suddenly he was wrapping things up, gathering up his papers, and the meeting appeared to be over.

I said, "Excuse me, but I'm going to be briefing the issue of the legal insufficiency of the indictment. It doesn't allege a criminal offense." I knew Tom Hagemann, who was participating by telephone for Bayly, had hammered on that issue pretrial, as had the Brown team. I called out to Tom on the speakerphone and said, "Tom, your honest services issue is the winning issue! That's what I'm going to be briefing as the primary issue for Brown. And since when is a Merrill employee criminally responsible for the books and records at Enron? There were no bribes or kickbacks here, and they didn't take anyone's money or property. This indictment doesn't state an offense."

Larry Robbins continued packing up his things to leave and spoke as if the icemaker had just unloaded into the freezer. "You just need to go read the Supreme Court's decision *United States v. Mechanik*. All indictment issues wash out with the trial."

I had been up most of the night reading every Fifth Circuit case I could find on this honest services allegation, and there wasn't a single one that supported the charges in this indictment. The convictions the task force had obtained against our clients would not hold up on appeal. This prosecution was crap, so I said, "No, this one doesn't. You can read and read it and not find anywhere it alleges conduct that any court has ever before found to be a federal crime. There isn't one in there. This case has to be reversed on appeal because of the indictment." Everyone at the table either stared at me or kept packing up.

Most everyone said good-bye and left. I stayed around a few minutes and thanked John Nields for his hospitality. I visited with Ike Sorkin and his associates who were friendly, open, and interested in the arguments and what I had found. I promised to send them some of the language from the cases I had pulled, and then I packed up and returned to Asheville.

I sent memos to everyone on the case so they could convince Robbins of the correctness of the honest services argument. It was very clear that he wasn't going to be listening to me. Not only was I female, but also I was almost a foot taller, years younger, a solo practitioner, and I didn't have an Ivy League degree, a Supreme Court clerkship, or a stint in the solicitor general's office on my resume. Even worse, I had been president of the American Academy of Appellate Lawyers, the youngest attorney ever inducted, and for unknown reasons, he had not yet been invited into the Academy. I couldn't possibly have identified a winning issue that he and his brilliant team of five had completely missed.

I also identified clear points that required reversal on everything from the indictment through the jury instructions that redefined the very basis of the entire case—the conspiracy charge. By the time Jim was sentenced and briefing began for the Fifth Circuit, I had the assistance of a very bright recent law school graduate, Torrence Lewis, from Indiana University Maurer School of Law in Bloomington. Torrence excelled in finding cases with the exact language I wanted and was an excellent technician. We had more real issues than I had ever seen in 350 criminal cases.

Seth Waxman and his team from the WilmerHale firm did a brilliant brief for young Bill Fuhs, arguing that the evidence against him was insufficient, and he should be acquitted. It was the best sufficiency brief I had ever read—eloquent, easy to read, and solidly supported by the law and the record. Meanwhile Fuhs was still incarcerated in a maximum-security prison with the worst and most dangerous offenders and hundreds of miles from his young family. We proceeded with briefing the issues I had identified, beginning with the indictment itself. Robbins' team eventually took up the indictment issues also.

The Fifth Circuit granted our request for an expedited oral argument, and we soon received notice that the court scheduled the oral argument of the case for March 6, 2006. New Orleans was still reeling from the devastation of Hurricane Katrina six months earlier.

A week before the argument, we learned that our panel would include Judge Grady Jolly from Mississippi, Judge Harold DeMoss from Houston, and Judge Thomas Reavley from Houston. Reavley had been on the panel that had wrongly decided *Andersen* and been reversed by the Supreme Court. Unfortunately we had to divide our arguments among counsel for four defendants. The court allowed us forty minutes a side for argument, but to allow for rebuttal, we only had about seven minutes each for our opening arguments. That was not enough time to argue a case on a record this large or this complex.

The Fifth Circuit building at 600 Camp Street in New Orleans is a massive old Post Office building with beautiful granite columns, towering windows throughout the Great Hall and the courtrooms, marble floors, and steps with brass handrails. Built in the Italian Renaissance Revival style, the building was constructed between 1912 and 1915 from regional building materials. Ornate copper and bronze sculptures mark the four corners of the roof. Called "The Ladies," they represent History, Agriculture, Industry, and Arts. Weighing a ton each, they were made by the renowned Piccirilli Brothers, who carved the statue of Lincoln in the Lincoln Memorial. High ceilings with elaborate wood carvings and intricate paintings and moldings on the courtroom ceilings inspire reverence and awe. The building and its courtrooms are themselves fine art.

Much like the Supreme Court, arguing counsel is close to the bench of three judges. To gain entry, we had to send all our briefcases through the X-ray screener and go through all the usual security protocols when we arrived early to set up in the courtroom.

As with *Andersen*, I had known all three of these judges a long time. They had very different personalities, but I liked each of them. Reavley was like an extra "dad." I felt like he had raised me from a "baby lawyer." Jolly was more formal and aloof but polite and usually got it right. DeMoss was always a gentleman, warm, polite, and friendly. It was always a pleasure to have him on the panel. Both Reavley and DeMoss officed in Houston in the same building with Judge Werlein.

We expected the panel to be "hot"—to have a lot of questions for us. We did not expect abject hostility, but we got it. Reavley, in his late eighties at the time, had apparently decided from his work on the *Andersen* panel and what he had seen of this case that the entire deal was dirty. He bought the government's "cooked the books" argument hook, line, and sinker, and he blamed the Merrill defendants for it. He had a lot of the facts wrong, and there wasn't enough time to straighten him out on them—even if he had been willing to listen. What was most disappointing was that he was not at all open-minded during my argument. In two hundred oral arguments and more than five hundred briefs, I'd never advocated a position that I didn't believe was correct. I would stake my life on my credibility with the Fifth Circuit, and all the judges knew it. When I found any error in our briefs or my position, I would advise the court immediately. Thirty years of sterling accuracy and credibility with the court meant nothing that day.

Jolly, the presiding judge seated in the middle of the bench, was a little less hostile but not by much. Jolly and Reavley seemed angry with everyone—including the government for screwing up this big prosecution. They did seem to understand, but reluctantly, the problem with the indictment failing to charge a crime when none of these defendants had taken money or property from anyone, or taken any bribes, or paid any kickbacks. It was a most unusual indictment.

Judge DeMoss was the only one who understood this was a business transaction that evolved as the parties learned more and consulted with counsel. He got it. He acknowledged that all the discussions these defendants participated in were purely preliminary conversations and negotiations, that they were trying to understand what was proposed and what they could do legitimately, and that corporate counsel had documented the transaction and made sure it was all legal. As is standard, Merill and Enron counsel had included in the contracts a specific clause that no one on either side of the transaction could rely on any oral statements any of the businessmen had made. Judge Werlein had not let trial counsel defend on that basis at all.

DeMoss understood the defense, and he as much as said that he could not see how any of this conduct was criminal. He also understood that Jim's grand jury testimony about his personal understanding of a telephone call that Jim had not even been a party to was not proper subject matter for a perjury or obstruction of justice conviction. Judge

DeMoss believed Jim was innocent and that his grand jury testimony was true. After all, Weissmann himself had instructed Jim to share with the grand jury his personal understanding of the transaction—whether it was "accurate or not." How could someone be convicted of perjury and obstruction when his answer to the questions expressed his personal understanding—regardless of its accuracy?

Could DeMoss persuade Jolly to acquit? It didn't look like Reavley could be persuaded. That fact alone crushed me. I had always counted on Judge Reavley to get it right. He'd already been reversed by the Supreme Court on *Andersen*. Was this going to be a two-to-one decision of the court? Was Reavley going to persuade Jolly to affirm the convictions?

Remarkably and fortunately, the entire tone of the panel changed when Seth Waxman stood up to argue that the evidence was insufficient to sustain the conviction of Bill Fuhs. The voices and body language of Jolly and Reavley softened completely; they relaxed, sat back, and all combativeness left them. It was a kinder, gentler panel in every respect. Waxman was eloquently winning the acquittal of Bill Fuhs. They had read his brief and found it persuasive. They all seemed to get at least that much. We could see it and feel it.

Stephan Oestreicher for the government presented his argument. Reavley and Jolly were mostly sympathetic to it, but Jolly at least expressed concerns about the "honest services" charge. When we had our brief rebuttal, Jolly and Reavley were back to acting like kids who had been crammed in the backseat of a Volkswagon on a cross-country trip with their parents—angry at everyone and wanting to get out of there. I left the courtroom knowing we were right on the law but with an abiding fear that only DeMoss understood this case. Reavley and Jolly were way off track. It felt like they were angry that they were going to have to reverse Counts One, Two, and Three—the "honest services" conspiracy and wire fraud charges—when they would rather affirm them. They were angry with the defendants for making this deal, and they were angry with the government for making all those mistakes.

One week after the argument, Waxman filed a motion with the Fifth Circuit renewing Fuhs's motion for release pending appeal. Nine days later, the Fifth Circuit requested a response from the government. That request was a very good sign for Fuhs and a bad one for the government. The court wouldn't request a response from the prosecution unless it was considering granting the motion.

The government vehemently opposed Fuhs's motion for release. Oestreicher, who had argued the case for the task force, pointed out how many times Judge Werlein and the court had already refused to allow Fuhs out on bond pending appeal, finding that he did not raise a "substantial issue for appeal." According to the government, the oral argument had not changed that. Oestreicher must have been at a different oral argument than we were—or he was forced to toe the task force line. While our case was pending in the Circuit, Friedrich had soared to the right hand of Attorney General Alberto Gonzales and was testifying before congressional committees or refusing to testify—as the case may be—on various controversial issues such as prosecution of the press for "leaks."

Oestreicher strenuously argued that the evidence was more than sufficient to sustain Fuhs's convictions, and certainly did not "raise a substantial doubt as to the outcome of its resolution." The prosecutors still claimed that Fuhs deliberately and knowingly helped document the Barge transaction without reference to Enron's oral guarantee that Merrill would be bought out of the barges within six months at a guaranteed rate of return. Oestreicher pounded the Fifth Circuit with the fact that "it was precisely that guarantee that rendered the deal a sham; it therefore had to be kept from Enron's auditors and Merrill's attorneys." Their inexorable mantra was that Fuhs knew of the guarantee and hid it from the attorneys.

According to the government, Fuhs had taken the language out of the engagement letter between Enron and Merrill to hide the crime from Merrill's own lawyers. Oestreicher argued that every issue the Merrill defendants had raised was wrong, and Fuhs's motion should be denied. The deplorable and severe conditions of Fuhs's confinement and the hardship on his family were merely "an unfortunate fact of life for nearly every convicted defendant."

In only three days, the Fifth Circuit granted Waxman's motion and ordered that Fuhs be released immediately on bail.

Finally a glimmer of justice. We all knew that meant only one thing: Bill Fuhs was coming home, and from what we had heard at argument, Fuhs was being acquitted of any wrongdoing whatsoever. Oestreicher had regurgitated Friedrich and Ruemmler's mantra, but there was no evidence that Fuhs knew anything was wrong with the transaction. We knew it was because the deal was lawful. Would the panel figure that out?

By the time Bill Fuhs was released from the maximum-security hellhole in Oklahoma, he had served 156 days in prison. All of those weeks, days, hours, and minutes were lost from his children's lives forever, while he was not guilty of any wrongdoing. Nothing could ever make up for that. I wondered if my friends, Judges Carl Stewart, Jacques Wiener, and Pete Benavides, along with Ewing Werlein, who had denied all our motions for release twice, even knew, considered, or cared about what their wrong decision had done to this young man and his family.

As of March 30, 2006, when Fuhs was ordered released, of the three cases the task force had actually taken to trial, first, *Andersen* had been reversed by the Supreme Court 9–0, after blatant failures of the district court and the Fifth Circuit to handle the legal issues properly. Second, David Duncan, the Enron auditor from Andersen who had been the key witness against Andersen in its trial, had been allowed to withdraw his guilty plea because his conduct was not criminal—just as Andersen's was not. Third, at the Barge trial, the jury had acquitted Sheila Kahanek—the midlevel Enron employee who said no; and fourth, now Bill Fuhs was being acquitted by the Fifth Circuit Court of Appeals. These people had been dragged through hell for years. I could only imagine what Fuhs had suffered in a maximum-security prison. And lastly, the Broadband trial was a complete failure.

At the same time, though, the task force prosecutors were being promoted, honored, and lauded for their work. Leslie Caldwell was heading the white-collar practice at Morgan Lewis. Friedrich was on a high-speed escalator up the ranks of the department. Weissmann ultimately landed at Jenner & Block. Ruemmler was prosecuting Lay and Skilling in Houston.

Time crawled for Dan Bayly at Petersburg, Robert Furst at Seagoville, Texas, and Jim Brown at Fort Dix. It dragged even more slowly for their families. These men were not incarcerated in the "camps" that people like to think white-collar criminals "enjoy." No, Jim shared a cell with thirteen people for a while. One of Jim's cellmates was set on fire while he slept one night.

They lived in daily fear of being attacked—by the guards as much as by the inmate population. They knew former Enron Treasurer Ben Glisan had been put straight into the "hole" when he had refused to "cooperate" with the task force. Everyone knew the hole was even worse. There was no privacy anywhere—not to shower or use the toilet. The filth and bugs were so bad that Jim, whose job within the prison was as a plumber, shaved his head and mustache as a sanitary measure. Prison was total sensory deprivation and daily degradation among people with whom they had nothing in common. Many hated them if for no other reason than that they weren't like everyone else. They were the despised, and the task force had done everything possible to make every minute of their existence as miserable and frightening as possible.

On the appellate litigation front, Robbins and Nields decided that there was a strong possibility that the Fifth Circuit was going to reverse the conspiracy and wire fraud charges against their clients, or that at the least, the court would order a new trial for Bayly and Furst. Among his errors during the trial, Judge Werlein had admitted into evidence an e-mail—made up of multilevel hearsay—that had been written by Jim Brown about an unrelated deal more than a year later. That e-mail made an erroneous reference to the Barge deal, and the prosecutors had used that extensively against all of the defendants to get the convictions. The use of that e-mail—especially against Bayly and Furst—was another clear constitutional error by Friedrich and Ruemmler. At a minimum, Robbins and Nields knew that the court would reverse the convictions of their clients for that error—even if the court affirmed the indictment as a whole and the two additional convictions against Jim for perjury and obstruction of justice.

We all filed renewed bail motions on March 31, 2006. This time, the government filed its oppositions in only four days, and we filed our replies to their oppositions the very same day.

⸻

Days and then weeks passed, with no word from the Fifth Circuit, which usually issues its opinions within ninety days of oral argument. Our worst fears intensified. Could it be that only the case against Fuhs was going to be reversed? Would Bayly, Furst, and Brown have to spend three to four years in prison? Was the panel split?

Back in Houston, the home of two of our three judges, the city was awash in all bad things Enron on a daily basis. The trial of Ken Lay and Jeff Skilling was proceeding there amid myriad allegations of prosecutorial misconduct against lead prosecutors Kathryn Ruemmler and Sean Berkowitz by Daniel Petrocelli and his team for Skilling, and Mike Ramsey and his team for Lay. Simultaneously Skilling and Lay were vilified daily in the press.

One *Houston Chronicle* columnist wrote that "the Enron prosecution has one true measure of success: Lay and Skilling in a cold steel cage." Despite the omnipresent negative publicity in Houston excoriating both men, and the fact that 80 percent of the jury pool reported adverse feelings toward the defendants, federal Judge Sim Lake allowed an average of only three minutes per juror to pick the jury and got right on with the trial.

Same song, different verse. Once again, it was the task force's show. Defense counsel were pleading for *Brady* material, witness statements, prior testimony, or agents' notes of their interrogations of key witnesses, including Fastow, whom the agents had admittedly questioned for thousands of hours. Instead what the task force gave the defense was a highly unorthodox FBI form 302—a report of an interview. It wasn't even the usual 302. The task force finally admitted that this was a "composite" 302 that had been cut and pasted and otherwise edited repeatedly. Worse yet, contrary to explicit FBI and Justice Department policy, the FBI had destroyed the original 302s. Despite this grossly improper procedure, Judge Lake did not make the task force produce the Fastow notes to the defense.

Instead the judge adopted the procedure of having the task force give him the notes, as if he were omniscient and could tell how they were relevant, favorable, and exculpatory to the defense as it went along, or how Petrocelli and Ramsey might use them—when Petrocelli and Ramsey had no clue what was in them. This wasn't just a couple of notes that were easy to read either. It was multiple notebooks—a voluminous amount of barely decipherable handwritten notes by multiple federal agents that would take anyone weeks to understand under the best of conditions. Judge Lake said that he would read them as the trial went along or if the defense required something in particular, and he would decide if any of it was favorable to the defense and had to be produced as *Brady*.

The assertion was unbelievable and literally impossible. The procedure Judge Lake instituted, but could not possibly perform, effectively insulated the task force from reversible error for their failure to produce the raw notes to the defense at the same time it denied the defense any access to them. It was a win-win for the task force and a complete "screw you" for the defense. As in the Barge case, the defense didn't know to ask about what they didn't know. Judge Lake would have had to spend twenty-four hours a day during the trial to try to plow through the notes and still could not view them as a defense lawyer armed with their contents would have done. The defense was deprived of significant preparation it could have used to begin to level the playing field.

Petrocelli was enraged. The defense could not do anything meaningful in cross-examination with this fabricated 302 that smoothed, resolved, or slanted assertions and inconsistencies in Fastow's many narrations and no doubt favored the task force's view.

While the Lay–Skilling trial was raging, the Brown team and the appellate team in general came to believe, as revolting as even the mere thought was, that the Fifth Circuit would not render a decision in the Barge case until the jury had issued its verdict in the Lay–Skilling trial. The Barge transaction was an underpinning of the Lay–Skilling case and was recited as one of the wrongs in the Lay–Skilling indictment.

We hated to think it, but we wondered if the Fifth Circuit was taking its time to avoid upsetting the apple cart and telegraphing anything that might affect the convictions of Lay and Skilling.

The Lay–Skilling jury returned its verdict on May 25, 2006, finding Lay guilty of all six counts against him and Skilling guilty of nineteen of twenty-eight counts. Within two weeks of the jury's conviction of Lay and Skilling, on June 7, 2006, the Fifth Circuit ordered the release of Bayly and Furst, with the same language it had used to release Bill Fuhs: forthwith.

The court denied Jim Brown's motion. Torrence, Hellen, and I were in shock. While we were elated for the others, it was devastating for us. We knew that it meant at the least that Bayly and Furst would get a new trial at which they could prove their innocence. Was the court reversing only on the issue of the e-mail? Or was it going to reverse on the indictment—as it should—but left Jim in prison because of the perjury and obstruction charges? The Brown team was crushed.

Bayly and Furst went home in a few days. The pain of telling Nancy and then Jim that everyone had been released except for him and that his motion had been specifically denied was oppressive. Nancy drove to the prison to tell him in person. It was a dark, dark day. Personally and professionally, I was heartbroken. I was losing respect for a court I had loved and admired even before I began practicing law. How and why had the great Fifth Circuit become so grudging in protecting individual freedom against blatant abuses and overreaching by the government?

We had no way of knowing what it all meant. It could have been any number of things. It could have meant that all Jim's convictions were being affirmed, and everyone else was being acquitted. That would have been the worst possible result and the ultimate irony for the one person who steadfastly urged his superiors not to do this deal. Reading the tea leaves wasn't working for any of us. All we really knew was that everyone was out of prison except for Jim, and that was unbearable, wrong, and unacceptable.

These were the darkest days for all of the Brown team—and especially for Jim, Nancy, Chris, and Lauren. Nancy and I spoke on the phone frequently, just to try to keep our spirits up and share our frustrations. Nancy went to see Jim at least once a week to try to keep his spirits up.

Jim, the prison plumber, in keeping with his promise to God in the hospital chapel, had volunteered to teach a class on basic financial skills—helping inmates learn what a bank account was, how to set one up, and how to write a check. He also taught inmates how to read. Nancy would bring him materials to use in the class. That helped keep him going. For the most part, he had made friends with everyone from the Mafia inmates whom he had taught to read the financial sections and statements to the octogenarian who had been the subject of the movie *Blow* starring Johnny Depp. The old man had been the largest original cocaine importer into the United States. In between his plumbing and teaching, Jim waited in line for more than an hour every night to get three minutes on the phone with Nancy.

Jim told her that one of the biggest men he had ever seen in his life wanted more than anything to learn computer skills. Educational programs in prison were a farce. Nancy bought the "big guy" a $250 book on computer programming and usage. She hand-delivered it to him on her next visit. When she gave it to him in the prison visiting room, this tremendous mountain of a man broke down in tears and hugged her.

Jim had faced some serious challenges to his own safety and to his psyche, but he had kept the promise he made to God. I believed that God would honor that and help Jim find the strength to deal with whatever he needed to deal with until he could be released, and I told Jim so every chance I got. I tried to speak with Jim at least once a month while he was in prison. I had always believed that an attorney could speak with a client virtually any time. That proved false. The prison officials fought hard against giving me any telephone time with Jim, and he was never left alone to speak with me. Every conversation we had was monitored. It usually took several blistering faxes and threats to take their denial of his right to counsel up the line and to the Fifth Circuit to even be permitted an occasional, monitored phone call. Each attempt to speak to Jim required this kind of ordeal. It was never easy or straightforward.

On July 25, we received astonishing news that made the front page of all the papers and live news broadcasts: former Enron Chairman Ken Lay had died of a heart attack while vacationing with his family in Colorado. Rumors of suicide started flying, along with rumors of a death hoax and escape to an island with a change of identity. In truth, Ken Lay was dead. He had had a bad heart. Perhaps he had stopped taking his medication. If so, that was his right. He knew he was facing the remainder of his life in prison. He knew there would be no bail pending appeal. Under all of that stress and at a high elevation, it was easy enough for his heart to give out. In essence, the government had gotten the death sentence for Ken Lay. Now Jeff Skilling faced sentencing alone for all of the wrongs at Enron.

We were still awaiting a decision from the Fifth Circuit on our appeal. We thought the release of everyone but Jim at least meant that a decision would be coming soon, but of course, there was no way of knowing when that would be. I had planned to take my aunt to her favorite place on the coast of North Carolina and then take her parasailing around Cape Lookout for her eightieth birthday. We drove from one end of North Carolina to the other.

On the latter part of the drive to the quaint little fishing and sailing village, Oriental, North Carolina, my cell phone rang. It was Hellen. The Fifth Circuit had just issued its opinion in *Brown*. She was highly excited but unsure of all the ramifications of the long decision, and she had Torrence call me to discuss the details. Of the fourteen counts of conviction against all of the Merrill defendants, the court reversed twelve. It affirmed only two—the perjury and obstruction charges against Jim. The court reversed all the conspiracy and wire fraud convictions against all of the defendants, including Jim, on the grounds that the indictment did not allege a valid conspiracy or wire fraud. The defendants' conduct was not criminal under the "honest services" provision. The court pronounced the indictment "fatally flawed."

Finally the right result on the law, with a touch of personal vindication of my consistent analysis on the side. It was even sweeter after the fight I had with my illustrious appellate cocounsel to recognize the importance of the argument. The three-judge panel unanimously ordered the acquittal of Fuhs, but the panel split on Brown's perjury and obstruction convictions. Judge DeMoss would have acquitted Jim, but Judges Reavley and Jolly affirmed those convictions. We missed getting Jim acquitted by only one vote.

I set to work drafting a motion for Jim's release *instanter*, a petition for rehearing to the panel to address their many factual errors, and suggestion for rehearing *en banc* to address the errors of law in their decision on the perjury and obstruction convictions. Torrence had also started on it. The Fifth Circuit obviously didn't realize that Jim's sentence was based on the sentencing guidelines for the conspiracy and fraud as the higher level, base offenses. That basis increased his sentence by three years or more over the maximum sentence he would have received had he been convicted only of perjury and obstruction, and DeMoss would have acquitted him of those. Holly Kulka, the associate from Heller Ehrman who had helped Larry Zweifach represent Jim in the ill-fated trial, called me to make sure I knew the effect that the reversal had on Jim's sentence. We both knew Jim had served all of the time to which he could have been sentenced on the only two counts that were affirmed—even if we could not get them reversed.

I called Nancy and let her know what we saw and were doing. She listened, but she held out no hope for any change. She had believed that Jim would not be indicted because he had told the truth in the grand jury, to the SEC, and to the bankruptcy examiner. Each time he testified voluntarily. She had believed the charges would be dropped months before trial when the front page of the *Houston Chronicle* announced that Fastow said there was no guarantee. She had believed that Judge Werlein would give them a fair trial, and that they would get to introduce the evidence they needed for their defense. She had believed that the jury instructions would be fair. She had believed that with a fair trial, Jim would be acquitted by the jury.

When all that failed, she had believed, in part due to my prior experiences with the Fifth Circuit, that the appeals court would straighten out this mess. She believed the judges would grant him bail pending appeal instead of requiring him to report to prison. When that didn't happen, she still believed that the Fifth Circuit would reverse all his convictions. When they released Fuhs, she had hopes again that the Fifth Circuit would reverse all the convictions. With the denial of Jim's release and the affirmation of his convictions on the perjury and obstruction convictions, we had long passed the point where she, Jim, their children, or any of their friends could believe the system of justice they had respected all their lives could or would work at all anymore.

Torrence and I had already been looking into the law on the sentencing and release issues that might apply to Jim after Fuhs was released. I'd had an inkling that the court would not realize Jim was entitled to release, so we got the motion for Jim's release instanter drafted and filed in two days—by August 3.

Once we filed it, I called Nancy again. She and Jim had become completely resigned to the fact that Jim would spend the next three years in prison while everyone else was out. It was heartbreaking—and for Chris and Lauren too. She decided that she wouldn't mention a word of this to the kids. Chris was still at home trying to recover from his accident. Lauren was in college. They had enough on their plates without having their hopes shattered again. It was better not to tell them anything.

Just in case, though, Nancy decided that she'd better make a special trip to the prison to let Jim know what was going on. He'd been feeling a bit rebellious since the others were released. She was concerned for his safety more from the guards than the other inmates now.

Nancy called to tell me she was going to go to the prison to visit Jim and warn him. She said she just knew they would try something. She told me for the first time, "They've really been hard on him in there, and they hate you!"

I told her I was so sorry. "Yes, go warn him. Nancy, Jim will be coming home soon."

Nancy made the three-hour drive to the prison to see Jim, her thoughts racing over all they had endured as she drove, wondering what she would say to Jim.

Their conversation was muted and careful in the visitors' room. Nancy was adamant. "Jim Brown, you keep your nose clean in here and be very careful. Sidney's filed a motion for your immediate release. She says you've served the maximum possible sentence for perjury and obstruction under the sentencing guidelines. They will have to resentence you to time-served."

Nancy's positive attitude didn't matter. Jim was completely de-feated. "It won't make any difference. They're not going to let me out of here. The court will come up with something or the prison will. I know I'm stuck. Someone's got to take the fall for this. It's me."

Nancy was inexorable. "No, Sidney says they have to release you soon. We don't know when it will be. Just keep your mouth shut, watch your back, and don't do or say anything stupid."

Jim not only had no hope by this time, he didn't want any at this point. He was better off resigned to his years in prison than to have hope and be crushed again. "All right, but it's not happening."

We filed our motion for his immediate release. Four days later, on August 7, my adventurous eighty-year-old aunt and I were in our car on the ferry crossing the three-mile-wide Neuse River from Minnesott Beach to Cherry Point, North Carolina, to go parasailing for her birthday. She was enjoying the view from the ferry and watching the seagulls; I was thinking about Jim and the court when my cell phone rang. Cell phone reception is challenging enough on the coast of North Carolina, but I sure wasn't expecting it to ring in the middle of the Neuse River.

Hellen was breathless, and she speaks very fast and with a heavier Spanish accent when she's excited. "The government's agreed."

"What?" I screamed over the roar of the ferry engines and the squealing of the flock of seagulls catching bread other travelers were tossing to them.

"The government's agreed to the motion you filed. They filed a response today saying that they agree that Jim should be released immediately. They agree with your calculations. He's served the maximum time and is entitled to be resentenced."

"Read me the entire response."

So she did.

I yelled again, "Tell Torrence to call me as soon as possible. This is amazing. It's about time. Who signed it?"

"Oestreicher."

"Hallelujah! Finally one person acting as a real US Attorney should," I proclaimed.

We got off the ferry at Cherry Point, and I pulled over to the side to call Nancy. She didn't believe me. "Something's going to go wrong. The Fifth Circuit won't grant it."

"Nancy, the court will grant it," I assured her. "The government has agreed to it. Jim will be out in a few days. Oestreicher did the right thing."

"I'm not saying anything to anyone," she said. "It's not going to happen."

Inside Fort Dix, every day the week of August 8 was just like all other days. Jim had been let out of his cell for breakfast and was making his daily rounds unstopping toilets from the worst human filth. He had not received the copy of the motion I had sent him, nor had he been informed of any of my calls to the prison and my many recent attempts to speak with him. He felt the intense scrutiny of the guards, and the pressure on him had ratcheted up significantly. They were glaring constantly and shoving him at every opportunity. He tried to keep his head down and just keep doing what he'd been doing. It was tense, he knew that much, but he had no idea what was really going on.

The next day, the Fifth Circuit called me. The court had granted Jim's motion for release instanter. The Fifth Circuit first faxed the order requiring Brown's immediate release to the Department of Justice. Then after what seemed like hours, it faxed the order to the Bureau of Prisons and finally to Fort Dix.

I called Nancy. She was in complete shock. Hellen got my plane ticket to go to New Jersey. The court called me to tell me they had notified the prison.

I called the prison again and requested to speak with my client about an urgent legal matter. I got the runaround. They said he "wasn't available."

"Well when will he be?" I asked angrily. "This is his attorney. The court has entered an order. I need to speak with my client."

They repeatedly refused to let me speak to Jim. I told them that the US Court of Appeals had ordered Jim's immediate release and I needed to speak with Jim urgently. They told me they knew nothing about it. Hellen sent them several faxes to confirm my attempts to call and speak with Jim and another copy of the order.

I verified with a call back to the clerk of the Fifth Circuit that the order had been faxed to the prison, and I informed the Fifth Circuit that the warden at Fort Dix would not allow me to speak with my client.

Finally an assistant US attorney from the office closest to Fort Dix called me and said that she had been given the case. Jim would be brought to the federal courthouse on August 11 for a hearing. I was to be there by 10:00 a.m.

I never was able to speak to Jim to let him know they had ordered his release, and he was not able to call Nancy again.

Back in the Connecticut suburb of New York the Browns called home, Chris Brown started to believe that the dad he adored would come home when he and Nancy left to pick me up at the airport in Newark on August 10. None of us had been able to talk to Jim in two days. We were very concerned. I had papered everything as well as I could to protect Jim from harm, and I did not want to convey my concern to Chris and Nancy. We drove to the courthouse early the next morning. I wondered what Jim would look like after a year in prison and if he would even be able to talk about what he had endured.

Fort Dix was not a nice place. We already knew that. Jim had experienced several close calls. He had to be alert constantly. On August 11, the morning we were to meet in court, Jim returned to his cell from his morning work detail. He was still unaware that he had a court date scheduled, much less that his release had been ordered by the Fifth Circuit. His orange jumpsuit with his prisoner number on the back was already nasty from his morning duties. Suddenly three very large, no-nonsense, angry guards appeared. One shoved Jim against the back wall. The other two parted as the warden himself entered behind them. One of the guards—a huge man with a tattoo on his arm—was slapping his nightstick against his hand.

The red-faced warden angrily ordered Jim to stand facing the wall with his hands behind his back. The biggest guard shoved Jim again, mashing his face against the wall, and roughly and tightly cuffed Jim's hands behind his back.

As Jim stood there, face against the wall, the furious warden personally began tearing apart Jim's cell. He flipped the thin mattress off the metal frame, tore down Jim's poster, felt all over the mattress, and searched each of Jim's few books. The warden was enraged. Jim was terrified and sure that he was going to be sent to "the hole."

"We've got nothing here," the warden growled. "Take him down the hall."

The three guards shoved Jim out of his cell and took him down the hall to a different cell. They pushed him through the door and slammed the cage shut behind him. They told Jim nothing. He was alone.

Thirty minutes later, which seemed an eternity, two more guards entered. They put shackles on Jim's ankles, changed his cuffs from behind his back to in front, then chained his cuffs to his ankle shackles. "Come with us," they commanded. They pushed Jim out of the cell down a dimly lighted hall and through a door into what looked like a big garage. Then they shoved him into the cage of a waiting prison van.

⚬⚬⚬

At the New Jersey federal courthouse, I sent Chris and Nancy to wait in the courtroom. I was intent on seeing Jim. At my request, Nancy had assembled a suit and tie for Jim to put on before appearing in court. I didn't want Chris and Nancy to see him in the chains and jumpsuit I knew he'd be in. I went to speak to the marshals and give them the clothes, but the marshals refused to let him change. Finally I was able to speak with the assistant US attorney. She instructed the marshals to let me see Jim in the holding cell before we had to go into the courtroom.

The door of the holding cell opened and I walked in wearing the all-white suit I had worn the day we first met.

"You look like an angel," Jim said and smiled.

I smiled but I was shocked at what I saw, and I hoped my face didn't show it. Jim looked very different from a year earlier. He was shackled and in the standard orange prison jumpsuit. His head and mustache were shaved bare. He had lost at least thirty pounds. He was so pale he looked dead, and his eyes seemed hollow. He was a shell of the man I had originally met. He told me a bit of what he had just been through, that he had almost missed the transport, and that he was not even told what was going on.

"Jim, we're taking you home today."

"I can't believe it."

"We are," I said reassuringly. "Chris and Nancy are waiting for you in the courtroom. The Fifth Circuit ordered your release immediately. We are taking you home today. The worst is over."

159

The marshals made me leave. I proceeded to counsel table in the courtroom and waited some more. I whispered to Chris and Nancy that he was OK but to be prepared for the ridiculous chains and jumpsuit.

It wasn't long this time before the judge came in and called the case. The marshals brought Jim into the courtroom, still shackled.

The judge, a woman, looked at me and said, "Ms. Powell, I've never seen a situation like this. Can you tell me where things stand?"

"Yes, Your Honor," I said as I stood. "According to the Fifth Circuit Court of Appeals, this court is to set the terms of Mr. Brown's release. He should be released on his own recognizance. He was on his own recognizance prior to and throughout his trial and sentencing. He then voluntarily reported to prison after being denied bail pending appeal. Now the Fifth Circuit has held that the government's indictment did not allege facts that constituted a federal crime. The government agreed that he should be released *instanter*, and the Fifth Circuit ordered his release. His family is here to take him home now, and we request that he be uncuffed and unshackled immediately."

The judge said, "Very well. Does the government agree?"

The young assistant US attorney replied, "We do, Your Honor."

The judge was competent, conscientious, and concise. "Mr. Brown, the court hereby orders you released on your own recognizance pending further proceedings in Houston or the Fifth Circuit. We'll get the paperwork done as quickly as we can. You'll need to go with your counsel to the marshal's office, and they will process you out."

"Thank you, Your Honor," I replied.

With that, the marshals uncuffed and unshackled Jim Brown. I accompanied him to the marshal's office, and we waited a ridiculous three hours or so for them to do whatever it was they were doing to complete his release, while Nancy and Chris languished in the hall.

Jim was in shell shock, and Nancy and Chris weren't far behind. Jim told us about his last several days and the warden tossing his cell. He laughed when he told me how much the prison officials hated me for demanding to speak to him. As we drove toward the airport for me to catch a flight before they took Jim home, Jim asked to stop and get a hamburger. We pulled into a mega-rest stop with a McDonald's and several other eateries.

Nancy and Chris headed toward the restaurant. I saw Jim was having a hard time, so I called out to them to go ahead. Jim and I stood at the back of the car and waited for them to bring us back a couple of bacon cheeseburgers. Jim was "whelmed-over." He was frozen at the back of the car.

He had been so sensory-deprived in prison that being out, actually being free, seeing the daylight, feeling the sunshine, and hearing the buzz of traffic and the crowd of people—all was a huge shock, a different kind of trauma. He was struggling to process it. He couldn't walk across the parking lot. I could only try to imagine his journey the past year and the adjustments that he and his family would have to make to integrate their experiences of Chris's near-death and abiding injuries, Jim's imprisonment, and Nancy's dealing with all of it into each other's lives again.

We got back in the car and ate our burgers. Nancy drove me to the airport and torpedoed me out barely in time to catch the flight. Nancy and Chris took Jim home to a house that had been decorated with all kinds of "Welcome Home" banners and balloons by their many friends.

Four weeks later, on Wednesday, September 12, 2006, hundreds of attorneys and other law enforcement officials connected with the

Department of Justice swarmed like ants to Constitution Hall in Washington, DC. It was time for the attorney general's 54th annual awards ceremony. The hall was magnificent, and the flags were flying. The scene was grand indeed. The attorney general's annual awards ceremony provides an opportunity to recognize the extraordinary accomplishments of a number of Department of Justice employees, as well as individuals from outside the department. It was a huge event.

Deputy Attorney General Paul J. McNulty joined Attorney General Alberto R. Gonzales in presenting the department's highest award—the attorney general's Award for Exceptional Service—"to the outstanding members of the investigative and trial team of the Enron Task Force." The attorney general honored them for "their exceptional service to the American public and the department in the investigation and successful prosecution of the individuals who were most responsible for the Enron fraud. The team's unparalleled dedication and teamwork over a period of years has made a significant contribution to restoring confidence in the nation's securities markets."

"Today's award recipients make me proud to be their colleague. They make me proud to be an American," added Attorney General Gonzales. "Their dedication and achievements remind me why it is an honor to serve at the Department of Justice."

Soon he called up the award recipients, including Sean M. Berkowitz, Kathryn H. Ruemmler, Leslie R. Caldwell, Andrew Weissmann, Samuel W. Buell, and Matthew W. Friedrich, who was then principal deputy assistant attorney general and chief of staff, office of the assistant attorney general.

On October 23, 2006, about a month after receiving the attorney general's highest award, Ruemmler appeared in Houston before Judge

Sim Lake and argued for the life imprisonment of Jeffrey Skilling. Judge Lake brushed aside serious allegations of a defective indictment, prosecutorial misconduct, witness intimidation, and failure to disclose *Brady* evidence, just as Ewing Werlein had done. Judge Lake sentenced Skilling to twenty-four years in prison.

Several months later, early in 2007, Ruemmler left the Department of Justice to join Alice Fisher, former assistant attorney general for the Criminal Division, at the prestigious Washington office of Latham & Watkins. Former Enron Task Force chief Sean Berkowitz had also joined Latham after leaving the task force and headed Latham's global litigation section. I couldn't help but wonder how Maureen Mahoney—a person of the highest integrity—felt about having former task force prosecutors as law partners given what she'd seen them do with Andersen.

Meanwhile the Department of Justice, where Friedrich had been honored and promoted, assigned a new prosecutor to the Barge case. He declared that they were going to prosecute Jim Brown, Dan Bayly, and Robert Furst for conspiracy and wire fraud all over again.

– 9 –

BOHICA

Shortly after Ruemmler left the Department of Justice to join Latham & Watkins, on March 19, 2007, the Fifth Circuit issued its decision in *Regents*. This was the multimillion dollar plaintiff's civil suit against several large banks that had done transactions with Enron, specifically including Merrill Lynch and its bankers in the Barge transaction. In *Regents*, the Fifth Circuit reversed Judge Melinda Harmon and held that the banks and their bankers had no civil liability or duty to Enron or its shareholders. The opinion in *Regents* was authored by Houston Judge Jerry Smith and joined by Judge Jolly. The third panel member, Judge James Dennis, agreed with the decision to reverse, but he did not join Judge Smith's decision. The opinion essentially adopted the arguments we had been making in the criminal case, and it stopped a huge civil suit on behalf of countless plaintiffs dead in its tracks.

How could the same court hold that the Merrill defendants should be prosecuted criminally when they did not even have civil liability, any duties to Enron, or responsibilities to Enron or its shareholders? We took the *Regents* decision as a good sign, but it seemed inconsistent with the court's holding in the criminal case.

Notwithstanding *Regents* and the illogical inconsistency, Judges Jolly and Reavley made short order of our requests for rehearing on

Jim's perjury and obstruction convictions. We were sent back to Judge Werlein's court. The Brown team decided to ask the Supreme Court to review the perjury and obstruction convictions, but that did not delay the government's efforts to pursue a second trial on the conspiracy and wire fraud. In fact, the new prosecutor decided to proceed on the very same indictment that the Fifth Circuit had just held was fatally flawed. These were the same factual charges that the *Regents* panel had held did not even warrant civil liability where the burden of proof is much lower—a preponderance of the evidence. Obtaining a criminal conviction requires proof beyond a reasonable doubt and criminal intent. The logical contradiction was maddening.

Judge Werlein called us all in for a status conference on April 4, 2007. Fortunately he did not require our clients to attend. Our new prosecutor, Arnold Spencer, was an assistant US attorney from the Eastern District of Texas. We heard he had originally interviewed for the Enron Task Force but didn't make the cut. He was already in over his head in this case. As of the morning of the hearing, we still did not have the indictment that we had been told the government would proceed on. We all knew that there were many things that, at a minimum, would have to be removed from the original indictment, but Spencer hadn't even done that yet.

He filed a motion that morning but left out page 13, and he had failed to confer with us on the motion as was required by the local rules. Judge Werlein wasn't used to government counsel who didn't know how to take over and run the courtroom. The judge was irritated. Then we got to the *Brady* issue. I had listened to Arnold Spencer jabber about how much evidence they had already given us in the first trial as long as I could tolerate. I stood up.

"Ms. Powell?" Judge Werlein noted.

"Judge, I'm very concerned that there were not full disclosures made in the first litigation. From what I understand from my prior cocounsel in New York, full discovery was not provided by the task force. We need all the *Brady* material—the evidence favorable to the defense—that the defense did not receive in the first trial."

Judge Werlein responded, "I've never heard of a *Brady* claim being made."

It took me a moment to recover from that announcement. I had read the record including the repeated *Brady* requests by the defense, countless motions requesting *Brady*, arguments at several hearings, and vehement denials by the task force. "Judge, we repeatedly asked for *Brady* material from Mr. Fastow and others, and that was never produced. We understand from Fastow's testimony in the Lay–Skilling trial, part of which I have seen, that there were multiple volumes of Fastow's 302s. And we don't know how many of those pertained to the Barge trial because we still haven't been given those. So I think there is some—"

Werlein cut me off. "Well, he didn't testify in the Barge trial."

"I understand that. But that doesn't mean what he told the government wasn't *Brady*. The government certainly used statements by him against the defendants throughout the Barge trial by the hearsay testimony of the coconspirators. That testimony could have been impeached with Fastow's 302 material or notes of his interviews. We do know that Fastow has given testimony that would be favorable to the defense in this case and in the Lay–Skilling trial. Obviously the government withheld *Brady* material."

"All right," Werlein replied tersely, as if I should be finished.

I wasn't. "And we don't know the full extent of all Fastow's possible *Brady* material because the government has never provided the notes, 302s, and statements that it has."

Werlein was astonished, "Well this is the first I've ever heard of any *Brady* claim being made against the government in connection with this."

The "hearing" was over shortly. We started pounding the government with motions demanding that Spencer produce *Brady* material—especially whatever the prosecutors were withholding that they had learned long ago from Merrill counsel Zrike and Gary Dolan and Enron's Fastow and McMahon. They were the very essence of the defense, and the government's case was so weak and contrived, I knew they were hiding something.

Werlein ignored our motions, and so did Spencer. The closer it got to a possible trial date, the more Spencer rattled his saber. The Supreme Court denied our petition for *writ of certiorari* and refused to look at the perjury and obstruction convictions. That was disappointing but not a huge surprise. As ridiculous as those two convictions were, the issue was neither exciting nor burning, so it was not likely to attract the attention of the court.

Spencer ratcheted up the pressure on Jim in particular. For weeks, he had tried to coerce a guilty plea out of Jim and force him to testify in the second trial against Bayly and Furst. Spencer told Furst's appellate counsel, former US Attorney Paul Coggins, that he "had tremendous leverage over Brown." According to Spencer, Brown still had three years to serve on his original prison sentence. Spencer didn't care that the Fifth Circuit had reversed the three counts of conviction on which that sentence had been based, or that the government had immediately agreed to Jim's release from prison exactly one year earlier and had agreed that Jim was entitled to be resentenced.

Jim would not "cooperate" despite Spencer's threats to send him back to prison. Jim would not even consider pleading guilty to a crime he did not commit, so Spencer played his trump card. On August 10,

2007, the eve of the one-year anniversary of Jim's release from prison, Spencer filed a motion to send Jim back to prison "to serve the remainder of his forty-six-month term of imprisonment."

Spencer's contention was specious, spurious, and unethical. He failed to cite the controlling Fifth Circuit decision or the Supreme Court authority that applied. It was a dirty tactic that, no matter how baseless, was terrifying to the Brown family.

Werlein set a hearing in Houston on Spencer's motion for November 16, 2007. He had also set other defense motions for hearing at the same time. All the defendants were required to be present, but only Jim had the specter of immediate imprisonment hanging over his head again.

The marshals were in the courtroom again too. They looked more ominous than usual.

The stress on Jim and his family was off the charts. The military's "black ops" handbook contains a special acronym for this situation: BOHICA. It means: "Bend Over, Here It Comes Again."

More than a year after Jim's release from prison, here we were in Houston, heading for Ewing Werlein's courtroom yet again, at the command of His Honor and the government, now represented by Arnold Spencer.

All the defendants and their new trial counsel and some appellate counsel gathered in the courtroom. Spencer began with his motion to send Jim back to prison. At some level, I must have thought he really wouldn't go through with it. I never thought I would hear anyone representing the United States of America stand before a federal judge and flat-out ignore the law in such a blatant abuse of power. I had warned Spencer of all of this in extensive correspondence.

I felt my blood pressure spike a good thirty points. In two long strides, I reached the now-familiar podium in Werlein's large dark-paneled courtroom. I gripped its sides so fiercely with both hands that my fingerprints are probably embedded in it. My temples throbbed with rage. I was so angry I literally could not speak. I just stood there.

Judge Werlein's law clerks, seated at a table to my left, stared at me. At least eight other lawyers were present for codefendants Bayly and Furst. They were staring at me, too.

The clients and their families were also staring at me—Dan and Pam Bayly; Rob Furst, his wife, and his parents; and Jim and Nancy Brown—as well as Juan Lozano of the Associated Press; Kristen Hays with the *Houston Chronicle;* and Laurel Calkins with Bloomberg, among others.

All eyes in the courtroom were fixed on me. I wondered if they could see the smoke coming from my ears. Werlein, who rarely looked at me anymore, was staring down and shuffling papers.

My silence was deafening. Still I said nothing. Still I was too angry to speak.

Judge Werlein finally raised his head and stared. I stood straight and still, square at the podium, and glared at the judge.

Then I turned and looked behind me at Jim and Nancy. They sat, frozen, on the first row of benches behind the bar.

Then I looked to my right at the prosecutor, who had just told Judge Werlein that Jim Brown needed to be remanded into custody—sent back to jail now to serve another three years in prison on counts of conviction that had been reversed. Above and beyond Spencer's head hung the portraits of three of the greatest judges who had ever sat on the Fifth Circuit. Two of them, Thomas Gibbs Gee and former Chief Judge John R. Brown, I had known a long time. They would not have tolerated this unethical tactic from an assistant US attorney for two seconds. They would have excoriated him and sent him packing. Spencer had already made it clear that he had no decision-making authority in this case. That itself is a violation of the local rules for the Southern District of Texas Court in which we stood. The rules required that whoever appears for the United States in a federal courtroom has the authority to make decisions for the prosecution. Yet Spencer couldn't take a bathroom break without permission from someone in the department.

Spencer had not contrived this argument until Jim "refused to cooperate." I wondered if Spencer had thought it up at all. Regardless this assistant US attorney was now telling a federal judge that Jim Brown had to be sent back to prison for three more years to serve an "unfinished sentence" that was imposed based on charges that had been reversed.

According to Spencer, when the Department of Justice had agreed that Jim was entitled to be released from custody immediately and should be resentenced, it had simply made a "mistake" that was "embarrassing." The government's agreement that Jim had already served the maximum term of imprisonment was an "error" made in haste.

I wondered where Spencer got the authority to countermand Deputy Attorney General for the Criminal Division Alice Fisher, whose name was on the agreement for Jim's release that Oestreicher had filed in the Fifth Circuit. *How was it,* I thought, *he could undo a binding "judicial admission" that the Department of Justice had made and upon which the US Court of Appeals for the Fifth Circuit had ordered Brown's release within three days?* Someone way above Arnold Spencer had to have authorized this maneuver. Spencer was someone's puppet and a pathetic one at that. If I hadn't been so angry, I might have felt sorry for him. He was way out of his league and stumbling every time he did anything.

Finally I managed to speak—without yelling—although my tone barely, if at all, hid my rage. Frankly I didn't want to hide it. I had hit

Refrigerator Rule #6: Enough is enough. I started with a blast. "The position Mr. Spencer asks you to adopt in this instance was so wrong that the Fifth Circuit—in a *pro se* appeal—acknowledged its own error and changed its own mandate in circumstances that control this decision. I think this court has correctly read the *Bass* decision. . . . The presentence report and this court's sentencing hearing transcript show without a doubt that Mr. Brown's sentence was 'bundled.'. . . The wire fraud offense was the greatest offense. The government does not even dispute the fact that our sentencing calculations are correct and that Brown has effectively served a full term of imprisonment for the offenses of perjury and obstruction."

Judge Werlein was not favorably impressed by Spencer any more than anyone else in the courtroom, but he still had questions and seemed determined to play devil's advocate: "Well what do I make of a decision by the Fifth Circuit to affirm the judgment on perjury and obstruction when he's been sentenced to serve whatever number of months it is on those offenses?"

I replied as vehemently as I had begun, "It was within forty-eight hours of our motion after the Fifth Circuit rendered its decision that affirmed those offenses that the Assistant Attorney General for the United States Department of Justice agreed unequivocally that Mr. Brown was entitled to be resentenced and entitled to be released."

Werlein countered with Spencer's argument. "But they didn't bother to check the law out on that. That was a mistake, as Mr. Spencer has explained. And then the decision comes down and then these judgments of conviction and sentences are affirmed."

That just made me more resolute. "There was no need for us to seek rehearing to correct that erroneous language in the Fifth Circuit's decision because the Department of Justice had already agreed to Mr. Brown's immediate release."

I was swinging back hard with irrefutable facts. "The sentences were affirmed and the decision rendered by the Fifth Circuit on August 1. Two days later we filed our motion for his release *instanter* based on the correct calculations of the sentencing guidelines that would apply to the only counts of conviction that were affirmed by the Fifth Circuit. Within hours of that, the government agreed with our calculations and with our motion to release, and with the fact that Mr. Brown was entitled to be resentenced. Counts One through Three were not reinstated on rehearing, as this court knows. Mr. Brown is entitled to be resentenced. . . ."

Then I finished with, "As a former Assistant United States Attorney of ten years' experience, I continue to be appalled by Mr. Spencer's efforts to pursue this motion. It is patently invalid and frivolous. I am confident that when the court has an opportunity to look at the cases, it will deny this motion. Thank you."

Still fuming, I sat down at counsel table. As I took my seat, my ears felt like they would explode from a high-pitched whine. My blood pressure really had spiked.

Spencer stood up to whine about his hurt feelings. "At some point, I would like the court to address the allegations that my conduct is appalling." I just shook my head in disgust.

Werlein wanted Spencer to sit down, and muttered something about expecting counsel to argue appropriately and if he found something he needed to remark on, he would.

Spencer kept on. Now he was claiming the court didn't have jurisdiction to resentence Jim and that Jim would have to go back to prison now to serve three more years and could only file another kind of motion to try to get out.

Werlein was getting annoyed. "All right," he remarked brusquely, which meant he had heard enough, but Spencer was oblivious.

Spencer either had his marching orders from on high or he couldn't or wouldn't take a hint. Most of us—at least the defense lawyers in the courtroom—could see that he was digging his own hole deeper.

He continued, "So notwithstanding the fact that it's embarrassing and we wish we hadn't done it, that doesn't mean that this court has jurisdiction as a result of that. It is not a statement in a plea agreement. It's not something that Mr. Brown relied on."

No, I mused silently, my thoughts dripping in sarcasm. *It was just a statement in a filing by the Assistant Attorney General of the Department of Justice of the United States of America to the court that is only one notch under the Supreme Court. On the basis of that representation, the Fifth Circuit ordered Jim's immediate release. The judge in New Jersey held an immediate hearing and ordered Jim's release on his personal recognizance. Jim went back home to his family, found work, and had resumed his place in society for an entire year. No—no one relied on the government's statement in that filing.*

If Werlein did follow the law this time, would he hold the prosecutor accountable for the stress and anxiety he had put the Brown family through over this abusive tactic? Would he make the government reimburse the attorneys' fees unnecessarily incurred to combat this outrage? Would this ever stop?

Werlein's tone, if not his words, sounded as if he were catching on—it seemed. "So you're wanting to revoke the bond and remand Mr. Brown?"

Spencer replied, "Yes, sir."

Werlein continued as Jim and Nancy watched, terrified. "As I understand it, after the government indicated that Mr. Brown would need to be resentenced, the defendant had moved to be put on bond, I think, and the Fifth Circuit ordered Mr. Brown's release and that he be placed on bond. Is that right?"

Spencer meekly replied, "I believe that's correct, Your Honor."

Werlein was sounding irritated, a rarity when speaking to government counsel. "And now you're asking me to sort of reverse the Fifth Circuit, I gather."

Spencer recoiled at the thought. "No. To the contrary. I am asking you to enforce the Fifth Circuit's ruling."

Werlein was puzzled. "Well they put him on bond, didn't they? Well when he was sentenced he was sentenced, was he not, on the basis of several convictions, not just the one that has been upheld?"

Spencer didn't want to admit that, so he tried to parry. "He was put on bond at a time when the Fifth Circuit—or a time the government was considering petitioning the Fifth Circuit for rehearing *en banc,* and he was put on bond as he was taking his motion up to the Supreme Court for *writ of certiorari.*"

Werlein caught that inartful dodge. "I asked, though, when he was sentenced?"

Spencer was shrinking by the minute. "I'm sorry."

Werlein continued—in the best form I'd ever seen him. "He was sentenced, was he not, based upon jury findings of conviction on several counts, not just the one count or whatever it was—I think there was one count—that was upheld by the Fifth Circuit, the count of conviction. Is that right?

Spencer couldn't give a straight answer to save his own life. "There were five separate sentences that were ordered by this court, sir."

Werlein had to take him one baby step at a time. "And how many of those were upheld by the Fifth Circuit?"

"Two of them." Spencer got that much right.

"Two of them were upheld. All right. So the sentence at the time it was imposed did not separate out those two to be sentenced for so much on these two crimes and then sentenced so much on these that the Fifth Circuit has set aside, did it?"

"To the contrary, it did, sir."

Spencer had misled Werlein again. The judge was in the ballpark but wasn't completely on top of this. "I thought it was one combined, as I recall—and I spent a lot of time on this—that we had PSRs that had all of these different offenses and they knew the combination that was required by the guidelines and still is in order to ascertain a range, an offense level, and a criminal history category and a recommended range. Isn't that the way it went?"

"Right up until the end, Your Honor."

"What do you mean 'up to the end'?" Werlein asked.

"Well, that was the procedure that the court followed coming up to entering its judgment and conviction. . . . In the judgment and the conviction, the controlling order, it specifies five separate sentences and each of those sentences are for an independent amount of the time."

We sat there wondering if Spencer really was this stupid or if this was just the logical consequence of trying to defend the indefensible. This felt like "Sentencing 101" for someone who had never handled a criminal case before.

"That's right. And they ran concurrently, didn't they?" Werlein asked.

"They run concurrently, but they are independent of one another."

Spencer was beyond hope. This could have ended thirty minutes ago if Werlein had just done his job and denied Spencer's motion, but he didn't, and Spencer kept going. "I don't know the manner in which they were reached, Your Honor."

Apparently Spencer had not read the record of the prior sentencing or even heard what Judge Werlein had said earlier.

This was torture, but Werlein wouldn't end it. "Are you suggesting that the same sentence would have been imposed had the convictions only been for obstruction and perjury?"

"That question was not reduced to the record for the Fifth Circuit to consider."

Werlein was bumfuzzled. "Well then, that's something that hasn't been considered, has it?"

Creating even more confusion, Spencer said, "No, sir. I believe it has been considered."

Werlein interrupted him. "That's when the government suggested to the Fifth Circuit that Mr. Brown should be resentenced? And the Fifth Circuit released him on bond?"

Spencer could not take a hint. "And after the government misstated that he would be able to be resentenced under the law."

Finally it seemed Werlein had heard more than enough. "OK. Any other argument on that, then?"

Still Spencer went on and on and on—now it was back to how Jim would have to file suit under a different statute to get his sentence fixed. I was rolling my eyes and shaking my head. Werlein was shuffling papers. Other defense counsel were all but chortling.

Spencer finally said thank you and sat down.

Werlein wisely did not even look at me to give me a chance to speak again, but called on counsel for a codefendant on another topic. Werlein's body language spoke volumes. He did not need to hear any more on this subject—and certainly not from Arnold Spencer. For the first time since I had appeared in Werlein's courtroom, I was confident he would get this one right.

Jim and Nancy Brown sat behind counsel table, stiff as boards and horrified at the possibility that Jim would be ordered back to prison. Jim's children had lived through their teens under the stress and threat of their father being declared a criminal, then imprisoned, then released, and now threatened with prison again. It was already a six-year ordeal for them. Lesser families would have disintegrated long ago. I could only admire Nancy Brown. She was a pillar of strength. She inspired me every day.

Next we got into a big argument with Spencer over *Brady* material. I sat still as long as I possibly could, listening to Spencer claim that he had "consulted with the task force attorneys" and "believed they acted in good faith," and there was no *Brady* material to give us.

I stood up, and stood, and stood, until Werlein acknowledged me to speak. Then I cut loose again. "Mr. Spencer's view of *Brady* to date discloses nothing more than the fact that he can't even define what it is. *Brady* includes exculpatory and impeaching information. The Supreme Court held that Mr. Spencer has a duty to learn of and to disclose all exculpatory or impeaching information from any department within the government. On April 4, now eight months ago, Mr. Spencer committed to this court that he would personally review all of the documents that the government had reviewed the first time, and the additional documents even though we were talking about the volumes of the Fastow 302s that are still out there. He has not done that. He said he would produce supplemental discovery by August 1. We got nothing."

I barely breathed and just kept going. "And we still don't have the material underlying the 302s, which I'm sure is also *Brady*. Over the government's repeated objections, Judge Higginbotham and the Fifth Circuit just ordered that the prosecutors produce to the Skilling defense all of the notes underlying the highly unorthodox 'composite' 302 the government prepared of Fastow's thousands of hours of debriefings. We have no doubt that anything that Mr. Fastow said in regard to the Barge transaction, Merrill Lynch, and LJM2 is exculpatory and/or impeaching information benefiting these defendants."

Werlein then did something we had never seen before. He recessed and called us all back into chambers to discuss "scheduling."

Jim and Nancy were still afraid, but I turned to assure them of my belief that Jim was going home that evening—for whatever good that might do. Dan Bayly patted me on the shoulder as I left the courtroom and whispered, "Good job." He seemed delighted that someone showed some anger over the department's deplorable tactics.

We went back into Werlein's office where there were more lawyers than chairs. He hemmed and hawed a bit, trying to encourage us to settle the case—meaning work out a plea deal. I told him that our client was innocent, and there wasn't anything we could plead guilty to.

Finally he gave that up. The only thing that was clear was that Ewing Werlein did not want to try this case again. Would he ever see that we'd given him plenty of valid legal reasons to dismiss it?

We left the courtroom that day with nothing resolved. Werlein did not rule on any of the pending motions. We still had no *Brady* order, no order on Jim's remand into custody—nothing . . . nada . . . zip . . . zero.

Spencer had made clear that he was going to put us all through another trial on this indictment for conspiracy and wire fraud. This case never made sense, but so far the government had spent tens of millions of dollars, and four men had spent up to a year in prison for conduct that wasn't criminal. The department and Spencer were continuing to spend tax dollars like water. Someone high up in the Department of Justice was pushing things hard, and it was completely irrational. Why would they continue to spend money and pursue this case . . . unless . . . they were protecting someone—but whom? And from what? The task force had disbanded, but Spencer had just admitted in open court that he had consulted with them—and apparently more than once. They had convinced him that they "had acted in good faith," as he said, and they had disclosed everything. I was certain they had not. They were fighting way too long and too hard. They were covering up something.

Former task force director Weissmann was at megafirm Jenner & Block, heading up its white-collar defense practice. Ruemmler had left the department in February 2007 and became a partner at Latham & Watkins. As Kristen Hays reported in the *Chronicle*, "Task Force Prosecutors Are Prospering."

Matthew Friedrich's path was even more interesting. Weissmann and Ruemmler were definitely with high-powered law firms, but Friedrich was with the most high-powered of all. Friedrich became special counsel to Attorney General Alberto Gonzales. Friedrich was smack in the middle of all the action in the department, including the enormous political controversy that erupted over Gonzales's decision to fire US Attorneys from around the country in the department's own version of Pearl Harbor Day in 2006. When Gonzales resigned in August 2007, Friedrich remained unscathed. Friedrich stayed on as special counsel to the attorney general during two interim appointments, and when Michael Mukasey was finally confirmed as the new attorney general in November, Friedrich became his deputy chief of staff.

By the time Arnold Spencer was trying so hard to send Jim Brown back to prison for convictions that had been reversed—fighting tooth and nail and stalling like crazy to keep from producing any *Brady* material—Matthew Friedrich was sitting at the right hand of Attorney General Mukasey.

Little did anyone know that Friedrich would soon be deep into manipulating another extremely high-profile case, to which he would apply all the dirty tricks he, Weissmann, Ruemmler, and others had used so effectively to achieve wrongful convictions while they were on the Enron Task Force.

Meanwhile all we could do was keep defending Jim and wait—in blind ignorance of what was happening in the Department of Justice and what had really happened to Jim Brown and his codefendants.

– 10 –

MORE SURPRISES

The absence of any decision from Judge Werlein; the threat of an impending second trial for Bayly, Furst, and Brown; Spencer's motion to send Jim back to prison immediately; and the endless nightmare of it all cast a pall over the holidays for these families and carried into the new year of 2008. While enormously grateful to be out of prison and to celebrate Christmas with their families, the emotional, psychological, and physical consequences of the stress and anxiety were more than anyone who has not been through such an ordeal can imagine.

On January 7, 2008, we received an order—finally—from Judge Werlein. He denied Spencer's motion to remand Jim into custody. In an unexpected and favorable development, Werlein punted the case back to the Fifth Circuit. He certified an issue for interlocutory appeal. This was an unusual step but one we had requested—to ask the Fifth Circuit to decide whether it would violate double jeopardy to try Bayly, Brown, and Furst on the same indictment for a second time.

Thankfully, in one sense, this meant there would be no second trial anytime soon—for at least a year—while we went to the Fifth Circuit the second time on the conspiracy and wire fraud counts. As important for Jim, Werlein had granted our motion for severance, which meant that Bayly and Furst would be tried together, without Jim and before Jim was tried. This development gave us a sense of relief also; we knew we would get to see the government's trial run before facing our own trial—if it ever came to that.

Werlein's order granting the interlocutory appeal would also give us more time to get the *Brady* material that we were still being denied so we could actually present a defense if we did have to try the case again. In addition, this gave the Fifth Circuit another opportunity to look at the purely legal issues with more distance from the heat of Enron than existed in the first appeal during the Lay–Skilling trial. There was nothing new or different in the indictment or the case from what the Fifth Circuit had already held was not a crime. How could Jim and the others be forced to stand trial again for exactly the same charges, actually even fewer than the first case? That's double jeopardy.

It was undisputed that the Merrill defendants did not take money or property from anyone. Those were the only two things that would support a conviction for wire fraud in the absence of the failed "honest services" allegation. This indictment never alleged a crime.

Meanwhile after three orders from the Fifth Circuit in the *Skilling* case, over repeated objections by the government, and our repeated demands on Spencer, he finally produced to us the raw notes of the government agents' hundreds of interviews of Andrew Fastow. Many of these notes did not include an agent's name or a date or were written in chicken scratch, but they were sufficiently decipherable for us to understand why Friedrich and Ruemmler did not call Fastow to the witness stand in the Barge trial.

There were astonishing revelations in the notes that had not made it into the heavily edited "composite 302" revised repeatedly by FBI case agents, especially Bhatia. The notes also clarified why the prosecutors fought so hard to keep the notes away from any defense attorney.

Fastow had told the government very clearly that there was no guarantee in the Barge deal. In fact, he said that he had been extremely careful to avoid making a guarantee. On top of that, he told the agents and the task force lawyers that he had used different language within Enron than he had with Merrill. With his Enron subordinates, Fastow called it "a guarantee" to "light a fire" under Glisan and Kopper to remarket the barges faster to another company. Those were the very people on whom Ruemmler, Friedrich, and team had relied to say there was a guarantee. The notes dramatically contradicted and undermined that testimony. Fastow said he had not made a guarantee to Merrill, and that what he had said to Glisan and Kopper was different from what he had actually told Merrill.

Time was now on our side. As the years had passed, the statute of limitations would apply and bar additional Enron prosecutions. Former Treasurer, President, and Chief Operating Officer Jeff McMahon—who had lived for years with repeated and sometimes daily threats of being indicted—finally knew he would not be indicted. At that point, we were able to obtain two memoranda through Tom Kirkendall, highly respected Houston counsel for McMahon. Written to the Department of Justice and to the SEC years earlier, both documents stated flat out that McMahon never made a guarantee in the Barge case. Significantly McMahon, who was also on the phone call on December 23 between Bayly at Merrill and Fastow at Enron, said that Fastow didn't make a guarantee either. Weissmann, Friedrich, Ruemmler, Hemann, Spencer, and the later prosecutors had never produced this information from the task force files, which would have shown exactly who received it and when.

Even more shocking, in McMahon's second memorandum—after the Barge trial and before any of the Merrill defendants went to prison—McMahon told the Enron Task Force that he had reviewed

Ben Glisan's testimony in the Barge trial and that Ben Glisan had lied about McMahon having made a guarantee.

Not only was that *Brady* evidence that the government had been constitutionally required to produce—even after the trial—it raised a serious question as to whether Weissmann, Friedrich, Ruemmler, and Hemann, or any combination thereof, had knowingly suborned perjury. They certainly had been told by one of the few people whom they never indicted that Glisan had lied in the Barge case. They had concealed that crucial fact while Dan Bayly, Rob Furst, Bill Fuhs, and Jim Brown reported to federal prisons and spent eight to twelve months there. They also hid the Fastow notes that corroborated what McMahon said. Fastow had told Merrill there was no guarantee while he had told the government witnesses there was one—for his own reasons. We now had evidence that the prosecutors knew all of this while they vehemently opposed release pending appeal, told two courts there was "no substantial issue for appeal," and before our clients went to prison.

We immediately went to work and filed a blistering motion for a new trial on Jim's behalf. These Fastow notes and McMahon memoranda were favorable, exculpatory, and material to the defense. It was *Brady* evidence under any objective definition. All defense counsel were shocked at the clarity, specificity, and force of this information. Both Fastow and McMahon—on whose "guarantee" Weissmann, Ruemmler, Friedrich, and Hemann had built their entire criminal case and convicted and imprisoned the Merrill defendants—had said long ago that they did not make a guarantee to Merrill in this case.

These astonishing revelations, however, did not slow any process inside the Department of Justice or seem to matter to anyone. On May 22, 2008, on the recommendation of Attorney General Mukasey, President Bush promoted Matthew Friedrich from Mukasey's chief of staff to acting Assistant Attorney General for the Criminal Division of the Department of Justice. Friedrich's career had skyrocketed after his convictions of Arthur Andersen and the Merrill Lynch executives.

No one seemed to notice—much less care—that Friedrich had played a significant role in causing the errors that led to the reversals in *Andersen* and in *Brown*—while wasting millions of taxpayer dollars and causing substantial harm to countless people. No one was paying any attention to the fact that these prosecutors had hidden evidence from the defense either. Our motion for a new trial languished on Werlein's docket.

Matthew Friedrich definitely had connections. Tall, with receding light brown hair and a boyish face that easily appeared smug, Friedrich had been practicing law only since 1995, after a one-year judicial clerkship. Friedrich had a total of only fourteen years' experience as an attorney when he took command of the criminal division and its seven hundred attorneys. It couldn't have hurt that in 2001, Friedrich married Dabney Langhorne. She was an assistant US attorney in the Eastern District of Virginia, who just happened to be a "Virginia blue-blood" from the wealthy and politically powerful Langhorne–Astor families. In fact, Friedrich's wife was associate counsel in the White House from 2003 until 2006. President Bush nominated her for a federal judgeship, but her nomination stalled in the senate. She was appointed to the Sentencing Commission in 2006, and President Obama reappointed her to the commission in 2010.

Once Friedrich became head of the criminal division, he brought in Rita Glavin to work as his deputy. It would later prove ironic that Glavin began her career with the department in its Public Integrity

Section in 1998. She was assigned briefly to the Eastern District of Virginia in 1999, where it appears that she and Friedrich became friends—if they weren't before. She was a 1996 graduate of Fordham and completed a two-year judicial clerkship. In 2003, she moved to the US Attorney's Office for the Southern District of New York as a line prosecutor before returning to DC as Friedrich's deputy at the Justice Department in 2008.

A slender woman with long black hair, sharp features, an easy smirk, and an affinity for androgynous attire, Glavin had practiced law only ten years when she became second in command of the criminal division. Just like the Enron Task Force and its "young gun" lawyers, there was no adult supervision of the new command of the criminal division.

Within days of taking up residence in their new offices, Friedrich and Glavin inserted themselves into the work of the department's Public Integrity Section (PIN) and its investigation of public corruption cases in Alaska, nicknamed Operation Polar Pen. PIN attorney Nicholas Marsh, who had practiced law as long as Glavin had, and his team had already obtained convictions of seven Alaska businessmen and legislators. Several of the most prominent cases were *United States v. Weyhrauch*, *United States v. Kott*, and *United States v. Kohring*. Of great interest to Friedrich and Glavin was a draft of an indictment against United States Senator Ted Stevens.

After sometimes daily meetings with PIN management, Friedrich and Glavin soon summoned all the Polar Pen attorneys for a meeting on July 14 to discuss the case against Senator Stevens. A heavily decorated World War II pilot, Stevens was a legend and a hero to most Alaskans. He had served in the senate for forty years, and he had helped build Alaska.

Dutifully the exhausted Assistant US Attorneys, Joseph Bottini and James Goeke, made the long trip from Alaska to join PIN Deputy

Chief Brenda Morris, PIN Chief Bill Welch, and PIN trial attorneys Nick Marsh and Edward Sullivan for the big conference. They had been commanded to put on a dog and pony show for Friedrich and Glavin like they had recently done for Friedrich's predecessor, criminal division head Alice Fisher. Wisely Fisher had returned to her comfortable partnership at Latham & Watkins without approving the indictment of Stevens.

The trial lawyers did not know what to expect from the new "front office" of the department. They assumed they would be doing the same presentation they had done for others, including Senator Stevens's defense counsel Brendan Sullivan. At Brenda Morris's suggestion, Marsh was rather casual about the presentation to Friedrich and Glavin. Consequently Marsh impressed Friedrich and Glavin—just not favorably. The meeting ended with nothing resolved. Friedrich and Glavin continued having frequent meetings with Morris and/or Welch, but no word filtered down to the trial lawyers.

Over Welch's objections, Friedrich reconstituted the trial team just two days before issuing the indictment. Friedrich and Glavin installed Morris as lead counsel and relegated Marsh to a supporting role. Marsh went from the star of the show to a minor supporting actor, and he had no idea why. The younger attorneys, Sullivan and Goeke, were exiled to a back-office support position. Adding to the conundrum, Morris said she did not want the assignment. Everyone in the Public Integrity Section had told Friedrich and Glavin it was too late to change roles among the trial team. It was terrible for morale and inefficient at best, and that was only the beginning of the problems the Friedrich–Glavin front office caused in the case.

Two days later, on July 29, 2008, a smug Matthew Friedrich swaggered into the Justice Department press room, where he mounted the podium to face a room full of reporters, television cameras, bright lights, and strobe flashes. As he stood in front of the cobalt-blue curtain, the seal of the United States Department of Justice formed a halo behind his head and the flag showed over his left shoulder. Friedrich could barely suppress his urge to grin as he read the public corruption charges just returned by the federal grand jury against the longest-sitting Republican in the United States Senate—Ted Stevens. This indictment was issued only four weeks before the primary election in Alaska.

Friedrich had enjoyed the daily presence of microphones and cameras throughout his prosecutions of Arthur Andersen and the Nigerian Barge case during his task force days. He seemed to relish the opportunity to conduct the press conference that was broadcast live on national news.

The reporters didn't notice. They were all facing Friedrich, but standing in the back of the packed room, Nick Marsh was glowering. His arms were crossed across his chest and his jaw was clenched. He seethed with rage while the new acting Assistant Attorney General Friedrich trumpeted the Stevens indictment.

Senator Stevens was defended by a powerful and prestigious team led by Brendan Sullivan and Rob Cary at Williams & Connolly in DC. Both had impressive records, stellar reputations, and the support and resources needed to handle such an important and public case. They were the best, and they demanded a speedy trial. The senator wanted his name cleared and the case tried before the presidential election on November 4. The race for his senate seat was tied to it and closer than usual. Stevens's seat was widely regarded as a target for the Democrats to reach the sixtieth seat they needed to control the senate, and Obama was favored to win the presidency.

Stevens's indictment and pending trial provided a media piranha-feeding frenzy. It was in the middle of Washington, DC. It had been brought by the Public Integrity Section of the Department of Justice. It was just before an election that could change the balance of power in the senate, and it was about a living legend in the state of Alaska accused of public corruption in such a way that it sounded like bribery.

The case fell onto the docket of federal District Judge Emmet Sullivan. An experienced trial judge, Sullivan was a distinguished man and widely held in high regard. He was no ordinary federal judge; he had worked hard all of his life on several different courts and had been appointed by three presidents representing both political parties. He had worked extensively on issues affecting juveniles, and he cared about justice and legal ethics. Appointed to the federal district court bench by President Clinton in 1994, Judge Sullivan had no tolerance for criminals, but he had great respect for the rule of law and strived to apply it equally and fairly in all cases in his courtroom.

Judge Sullivan expected those entrusted with the power of the sovereign and privileged to represent the United States in its courts to be correct on the law and the facts when they threatened someone's life and liberty. Long ago, in a case called *Berger*, the Supreme Court set the standard for the conduct of US attorneys:

> The United States Attorney is the representative not of an ordinary party to a controversy, but of a sovereignty whose obligation to govern impartially is as compelling as its obligation to govern at all, and whose interest, therefore, in a criminal prosecution is not that it shall win a case, but that justice shall be done. As such, he is in a peculiar and very definite sense the servant of the law,

He may prosecute with earnestness and vigor—indeed, he should do so. But, while he may strike hard blows, he is not at liberty to strike foul ones. It is as much his duty to refrain from improper methods calculated to produce a wrongful conviction as it is to use every legitimate means to bring about a just one.

Judge Sullivan believed that all lawyers should practice by that code—especially federal prosecutors whose only real job was to seek justice in the highest sense.

The Department of Justice indicted Senator Stevens on seven counts of making false statements on the forms he was required to file with the senate to report all gifts. At the senator's arraignment on Thursday, July 31, 2008, Brendan Sullivan requested a speedy trial and an October trial date, so that Senator Stevens could clear his name before the general election on November 4. The government agreed to the request—and an even earlier date, so the trial began on September 22. The defense made repeated requests for *Brady* material, and the prosecutors repeatedly represented they had complied fully with *Brady*.

According to the government, a prominent and wealthy builder in Alaska, Bill Allen, had given Senator Stevens numerous "gifts" during the process of remodeling the senator's house. The prosecutors said that the senator had failed to report the true value of those gifts as required by senate ethics rules. The prosecutors strongly implied that these "gifts" were in exchange for various favors and really were bribes, but Friedrich and PIN did not indict the senator for bribery. Rather as Friedrich had done in the Enron cases, the prosecution was content to besmirch the senator with the stench of an offense the government couldn't prove and obtain a conviction from a jury who would believe it smelled bad, and therefore, he must be guilty as charged.

Senator Stevens, on the other hand, always said that he had paid every bill he had been given, had intended to pay for everything, and believed he had paid for everything—totaling more than $165,000—for what really did not look like much of a remodeling job. As a "serial remodeler" myself, it looked to me like the senator had been taken advantage of by his builder. The photographs didn't evidence $165,000 worth of remodeling to me.

Throughout the Stevens trial in late September and October 2008, which Glavin often attended, sitting in the gallery, the defense team managed to catch the prosecutors in one embarrassing and damning "oversight" and "mistake" after another. As Judge Sullivan became increasingly perturbed, he ordered the government to provide more and more information that the defense had requested all along. That information, once produced, led to evidence of further "mistakes" by the prosecution until Judge Sullivan was boiling mad.

At the beginning of the trial, prosecutors sent key witness Rocky Williams back home to Alaska, ostensibly because his health was so bad. Williams was the lead employee on the remodeling project for Allen's company, VECO. It looked like the prosecutors sent him away to keep him from testifying for the defense. Williams was not in good health, but the defense had subpoenaed him too, and the prosecutors didn't tell the defense that they had sent Williams back to Alaska.

On October 8, during the third week of trial, Morris tried to excuse their mistakes by reminding the court about the accelerated trial schedule. Morris's excuses infuriated Judge Sullivan. He cut her off. "Stop. Counsel . . . It is not about the pace of litigation, it's about the fairness of the proceeding. You know, we don't sacrifice fairness for expediency sake. We don't do that." Apparently, although Morris said they could be ready in time, and at the direction of the "front office" had requested an even earlier trial date, the prosecutors really did not expect or plan to give Stevens the speedy trial to which he was entitled by the Constitution.

By the end of the trial, the prosecution team had lost all credibility with the judge. The defense was hammering the prosecutors with motions to dismiss for prosecutorial misconduct and for the government's failure to produce *Brady* information favorable to the defense or that would call into question the testimony of any government witness. Still the jury returned its verdict of guilty against Senator Stevens on October 27, 2008—just one week before the final election for Stevens's senate seat.

Despite all the prosecution's problems during the trial, and the judicial tongue-lashings the prosecutors took, Friedrich called a press conference on the steps of the federal courthouse to gloat about the jury's guilty verdict. Morris walked out of the courthouse with a big smile; Marsh was smirking. They had just convicted a sitting US senator of hiding his receipt of gifts from a wealthy and powerful constituent. Despite all the problems with the case, they had won.

Friedrich strode purposefully out of the stately granite E. Barrett Prettyman Federal Courthouse, with his entourage in lockstep behind him. Most of them walked through the cold rain with no overcoat or umbrella. Friedrich stepped to the microphone stand about ten feet in front of the courthouse steps. Only fourth-chair prosecutor Edward Sullivan had an umbrella open as he crossed the plaza. Sullivan closed it as if on cue when he approached the reporters and his place in the formation. Friedrich's subordinates assembled behind him in a semicircle on spots obviously assigned to them. Friedrich turned back only to direct them to come down three steps to stand several paces behind him.

To Friedrich's right, about three feet behind his shoulder, lead trial counsel Brenda Morris straddled her bulging leather briefcase, first with her arms crossed over her chest, then in the fig leaf pose. She looked uncomfortable either way. Marsh, in a dark suit, stood expressionless, his jaw clenched, his hands shoved in his pockets. Marsh was a row behind Morris, with second-chair and poker-faced Assistant US Attorney Bottini and FBI Case Agent Mary Beth Kepner. Behind them were PIN attorney Edward Sullivan, who appeared completely uninterested in Friedrich's spectacle, and PIN chief Bill Welch, who was largely hidden by Friedrich's frame. Assistant US Attorney Goeke, who had been relegated to back-office support for the trial team with Edward Sullivan, was already on a plane back to Alaska as soon as closing arguments began. The trial had been brutal.

Friedrich, at about six foot two, dwarfed the trial team members behind him as he faced the television cameras, the microphones thrust toward him, and the hundred or so reporters huddled around in the cold, steady rain. Friedrich and his minions stood there as if the sun were shining.

With the authority and bravado that only a fool or narcissist could muster after the repeated beatings the government had taken from Judge Sullivan and the defense throughout the trial and its countless "mistakes," Friedrich proclaimed:

"The jury convicted Senator Stevens . . . of hiding from his constituents and the public hundreds of thousands of dollars of freebies from an Alaska corporation and its chief executive officer. This corporation was not a charity. And it in fact, solicited Senator Stevens for assistance in numerous areas during the same time frame that it provided Senator Stevens with these gifts and things of value. . . . The department is proud of its team—not only for this trial but for the investigation that led to it. This investigation continues as does our commitment to hold our elected officials accountable when they violate the law." Friedrich was in his glory. He was untouchable. He had orchestrated another conviction, and no one would ever know.

– 11 –

THE DEPARTMENT OF *IN*JUSTICE:
POLAR PEN MELTS

In late 2008, only two months after the Stevens trial ended amid outcries of prosecutorial misconduct, another bombshell shook the department. FBI agent Chad Joy, a young agent on the Stevens case, had done the unthinkable. Agent Joy filed a complaint with the Justice Department's Office of Professional Responsibility. Joy, who had worked on Polar Pen with fellow agent Mary Beth Kepner and the trial team, said the prosecutors hid evidence. Joy disclosed a number of discussions that had occurred during the prosecution, and he alleged that lead agent Kepner had an inappropriate relationship with the prosecution's star witness Bill Allen. How was the department going to keep the lid on this one? Agent Joy had requested the protection of "whistle-blower status" within the FBI, but it was unclear if he was protected.

Among many shocking revelations, Joy said that prosecutor Marsh had concocted an excuse to keep witness Rocky Williams away from the defense because Williams couldn't handle cross-examination and had flunked his mock testimony. If Williams had testified, his testimony would have hurt the government. Joy said Marsh hatched a scheme to send Williams back to Alaska out of "concern" for his health—regardless of the fact that Williams was under a defense subpoena to testify for Stevens. As if that were not enough, Joy singled out Marsh as the prosecutor who had deliberately hidden specific, favorable evidence from the defense. Marsh could be prosecuted for obstruction of justice, subornation of perjury, and criminal contempt of court, and could be disbarred. Remarkably, despite Judge Sullivan's orders, the Department of Justice was trying to keep Joy's complaint under wraps—but it couldn't for long. Prosecutors disclosed it to the defense about a week after the defense's deadline had passed for filing posttrial motions—even though the prosecutors had it for at least a week before.

About the same time that the Joy complaint hit the fan, Friedrich quietly left the department during the transition to the Obama presidency. In the meantime, the word leaked that Kathryn Ruemmler was leaving Latham & Watkins and returning to the Justice Department to join Deputy Attorney General David Ogden, second in command of the department behind the attorney general. Ruemmler took office on January 16, 2009, as principal associate deputy attorney general.

Judge Sullivan was irate upon learning the facts recited in Joy's complaint and the prosecutors' continued gamesmanship in not producing evidence to the defense, even after being ordered to do so by the court. On February 3, 2009, in the middle of the complete meltdown of Operation Polar Pen, the Stevens prosecution, and the scandal with the FBI and the prosecutors, Eric Holder took the oath of office as attorney general. Holder was a partner at the powerful DC firm of Covington & Burling. He had barely unpacked his wife's picture and put it on his desk in his wood-paneled, elegant, historic, and expansive suite of offices on the top floor of the department when he was forced to address the disaster of the Stevens prosecution. The press had exploded with all of the news, giving the department a whopping black eye.

The issues of the prosecutors' suppression of evidence and Agent Joy's complaint were major news. On February 13, in a judicial version of the Valentine's Day Massacre, Judge Sullivan held three Department of Justice lawyers in civil contempt for failing to produce evidence to the defense. The attorneys were PIN chief Bill Welch, lead trial counsel Brenda Morris, and Appellate Section Chief Patty Stemler. The contempt order triggered a department requirement to appoint new prosecutors immediately—to start over through the government's files and to investigate for anything else Morris and her team might have missed.

The new team took only a couple of weeks, as they were preparing for a hearing on April 15, to find notes written by two of the prosecutors of an interview of key government witness Bill Allen back in April 2008 before Stevens was indicted. The prosecutors' own notes were exculpatory to the defense. They revealed that Allen had given the prosecutors information in his pretrial interview that contradicted his testimony at the trial itself.

This was exactly the kind of information that the defense was entitled to receive and could have used to cross-examine Allen and impeach or undercut his testimony to the jury. Allen's statements, as reflected in the notes of two of the prosecutors, went to the heart of the government's case against Senator Stevens—the value of the work Allen performed on Stevens's house and Stevens's payments for it.

At the same time the prosecutors had Allen testify that he did $250,000 worth of work on the house and indicted Stevens for not reporting that amount on his ethics forms, their own notes reflected that Allen himself had told them that the real value of the work was only $80,000. Allen also had told the prosecutors—as their notes reflected—that the workers had not put in the time on the job that the prosecutors had claimed. In addition, the government had withheld evidence supporting Stevens's defense that he would have paid additional bills if Allen had sent any—just as the senator had always said—and that prosecution-sponsored testimony to the contrary during the trial had just been made up, or, as lawyers say, "was recently fabricated."

Not surprisingly, Stevens's defense attorneys were outraged when they got word of the attorneys' notes. The usually unflappable Brendan Sullivan was so angry he worked in a silent rage for about three days.

By the time this new team of department lawyers found more evidence that the Polar Pen team had failed to give to the defense, it was obvious to any savvy observer of federal courts and judges that Emmet Sullivan had heard more than he needed to dismiss this case for prosecutorial misconduct and *Brady* violations. It was even more obvious that Emmet Sullivan was the rare federal judge who would dismiss the government's case. It was beyond dispute that the prosecutors had failed to produce evidence that was favorable to the defense and had violated their constitutional, legal, and ethical duties to do so.

All the negative publicity and Judge Sullivan's outrage gave Holder a perfect political opportunity. Holder could ride in on a white horse, be the "good guy," stand up for true justice, and move to dismiss the case against Stevens. After all, it was filed and prosecuted while George W. Bush was still president. Here Holder was the first black attorney general—and a Democrat no less—standing up for an eighty-five-year-old Republican senator because he had been denied a fair trial by the Republican-appointed prosecutors. It couldn't have been scripted any better by Michael Moore.

It wasn't Holder's problem, but Holder could sure take all the credit for doing the right thing. Holder didn't care whose heads rolled well below him. Friedrich's golden parachute had worked. He was gone already. There would be a big, favorable splash in the press, and Holder would "restore confidence" in the Department of Justice. He would send a message throughout the department that his lawyers must follow the rules. If Holder himself moved to dismiss the case against such a prominent Republican, he could turn all that negative press in his favor. He would rake in the accolades. The country was desperate for "change" and for nonpartisan justice. This would look just like that—a Democrat protecting the rights of the longest-serving Republican in the senate. The press and the public would eat this up.

In truth, and what most people would not realize, Judge Sullivan left Holder with no choice whatsoever. The judge was going to dismiss the Stevens case and excoriate the Justice Department if Holder had not dismissed it himself. That would have looked terrible for the new attorney general. The astute Holder simply turned the situation to his advantage.

When the defense team received the third set of startling disclosures from the new prosecutors, Brendan Sullivan and Rob Cary called the department and demanded an appointment with Holder. The defense attorneys and the new prosecutors knew that the evidence of statements the government's key witness had given the prosecutors during a pretrial interview would have been devastating to the government's case—if it had been provided to the defense before trial as the Constitution, the Supreme Court, and legal ethics required.

The defense team had motions to dismiss already on file based on agent Joy's revelations and other discoveries of the government's "mistakes." This was the last straw. There were no circumstances under which any institution pretending to seek justice could proceed with this prosecution. The case should never have been brought. This information was obviously known to the trial team—and they didn't produce it. On top of that, they elicited testimony from their witnesses and repeatedly argued the opposite. We had seen the same in *Brown*, but no one cared. Judge Sullivan was different.

Holder had to move quickly. He was not going to meet with Brendan Sullivan and Rob Cary. The dismissal needed to appear as if it were being done solely because he had decided to do the correct thing—not because he was forced to dismiss it by the judge or persuaded to do so by the defense.

Figuratively wrapping himself in truth, justice, and the American way, Attorney General Holder issued a statement on April Fool's Day— no joke—only eight weeks after he was sworn in. Without admitting that any attorney in the department had done anything wrong, Holder announced that he was dismissing the case against Senator Stevens "in the interest of justice."

He pledged a "thorough review by the department's Office of Professional Responsibility." However, he hedged, "this does not mean or imply that any determination has been made about the conduct of those attorneys who handled the investigation and trial of this case." He said that the department "must always ensure that any case in which it is involved is handled fairly and consistent with its commitment to justice."

Holder's play was masterful. NPR's Nina Totenberg was already reporting that Holder wanted "to send a message throughout the Department of Justice. Do not play fast and loose with the disclosure rules, because we won't tolerate it." In a conversation with noted broadcast journalist Judy Woodruff, Totenberg opined that this would send a "very loud signal within the department. These are the kinds of things that make everybody suck it up, and look at their notes one more time, and look at the files one more time, and say, 'Have we done everything we possibly could?'"

Shortly after Holder's announcement that the government was dismissing the indictment, a somber and furious Brendan Sullivan, with Rob Cary at his side, briskly walked to the podium in a conference room packed with reporters in the stately offices of Williams & Connolly in DC.

The bespectacled and distinguished Sullivan was loath to make statements to the press, but he could no longer be quiet. This wasn't the first time the government had hidden evidence that was favorable to a defendant, and Sullivan and Cary knew just how close to impossible it was to prove the government was hiding evidence. It is impossible for the defense to know what it doesn't know. Frankly they had been especially fortunate to discover any of it—and Agent Joy's whistle-blower complaint was a miracle. Neither experienced litigator had ever seen an FBI agent come forward like that. It was unheard of.

Under bright lights, and with cameras clicking, Sullivan spoke forcefully. He expressed his gratitude to the attorney general and lauded his decision—"justified by the extraordinary evidence of government corruption in the prosecution of Senator Stevens."

"This jury verdict was obtained unlawfully," Sullivan continued. "The government disregarded the Constitution, the Federal Rules of Criminal Procedure, and well-established Supreme Court case law." In "stunning" misconduct, "the government presented false evidence on a key matter when it elicited testimony from its principal witness—Bill Allen—that a crucial handwritten note by Ted Stevens was an effort to 'cover his ass.' This testimony was false and a 'recent fabrication.'"

Defense counsel Brendan Sullivan explained, "In essence, the government tricked the jury into returning a tainted verdict against the senator based on false evidence." He called Judge Emmet Sullivan a "hero," noting that "had Judge Sullivan accepted the word of government prosecutors as is done often in our courts, the extraordinary misconduct would never have been uncovered, and the trial verdict might have survived appellate review. Judge Sullivan prevented such a tragic outcome." And, like all the media, now Brendan Sullivan could only describe the new Attorney General Eric Holder as "a pillar of integrity in the legal community."

Noting how truly dangerous and destructive prosecutorial misconduct is, Mr. Sullivan said, "This case is a sad story and a warning to everyone. Any citizen can be convicted if prosecutors are hellbent on ignoring the Constitution and willing to present false evidence."

The dismissal of the Stevens case because of the "corrupt prosecutors" blanketed the news. Nick Marsh felt an increasing sense of dread and doom. The next morning's *Wall Street Journal* editorial read: "The government's lawyers likely miscarried justice and should be held to account."

We, the Brown team, were watching the developments in the Stevens case with great interest. It sounded like Judge Sullivan would actually do something. He had scheduled a hearing for April 7. We hoped it would spill over to Judge Werlein. Maybe this was what it would take to wake up Judge Werlein and bring change within the department.

We felt renewed hope. Now, under Holder's leadership and with his proclamations and new procedures, we would be able to get all of the *Brady* evidence we had requested and an independent review of the proposed second trial against Bayly, Furst, and Brown. After all, Holder had told the public and various senate committees that he was "serious" about *Brady*. He wanted "to prevent those kinds of mistakes from happening again." Holder recognized that "there is a legitimate public interest in knowing as much as we can about" these *Brady* violations. He had proclaimed that anyone with serious *Brady* allegations should bring them to his attention. The attorney general told CBS News he wanted "to tell the world" that "this is not the way in which this Justice Department will conduct itself."

Judge Sullivan's hearing on the government's motion to dismiss was only days away. The new prosecutors would handle it, but they all dreaded it immensely.

I would have paid admission to be in that courtroom.

– 12 –

THE MOTHER OF ALL HEARINGS

April 7, 2009, was a momentous day in legal history—especially for criminal defense attorneys and anyone who cares about individual rights. Because he saw government lawyers in his courtroom day in and day out, and he knew that they knew his expectations, Judge Sullivan preferred to give the government the benefit of the doubt, and he expected to be able to do so. In this case, though, there had been far too many problems. The judge could not believe anything the Stevens prosecutors said anymore. Their conduct was an affront to the integrity of the court and the judicial process.

Judge Sullivan had worked countless hours dealing with the defense motions and the government's mistakes. The prosecutors had exceeded his capacity for excuses, which became more lame and less credible with each additional attempt. Judge Sullivan knew that the prosecutors all knew better—and certainly should have done better. Agent Joy's complaint iced the corrupt cake of a case the prosecutors never should have indicted.

Judge Sullivan's courtroom could not hold another reporter, spectator, or member of the bar. At least a dozen members of the Williams & Connolly defense team were present. Despite the cramped conditions in the courtroom, there was an excited and apprehensive buzz among onlookers as they waited for the judge to enter. It was as if everyone in the gallery—predominantly Stevens's supporters—were solemn but empowered as they waited for the government to dismiss the indictment and take its beating from Judge Sullivan. Anticipation and emotions were running high in the Stevens's camp.

The new prosecutors' obvious discomfort grew as 10:00 a.m. approached.

The senator wore a classic dark blue suit and white shirt with the perfect single Windsor knot of a red print tie barely showing from beneath his sweater vest. He was surrounded by the full team of William & Connolly lawyers, led by Brendan Sullivan and Rob Cary, and by his wife, Catherine, and their daughters.

The thunderous bang of the knocker on the door from the judge's chambers into the courtroom jolted the already edgy participants and spectators to their feet as the Honorable Emmet Sullivan, US district judge, stepped briskly to the bench. He was as solemn and stern as anyone had ever seen him. He sat down in his high-backed black armchair and looked at government counsel. It wouldn't take much to set him off today.

The new prosecutors stood stiffly and looked up at him. Paul O'Brien announced their names for the record: "Paul O'Brien, David Jaffe, and Bill Stuckwisch for the United States."

These were the prosecutors assigned to the case after Judge Sullivan had held their colleagues in contempt. After only a couple of weeks of reviewing the case files almost around the clock, they had found the remarkable notes of the trial team's interview of Allen that contradicted his trial testimony but had not been disclosed. Even though the new prosecutors were not responsible for the wrongful prosecution of Stevens, they knew this was going to be the most difficult hearing they had ever participated in. They had hoped that Attorney General

Holder's public dismissal of the indictment would suffice, but that was pure hope. They were at high risk for a very public and publicized verbal lashing for the trial lawyers and the Department of Justice. Any misstep could result in more of the court's wrath. They had to clean this up as quickly as they possibly could. They were sleep-deprived and pale.

Even Judge Sullivan's terse "Good morning" sounded ominous. Even though the charges against the senator were being dismissed, irreparable damage had been done. Senator Stevens and his family had borne the incomprehensible anxiety, stress, and slander of the charges and public trial. He had lost the senate seat he had held for more than four decades. The balance of power had changed in the senate. Their lives would never be the same. Emotions were high. Nothing could make up for what this wrongful prosecution had wrecked.

Rob Cary, in a solemn and serious tone, introduced some of the defense team members who were present. "Good morning, Your Honor. Joe Terry, Alex Romain, Beth Stewart, Brendan Sullivan, and Rob Cary for Senator Stevens, who is present."

Cary had not even resumed his seat when Judge Sullivan began with force and determination. No one dared utter a sound.

After a "Good morning," he commenced, "This is indeed a dramatic day in a case that has had many dramatic and unfortunately many shocking and disturbing moments. For nearly twenty-five years I have told defendants appearing before me that in my courtroom they will receive a fair trial and that I will make sure of it."

The judge was just getting started, and he was livid. "In nearly twenty-five years on the bench, I've never seen anything approaching the mishandling and misconduct that I've seen in this case. Before we hear from the parties this morning, the court believes it is important to take a few minutes to share some thoughts about what we, as a legal community, need to do to safeguard the integrity of our criminal justice system."

Judge Sullivan had thought about this a great deal. He was extremely troubled by what he had seen. He spoke to the government's "obligation to pursue convictions fairly and in accordance with the Constitution. . . . When the government does not meet its obligations to turn over evidence, the system falters."

He catalogued the government's multiple failures and excuses. They were the usual "mistake," "unintentional," "inadvertent," or "immaterial." He was especially and rightly critical of the department's outrageous response to FBI Agent Joy's complaint of government misconduct. "Not only did the government seek to keep that complaint a secret, but the government claimed that the allegations had nothing to do with the verdict and no relevancy to the defense; that the allegations could be addressed by the Office of Professional Responsibility's investigation; and that any misconduct had already been addressed and remedied during the trial."

Everyone in the courtroom was hanging on Judge Sullivan's every word. Senator Stevens and his defense team knew this would have ramifications across the country and throughout the department—or, at the very least, it should.

Of course, Stevens's defense team and every experienced criminal defense attorney also knew that the Justice Department would never do the same kind of investigation or reach the same conclusion as would a truly independent prosecutor. The department was way too political, incestuous, self-serving, and self-institutionalized to do so. Some lawyers opined that it really needed to be cleaned out from top to bottom with bleach and fire hoses. Too many people had been there too long. A select few merely moved in and out of the upper echelon of the department depending on the political party in power. "Main

Justice," as insiders called it, had descended to inbreed arrogance and political abuse of power, and the narcissists who wielded it produced disregard for the rule of law.

Judge Sullivan paused, glared at the prosecutors, and then continued. "In fact, as recently as February 6, the government told the court that there was no need for any posttrial discovery and that the government was, and I quote, 'confident that its response to the defendant's posttrial motions would resolve the need for further inquiry into the allegations as they relate to the trial and the convictions of the defendant'. . . ."

Judge Sullivan continued, "And yet, after the court held three senior attorneys in contempt for blatantly failing to comply with this court's order to produce documents, and a new team of prosecutors was assigned to the case, we learned for the first time what may well be the most shocking and serious *Brady* violations of all—that the government failed to tell the defense of an interview with Bill Allen in which Allen stated that he did not recall a conversation with Bob Persons about sending the senator a bill and that Allen estimated the value of the VECO work on the senator's home at $80,000, far less than the hundreds of thousands of dollars the government had alleged at trial."

The judge was angry about what he had seen. If Judge Sullivan had not held the attorneys in contempt, triggering the appointment of new prosecutors, the original team would have buried the exculpatory evidence forever. It was only the pressure the judge put on the department that caused the truth to surface, and he couldn't be sure that he had all of it yet.

He continued with great emphasis: "This is not about prosecution by any means necessary." Moreover "the fair administration of justice does not depend on the luck of the draw or a lucky day or a lucky continuance. Indeed it should not depend on who represents the defendant, whether an FBI agent blows a whistle, a new administration, a new attorney general, or a new trial team. The fair administration of justice depends on the government meeting its obligations to pursue convictions fairly and in accordance with the Constitution."

Judge Sullivan took those obligations seriously, and he intended that the prosecutors do so as well. "The importance of these obligations cannot be overstated. As the Supreme Court explained in its 1999 decision in a case of *Strickler v. Green*: 'In *Brady*, this court held that the suppression by the prosecution of evidence favorable to an accused upon request violates due process where the evidence is material either to guilt or to punishment, irrespective of the good faith or bad faith of the prosecution.'"

Judge Sullivan continued, "These cases, together with earlier cases condemning the knowing use of perjured testimony, illustrate the special role played by the American prosecutor in the search for truth in criminal trials." Quoting the Supreme Court's decision in *Berger*, he said, "the United States Attorney is the representative, not of an ordinary party to a controversy but of a sovereignty whose obligation to govern impartially is as compelling as its obligation to govern at all, and whose interest, therefore, in a criminal prosecution is not that it shall win a case, but that justice shall be done."

He was not finished. "We must never forget the Supreme Court's directive that a criminal trial is a search for the truth. Yet in several cases recently this court has seen troubling failures to produce exculpatory evidence in violation of the law and this court's orders.

"Whether you are a public official, a private citizen, or a Guantanamo Bay detainee, the prosecution, indeed the United States government, must produce exculpatory evidence so that justice *shall* be done."

Then Judge Sullivan expressed a much-needed and wise word of caution for his colleagues on the bench across the country. "I, therefore, urge my judicial colleagues on every trial court everywhere to be vigilant and to consider entering an exculpatory evidence order at the outset of every criminal case, whether requested to do so or not, and to require that the exculpatory material be turned over in a useable format because, as we've seen in this case, the use of summaries is an opportunity for mischief and mistake."

He encouraged the new attorney general "to require *Brady* training for new and veteran, experienced prosecutors throughout the country." He also asked Holder to "open dialogue between defense attorneys and prosecutors regarding these discovery obligations."

He urged the president, the attorney general, and the senate to consider this issue in the appointment and confirmation process for new US attorneys, and to obtain from nominees a commitment to fulfill their *Brady* obligations.

Judge Sullivan thanked O'Brien, Jaffe, and Stuckwisch for their massive effort.

With that direct cue, O'Brien stood. "The United States respectfully moves this court to set aside the verdict and dismiss the indictment with prejudice." He went on, though, with prepared remarks, still trying to make the department look better than it did—or was.

O'Brien credited Rita Glavin, then acting criminal division head, with appointing the three new attorneys in February 2009 to handle the "litigation arising from the complaint filed by Special Agent Joy." O'Brien wanted everyone to know that they had conducted interviews and started the "investigation" in response to Agent Joy's complaint, then wanted to "be as transparent as possible with the court and with the defense." He claimed that was why they "voluntarily produced the

302s generated from the witness interviews" as they were preparing for a possible hearing.

These comments prompted more than one sideways glance, eyebrows raised, among the observers. This was sounding like a defense of the indefensible—and definitely not a wise move at this point. Judge Sullivan leaned forward, appearing somewhere between puzzled and peeved.

O'Brien got back on track. He explained the process of their review at the time they found the notes of the Allen interview. He admitted that the "government was obligated to produce the information from the April 15, 2008, interview with Mr. Allen to the defense, and they did not do so."

Judge Sullivan brusquely interrupted, "So what you did was, you did what should have been done months ago."

O'Brien was struggling. Obviously he was trying to avoid out-and-out admitting a *Brady* violation.

The judge was not happy, and his voice got louder. "At least a year ago, almost a year to the date, April 15, is that correct?"

Judge Sullivan, wisely, was going to pin O'Brien down and was annoyed that he had to work to do so. O'Brien could do nothing but admit the judge was correct. With that discovery, O'Brien explained that their focus shifted from trying to defend against the defense's motions to whether the case should be retried or the indictment dismissed by the government itself.

Finally O'Brien apologized to the court but not to Senator Stevens. "On behalf of the department, we deeply, deeply regret that this occurred. . . . Again, I apologize to the court, and we deeply regret that this occurred."

This was some of what Judge Sullivan wanted to hear but not all of it. He was not satisfied, nor should he have been. He wanted precise admissions of misconduct. O'Brien had yet to admit a *Brady* violation.

Staring right at O'Brien, Judge Sullivan said in a no-nonsense tone, "Let me ask you this, counsel, and I need a very precise answer to this question. The government counsel will concede, will it not, that the failure to produce the notes or information from the April 15, 2008, interview with Bill Allen in which he did not recall having a conversation with Bob Persons about sending the bill to the senator was a *Brady* violation?"

O'Brien should have known it wasn't going to be as easy as he had hoped.

The judge forced him to confess. "It was a *Brady* violation. It was impeaching material, and the court knows that *Giglio* is a subset of *Brady*."

The lawyers in the gallery couldn't help but wonder why O'Brien was bothering to make that distinction. The Supreme Court had long required the government to disclose all favorable information—whether it could be used directly or as impeachment. It was a distinction without a difference. One could only surmise that O'Brien was still following instructions from "on high" in the department. Glavin was still there. She had selected him for this task.

O'Brien confessed that they also found information about the value of the work performed on the senator's house—the point on which most of the government's allegations turned.

Judge Sullivan hammered that home, as well. "And that was going to be the second question. Indeed, was that a *Brady* violation as well?"

O'Brien hedged again. "I believe that was. At a minimum, it was favorable evidence to the defense that should have been turned over pursuant to the instructions that Your Honor previously mentioned."

Judge Sullivan still had to work to make sure the record reflected that this information had been found in the notes of the prosecutors themselves. After confirming that the Justice Department was conducting its own investigation, which would be disclosed to the court, Judge Sullivan turned to the defense.

Tall, thin, distinguished Brendan Sullivan stepped to the podium. After thanking the court and its staff for their extraordinary hard work during this case, he reinforced Judge Sullivan's point that prosecutors "have this tremendous power and tremendous duty and responsibility to make sure our system is fair."

Defense counsel Sullivan also wanted to make a record of the prosecutors' failures. "Four Assistant US Attorneys and one FBI agent participated in the interview of Bill Allen, yet failed to disclose the information that contradicted their case. There had even been an e-mail chain of discussions between the prosecutors about not being satisfied, basically, with what they heard from Mr. Allen and pushing him or finding a way to push him."

Brendan Sullivan went on to explain the importance of that interview on the defense's most important piece of evidence—the "note upon which we based the foundation of our defense, because all of the words in the note screamed out that the author of the note had no criminal intent and was innocent of the charges that the government had brought."

The day after that note was produced, O'Brien had another document delivered to the defense—the handwritten notes of one of the assistant US attorneys who participated in the trial. "And the key *Brady*, the heart of it all, in the prosecutor's handwritten notes 'Bill does not recall Bob Persons talking to him about a bill for Ted Stevens.'"

Brendan Sullivan, outraged, continued. "The next day, March 26, Mr. O'Brien delivered another set of handwritten notes from a second prosecutor. Similarly on the key sentence, it read, 'Bill Allen recalls receiving a note from Ted Stevens, doesn't recall talking to Bob Persons regarding Ted Stevens's bill.' It went to the heart of what we call the lie about Ted Stevens covering his ass. The most explosive testimony in the case, the recent fabrication, as we told the jury, and these materials were denied to us in cross-examining this witness and in arguing to the jury our foundation principle."

The impassioned defense attorney was on a roll. "But there was even more in these short notes of the prosecutor that would be called *Brady* or *Giglio*, and the court referenced some of it, but it was stunning, given the way the government presented the case. For example, statements such as from Bill Allen, 'Rocky and Dave screwed this up because they were always drunk.'

"Another statement in these same notes: 'David Anderson and Rocky Williams always drunk, screwed up the project, allowed the workers to waste time, sit around, inefficient, didn't supervise well, but if they had done it efficiently, maybe the fair value would be $80,000.'"

The prosecutors had argued repeatedly to convince Judge Sullivan that one of the key documents in the case was a business record. At the same time they knew it was false, and that Allen himself had said the fair value of the renovations was only $80,000 when Senator Stevens had paid $160,000.

Defense counsel Sullivan explained that the e-mail chain only recently disclosed showed that the government prosecutors had taken a "kernel of an idea" and "fabricated testimony" by pushing Allen to provide what was "bombshell testimony" against Senator Stevens.

They pushed Allen to testify, essentially, that Senator Stevens's note indicating that the senator wanted to pay all of his bills was meaningless. Even worse, they had stood it on its head. They used it against Stevens, claiming it was part of Stevens's plan to just act like he wanted to pay.

After being pushed by the prosecutors, Allen said that Bob Persons had told him, "'Oh Bill, don't worry about getting a bill.' He said, 'Ted is just covering his ass.'"

The defense believed strongly that Allen had just made up that testimony under pressure from the prosecutors and to avoid more jail time himself or additional charges, but at trial, the defense had no way to prove it. They could have proved it with these notes and even more that would not be discovered for another two years.

Sullivan continued. "I said in opening statement how important Ted Stevens's handwritten note requesting a bill was. I built the defense on it. I didn't know the CYA statement was coming. That was false testimony. They knew it was false because they sat there and heard Bill Allen say he had no recollection of talking to Persons about the document." On cross-examination, Allen even denied that he had only recently made up that testimony. Then in closing arguments, the prosecutors had told the jury how believable Allen's statement was—that Ted was just "covering his ass."

Defense counsel continued, rebuking anyone who dared minimize this concealment as a mere technical violation of the rules. "It is clear from the evidence that the government engaged in intentional misconduct, which violated *Brady*, the Federal Rules of Criminal Procedure, and the Constitution, not to mention a few court orders." He was very specific. "While there could have been some mistakes in there, most of it was clear, intentional, devious, and willful. Sometimes the government failed to produce *Brady* that was clearly *Brady*. Sometimes they redacted *Brady*. Sometimes they did a reinterview so as to hide the *Brady* rather than provide it." In one instance, the prosecutors even completely changed the meaning of a crucial sentence by inserting the word "not"—and then they introduced that record for reliability.

Everyone in the courtroom supporting Senator Stevens wanted to cheer on his counsel, but Brendan Sullivan didn't need cheering. No one had ever been more determined to expose the corruption that had embroiled them all in this living hell for over a year and cost his client his senate seat.

Then Sullivan got to the crux of the problem—especially in a high-profile prosecution. "They had a duty to provide these materials, but of course, how could we even think for a moment that they would? . . . I guess it's expecting too much to produce the *Brady* that would allow us to show that the testimony they had just put on was perjurious. . . . I don't think there is anything worse than our government presenting false evidence, manufacturing evidence to suit the occasion in order to get the upper hand. They dealt with witnesses like Bill Allen, of course, who was well rewarded for his testimony and was susceptible to being pushed." The prosecution used a combination of rewards and threats—financial and otherwise—to manipulate him.

Brendan Sullivan spoke to the "insidious nature" of the government's wrongdoing—hiding that meeting and its substance despite being reminded frequently by the court of their *Brady* duties and by "our repeated, jackhammer-like requests for *Brady*. But they countered all of our best efforts, the court's and ours, by misrepresentations and outright lies."

The prosecutors repeatedly claimed, "We understand our *Brady* and *Giglio* obligations, and we will continue to provide you information pursuant to these obligations." They claimed *Brady* required nothing more than what they had provided, and then two weeks before trial, more *Brady* dribbled in.

One of the same prosecutors who participated in the hidden April 15, 2008, interview of Allen, only a few months before Stevens was indicted, claimed, "We have made substantial *Brady* disclosures. We provided a *Brady/Giglio* letter, we've attached a number of attachments."

"It's not accurate," insists that same prosecutor, "to say the government is sitting on some treasure trove of *Brady* material that we're essentially not passing onto the defendant." Remarkably, however, Sullivan said, "New prosecutors found that very treasure trove in just a few weeks."

The statesman of the defense poured it on. "The prosecutor says, 'We've represented to the defense that we are continuing to go back and we'll go back again, and have. If there's anything to turn over, we'll turn it over,' and it went on and on and on."

This all sounded painfully familiar to me. This was exactly the same song the Enron Task Force and Arnold Spencer had sung to Judge Werlein in Jim's case. It had lulled Werlein to sleep. Brendan Sullivan was quoting the prosecutors' refrain. What it took me another two years to uncover was that song had the same composer and conductor in *Brown* and in *Stevens*.

The "frightening part," as Brendan Sullivan described it, was how close the prosecutors came to succeeding.

Then defense counsel got to the most important point—the crucial difference that very few defendants have ever experienced. "But for a judge that pressed harder than I'd ever seen a judge in all of my years press for discovery, press for *Brady* obligations, we would be meandering through our motions."

Sullivan brought it home with his personal reaction when he saw the three crucial documents that the original trial team could only have deliberately concealed. It was emotional.

"You'd think after a long, hard fight, [we would feel] jubilation, that we'd be high-fiving each other around the office—we finally got them, we were right. That was not the reaction. My reaction was sick.

I was sick in my stomach. How could they do this? How could they abandon their responsibilities? How could they take on a very decent man like Ted Stevens, who happened to be a United States Senator, and do this? It was revulsion. The revulsion turned to anger."

Brendan Sullivan said he finally picked up the phone and called O'Brien to end the case. "I was going to have a meeting in his office . . . and ask them to dismiss." That meeting was scheduled for April 1 at 10:00 a.m., but Sullivan's phone rang at 9:00 a.m. that morning. O'Brien called and told him that the attorney general would dismiss the case.

Brendan Sullivan then turned to the conduct of Matthew Friedrich, acting assistant attorney general of the criminal division, who had held the press conferences to gloat over Stevens's indictment and then the jury's verdict of guilty. Without mentioning Friedrich's name, Sullivan had some choice words for the man in front of the cobalt-blue curtain and who, we would learn much later, was pulling all the strings behind it.

One of "the most remarkable things is that despite this court's many admonitions to the government throughout this process, some amounting to virtual public censures for their conduct," the "acting assistant attorney general of the criminal division of the United States Department of Justice goes out to the steps" of the courthouse after the verdict, gathers the prosecutors "in a family photo," and "says to the world, 'The Department of Justice is proud of this team. . . .' If he had just read the newspapers, how could the leading attorney of the Department of Justice over the criminal division make such a statement? . . . There is the failure of leadership. It's to prosecute to win at all costs, and wrongdoing can flourish when that's the attitude of a leader."

Little did Brendan Sullivan know even then how much evidence was still buried within the department, how it would be uncovered, how far back it went, and how many cases Friedrich and his cronies had corrupted.

Clearly once the senator was indicted, the trial team had to win, Sullivan continued, because "a loss in such circumstances blights a career and maybe even ruins it, and so they abandoned all decency to win a conviction. Unfortunately the theme of some is 'get a conviction; we'll worry about the appeals later' because there's so little chance often that wrongs can be remedied." Sullivan said, "The fear of loss drove them to do what they did. The chances of being caught were small, even with a diligent and skeptical judge and even with a vigorous defense."

Then Sullivan exposed the painful reality that everyone wants to pretend does not exist: "If the government is not honest, it can trump even the best efforts of those of us who work in the system. . . ."

That truth certainly resonated with me. I was certain the prosecutors were still hiding evidence in *Brown,* but Judge Werlein was no help at all, and nothing had changed yet in the department.

The distinguished attorney's last request was that Senator Stevens be allowed to speak. Of course, Judge Sullivan agreed.

Ted Stevens, refreshed and empowered with these astonishing and vindicating developments, stepped to the podium.

The former senator graciously thanked Judge Sullivan and his staff for their hard work during "many late nights and weekends and holidays." He acknowledged that "without your experience and vigilance, the truth would never have been known." He graciously thanked the new prosecutors for their competence in uncovering and providing the favorable evidence.

Judge Sullivan nodded and gently interrupted only to say that he had noticed.

The former senator continued. "Yes. I'm full of giving thanks this morning, but I do also thank the Alaskans. As I traveled throughout the state, Your Honor, almost every Alaskan said, 'I've said a prayer for you, Ted.'" He thanked his "senate colleagues, former staff, and close friends for their support. Many of those friends attended these proceedings every day and some of them are here again this morning. Their friendship has been a humbling source of strength to me through this ordeal."

His voice was emotional as he expressed his gratitude, and when he mentioned his wife, "Catherine . . . who stood by me through this whole process, and my children, my entire family, three of my daughters are here this morning, for their unwavering support in these troubled times, I'm—I'm really fortunate and I love each one of them."

Then he spoke to the great tragedy—how much the rule of law meant to him and how close it came to being completely destroyed:

I've served the United States for many years. I served as a pilot in World War II in China. I served as a United States Attorney in the Territory of Alaska. I was Solicitor of the Department of Interior, and I've been a senator for forty years. It was my great honor to be a member of the Bicentennial Commission on the Constitution of the United States with Warren Burger, Chief Justice Warren Burger. I've been deeply committed to the rule of law and the Constitution, and I support it to the best of my ability.

Until recently, my faith in the criminal system, particularly the judicial system, was unwavering, but what some members of the prosecution team did nearly destroyed that faith. Their conduct has consequences for me that they will never realize and can never be reversed. But today, today, Your Honor, through your leadership and persistence and commitment to the rule of law, my faith has been restored, and I really can never thank you enough.

Your actions gave me new hope that others may be spared from similar miscarriages of justice, and it is my hope that when the dust settles, I may be able to encourage the enactment of legislation to reform the laws relating to the responsibilities and duties of those entrusted with the solemn task of enforcing criminal laws.

I deeply appreciate your service. Thank you.

With that, Ted Stevens turned, smiled, and returned to his seat.

"Thank you, sir," Judge Sullivan sincerely replied. Then the judge looked at Brendan Sullivan again. "Mr. Sullivan, you got away from the podium without me asking you one question. . . . On October 28, the day after the verdicts were returned, you delivered a sixteen-page letter to then-Attorney General Michael Mukasey, detailing at length many of the events recited today and asking the attorney general to commence a formal investigation into the prosecutorial misconduct in this case. Did you ever receive a response?"

Brendan Sullivan stood in place and responded with painful clarity. "Your Honor, I had actually sent three letters to the Attorney General of the United States, Mr. Mukasey. I never received an acknowledgment that they were even received in the office. I received no word back."

Judge Sullivan coldly replied. "Shocking."

After thanking all his clerks and staff, Judge Sullivan unsealed all bench conferences during the trial and made them part of the public record.

Then came a real shocker. "Finally the court has repeatedly been told that the Office of Professional Responsibility at the Department of Justice is conducting an investigation into the investigation and prosecution of this case. . . . That was six months ago. The court next heard about the OPR investigation when the government assured the court that it need not take any action based on the Joy complaint because

OPR was conducting a thorough investigation. That was four months ago. And yet, to date, the silence has been deafening. Similarly the defense tells us just moments ago they received no response to their numerous letters to former Attorney General Mukasey urging him to commence a formal investigation." He referred to this irrefutable fact as "shocking, but not surprising. . . ."

Judge Sullivan was not going to let this go unanswered. He said "the events and allegations in this case are too serious and too numerous to be left to an internal investigation that has no outside accountability. This court has an independent obligation to ensure that any misconduct is fully investigated and addressed in an appropriate public forum."

Judge Sullivan paused to breathe—and for effect. Anyone taking notes stopped and looked up. The air seemed to have left the room. The prosecutors could hear their own hearts beating and feel their temples throbbing. No one saw this coming.

– 13 –

MOVE OVER, DOJ:
THERE'S A NEW SHERIFF IN TOWN

Judge Sullivan looked up. He seemed to be absorbing the full effect of the throng gathered and the importance of the moment. He knew this would make national news and legal history. He saw every eye in the courtroom on him. There wasn't a sound. Then Judge Sullivan spoke with great emphasis:

"Accordingly the court shall commence criminal contempt proceedings against the original prosecution team, including William Welch, Brenda Morris, Joseph Bottini, Nicholas Marsh, James Goeke, and Edward Sullivan . . . based on the failures of those prosecutors to comply with the court's numerous orders and potential obstruction of justice."

The reporters in the courtroom were writing furiously. Those in the media room on the second floor where they had wireless access became animated. This was quite a turn of events. Unprecedented.

Judge Sullivan paced his words. "The interest of justice requires the appointment of a nongovernment, disinterested attorney to prosecute that matter."

There was an audible, virtually collective gasp. This was even better than the defense could have hoped. Brendan Sullivan and Rob Cary exchanged an appreciative sideways glance behind their professional poker faces. Tears were welling in the eyes of many of Stevens's defenders and friends. This should make a difference. Those close enough patted Ted Stevens on the shoulder.

Judge Sullivan was taking the extraordinary step of appointing a special prosecutor. He chose highly respected DC attorney Henry Schuelke III to investigate the prosecutors for possible criminal charges. The judge ordered the department to preserve all of its files, electronic correspondence—everything—and cooperate fully in the investigation, including providing Schuelke access to investigative files and all witnesses.

Schuelke, known to his friends as "Hank," was a lawyer's lawyer. He had represented any number of high-profile clients, many of whom no one knew he had ever helped. Schuelke even looked the part of a sheriff. He was tall, with rugged good looks, steel blue eyes, a full head of salt-and-pepper hair, and a matching moustache. Given the right Stetson, Schuelke could have easily been at home riding into a Wild West town on a palomino stallion, with the sun at his back and a six-shooter strapped to his side. He was just the man Judge Sullivan needed to cut through the cover-up, protectionism, arrogance, and entrenched self-preservation within the Department of Justice and find out what really happened in the Stevens case.

Before concluding, Judge Sullivan joined the chorus, praising Attorney General Holder, for whom "the court has the highest regard," for his "impeccable reputation as a lawyer firmly committed to fairness, integrity, and the rule of law."

That seemed a bit much, certainly to the Brown team and other Merrill defense lawyers, who were still being stonewalled, but at that time Judge Sullivan didn't know what we knew. We still didn't know the extent of what we didn't know, and no one knew all the truth in the Stevens case yet either.

With little flourish but obvious satisfaction behind his judicious expression, Judge Sullivan emphatically granted the government's motion to dismiss the indictment with prejudice—"in the interest of justice." Some members of the senator's family openly sobbed, the courtroom erupted in applause, and friends mobbed the senator with congratulations. Senator Stevens raised a clenched fist in a sign of victory.

Court was adjourned at 11:48 a.m. Television cameras, reporters, and photographers were lined up outside to record every move the senator and his family made as they left the courthouse. They paused and smiled for a family photo. This time, the senator had more of a spring in his step and a slight smile on his face. He was determined to enjoy this day, but their smiles barely masked the rage and stinging pain he and his entire family still felt.

Judge Sullivan's decision to order an investigation necessitated that the Justice Department's Office of Professional Responsibility ramp up its own investigation. The criminal division was also conducting its own investigation—whatever that meant. In any event, Judge Sullivan's appointment of an independent investigator was going to require the department to take this much more seriously than it had planned. Judge Sullivan had kicked over the large bucket of whitewash they had in stock.

—✥—

The news of the court's initiation of its own criminal investigation and the appointment of Hank Schuelke as a special prosecutor rumbled through the department like a 9.8 earthquake, shaking everyone. The trial prosecutors were traumatized. Nick Marsh felt he was getting it from all sides. The last seven months had been unbearable, and now it would only get worse. The ramifications of an investigation by a special prosecutor went deep and wide. It was really unthinkable. He couldn't believe this was happening. Prosecutors being prosecuted? Had this ever happened before? Prosecutors have always had immunity from suit for doing their jobs. Judges rarely pushed back at all against their assertions that they had complied with *Brady.* Bar associations usually just dismissed any complaint as a maneuver by a disgruntled criminal who was rightly convicted.

The department allowed all the prosecutors named by Judge Sullivan in his February contempt order and this new order to retain counsel. On the taxpayers' dime, they all hired the best criminal defense attorneys in the DC Bar—most of whom had also been Department of Justice officials at one time or another.

Marsh hired the same lawyer Karl Rove had hired in the Valerie Plame case—Robert Luskin—who cochaired Patton Boggs' litigation practice.

Appellate Chief Patty Stemler hired the WilmerHale firm, including former Solicitor General Seth Waxman, who had obtained the acquittal of Merrill executive Bill Fuhs in our Barge case. The current Deputy Attorney General David Ogden had been a partner at WilmerHale. Stemler was soon cleared of any wrongdoing.

Bottini hired O'Melveny & Myers partner Kenneth Weinstein, who had recently served as President Bush's Homeland Security adviser and head of the National Security Division of the Department of Justice.

Another prosecutor hired attorneys from Covington & Burling—the firm at which Attorney General Holder and Assistant Attorney General Lanny Breuer had been partners before ascending to the department.

I could only wonder how these big firms and the Department of Justice could evaluate and resolve potential conflicts of interest. They were so intertwined—if not incestuous.

It turned out that the top Justice Department officials—Holder, Breuer, and Ogden—obtained "ethics waivers" that allowed them to review matters related to the *Stevens* prosecution investigation even though their former firms were representing the subjects of those investigations and the administration's ethics rules required Justice Department appointees to recuse themselves from official matters involving their prior firms.

Marsh absorbed another powerful blow to his life and his career on June 4. The Department of Justice informed the Ninth US Circuit Court of Appeals that the defendants in the *Kott* and *Kohring* cases, involving two legislators that Marsh, Edward Sullivan, Bottini, and Goeke had recently tried and convicted in Alaska in Operation Polar Pen, were entitled to a hearing on "newly discovered evidence" and "possible" *Brady* violations. They admitted that the cases should be returned to the district court for consideration because the prosecutors had failed to provide the defense in those cases with favorable evidence regarding some of the same issues and witnesses as in the *Stevens* case. Astonishingly and despite what Judge Sullivan had said, the department still did not admit there was an actual *Brady* violation in those cases. Instead the government continued to argue that the evidence was not "material" to the defense and that the defendants would have been convicted regardless.

Even so, two more of Marsh's hard-fought convictions were being scrutinized and could be reversed. Obviously he would be or was being blamed for not giving the evidence to the defense. Bottini, Sullivan, and Goeke were in the same boat with him on those cases, as well.

The same day Marsh was told of the department's position in *Kott* and *Kohring*, the Department of Justice transferred Marsh and Sullivan to its Office of International Affairs, where they could not try cases.

Experienced defense counsel nationwide applauded Judge Sullivan's wisdom in recognizing that the Justice Department could not be trusted to investigate itself and for excoriating the prosecutors for hiding this evidence. It is far too rare to have any court do anything about a *Brady* violation even though it is little different from the crime of obstruction of justice—especially if the evidence is deliberately concealed.

Judge Sullivan had given Schuelke an Augean task, but it was crucial to the administration of justice, and Schuelke could handle it.

Sadly to all who cared about the department, who used to work there, and who wanted it to shine, the department could not be trusted. Some of us wondered if this would even make a difference. I still believed that it would.

Upon disclosure of the department's complete debacle in *Stevens*, Judge Sullivan's dismissal of the case, and Holder's proclamation that he wanted to be informed of *Brady* violations, we wrote a lengthy letter to the department. We took Attorney General Holder and his deputies at their word that they were motivated to clean things up and asked them to remedy the *Brady* violations in *Brown*. The newest prosecutor assigned to the Barge case after Spencer's debacles, Patrick Stokes from the Fraud Section in Main Justice, finally arranged a meeting for us with the "front office." He and young Albert Stieglitz III were now the third team of prosecutors that had been assigned to this case. Until we arrived in Washington that morning, Stokes had refused to inform us with whom we would be meeting.

Stokes liked playing things "close to the vest." We surmised that Stokes, who came from the Eastern District of Virginia, Friedrich's old stomping grounds, had been handpicked by Friedrich to take over from

Arnold Spencer. We had heard Stokes was a Friedrich "wanna-be"—except about a foot shorter—and always snide, sarcastic, and generally unpleasant—at least in dealing with me. Stokes had no ability to turn on the charm like Friedrich could.

———

It was a beautiful Washington summer day. I felt a touch of nostalgia as we walked over to the magnificent building that takes up the entire block bounded by Pennsylvania and Constitution Avenues and 9th and 10th Streets. It always inspired me. The monumental building is rich in classical design and includes Art Deco and Greek features, statues woven into the fabric of the building, sixty-eight murals painted throughout the interior, brilliantly colored concrete mosaic ceilings over the gated motor and pedestrian entrances on 9th and 10th Streets, and amazing, massive pocket and elevator doors crafted in Art Deco aluminum instead of bronze. The craftsmanship, sheer mass, and weight of its features alone emanate authority and evoke a solemn reverence for the law.

As we entered, the change since 9/11 slapped me in the face. I was shocked just at the process to gain entrance to the building that morning. I remembered walking freely in and out of the building, just showing my Justice Department credentials back in "the old days." Now the entrance looks like a multilevel, time-delay vault out of *Brave New World*. In addition to the usual airport security devices and procedures, Torrence and I had to go through two sealed-off, rotating tubes—like an airlock—to get into the main part of the building. Stokes met us downstairs after we passed scrutiny and led us to the "front office." Not much had changed beyond the entrance process. The hallways were still the same "Veterans Administration-hospital green" or off-white that they were years ago, and the individual office doors were the same, scuff-marked brown wood. Only when pressed, Stokes finally told us we'd be meeting with Deputy Assistant Attorney General Rita Glavin.

We had believed with the new administration and Holder's recognition of the problems in the *Stevens* case that we would now get a fair hearing of the multitude of problems in *Brown*. As they say, we assumed too much. Glavin was icy and bristling with hostility. Her already sharp features sharpened more with the clenching of her teeth, and she could barely stifle her rage in having to deal with us at all.

Glavin walked us into a typical bare government conference room. There we met Gary Grindler, whose role was never specified, but apparently he was Holder's designee of the day, and Steve Terrell, who we did know was chief of the Fraud Division. Terrell was the only polite one in the group. The rest of them all but hissed when they spoke to us. Grindler said nothing. Boy, were we naïve.

Not one of them would admit to being in charge or tell us who had the authority to dismiss the case. Not one of them had read the substantial motion to dismiss for government misconduct that we had filed, which was the reason for and subject of our meeting. Not one of them even seemed interested in doing so. At the five-minute mark of this conversation we had waited months to have and flown hours to attend, Glavin began asking "Is that all?" in her most terse and annoyed voice.

Torrence and I looked at each other, wondering why they had bothered to meet with us at all.

We listed and explained the *Brady* violations that we knew of at the time, and we asked primarily that someone who had no connection with Friedrich, Ruemmler, Weissmann, or the original task force be assigned to review the case independently and objectively consider the issues we had raised. We stressed the waste of taxpayer dollars.

The indictment alleged nothing new, and the defendants would never be sent back to jail—even if the government were able to get a second conviction. Glavin just glowered at us. If looks could kill, I'd be dead.

She couldn't wait to get us out of there. "I'll review your motion. Is there anything else?"

Maybe twenty minutes into the "conversation," this was the fifth or sixth time she had asked that question. Having at least obtained her "word" that she would read the motion, we felt that we had done all we could. It was painfully obvious nothing had changed, and we both had a strong feeling that something was very wrong.

We did not know that Friedrich had chosen Glavin to be his deputy. Likewise no one outside a small circle in the department knew her role or Friedrich's in the Stevens debacle. We were completely clueless. And it still remained to be seen how much Schuelke would find out. All we knew was that her reaction was so visceral and hostile, it had to be personal.

We left the building as quickly as we could. As I turned and looked back, I felt heartsick. The words chiseled into the Indiana limestone exterior of this million-square-foot monument to the Rule of Law captured the essence of the problem that has infected our system: *Justice in the life and conduct of the state is possible only as first it resides in the hearts and souls of the citizens.*

The people—the citizens—who made the decisions in the Justice Department had lost their hearts and sold their souls. The "change" we had been promised was a farce; it was even worse than before.

Within a few weeks, Glavin left the department to go into private practice. Terrell left also. We never received a response to our request for independent review. No one above Stokes had paid any attention to the issues we raised.

In the Barge case, Stokes made clear he was proceeding to prosecute Jim again. In pleadings and in court, Stokes continued to deny that there was any *Brady* material in the government's files or otherwise. As he had done before the Barge trial, Judge Werlein ignored our motions and did nothing.

Then on June 18, 2009, the Supreme Court handed the Enron Task Force its third reversal out of four cases taken to trial. It reversed the Enron Broadband cases of Yeager and Hirko because of a double jeopardy violation from prosecutors' efforts to prosecute them a second time for the same offense. This was the trial that had just gone to the jury when Weissmann resigned as task force director amid allegations of assorted misconduct by the prosecutors in that case.

A month later, in July 2009, Schuelke requested and received from Judge Emmet Sullivan the power to subpoena Public Integrity Section Chief Bill Welch; his deputy and lead Stevens prosecutor Brenda Morris; former PIN prosecutors Edward Sullivan and Nick Marsh; Alaska-based trial attorneys Bottini and Goeke; FBI Agent Mary Beth Kepner; and government star witness Bill Allen and his attorney.

What the Justice Department called a couple of "little mistakes"—in a hurried trial where Marsh was banished to a backseat—had snowballed into a damn avalanche. Now the judge, the press, the defense, and the department were all over the prosecutors—especially Marsh—or so he felt. Agent Joy had expressly singled him out, and it was convenient for the department to blame him. From Nick's perspective, this was a cluster-fuck if there had ever been one, and there was no end in sight.

At the same time that Marsh was feeling like the sacrificial lamb and contemplating the end of his career, if not his life, Friedrich landed a lucrative partnership with David Boies, the highly respected and successful attorney who represented presidential candidate and former Vice President Al Gore in *Bush v. Gore* before the Supreme Court. The Boies Schiller firm was widely heralded as one of the best litigation firms in the country.

One month later, on September 21, 2009, Brenda Morris quietly left Washington and the leadership of the Public Integrity Section to work in the US attorney's office in Atlanta. The department reported as subtly as possible that Morris moved "for personal reasons."

Meanwhile Schuelke was turning up the heat in his investigation. In October, he filed two motions, and Judge Sullivan issued an order under seal. The word was that Schuelke had begun interviewing FBI agents in the case, including whistle-blower Chad Joy.

The very next day, Justice Department Criminal Division head Lanny Breuer announced that veteran prosecutor Bill Welch was stepping down from his position as head of the Public Integrity Section and returning to Massachusetts "for personal reasons." Welch would remain an employee of the criminal division but as senior litigation counsel assigned to the US Attorney's Office in Springfield, Massachusetts, where he had worked before joining Main Justice.

As news of these dramatic personnel changes reached the defense bar, the general consensus was that the proverbial rats were fleeing the sinking ship of the "Public Integrity" Section because of their own lack of integrity.

———— ∞ ————

December 8, 2009, was a clear, cold day in Washington—way too cold to walk the few blocks to the Supreme Court building, so I bundled up in an almost floor-length coat and hopped into a cab.

I soon walked through the doors of the majestic building and took my place in the line for members of the Supreme Court Bar in the long marble corridor on the first floor of the building. Although the arguments did not start until 10:00 a.m., the line had begun forming at 7:45 to hear the oral arguments of the cases of media mogul Conrad Black and Alaska state legislator Bruce Weyhrauch—both of whom were arguing that they had been wrongly convicted of "honest services" fraud—as the Merrill defendants were. I immediately ran into one of Dan Bayly's trial lawyers from Houston, who spoke only to ask what I had heard from the government in Jim Brown's case since we had been sent back to Judge Werlein's court.

"Nothing," I replied. "Radio silence."

"Bizarre," he responded.

I moved through the line to the admissions desk. I knew the counsel arguing for both defendants. I warmly greeted the distinguished man who always managed the lawyers' line and directed counsel to their appropriate places. He let me proceed to the richly paneled attorneys' lounge adjoining the solicitor general's private office—just steps away from the courtroom.

The lounge was full with the defense teams for both cases. I briefly spoke to Miguel Estrada, who was arguing for Conrad Black, and chatted with Don Ayer, who represented Weyhrauch. Ayer was a former deputy solicitor general and a current officer in the American Academy of Appellate Lawyers. He and his team had drafted our original petition for *writ of certiorari* in *Brown* when we asked the Supreme Court to review the perjury and obstruction issues. They had done an outstanding job on it, but it was not a hot enough issue to attract the court's attention. When a court takes only sixty cases a year, it's hard to get on the dance card. Now, with Bruce Weyhrauch, another target of Operation Polar Pen, Don had a "hot issue"—the honest services issue we had won in the Fifth Circuit in *Brown*. I wondered how much the Enron Task Force had collaborated with the Polar Pen prosecutors and who had concocted all of these overly creative cases without crimes as bogus "honest services" allegations. The prosecutors had obviously cross-pollinated to produce baseless crimes and tortured law in both major investigations. The Enron Task Force cabal had about a two-year head start on Polar Pen, but the investigators and prosecutions overlapped for several years.

Veteran Deputy Solicitor General Michael Dreeben was arguing these cases in the Supreme Court for the government again. He was huddled with then-Solicitor General Elena Kagan in their office adjoining the lounge.

Dreeben, whom I had met for the first time when he argued for the government against Maureen Mahoney in the *Arthur Andersen* case, was wearing the required morning coat with tails. Although on the wrong side of these issues, Dreeben evoked my fond memories of former Fifth Circuit Judge Jerre Williams, for whom Dreeben had clerked. I could not help but think that Judge Williams would have granted Brown bail pending appeal and reversed all of his convictions.

In a moment, everyone was ushered into the magnificent courtroom and shoehorned into cramped, miserably uncomfortable straight chairs, squeezed elbow to elbow.

Estrada and Dreeben took their places at counsel tables on either side of the podium.

In a few minutes, the marshal entered the courtroom and instructed all to rise. As everyone stood in abject silence, the justices entered through the heavy red curtain that framed the courtroom behind their high-backed leather chairs at the bench. After the elderly Marshal, who looked like he had been with the court since it was created, boomed the ancient and familiar "cry" to open the court, Chief Justice John Roberts greeted everyone warmly, and then called the first case.

In an instant, Miguel Estrada, counsel for Lord Conrad Black, was at the podium. A highly regarded and accomplished Supreme Court advocate, Estrada was fairly short. He spoke with a heavy Spanish accent and was difficult to understand at times. He managed to make about a sixty-second, well-organized opening before Justice Scalia popped the first question.

From there on, Justices Scalia, Kennedy, Roberts, Alito, Ginsburg, Breyer, and Sotomayor peppered Estrada with mostly "friendly" questions—all indicating the court's serious concern with the breadth and creative uses to which the government had put this vague statute and what they should do about it. Because our first appeal in *Brown* had resulted in the Fifth Circuit's reversal of the convictions of the Merrill defendants on this very issue, our case was part of the discussion. It provided at least circuit precedent in support of reversing the convictions of Black and Weyhrauch. The only arguably better result would be for the Supreme Court to declare the statute unconstitutional because no one could tell what it meant. The second best result would be for the court to cabin the application of the honest-services statute to cases where there was proof of bribery or kickbacks—the defendant's self-dealing to the disadvantage of his employer.

The court's questions focused on where to draw the line. Should it be declared unconstitutional? Did Estrada request that relief? Where? Should they send it back to Congress to try to get it right again? That didn't seem like a good idea. Congress had now twice failed to get it right.

Estrada had good command of the law. He was making progress, and most of the court was clearly engaged and asking the right questions. Justice Thomas just sat there and said nothing—as always. Justice Alito noted the lack of consistency among the individual circuit courts that had tried to interpret the statute. Estrada pointed to the lack of notice in the statute of exactly what conduct it made criminal. In *Andersen*, Maureen Mahoney had argued that the law requires "fair warning" on what conduct is criminal. This "honest services" statute did not do that. There was no clear rule that anyone could follow—no fair warning of what conduct could be deemed illegal under it. Justice Sotomayor expressed a view that the statute might be limited to bribery and kickbacks, but Estrada countered "if that is what the statute says—but it did not." It provided no definition or limits to its application.

An avid textualist, considering the court bound by the precise words of the statute—or the failure thereof—Justice Scalia reminded his colleagues repeatedly that nothing in the text of the statute itself prohibits bribes and kickbacks. I was rooting for them to just declare it unconstitutional, but that meant that Congress would have another go at it. That thought was pretty scary, and no one really seemed to think giving Congress a third shot at rewriting the statute was a good idea.

Estrada's time seemed to evaporate—a problem that exists only for good advocates on the winning side.

Dreeben took the podium and uttered only two sentences, trying to direct the court away from the possibility the statute was unconstitutional, before Justice Scalia took him to that very issue. "But if I think the whole statute is bad, what, you know—why should I engage in—in this exercise?"

I caught myself grinning and nodding. Finally someone was hammering the government on its abuse of this statute to criminalize conduct that no one could foresee was a federal crime. Under the government's view, anyone who called in sick to work and played hooky instead had committed a federal crime—depriving his boss of his honest services.

Dreeben started to answer, "Well, Justice Scalia—"

Justice Scalia erupted again, "It doesn't make any sense to make me do that."

Dreeben became snide, which is never a good idea before the Supreme Court or any court for that matter. "Maybe you should wait for a Petitioner who presents the question, rather than granting relief to a Petitioner who chose not to raise the constitutional issue in this court."

I smiled. This was not going well for Dreeben.

Justice Kennedy interrupted. "Well, it's a little—it's a little odd that you—you would say that an argument that shows a way the statute can be saved cannot be—cannot be presented."

At one point, Justice Breyer asked if the issue of constitutionality was coming up in the *Skilling* case. That was interesting. I don't think I had ever heard, or heard of, a justice asking about an upcoming case. The court had just granted *certiorari*, agreeing to take the *Skilling* case a few days before this argument. We knew that meant that *Skilling*, the task force's ultimate prize, was going to be reversed—at least in part.

Dreeben was noticeably on the ropes. I wondered what he really thought of all of this prosecutorial creativity and if he was simply forced to make this ridiculous argument. I couldn't understand why a solicitor general would do that. It wasn't becoming of the "Tenth Justice."

Justice Breyer was animated. "What I wonder is, does the government feel, in order to have a full opportunity to brief constitutionality, that we should issue an order saying 'Please brief the constitutionality'?"

A clearly frustrated Justice Sotomayor was still trying to get a straight answer from Dreeben on the question presented by the pending *Skilling* case. With a brittle edge to her voice, she instructed Dreeben, "Directly answer this question: Does *Skilling* present the pure question or not?"

Dreeben was losing ground by the moment.

"No, because in *Skilling*, Justice Sotomayor, the question is whether an element of personal or private gain needs to be read into the statute in order to render it constitutional."

I shook my head in disbelief. Skilling had not even filed his brief yet. How could Dreeben possibly tell the Supreme Court of the United States that *Skilling* was not going to raise the unconstitutionality of this statute? Skilling's petition left that argument open.

Sure enough, Dreeben had to backpedal and quickly. "Now, in all fairness to Mr. Skilling, he has not filed his opening brief; the government has not filed its response. So that case—"

Justice Sotomayor immediately caught the problem. "We don't know if that's going to be—"

Dreeben looked foolish. "That case may present a—a different issue."

Chief Justice Roberts brought the point home. "Well, Mr. Dreeben, you agree that it would be very unusual if in June we announced the opinion in your case agreeing with you and then the next case announced that the statute is unconstitutional?"

Dreeben was stuck. He could say nothing more than "Agreed."

The entire courtroom erupted in laughter—at Dreeben's expense—just as it had in his *Andersen* argument.

Justice Scalia worked him over again. "You speak as though it is up to us to write the statute. We can make it mean whatever it—you know, whatever would save it or whatever we think is a good idea, but that's not our job."

One after another, the justices kept Dreeben hopping—generally with one foot in his mouth—for his entire thirty minutes at the podium. He was trying to defend the indefensible. Lord Black had not engaged in any conduct that had ever been punished under this statute previously. At least I could be grateful the Fifth Circuit had gotten that part of our case right—even if it had done so reluctantly.

As Dreeben squirmed and dodged, I realized I was shaking my head in disgust. I could not believe that the office of the solicitor general of the United States, with the Solicitor General Elena Kagan herself sitting in the courtroom, was making an argument this lame to try to save cases that should never have been brought. Kagan had an excellent reputation. For those who truly loved the law, and expected the solicitor general to live up to the highest standards as the "Tenth Justice," this was another heartbreak.

Dreeben finally used up all his time. He sat down with a sigh of relief that anything was left of his skin. Estrada popped up and slammed the government in an effective three-minute rebuttal. He had won. The argument in the first case was concluded.

―――――⁓∽∾―――――

Chief Justice Roberts called the next case—the one most like the case against Brown.

Don Ayer, a former deputy solicitor general with an impressive record of success before the court, rose with an augmented air of confidence to argue the second case for Alaska State Legislator Bruce Weyhrauch. Having had the benefit of listening to the first argument, Ayer had a keen sense of the justices' views, and his case was looking very good.

"Mr. Chief Justice, and may it please the court: When counsel for the United States defended the first honest services case before this court in 1987, the first thing he did was to acknowledge that many of the existing similar or 'intangible rights' cases contained what he called 'extravagant language' that, on its face, extended the doctrine far beyond the principle that one can be guilty of fraudulently denying others the performance of a clear legal duty that he owes. . . . I know that because the government lawyer was me, and that was the only thing I said that day that the 7-2 majority agreed with." Several justices nodded and smiled.

Ayer continued, "But twenty-two years later, and one twenty-eight-word statute later, the United States is now pressing to take that extravagant language of the pre-*McNally* cases to the bank. It does that by contending that a public official commits honest services fraud simply by failing to disclose an arguable conflict of interest, even though he has no legal duty to disclose it."

Then much as it had done in *Black*, the court poked and prodded—primarily with friendly questions—to explore where it should draw the line between what was criminal conduct, with fair notice that it was in fact criminal, and what was not. Ayer concluded his opening argument, and the justices knocked Dreeben back on the ropes again.

Justice Scalia was nowhere near finished with Dreeben. "Why didn't Congress say that instead of—instead of—of setting up this mush of language that doesn't even mention our decision in *McNally* [Ayer's 1987 case that he had just mentioned]? . . . That phrase does not appear, as I understand it, in any of the cases."

Dreeben was stammering in incredulity, "Justice—Justice Scalia, the phrase 'intangible rights' is at the center of the *McNally* majority opinion, the language 'honest services' is in the *McNally* dissent and in many of the pre-*McNally* opinions. For—"

Dreeben was right, but the language "intangible rights" and "honest services" still said nothing. No one could tell what those words in the statute meant. I was practically cheering—in silence. Justice Scalia was most annoyed. "What is the citizen supposed to do? He is supposed to go back and read all our old cases?"

Dreeben was floundering badly. "Well, I—"

When Justice Scalia is on a tear, one has to speak quickly and forcefully or he will miss the chance. Sure enough, Justice Scalia continued. "Why would it have been so difficult for Congress to say no bribes, no kickbacks, and—and—and the third thing, however you want to describe it?"

Again the courtroom erupted in laughter. The solicitor general's argument was nonsensical. Law is supposed to make sense.

Justice Scalia continued. "I mean, I think if you have a principle that the citizen is supposed to know that he is violating a criminal statute, this is just too much."

Dreeben finally found his own sense of humor. "I think we would all agree, Justice Scalia, that had Congress taken your counsel, I would not be here today—defending what the Congress attempted to do."

The audience laughed again. No truer words had ever been spoken.

What annoyed and offended me most was that the solicitor general did not have to defend these cases. She could have "confessed error," agreed the government had misused the statute, and thereby avoided losing these cases, protracting the litigation and expense, and making law adverse to the government's position. It was only a multi-million dollar exercise in poor lawyering by the department from the indictment through the solicitor general's argument—not to mention the toll on the defendants and their families, wasted time of multiple federal courts, and so on.

The solicitor general's argument was so bad that the justices got playful. Justice Breyer picked up where Justice Scalia left off and teased Justice Scalia at the same time. "I thought there was a principle that a citizen is supposed to be able to understand the criminal law that was around even before Justice Scalia."

The more Dreeben tried to save the statute or defend the government's overreaching prosecutions, the more he got hammered. Justice

Scalia's frustration bubbled up again. "But it's—it's not—it's not just one case of overreaching. One of the briefs in one or the other of these cases describes the great variety of pushing-the-envelope prosecutions that the Justice Department has, indeed, pursued, and they are all over the place. And if the Justice Department can't figure out what—what is embraced by this statute, I don't know how you can expect the average citizen to figure it out."

I and most of the attorneys in the courtroom were elated that the Supreme Court was finally dealing with this twenty-seven-year-old problem of a law so vague no reasonable person could tell what it meant. In recent years, it had been wrongly used by overly aggressive, headline-seeking, or politically motivated prosecutors to send people to prison for transactions and conduct that were not crimes at all. That was exactly what happened to all of the Merrill Lynch executives in the Enron Barge case. Finally, after letting the lower courts struggle with these issues and countless wrongful prosecutions for almost three decades, the Supreme Court was going to solve the problem and clarify the law. It actually gave me a glimmer of hope again.

The arguments in the two cases lasted two hours, at the end of which I was convinced that the cases would be reversed. However, it was hard to tell how many justices—like Justice Scalia—thought the statute was unconstitutional versus how many—like Justice Ginsburg—might try to save the statute by limiting its application to facts of bribery and kickbacks.

Either way, all of these cases that hinged on the government's expansive and creative applications of the "honest services" statute, including another Polar Pen prosecution and some of the *Skilling* convictions, would have to be reversed—just as *Brown* was—because of overreaching in the prosecutors' charging decisions. The defendants' conduct was not criminal. They did not engage in bribery or kickbacks, and the Supreme Court was finally going to say so. It was quite clear, however, that we would have to wait for a decision until after the court heard arguments in *Skilling* in March 2010.

———

Meanwhile Hank Schuelke and William Shields were conducting countless interviews and depositions of people in the Justice Department who were involved in the Polar Pen prosecution of Senator Stevens. They continued throughout the fall and into January 2010. The press was reporting that Schuelke was nearing the end of his investigation, but once he had gathered everything he wanted, Schuelke and Shields would still need time to analyze it all and write the report.

For those being investigated for the first time in their lives—the prosecutors—this process seemed endless. They were used to dishing out the agony to the target of an investigation with no thought of what their actions meant to the target, his or her family, or anyone else. With a target on their backs, however, there was a dramatic change of perspective.

Schuelke had not even deposed Nick Marsh yet. There were thousands of pages of materials to review, and no doubt every prosecutor had a different view of what happened and who was responsible. Someone was going to take the fall for this, but who? Just how far was the fall going to be? Was there a deep pool at the bottom—or just concrete?

– 14 –

ANOTHER TRY

Back in the Barge case, the Fifth Circuit had denied our interlocutory appeal on double jeopardy grounds, and the Supreme Court had just denied our petition for *writ of certiorari*. That would force us to face trial again on the same indictment, which was even more devoid of content after Bill Fuhs, "honest services," and other items the task force prosecutors failed to prove in the first trial had to be "whited out." The revised indictment now looked like a thin slice of Swiss cheese. It alleged even less than it had originally.

After hearing the oral arguments in *Black* and *Weyhrauch*, and seeing that the Supreme Court was so troubled by the honest services issue, I decided to try to reach out to Deputy Solicitor General Michael Dreeben in hopes of getting him to consider the misconduct and legal issues that warranted dismissal of the case against Brown. The Supreme Court had just handed Dreeben his own head. Dreeben was a good attorney. He knew he was going to lose. I was hoping that he had been in the solicitor general's office long enough to exercise the independence and shining integrity that used to be the hallmark of that office. Dreeben might have looked at our recent petition already.

I called Dreeben's direct line and introduced myself when he answered. "I heard that you clerked for one of my favorite judges, Jerre Williams," I added quickly.

I could hear him smile as he replied, "I did, and just the mention of his name makes me smile."

"Me too. I wish he were still there. I really miss him."

I proceeded to explain the current status of the *Brown* case and the prosecutors' attempted circumvention of the "honest services" defeat by taking Brown to trial again on the same but even more vapid indictment. I asked Dreeben if he had read our *certiorari* petition in *Brown*. Dreeben said that he had not looked at the recent issues in Brown's case.

"I'll bet you're one of those former 'AUSAs' who cites *Berger* in every brief," he needled.

"Well, usually not, but it's in most briefs in this case," I replied, with a hint of disbelief and annoyance in my voice. I gathered that he had either read the petition or heard about our complaints. In any event, he politely declined my invitation that he look into it at all.

I hung up with great disappointment in the long-touted independence and integrity of the solicitor general's office. After hearing the arguments in *Andersen, Black,* and *Weyhrauch,* I could see that the office wasn't what it used to be. They had always approved my requests for permission to confess error when I was a prosecutor. I knew they could do it. Apparently it had been turned political too. I failed to understand what was political about a commonsense and fair application of law to all citizens.

Next I called Alan Morrison—a good friend, prominent Supreme Court advocate, Fellow of the American Academy of Appellate Lawyers, and cofounder with Ralph Nader of Public Citizen. Alan had been teaching at Stanford Law School but was back in DC teaching at George Washington University. "Is there anything we can do?" I pleaded.

Alan said, "Look, Sidney, it is next to impossible to get rehearing from the Supreme Court, but in this case, as hot as the honest services issue is, it would certainly be appropriate to ask the court to grant rehearing merely to request a response from the solicitor general. . . . Dreeben told you that the SG has not paid any attention to Brown's case, and here they are, with three cases in the Supreme Court that may face the same problem as *Brown* if the court reverses them, as it appears it will do. I'll help you with a rehearing petition."

We had only a few days to get it done and filed by this point, but it was a simple approach and one that we thought was reasonable and could work. We identified the cases pending and the way the government was already trying to make an end run around the Fifth Circuit's holding in *Brown*. We asked the Supreme Court to request a reply from the solicitor general and to hold Brown's petition until the court decided *Skilling*. We filed the petition on December 23, 2009, and started the waiting process again.

Meanwhile the government and the district court were proceeding against Bayly and Furst. They were still taking no action against Brown even though the Fifth Circuit had issued its mandate, thereby returning jurisdiction to Judge Werlein. Bayly and Furst were set for a pretrial conference on January 14, 2010.

There was a lot of fallout from the public excoriation by Judge Sullivan in *Stevens*. There was enormous negative publicity and pressure, both inside and outside the Department of Justice. Of course, there was also Holder's proclamation that he was cleaning up the department—or so he said. Our little meeting with Rita Glavin and friends had already belied that.

On January 4, 2010, outgoing Deputy Attorney General David Ogden issued a formal memorandum establishing the Justice

Department "guidance" for federal prosecutors to review files and produce *Brady* material to the defense. It proclaimed "to establish a methodical approach to consideration of discovery obligations that prosecutors should follow in every case to avoid lapses that can result in consequences adverse to the department's pursuit of justice." The memo noted, "Providing broad and early discovery often promotes the truth-seeking mission of the department and fosters a speedy resolution of many cases. . . . Exculpatory information, regardless of whether the information is memorialized, must be disclosed to the defendant reasonably promptly after discovery." The Ogden memo also announced that the department was providing additional training for prosecutors nationwide on their duty to disclose *Brady* material.

Odgen left the Department of Justice the next day.

Ogden's memo drew attention, notably for what it did *not* contain. It did not provide any enforcement mechanism or actual deadlines for production of anything. It was not enforceable by the defense. Worse yet, it still allowed prosecutors to decide how important the evidence might be to the defense (whether it is "material"), meaning a prosecutor could conceal evidence from the defense if the prosecutor didn't think it was important or "material" enough to the defense. At the same time, the defendant has no way of knowing what evidence the prosecution has. So the defense doesn't know what the defense doesn't know—but the prosecutor still does. This means the prosecutors can still be the judge and jury and completely incapacitate the defense.

I was working at my computer when an e-mail came in from the electronic filing system for the Houston court. It was late Friday afternoon, January 8, 2010. No motions were due and nothing was expected.

I couldn't open the document fast enough. I yelled for Hellen. "The government has just filed a motion to dismiss all counts of the indictment against Dan Bayly."

"What?" she exclaimed in reply. "Why? How?"

"I have no idea. The defense didn't even file a motion to dismiss it. They've obviously cut some kind of deal. You know, Lanny Breuer, the assistant attorney general for the Criminal Division of the Department of Justice, represented Bayly very early in this case. He knows Bayly was innocent."

I picked up the phone and called my friend Paul Coggins, a former US attorney and counsel for codefendant Furst. Paul said he was just as surprised as I was and had heard nothing from cocounsel or the government before Stokes moved to dismiss against Bayly. Paul and I surmised that Bayly and the government had made a "secret side deal" to dismiss the criminal case once Bayly paid the SEC and settled the civil case against him. Another irony: Brown, like Bill Fuhs who had been acquitted by the Fifth Circuit, wasn't even charged by the SEC in its case.

Brown and Furst were entitled under *Brady* to the details of any government agreement with Bayly, so we added that to our list of information to request from Stokes.

We couldn't help but speculate on how the government could possibly proceed to a second prosecution of Brown—who had told Bayly and Furst not to do this deal—when it had just dismissed all of the same charges against Bayly, who had supposedly made the unlawful agreement with Fastow in the phone call Brown did not join.

We knew that Bayly was innocent, and we were delighted the government had ended his persecution, but in view of the fact that the prosecutors had repeatedly said Bayly was more culpable than Brown and Furst, we wondered if Brown would enjoy the same dismissal.

Surely, we thought, this meant that someone in the department was finally paying attention to our case, and all charges would soon be dismissed against Brown and Furst.

We agreed to keep each other informed of any developments on either side, and we planned to meet in DC at the *Skilling* argument in the Supreme Court. Meanwhile Paul was preparing his own heated motion to dismiss the same conspiracy and wire fraud charges against Furst because the same evidence they had hidden from us showed Furst was innocent also.

Then promptly on Monday morning, another e-mail came from the court. Judge Werlein had already signed an order dismissing the indictment as to Bayly alone. Something had happened behind the scenes—but what was it? Stokes wasn't telling us anything, and neither were our former cocounsel.

Furst had a motions deadline of February 15, and Paul filed his potent motion to dismiss. Still the Brown team heard nothing from the government.

At the same time Ogden left the department and the case against Bayly was suddenly dismissed, Kathryn Ruemmler, former deputy director of the task force and one of the lead prosecutors against Bayly, the Merrill defendants, Jeff Skilling, and Ken Lay, moved from her position as David Ogden's deputy over to the White House to serve as deputy White House counsel.

The Supreme Court denied our rehearing petition on the double jeopardy argument in late January. They did not agree to hold the petition or ask the solicitor general for a response. All possibilities exhausted, we awaited a setting from Judge Werlein.

All of this, we knew. What we didn't know—and no one outside the department knew—was even more interesting and illuminating.

Behind the encampments of self-preservation and the concrete bunkers of bureaucracy within the Justice Department, Hank Schuelke was drilling deeper. Nick Marsh swore to "tell the truth, the whole truth, and nothing but the truth" on February 2, 2010. That seems to have been a secret watershed inside the department that would be revealed to the rest of the world only if one read Schuelke's more than five-hundred-page report when it eventually came out on March 15, 2012—two years later.

Nick had to admit that every lawyer was responsible for identifying *Brady* material, and that he had said he "didn't want to make document discovery easier for the defense." Even though Nick had always told PIN Chief Bill Welch that they had the discovery ready, Nick said he really didn't know if *Brady* review had been completed by September 9, 2008. That was the day Brenda Morris sent the "*Brady* letter" that Nick had edited. The prosecutors wrote that they had completed their review of evidence favorable to the defense. Nick conceded that the use of other attorneys from the Public Integrity Section to review evidence for *Brady* material was, in hindsight, "not a procedure calculated to be successful."

Such a self-evident truth would be one of the reasons that task should not be left to the prosecutors. The process the prosecutors had employed to meet the constitutional right of the defendant might be laughable had it not resulted in the wrongful conviction of a sitting senator and helped change the balance of power in the senate.

Nick Marsh and his fellow Polar Pen prosecutors had been in the grand jury with many witnesses. The prosecutors in the grand jury know what the witnesses have said, are trying to formulate the criminal charges, usually draft the indictment, and often try the case. These prosecutors had tried other cases involving many of the same witnesses.

So had Bottini and Goeke.

Nick had tasked the FBI and IRS agents with reviewing their notes and 302s for *Brady* material. Welch hadn't heard about that delegation until he saw FBI Agent Joy's complaint. Every prosecutor knows or should know that it is his or her responsibility to review all the information and provide the defense everything to which it is entitled under the Constitution.

Nick also had to admit that he "didn't have a tremendous familiarity with what had gone on in the *Brady* review process." He just trusted his colleagues to do their jobs. He "didn't know what review had been conducted." Nick's excuses sounded really lame as he gave voice to them. They had not expected Senator Stevens to ask for a speedy trial, and Friedrich and Glavin had instructed Morris to agree to go to trial quickly—even sooner than the defense had requested.

Nick had also been on the phone call when the government's key witness, Bill Allen, was interviewed in person by Bottini and Goeke in Alaska, not long before Stevens was indicted. That later proved important for the defense, but Nick had no recollection of hearing Allen's exculpatory remarks. Instead the prosecutors pushed Allen to testify that Senator Stevens was "just covering his ass" with a note he had written about paying for all the renovations.

Nick and the other prosecutors had also failed to mention to the defense that the government had significant other information that would have caused the devastating impeachment of Allen. Nick and his colleagues knew that Allen was seriously implicated in sex crimes— with minors—including one from whom Allen had sought a false statement. The Anchorage Police were investigating Allen for all of it.

Not until Schuelke's report was published did we learn who was really responsible for withholding that remarkable impeaching evidence. At the same time, we did not know what Schuelke knew, and Schuelke did not know what we knew.

———— ✺ ————

By the morning of March 1, 2010, Torrence and I were back in Washington, walking through the marble corridors of the Supreme Court building. Paul Coggins had something come up in one of his other cases and could not attend the *Skilling* argument.

The tall distinguished man who presides over the seating for members of the Supreme Court Bar recognized me and ushered me to the attorneys' lounge where the arguing attorneys met before taking their places at counsel table in the great chamber. Dan Petrocelli, Skilling's lead counsel, was there with the trial team from O'Melveny & Myers—Matt Kline and David Marosso. They introduced me to Sri Srinivasan who was going to argue Skilling's case this morning before the Supreme Court. Sri, an appellate partner with O'Melveny & Myers, would subsequently be confirmed as a judge on the Court of Appeals for the District of Columbia Circuit. As I walked over to speak to Sri, Solicitor General Elena Kagan came barreling out of her adjoining office and almost ran into me—slightly above my elbow—as she hurried through the lounge. Kagan spoke only in passing to Sri, who had been recruited by O'Melveny from the solicitor general's office.

Sri was calm, composed, and clearly very well-prepared. I wished him well, chatted with the trial lawyers, and waited for the courtroom to open for seating. It was going to be a great argument.

Michael Dreeben was arguing for the United States yet again. This would be his third honest services argument in four months, having argued the last two back to back on the same morning. This had to be a record. Having witnessed the flogging Dreeben took from the court in those two cases, I expected this would be the same, if not worse.

Dreeben stepped quickly through the lounge. He looked more

pale than usual. I couldn't fathom what he was really going to argue.

Our courtroom deputy came to escort us into the chamber. I took my seat a couple of rows behind Skilling's counsel table. Not far to my left was Walter Dellinger - University of North Carolina undergraduate, Yale Law graduate, Duke law professor, speaker at our Fifth Circuit seminar, former acting solicitor general under Clinton, and chair of the O'Melveny appellate section. Because he is an amazing and veteran Supreme Court advocate, I assumed Walter had helped Sri prepare for the argument.

After the ceremonial entry of the justices and "the Cry," Chief Justice Roberts issued his usual welcome, and Sri took the podium. A handsome, brilliant, and elegant dark-skinned man, he had a wonderful and comfortable presence before the court.

He began with the issue of a prejudiced jury pool, on which the Fifth Circuit had made some helpful findings. The trial court had refused to move Skilling's trial to a different city and had spent little time selecting the jury. Sri tried to set the stage for the court of the extremely hostile environment that existed in Houston upon Enron's collapse. Pure hatred permeated the city and the jury pool through all the Enron related cases. The *Houston Chronicle* helped whip it to full froth upon the indictment and trial of Lay and Skilling.

Sri looked at each justice as he spoke. "The dramatic collapse of Enron had profound reverberations experienced throughout the Houston economy and citizenry. Sixty percent of the jury *venire* affirmatively acknowledged in the responses to questionnaires that they would be unable to set aside their deep-seated biases or doubted their ability to do so, or said that they were angry about Enron's collapse." That anger was "manifested in the vitriolic terms" against Petitioner Jeff Skilling. "In those conditions, the court of appeals was correct in unanimously concluding that this was one of the very rare cases in which, because of the degree of passion and prejudice in the community, the process of *voir dire* cannot be relied upon to adequately ferret out and identify unduly biased jurors. And—"

Justice Sotomayor cut him off with a question.

Sri reminded the court that "no juror could be seated in this case because the process of *voir dire* couldn't adequately be relied upon in these conditions. . . . And just to give this a frame of reference, the entire *voir dire* process in this case took five hours, and the trial judge interviewed each juror for approximately four and a half minutes."

Most of Sri's argument felt bogged down in discussing the parameters for selecting an impartial jury because an entire city came to loathe Skilling and Lay overnight and continued to loathe them. It seemed that the court had decided the fate of the "honest services" statute.

Justice Ginsburg cut in with a question, indicating her belief that the trial judge, Sim Lake, had given trial counsel more time to ask questions.

Sri explained how little time it was and how little it meant. "And just to paint the picture a little bit, the potential jurors were brought before the bench, and they were left standing, which I think reinforced the concept that this was going to be a rather quick affair, and it was not going to allow the kind of extensive, meaningful follow-up that we thought was required."

Sri continued, and the court was listening. "And to give it a frame of reference, in the Oklahoma City bombing case, the prosecution of Timothy McVeigh, that proceeding was transferred for trial from the city of Oklahoma City to Denver, but even after the transfer, the trial judge conducted an eighteen-day *voir dire* with an average of one hour of interviews per juror; eighteen days and one hour as compared with five hours and four and a half minutes. And we think the Oklahoma City experience is much more befitting of the kind of *voir dire* that's necessary in circumstances of community prejudice and passion of the kind that existed here."

Justice Ginsburg leaned forward and cut in again. "You made a change of venue motion at the outset, right?"

"We did," Sri replied. "Our argument is not . . . that pretrial publicity caused the passion and prejudice in the community. This is—is very much a case in which pretrial publicity was a symptom rather than the cause. Now pretrial publicity, to be sure, stoked the passions that—that already lay within the community, but really this was a case in which the passions existed regardless of pretrial publicity."

Sri and Justice Breyer got into a lengthy discussion of where to draw the line, so that trial judges could seat a jury without taking days, then Justice Sotomayor asked, "Is there any place in the record I could look to see questions that you would have posed absent the judge's limitations?"

Without batting an eye or even looking down at his notes, Sri cited the very page from the enormous record where Skilling's attorneys had explained what should be done to have a fair jury. Walter Dellinger almost gasped at Sri's mastery of the record and shook his head in amazed pride, just beaming over the brilliance, command of the record, and finesse of his young partner.

Finally Chief Justice Roberts interrupted to turn the conversation to the honest services statute. "Counsel, can I—perhaps it's time for you to shift gears, if I could—and move to the statutory question."

"Sure."

The chief justice, with a slight smile and a mischievous twinkle in his eye, asked, "I don't understand why it's difficult? The statute prohibits a 'scheme to deprive another of the intangible right of honest services.' Skilling owed the Enron shareholders honest services. He acted dishonestly in a way that harmed them. But I don't understand the difficulty."

Some of us could see that he was teasing the young man he probably knew from the solicitor general's office. It is much harder to see that as the only one who can respond to the question. I was thinking, *Yes, and therein lies the problem. No one understands "the difficulty" or anything from the text of the statute.*

Sri took it seriously and handled it well. Before long, he was reserving the remainder of his time for rebuttal, and the honest services statute was going onto the *McNally* decision scrap pile.

Dreeben stepped to the podium, seemingly safe at least on the question of jury selection—or so he thought.

But no sooner had the words "I don't think that there is any problem with this *voir dire*" left his lips than Justice Breyer leaned forward and let him have it. "There's no problem? I went through the two hundred pages, and I counted—this is only my own subjective recounting of it, but I counted *six* of whom only one lasted, but I counted five others that they had to use peremptories on that including one juror, twenty-nine, who herself was a victim of this offense to the tune of $50,000 or $60,000. And, the judge said, 'I will not challenge her for cause.'"

Justice Breyer was extremely animated. "I counted another, juror—what's this one—juror number—number's seventy-four, who when he looked her square in the eye and said, 'Can you be fair?' she said, 'I can't say yes for sure. No.' OK? So, in my own subjective account, there were five here, maybe six, certainly three, that perhaps if they'd had an appeal on peremptories, which apparently they don't, they might have said these should have been challenged for cause. So I'm concerned about the five hours, about the lack of excusal for cause, about the very,

very brief questions that he provided to people who had said on the questionnaire they could be biased. They said we think he's guilty, for example."

Justice Breyer was still leaning forward and very concerned, "And all those are cause for concern. At the same time, I'm worried about controlling too much a trial judge. I've expressed those concerns. I know this is a special case. Half, almost, of the jury questionnaires, they just threw out. And the community—you know all the arguments there. You see what's worrying me. And I'm worried about a fair trial in this instance and to say—and I'm genuinely worried, and—and I'd like to hear your response to the kind of thing I'm bringing up."

So here Dreeben was, on the ropes yet a fourth time in as many cases and on both issues. The jury selection process was now in serious doubt, and the honest services conspiracy charge was definitely going on the task force garbage heap of failed prosecutions and overreaching.

When the argument concluded, Skilling's honest services conviction was going to be reversed, but it was still unclear whether the statute would be declared unconstitutional or limited by the court's decisions to cases of bribery and kickbacks. Justice Scalia would prefer it declared unconstitutional because nothing in the text of the statute itself defined it. Justice Ginsburg did not want to give Congress another chance to make it worse, and she seemed to believe the court could roll it back with previous decisions.

The justices were scattered on the issue of whether a fair and impartial jury was seated to hear the case. I couldn't tell if the court might reverse more than the conspiracy conviction, but it was looking more limited. A number of other counts of the indictment and convictions of Skilling were tied to the conspiracy count, but the justices did not seem very concerned about that. As usual, Justice Thomas never uttered a word.

I returned from the argument in DC and still neither the government nor the district court had issued so much as a scheduling order regarding Brown. Furst had long been scheduled for a pretrial conference on April 16. It was as if Brown didn't exist.

Paul Coggins called in a week or so and told me that the government was offering Furst a "deferred prosecution agreement." This meant that as long as Furst did not commit any other crime for one year, all charges against him would be dismissed. Paul also said that Stokes had asked him if he thought Brown would settle. Paul suggested that Stokes discuss that with me. Still I heard nothing from Stokes—or from the court.

We had already been researching the Speedy Trial Act, which generally requires the government to bring a defendant to trial within seventy days of remand by a court of appeals. There were certain exceptions, but none of them applied here. It had been way too long with nothing done on Jim's case by the court or by the government. We determined that the Speedy Trial Act alone entitled Jim to a complete dismissal of the conspiracy and wire fraud charges. It was mandatory; Judge Werlein would have no discretion. It was a clean, purely legal argument. The government had done nothing to bring Jim to trial in more than two hundred days—since the Fifth Circuit returned jurisdiction to Werlein back on August 13, 2009. The government had specifically objected to a stay of mandate pending our *certiorari* petition to the Supreme Court so there was no question that Stokes knew Werlein had jurisdiction since August 13. The clock had been running for more than seven months. Someone had to do something.

– 15 –

THE BIG OOPS

I n late March 2010, six years after Brown's trial, about ten weeks after the Ogden memo was released and Ruemmler moved to the White House as deputy counsel, after it was obvious that at least Skilling's honest services conviction would be reversed, and about six weeks after Schuelke grilled Nick Marsh in his deposition, the third team of Barge case prosecutors from Main Justice sent the Brown and Furst defense teams a small package with a letter.

> I am enclosing a disk containing documents numbered DOJ-ENRONBARGE-000001 through DOJ-ENRONBARGE-001005. The disk contains scanned copies of the witness statements, notes, and grand jury transcripts submitted to the court, pursuant to its request, on June 1, 2004. These documents formed the basis of the government's July 30, 2004, disclosure letter.

The disk contained more than fifteen hundred pages of documents. Most of it contained material we had been given a few months previously in another form. We were busy working on a motion to dismiss the case on several grounds. We were also wondering why the prosecutors had done nothing to proceed against Jim for almost 250 days now.

At the beginning of April, months after the deadline had passed for giving Jim Brown a new trial on the conspiracy and wire fraud charges still hanging over his head, we decided to wake up Stokes. The prosecutors had proceeded in a timely manner against Bayly and dismissed all charges against him in early January. A hearing was scheduled for Furst with whom they were working on a deferred prosecution agreement, yet they had flat-out ignored Jim Brown.

I contacted Stokes as we were required to do by local rule to see if he would oppose dismissing the indictment against Brown for a Speedy Trial Act violation. Of course, he did. Remarkably within an hour or so, we received a notice from Judge Werlein that we were required to be in Houston for a hearing in ten days—on April 16, 2010—the date that had long been set for the hearing for Furst alone. We filed our motion to dismiss for Speedy Trial Act violations.

As we arrived early at the Houston federal courthouse on April 16 and turned the corner to face the large double doors to Judge Werlein's courtroom, we almost ran into the laughing and smiling duo of Stokes and Stieglitz coming out of Judge Werlein's chambers. They sobered up instantly. Stokes became combative, accusing us of "lying behind the log" as if we were supposed to alert him that he was supposed to prosecute the case in a timely fashion. I told him that if it were my job to do his job, this case would have been dismissed long ago because there was no crime. Torrence was on the verge of decking him. Obviously our Speedy Trial Act motion had embarrassed him. He had dropped the ball—badly—and we'd caught the fumble and should have scored the game-winning touchdown.

We set up at counsel table, thinking that we had given Judge Werlein the perfect way to wash his hands of the retrial of Jim Brown—purely as a matter of law. There was nothing to dispute. The judge had been thrilled that the government had dismissed Bayly. He was delighted at the possibility that something was being "worked out" with Furst, and he was very clear that he did not want to retry any of these defendants. If nothing else, his startling decision to grant us the interlocutory appeal that took two years told us that much.

Before the bang of the knocker on the door from Werlein's chambers into the courtroom stopped thundering in our ears, he was flying onto the bench. He was not exhibiting signs of the joy or relief I had been expecting.

Nope, definitely not.

Werlein's speech was clipped. "I observed that there are some motions pending, several motions pending, apparently. But in any event, what I wanted first to do is to get a scheduling order on this with an amended docket control order, so we have a schedule in place. And I might start, however, by asking the government whether it anticipates, in view of the other developments that apparently have taken place, or are ongoing, whether this case is going to have to be tried or not?"

Stokes was right on cue—not surprising since he'd just left Werlein's chambers a few minutes previously. "Your Honor, we do need to set a trial date. We've not been able to have any productive talks with Ms. Powell. So I think we probably do need to have a trial date set."

Werlein acted like this was news. "Have you talked about a trial date?"

Stokes lied. "Your Honor, we tried to. Defense simply wouldn't— didn't have any dates to suggest."

Werlein was angry. "Well, let's talk, Ms. Powell."

I stood up and walked over to the podium and towered over Stokes, who came up to my shoulder if he stood on his tiptoes. "I'll be glad to, Your Honor."

"When can you be ready for trial?"

Werlein had no intention of considering our Speedy Trial Act motion, but I put it to him. "The first question that needs to be addressed is our Speedy Trial motion."

He turned his head to the side. "I've seen the motion and answer. And my clerk sort of pushed the government to file a quick answer, and I appreciate that. I'm not going to rule on that today. And I will give the government an opportunity to expand upon its response, if it wants to."

Of course he would, but I wasn't backing down. "And we'll need to file a reply to that motion."

"I will permit that, of course," said Werlein in his utmost judiciousness.

I kept going. "But that motion is dispositive of Counts One, Two, and Three because there is a clear Speedy Trial Act violation here. The motions on which the government is relying to say that they were pending were wiped clean by the interlocutory appeal and then the remand by the Fifth Circuit which started the clock anew on Speedy Trial grounds."

Werlein was looking down and shuffling papers, ignoring me completely.

He looked up long enough to say, "I'm not sure that's the case, but we'll reach that in time. Now when can you be ready for trial?"

As they say in the South, I could have used a dip of snuff right then. Why didn't he just get out his rubber stamp that said *Denied* and slap it on our motion? Neither he nor the government really wanted to try this case. They didn't have a case to try. It was all just to torture Jim, and Patrick Stokes hated my guts for raising the misconduct issues against his task force heroes and vigorously defending my client.

I stood firm. "We can be ready for trial, certainly, by September."

Werlein looked at Stokes. "Does that sound agreeable to the government?"

Stokes was distracted and missed his cue, so Werlein just went on. "All right. We've got . . . Well, we have some previously set cases that fill September and October that are lengthy trials, multiple-defendant trials. November 15. How does November 15 sound?"

I responded firmly, "Subject, of course, to our Speedy Trial Act objections, November 15 is fine."

"For the government?"

Stokes heard this one. "Your Honor, that's fine with the government. . . . The government would request that pending the court's ruling on the Speedy Trial issue, that the defense waive any further Speedy Trial Act claim if we are going to push the trial out to November. . . . So, I just want to make sure that the defense, if they are willing to go in November, that they are going to waive any additional time so we won't have any additional Speedy Trial Act claims after the motions and responses have all been filed. So subject to that."

I wasn't going to budge. I'd already caught Stokes coming out of the judge's office. Werlein had admitted he had contacted the government and pushed for an immediate response to our motion. Stokes had contacted Werlein's chambers or the clerk as soon as he hung up from talking to me when I called to confer with him on the Speedy Trial Act motion. They both knew we were right, and they knew it wasn't going to matter a whit. Our Speedy Trial Act motion was going to be denied regardless of the law.

I loomed over Stokes. "Well, Your Honor, that would be contrary to the Supreme Court's decision in *United States v. Zedner*, holding that a defendant cannot prospectively waive the protections of the Speedy Trial Act."

Werlein glared at me. "Are you agreeable or not?"

"No. I'm not going to waive any Speedy Trial Act issues," I said resolutely.

Werlein, disgusted, looked at Stokes. "She is not agreeable to that. How long is this going to take to try?"

Stokes was chapped and caught flat-footed by the speedy trial issue. "Your Honor, I would anticipate the trial would be two to three weeks. I would point out that under the case law we've cited that the Speedy Trial Act is tolled through the period of time through which the government—its responses are filed and the defense has its opportunity to file its replies, and there's a hearing. So we think that the November trial date could work. But I just want to make the Speedy Trial Act issue clear to the court."

Werlein was blistered. He and Stokes had both dropped the ball on this one, but neither wanted to blame the other or do what was right.

Werlein had his back up. "Well, it may be that—it may be that you will even be able to get another judge because I can't accommodate you."

Werlein must have seen an unconscious flicker of hope on my face, or maybe he thought we would crater if he moved up the trial date. He quickly rethought that offer. "I think what I'll do, we'll move that up. Both sides, obviously, want to get this moved as early as possible. So let's move this up to August 2 for jury selection and trial at 9:00 a.m. We will reset that one to another time, and I think that way I will have time to get the responses on the pending motions and replies and to—and to get a ruling for you by July anyway. I will set this for August 2, 2010, at 9:00 a.m., estimating two to three weeks. Does that sound right to you, Ms. Powell?"

"That's fine, Your Honor." I was delighted to kick this case off high center. We had nothing to fear. *The sooner the better*, I thought. We needed a trial date to put Stokes's back to the wall and see if he had the guts to try this case. I certainly did. I could hardly wait to get all the truth out and actually put on the defense that the task force prosecutors' tactics denied the defendants the first time. With a trial deadline, we could push harder to get more *Brady* material produced, so I asked for a new motions deadline to add a little more fuel to the fire.

"Right now there are only two that qualify as pending under the Speedy Trial Act," I added.

Werlein wasn't going there. "Well—"

Stokes jumped in. "Your Honor, I think we have a significant disagreement on what motions are pending."

"I understand. I'm not going to rule on it no matter how many—right now no matter how many times Ms. Powell says it."

Werlein's attitude, Freudian slip, and comments overall made very clear there was no chance of him dismissing the case for a Speedy Trial Act violation. At least we had gotten this moving toward the resolution we wanted—a trial.

Werlein set more deadlines. Stokes agreed, and Werlein continued, "OK. Now I gather that the count of conviction that was affirmed by the court of appeals—was which count?"

In disbelief that Werlein still didn't know the results of the Fifth Circuit's decisions and Jim's status—and fury that Werlein was raising and reinforcing the government's threat of sending Jim to prison again—I responded emphatically, "Counts Four and Five."

Making it worse, Werlein then asked, "And what amount of unserved time is there yet on that sentence?"

My voice got louder with my disgust. "None, Your Honor. Actually Mr. Brown served what would have been more than the maximum possible length of time imposed under the guidelines for the offenses of which he stands convicted. So there's no remaining time to be served."

Stokes popped up again. "Your Honor, I believe, if I'm not mistaken—and I could be on this—but I believe he was sentenced to forty-eight months. I believe he served between nine and eleven months. There's—Ms. Powell has raised a dispute in the past about whether or not that sentence was appropriate. And the court determined—in an opinion back in January of 2008, ruled that it could not resentence him. But I believe the numbers I have are correct, that he is facing a sentence of forty-eight months in total on that."

Here we went again. Another Justice Department prosecutor—and now judge—terrorizing Jim and Nancy by waving the specter of prison, contrary to the agreement two years earlier, contrary to law, with Jim and Nancy sitting in the courtroom, their faces frozen in horror.

Judge Werlein started, "Well—"

I interrupted. "That was a bundled sentence, Your Honor. It has to be unbundled in light of *United States v. Bass.*"

Werlein had been through this before—at length. He had spent almost an hour on it with prosecutor Arnold Spencer at a prior hearing. Surely he remembered denying Spencer's motion to remand Jim to custody. Werlein did not like me making him work or challenging his rulings one bit. For my part, I know and have known many federal judges across the country, but I had never seen a judge work so hard, in the face of completely contrary law, to make sure the government could win—and preferably without making a ruling. I glanced to my right at the portraits of Fifth Circuit Judges Gee and Brown who had presided within the walls of this courtroom, and I wished they were here.

Fortunately Werlein's recollection was returning. "I think it was. I had thought when we had that discussion about whether he should be remanded at this time, and I declined to do that—and I haven't gone back and reviewed it—but my recollection is, is that it was rather set up for the government to go ahead and move to *mandamus* me at that time and get a determination from the Fifth Circuit. I gather the government has never done that."

Stokes had to admit that one. "That's right, Your Honor, we did not. I do recall that being a footnote."

"How does that get resolved?" Werlein inquired of the government.

I could have answered that easily, but he wasn't asking me. There was a document from the assistant attorney general in charge of the criminal division, Alice Fisher, agreeing that Jim was entitled to be resentenced. Judge Werlein could simply have held the government to it, and we would have been finished with that part back in 2006.

Stokes returned to pandering and lying. "Your Honor, we are certainly mindful of trying to resolve this case, like any case before trial. But as the saying goes, it takes two to tango."

Werlein turned to me, a chastising, patronizing tone in his voice. "Ms. Powell, I am somewhat disturbed when I hear from the government that they are having difficulties even having conversations with you. That is not a good thing."

I firmly replied, "I have had several conversations with Mr. Stokes, Your Honor." I explained to Judge Werlein that the government was trying to intimidate Jim with threats of being sent back to prison "on their unfounded argument that he is supposed to serve forty-six months for a bundled sentence" that included convictions that had been reversed. We were not going to be intimidated. And I reminded him, "We have significant legal issues here that need to be ruled on. And those rulings are imperative before we go any further."

Stokes misrepresented the situation again. "Your Honor, if I may, just briefly for the record, we have certainly not lorded anything over Ms. Powell or her client, certainly not any threat of her client going back to jail or prison for any period of time. I know this isn't the forum to discuss any resolution discussions the parties have had, but I would simply point out, Your Honor, that the government has been attempting to work out a resolution that would allow Ms. Powell to make the arguments she wants to make. But, again, we can only do so much on the government's end. And so, I think the government has been extremely reasonable in this. Ms. Powell has throughout this accused the government of misconduct, for example, in her most recent motion attacking the assistant attorney general without any basis in fact whatsoever. We are not—nonetheless, we are recognizing that it's Mr. Brown who is on trial, and so, trying to work out a reasonable resolution. But it is difficult when the allegations against the government are simply not founded in any fact, and it makes it difficult for us to negotiate in that sort of posture. We will continue to try to do so."

Werlein looked at me again. "I would encourage you to have— maybe put down some of the swords and armor and have some conversations about this."

I wasn't going to let that stand unchallenged. "Actually I called Mr. Stokes a couple of weeks ago and woke him up on this case, apparently. Because it was after that phone call, which I initiated to attempt to resolve this one last time, that he scheduled or arranged for this hearing."

I wanted Werlein to know that I knew Stokes had contacted the court through the judge's law clerk or otherwise—immediately after my phone call, before we filed our Speedy Trial Act motion.

Stokes tried to interrupt. "Again, Your Honor—"

But I wasn't stopping. "We have made efforts to talk to the government, and we have made efforts to resolve it."

Stokes was really squirming. "Again I would point out that Ms. Powell is operating without the facts. I think the court will be well aware of this, that we did not schedule this hearing."

Werlein came to his rescue. "Yes, that's right, I set the hearing. But in any event, I think the parties would be well-served by lowering the rhetoric, especially given what I have—I have been informed with respect to the—I don't know the terms of the disposition—but I know that the Bayly matter has been disposed of. I'm told that the Furst matter is going to be disposed of."

I had to speak again. Werlein's halting speech and backtracking caused me to believe he was protecting the government. "And we haven't been provided with the information as to what the terms of those dispositions are either."

Werlein became very defensive. "I don't know that—nor have I and it hasn't concluded with Mr. Furst. That's beside the point. It seems to me the fact of the matter is, the government at least has succeeded with other good lawyers and I would think that—where apparently both sides are satisfied with the results."

Werlein really wanted us to take this off his plate. "I've encouraged for the long time since this matter was first remanded that the parties try to work out some resolution, and I think that the parties will be well-served. I recognize that there's—there's some additional complication here because of the sentence imposed upon Mr. Brown that will need to be resolved in some way and either served or changed."

There was that threat again—of a sentence still to be served. My teeth clenched, I glared over at Torrence, who knew exactly what I was thinking.

Werlein continued. "I would hope that good lawyers would re-solve—would be able to guide me as to how that appropriately should be done. So let me give you encouragement, both sides, on that. We have a schedule. And I will get the briefing from you in due course—if that's the way you want to spend all of your time. I would encourage you to spend your time not writing such voluminous briefs, because I have quite a number."

Of course if he had ruled on any of the valid motions we had filed—many of which required dismissal of the case—or if he had resentenced Brown, this wasteful and needless litigation would have ended long ago. Werlein preferred to blame us and our briefing. Where had all the real judges gone? He refused to rule on the law if it meant it ended the prosecution.

I had to call him on it. "That's why our Speedy Trial motion is just three pages, correct on the law, and requires dismissal."

He couldn't have cared less. "Thank you for any brevity that you can bring to it. But I would really encourage you to work on—on a different level, perhaps, than trying to demonstrate all the nice skills that both of you have in terms of briefing matters."

The "hearing" was over. After yet another trip to Houston by four of us, the specter of reimprisonment raised yet again to Jim's face, two government lawyers coming in from DC, and an hour in court, Ewing Werlein had ruled on nothing. At least we had a trial date set. That was something.

Less than four weeks later, on May 14, 2010, the Justice Department entered into a deferred prosecution agreement with Rob Furst, Brown's only remaining codefendant. As long as Furst didn't break any other law for one year, Stokes agreed that they would dismiss the conspiracy and wire fraud charges against him at that time. Furst had already served almost a year in prison for something that wasn't a crime. He'd never committed a crime before, so going a year without committing one shouldn't be too hard. He avoided the endless trauma, anxiety, and humiliation of a second trial and threats of reincarceration.

When our irrefutable Speedy Trial motion went down in flames, we knew we would have to finish the Herculean task of identifying all of the exculpatory information the prosecutors had withheld. We would have to explain why it was exculpatory and file a huge brief, asking the court to dismiss the indictment for egregious prosecutorial misconduct.

Despite all of the documents we had reviewed and the work we had done, we still didn't realize just how egregious it was. There was even more.

As we were working on the mother of all motions to dismiss for prosecutorial misconduct, including the evidence from the fifteen hundred pages the government had given us in late March, Hellen and I went to the original disk Stokes had provided. Hellen made an astonishing discovery. There was yellow highlighting on some of these documents. She promptly told me of the highlighting and was concerned that it kept us from using the documents.

I knew what it meant and got a funny feeling in the pit of my stomach. I remembered from the record that just before the trial in 2004, the defense attorneys pounded relentlessly, asking Werlein to order the government to produce all of the information favorable to the defense. The defense attorneys repeatedly asked for *Brady* material and reported to Werlein that the prosecutors were threatening the witnesses so that no one—not even the defendants' own colleagues at Merrill—would speak to them. Friedrich had even insisted that if a Merrill employee agreed to be interviewed by the defense, a task force attorney would have to be present at the interview. Not surprisingly, there were no interviews, and the defense team had had no way to prepare for the Barge trial.

Finally after the task force disclosed in mid-2004, and the press splashed that Fastow himself had said he didn't give Merrill a guarantee,

Judge Werlein ordered the task force prosecutors to mark for him the material that had led the task force to list the names of people who might assist the defense. That information—exactly as it was submitted to Werlein—was on the disk in Hellen's computer. It contained the government's own yellow highlighting identifying the *Brady* information Werlein had told them to mark for him. It showed that Ruemmler, Friedrich, Hemann, and Weissmann knew before the trial that it was *Brady* evidence. In fact, it formed the basis of the "*Brady* letter" of summaries that Ruemmler herself signed when Werlein ordered the task force to do so.

I stood watching over Hellen's shoulder at the yellow highlighting on the computer screen as she scrolled through some of the documents. I knew that some of the highlighted statements had been included in the "*Brady* summaries" the task force had given the defense before the 2004 trial. But it looked like some of the statements the prosecutors had highlighted were not included in the court-ordered "summaries." We presumed that a "summary" was supposed to be accurate—not misleading. The defense lawyers before trial had asked specifically for the documents the task force had given to Werlein, and he refused to require the task force to produce them.

Now it was 2010, and we had just received this disk from the third prosecutor assigned to the case. Did Stokes know what was really on this disk?

We printed in color every page that had any highlighting. We needed to compare this line by line with the summaries the task force gave the defense before the trial. We pulled the letter that Ruemmler had written providing the "summaries" of these witnesses and the letter Stokes wrote when he sent us this disk.

First, I needed to make sure this was exactly what the prosecutors gave Werlein. Then we needed to determine if there was any difference between the summaries and what the task force had highlighted. I could already tell that there were differences. I thought they were significant, but we had to make sure. It would be tedious and take time to make a very careful comparison. I contacted Stokes, and he verified that the disk contained all the material in the exact form it had been given to Werlein.

I called Torrence. "You're not going to believe what they did."

Deep in the current draft of the motion, Torrence queried, "What in the world are you talking about?"

"The task force yellow-highlighted *Brady* evidence before trial. They gave it to Werlein and then they hid it from us. You've got to pull the disk and all the *Brady* disclosures. Start a line-by-line comparison. We need to know exactly what they yellow-highlighted and then omitted from the summaries. We need to know what was *Brady* material that they didn't highlight so as not to draw attention to it. I'm sure this disk is chock-full of evidence the defense attorneys should have had before the trial. Apparently no one else has even looked at it. We've got McMahon's notes too. They didn't give us those before. They're buried in here among a thousand pages they had given us the last time. McMahon's interview notes—pages of them—are totally exculpatory, and Ruemmler's '*Brady* letter' before the trial only gave the defense a four-line 'summary' of what McMahon supposedly said."

We had—in their own highlighting—the exact information that Ruemmler, Friedrich, Hemann, and Weissmann knew to be crucial to the defense. They had identified it for Werlein as *Brady* material. They damn well knew it was favorable, exculpatory, and material to the defense, and this proved that they knew it prior to Jim's trial.

This disk was the first time that we had seen the notes of the government's interviews of former Enron treasurer Jeff McMahon taken in 2002—eight years earlier. I devoured those notes, which revealed one startling fact after the other. Many of the statements directly contradicted the prosecutors' entire case. Some exculpatory statements they had highlighted, and some they had highlighted around.

We confirmed that Kathryn Ruemmler had personally signed the "*Brady* letter" to the defense attorneys. Now we could understand why the task force had threatened McMahon so intensively—keeping him in constant fear of indictment—to keep him from testifying in the Barge case. Now we also knew why they never indicted him for making the alleged guarantee for which the four Merrill executives served time in prison.

I felt nauseous. I knew the rage Brendan Sullivan felt when he saw the notes of the prosecutors in *Stevens*. I always knew that something was very wrong in this case. These prosecutors had worked way too hard to make something a crime that wasn't, and they had all fought producing the real documents and anything *Brady* way too long and too hard.

In addition, the use of summaries is an abhorrent practice. It's not used by any responsible US attorney unless there is real and reasonable danger to a witness or national security. Creating a summary is a lot more trouble and work than simply producing the evidence. No wonder Judge Emmet Sullivan in the *Stevens* case had referred to summaries as too great an opportunity for "mischief and mistake." This was cold, hard evidence in the government's own highlighted notes that showed they knew exactly what they were doing—and could have only deliberately hidden this evidence from the defense. They had prosecuted people for obstruction of justice for much less.

The more we compared the evidence on the disk given to us in 2010 with the summaries the prosecutors had given the defense in 2004, the more outraged I became. Judge Sullivan would have gone ballistic. This misconduct and *Brady* violation was even clearer than in *Stevens*—and four men had gone to prison because of it.

– 16 –

TRUTH BE TOLD

Long before the Barge trial, Ruemmler, Friedrich, Weissmann, and Hemann knew exactly what evidence the Merrill defendants needed for their defense. Several Merrill executives had testified before Congress, the SEC, and the Enron Grand Jury that they had made only a lawful agreement with McMahon and Fastow that Enron would use its "best efforts" to remarket the barges to a third-party buyer. That is all that they, and in consultation with Merrill legal counsel, agreed to do. Enron had told Merrill that an industry buyer in the power business was waiting in the wings to buy Merrill's interest in these barges. AES Corporation actually did buy them nine months later and still used them ten years later.

The prosecutors knew that a best-efforts agreement to remarket the barges was lawful. Friedrich said, "If it's just 'best efforts,' then it would have been OK. . . . There is nothing wrong with remarketing. . . . They could have gotten a sale and a gain treatment on this." It was undisputed these prosecutors knew the defense was built on the defendants' understanding that the only "side deal" was a lawful best-efforts agreement to remarket the barges, and that the Merrill executives relied on their legal counsel throughout the transaction.

As we combed the hundreds of pages of newest disclosures and found the prosecutors' highlighting, it became evident that the prosecutors had deliberately, and with the greatest care, kept the precise words out of the summaries of the crucial witnesses that would have proved the defense. The yellow-highlighted evidence they hid directly contradicted their witnesses and arguments. Ruemmler and Friedrich in particular fought relentlessly to keep exculpatory evidence from the defense at trial. Their protégés—Spencer and Stokes—continued the fight, throughout the appeals and impending new trial, to conceal the sworn statements, FBI 302s of interviews, and interviewers' notes of key witnesses that proved the opposite of the testimony these prosecutors elicited from the hearsay witnesses they had carefully prepared to testify at the Barge trial.

Now we had them cold—in black and white and yellow. It was irrefutable. Ruemmler, Friedrich, and Hemann, under Weissmann's supervision, had repeatedly denied the existence of *Brady* material. Just like the Stevens prosecutors, they told Judge Werlein time and time again that they had met their *Brady* obligations or exceeded them. They fought vehemently against producing anything to the Merrill defendants. Arnold Spencer told the judge there was no *Brady* material, and Patrick Stokes had repeatedly told Werlein there was no *Brady* material. Even at the last hearing, Stokes had whined that there was "no basis" for our misconduct allegations.

We had the proof now. When Judge Werlein ordered Friedrich, Ruemmler, Hemann, and Weissmann to produce summaries of the exculpatory evidence to the defense, the prosecutors further redacted even the *Brady* material they had themselves highlighted. They knew unequivocally that it was *Brady*. Yet they very carefully excised the crucial facts provided by witnesses who had actually participated in the deal. They removed key words that they had highlighted as *Brady*. They had also carefully avoided other crucial facts that were equally or even more exculpatory.

Not even Ewing Werlein, the most pro-government judge I had seen, could ignore this. Even he should be outraged about this; they had thumbed their noses at his order and made him look like a sloth, or at best, careless. He could not have made any kind of actual, meaningful review of the fifteen hundred pages they submitted to him—*highlighted*—before the 2004 trial and then approved the few-page letter Ruemmler signed, claiming it was the "summary" the court ordered the government to provide. "Summary," even as defined in a basic dictionary, means "a comprehensive and usually brief abstract, recapitulation, or compendium of previously stated facts or statements."

At trial, Ruemmler had vociferously and repeatedly told Judge Werlein, the jury, and the courtroom packed with reporters, "You know that Enron, through its Treasurer McMahon and Chief Financial Officer Fastow, made an oral guarantee to these Merrill Lynch defendants that they would be taken out of the barge deal by June 30th, 2000, at a guaranteed rate of return."

Ruemmler said, "So the key . . . was Jeff McMahon . . . Trinkle told you . . . and Glisan told you that Jeff McMahon confirmed to him that he gave that exact guarantee."

She went back to it again. "And during that conversation between Glisan and McMahon, Mr. McMahon confirmed to Mr. Glisan that he had, in fact, given an oral guarantee to Merrill Lynch."

Yet again, she said, "It was Bayly's job . . . to get on the phone with Mr. Fastow . . . and make sure that Mr. Fastow ratified the oral guarantee that Mr. McMahon had already given to Mr. Furst."

The evidence we received in March 2010 showed that Ruemmler and her team were hiding the notes taken by multiple government agents, who interviewed McMahon two years before trial. At least four government agents' notes, independently corroborating each other, confirmed that McMahon himself had said clearly, definitively, and unequivocally:

"No—never guaranteed to take out [Merrill Lynch] w/rate of return."

"Never made rep[resentation] to ML [Merrill Lynch] that E[nron] would buy them out at price or @ set rate of return."

"Andy said—Enron would help remarket in next six months."

"Andy said E[nron] would help remarket equity w/in next six months—no further commitment."

"AF [Fastow] agreed that E[nron] would help them [Merrill Lynch] remarket the equity six mo[nths] after closing."

"Disc[ussion] between Andy [Fastow] & ML [Merrill Lynch]. Agreed E[nron]would use best efforts to help them sell assets."

But that's not all.

At the trial, Ruemmler turned from her mantra that "McMahon made a guarantee that Fastow ratified" to mocking the defendants' assertions that this was a lawful agreement to use their best efforts to remarket the barges. Her second refrain was, "The written agreement between Enron and Merrill Lynch had no remarketing or best-efforts provision. You heard testimony . . . that there was some suggestion, made primarily through Ms. Zrike . . . that the Merrill Lynch defendants believed that all that Enron had committed to do was to remarket . . . Merrill Lynch's interest in the barges. . . . You can spend as many hours as you would like. You will nowhere in those documents ever find a reference to a remarketing agreement or a best-efforts provision. It's not there."

All along, Ruemmler, Friedrich, Weissmann, and probably Hemann knew and were hiding the evidence that Zrike had sworn as true in the grand jury. Merrill's in-house counsel, Kathy Zrike, had told the prosecutors and the Enron Grand Jury, long before the Barge trial, that "Merrill tried to put the remarketing agreement in the written agreement but Enron said it was inappropriate and it could not commit to it. The 'best-efforts' agreement for selling Merrill's position looked like Enron had to buy back Merrill's interest in the barges. Merrill was putting in real equity with only Enron to remarket its position." Zrike also "wanted a 'hold harmless' clause for Merrill but Enron rejected that because Merrill had to be at risk." Zrike "tried to insert a 'best-efforts' clause but Enron said that it was too much of an obligation and that they could not have this clause in the agreement."

Enron Task Force Director Andrew Weissmann had personally questioned Zrike in the grand jury for hours, if not days. He was also present six months earlier when the FBI interviewed her, and she said the same things. Friedrich questioned her at trial. He would have prepared to cross-examine her by reading all of her prior sworn testimony, the statements she had made to the FBI, her SEC testimony, and any interview notes. In her SEC testimony also, Zrike reaffirmed these statements under oath and explained even more. At the Barge trial, Weissmann sat right in front of her as she testified, staring at her, as if he were daring her to say anything that contradicted the deal he had made with Merrill. He already had her in fear of being indicted herself. The task force deal with Merrill required all Merrill employees to express only "the government's view" of "the facts" or risk the destruction of Merrill à la Arthur Andersen.

At the Barge trial, Matthew Friedrich argued last. He had the rebuttal after all the defense lawyers could not speak again. He pounded the jury with the fact that the documents didn't include best efforts or a remarketing agreement. Friedrich argued that the defendants were lying when they claimed that it was only a best-efforts agreement to remarket the barges. "They could have gotten sale and a gain treatment on this." And he poured it on, "If it was a remarketing agreement, there wouldn't have been a problem with that. . . . If it's a remarketing agreement, if that's all it is, why was it not put in writing?"

All this time, the prosecutors were hiding Zrike's sworn grand jury testimony, which they had highlighted. Zrike had testified under oath and they highlighted but omitted her statement that: "The fact that they would not put in writing an obligation to buy it back, to indemnify us, all those things were consistent with the business deal and were not things that I felt were nefarious [or] problematic."

Ruemmler included the sentences around this crucial evidence in her "*Brady* letter" but omitted the highlighted sentence that made it clear that Zrike knew exactly what the deal was.

Friedrich kept on and on, telling the Barge jury the defense was a lie, while Ruemmler nodded in agreement. "There is a suggestion . . . that what's going on is sort of a good-faith exchange between two parties as they try to negotiate different legal documents that sort of come back and forth, and sometimes language comes in, sometimes it's taken out, that kind of thing. This is not the average business case. This is not a case where people are trying to . . . put language into documents as some sort of good-faith negotiating process."

It took six years to find the evidence that they had hidden Zrike's sworn statement to the contrary. There were precisely such negotiations—Zrike participated in them, and Weissmann, Friedrich, and Ruemmler knew it.

Zrike had testified under oath: "The Merrill Lynch lawyers in my group and I did ask that we include two types of provisions that we thought would be helpful to us. One would be to indemnify us or hold harmless if there was any sort of liability like a barge explosion or environmental spill, loss of life, or something that was, you know, a disaster scenario. . . . The other thing that we marked up and we wanted to add was a best-efforts clause . . . that they would use their best efforts to find a [third-party] purchaser [for] Merrill's equity interest. . . . The response from the Enron legal team was that—both of those provisions would be a problem. . . . They kept coming back to the fact that it really had to be a true passage of risk. . . . We were not successful in negotiating that in with Vinson & Elkins."

What these prosecutors did to Bill Fuhs, Brown's young associate who spent eight months in a maximum-security transfer facility in Oklahoma, was even worse. The prosecutors told the jury that Fuhs had deleted the buyback language from the engagement letter, which, they said, showed he knew it was a crime. He suffered the worst conditions of confinement of all of the defendants and was imprisoned far away from his young children.

At trial, Bill Fuhs explained that he consulted counsel on everything, just as Jim had instructed him to do. But Friedrich mocked and excoriated Fuhs for that assertion. Friedrich said, "The lawyer has to know what's going on; they have to know all the facts. . . . there's no evidence that Mr. Fuhs made any efforts to talk to a lawyer or had any reliance on a lawyer about what was going on. . . . Fuhs gets copies, for example, of the engagement letter that had the offending language included, and that shows you what he knew at the time the deal was."

I ran to Hellen's office in a blind rage, shaking a highlighted piece of paper in her face. "Look what these bastards did. It was Merrill's counsel Dolan who took the buyback language out of the engagement letter—and they knew it. Look at this. They yellow-highlighted and omitted from their summary the most important sentence: 'Merrill in-house counsel Gary Dolan had said that it was he who objected to this language,' and it was Dolan—not young Bill Fuhs—who changed the engagement letter, precisely because Dolan knew 'that such an agreement would be improper because such a transaction could be viewed as a "parking" transaction.'"

"Oh, my God! How could they do this?" Hellen exclaimed.

The government's pretrial "summaries" totaled nineteen pages, including their misleading summary of Fastow's comments, and their four-line "summary" of pages and pages of McMahon's statements. No rational judge could find that these nineteen pages could possibly satisfy *Brady* while the prosecutors hid thousands of pages of evidence we had now—many with their own highlights of *Brady* evidence. The Enron Task Force and their puppets fought vigorously to hide these documents for as long as six years. Judge Werlein had allowed them to do so, despite the fact that this included sworn testimony of the primary witnesses who had personal knowledge of the Barge transaction and had tried to document the best-efforts agreement to remarket the barges.

If not strategically to engineer the defendants' convictions, why else would these prosecutors have refused repeatedly to produce the actual statements, notes, and prior testimony of these witnesses? Why else would they have gone to such time and trouble to create short and misleading summaries? Why else would they have made such careful, deliberate surgical edits and alterations of the material—even of what they had highlighted? Why else would they have spent time carving out even single words, short phrases, or an especially exculpatory sentence?

In one place, they edited out the word "subsequent" and the phrase that "Brown was worried," which indicated Brown's continuing objections and concerns of risk past the time they had claimed Jim joined the conspiracy merely because he was silent on the "Trinkle call." They edited out of Merrill counsel Dolan's statements that he specifically knew the concerns of a "parking transaction," which showed both Fuhs's reliance on counsel and that Brown's grand jury testimony and Fuhs's trial testimony were true.

And why edit out Zrike's knowledge of the buyback issue that the task force had already highlighted as *Brady* material? Why change or omit words and phrases to shift the evidence from declaratory statements to qualified "beliefs"—couching the "disclosures" by incorporating clauses like "did not believe," "did not recall," or "did not feel"—if not to obfuscate the truth and grossly minimize what the Merrill lawyers and call participants actually said and knew? Why else refer to what was plain truth as a mere "suggestion"—just as they had done in *Stevens*—if not to paint as a lie what they knew was the truth? Even if they did not believe any of the evidence they hid to be true, they had a constitutional and ethical obligation to produce the contradictions.

Why not disclose to the defendants that Zrike had tried her dead-level best to include the best-efforts agreement in the written materials, but Enron's lawyers would not allow it? And why not just give the defendants all the 302s, grand jury testimony, etc., in the first place? That kind of disclosure is made routinely by prosecutors who seek justice. These were not unsophisticated prosecutors. They were the cream of the department's crop. They were from the best schools, judicial clerkships, and law reviews. They were also experienced prosecutors.

The truth was that the withheld material undercut their entire case. They knew it, and they hid it. In sum, it is really this simple: the evidence the task force concealed of McMahon, Fastow, and Merrill's own lawyers contradicted the theory of the government's case at trial and every hearsay witness on whom their case depended. It contradicted the arguments they made to the jury at least two dozen times and the witnesses to whom they pointed at least fifty times. It eviscerated their mantra. The task force chose not to have a single participant in the Merrill–Enron call testify for one reason: they all contradicted the task force's contrived, hearsay, falsely premised, and falsely presented case—as Ruemmler, Friedrich, Weissmann, and Hemann knew. Even McMahan and Fastow, who despised each other, had long told the prosecutors, independently and at different times, they never gave Merrill a guarantee on the barge deal.

Finally armed with this much of the truth, and the task force's own highlighted *Brady* material, we finished our briefing with relish and eagerly anticipated Werlein's reaction at the hearing. No one could turn a blind eye to these astonishing revelations. Brown would get a new trial on all counts. Perhaps the case would be dismissed for this egregious misconduct.

– 17 –

THE BEGINNING OF THE END

The order from Werlein arrived fifty-eight days after the last hearing in Houston that foretold its result. Werlein refused to dismiss the second prosecution of Jim on the same conspiracy and wire fraud indictment that had failed once already. It didn't matter that the government had failed to proceed against him for 250 days—long past the Speedy Trial Act deadline of seventy days. It didn't matter that the indictment on its face did not allege an offense.

Judge Werlein's denial order, however, gave us reason to believe that we would get a hearing on the motion for new trial on the perjury and obstruction charges. In fact, Werlein's order said that he was denying the speedy trial dismissal because the court "expected to conduct initial hearings or additional hearings on these motions," including Brown's motion for new trial. Werlein reached back years to the motion for new trial Brown had filed before the interlocutory appeal to claim it tolled the time for prosecution. The only way he could refuse to dismiss the case on a Speedy Trial Act violation was both to ignore the law and to exclude "all time between the filing of a motion and any required hearing thereon." Therefore Judge Werlein said that "Brown's counsel expressly requested the court to set a hearing date for Brown's motion for new trial, which has yet to be heard."

Fine with us. We had to have a hearing and a new trial on Counts Four and Five, and we needed and wanted one. Those were the perjury and obstruction charges based on Jim's grand jury testimony about his personal understanding of a telephone call he was not a party to after Weissmann had instructed him to share his personal understanding—"whether accurate or not." Until we got those reversed, Jim would always be a convicted felon. He couldn't shoot skeet with his son. He couldn't vote. He had lost all his securities licenses, and he couldn't work in his lifelong profession again.

In a hearing on our motion for new trial, we should have been able to present evidence of what the witnesses had really told the prosecutors before trial and how the prosecutors had threatened McMahon and others to keep them from testifying for the defense, and we could prove the prosecutors' misconduct. If we had had a judge like Emmet Sullivan in *Stevens* or Judge Pregerson on the Ninth Circuit, or any of a handful of federal judges who hold the prosecution to the proper standards and impose accountability, we should have been able to subpoena the former prosecutors and agents. Then they would have to testify or take the Fifth. They would have to answer our questions about the yellow highlighting. They would have to explain their surgical omissions from the *Brady* letter Ruemmler signed. Chief Judge Alex Kozinski or Judge Betty Fletcher of the Ninth Circuit, whose opinions we had cited more than once, would have rearranged the anatomy of the prosecutors by now.

We enlisted the help of noted Houston attorney Daniel K. Hedges to work with us as local counsel in preparation for Jim's second trial and the misconduct hearing. Dan was a former US attorney for the Southern District of Texas with a stellar reputation. Dan and I wrote another and more lengthy letter to Attorney General Holder, and again requested an independent review of the case. We attached exhibits that included the yellow highlighting and had the letter hand-delivered to Holder and the chief at the Public Integrity Section of the department. Like Stevens's attorneys, we never received a response.

In the meantime, we could hardly wait for that hearing and began preparing immediately. We planned to subpoena documents and witnesses.

We still needed the government's notes of their interviews of Merrill counsel Zrike and Dolan. We had found huge discrepancies between the notes we had of Fastow, McMahon, and others, and what the task force had disclosed. We were certain Stokes was still hiding exculpatory evidence—despite the pressure from the *Stevens* case, the Schuelke investigation, and the protestations of "change" in the department. Like Judge Sullivan in *Stevens,* we could no longer believe anything the prosecutors said.

By 2010, the statute of limitations had expired, so no one else could be prosecuted on Enron issues. The task force had been disbanded. Witnesses were starting to talk to us—both about the validity of the Barge transaction and how the task force kept them in constant fear of being indicted if they said anything that contradicted the prosecutors' view of the facts and the case.

We had plenty of evidence that what the witnesses were telling us was true—both as to the transaction and the prosecutors' threats of perjury charges. Weissmann and team had indicted both Jim and Bill Fuhs for perjury or false statements and obstruction. Before the 2004 trial, however, Fuhs had been able to get those charges separated from the trial with Bayly, Brown, and Furst. After Fuhs was convicted of the conspiracy and wire fraud—and before the Fifth Circuit acquitted him—the task force dismissed the false statement and obstruction charges against Fuhs. And after the June trial date was postponed to August because of the revelation that Fastow said there was no guarantee, the task force superseded the indictment to add the two wire fraud counts against all the defendants and a false statement count against Enron employee Dan Boyle. That increased the stakes and likely the sentences for all of them tremendously. The task force was notorious for upping the ante for anyone who didn't collapse under their initial charges and threats.

According to the task force, whatever the prosecutors said was true and what anyone else said was perjury, obstruction of justice, or a false statement, punishable by years in prison and heavy fines. Wasn't that Nixon's self-rationalizing world view? If the president said it, it was the law—or something along those lines.

Every now and then, encouraging information would leak out from the Schuelke investigation of the Stevens prosecutors. We knew that he was deposing lots of witnesses under oath and interviewing others, and that he had access to internal department communications that we suspected would be quite revealing. If we could get the same, we knew we would find even more egregious and deliberate misconduct. It just wasn't possible to accidentally omit the precise exculpatory words or the most incriminating statements from a yellow-highlighted sentence. We anxiously awaited the Schuelke report—as did the rest of the lawyers in the country.

Then we got our first possible big break with a key witness. Well-known Houston attorney Tom Kirkendall and Jeff McMahon agreed to meet with us. McMahon had lived under task force threat of indictment for five years, despite the fact that Fastow and Skilling had demoted him from the treasurer's position because he disagreed with Fastow, would not do his bidding, and insisted they follow the rules. Like a scene from a movie, Dan Hedges and I met Jeff McMahon and Tom Kirkendall for dinner in a dark corner of a downtown Houston restaurant. McMahon was intelligent, professional, and articulate—quite likable. He would be a stellar witness.

Dan and I were filled with questions. Ruemmler had told the jury, "McMahon was the key." Well here we were, sitting with the key, and it turned out he really was.

Jeff McMahon was unequivocal as he always had been: there was no guarantee in the Barge case. He did not make one to begin with, and Fastow did not make one or ratify anything on the phone call. McMahon was also on that Fastow–Bayly call on December 23, 1999. There was no guarantee to Merrill. McMahon had consistently opposed guarantees and buybacks. Neither he nor Fastow made one to Merrill regarding the barges. The whole purpose of the deal was to unload some of Enron's risk and get some of its money out of that risky venture.

Even more importantly, he said he had told the government repeatedly—as far back as 2002—that there was no guarantee. He also confirmed that he had told the government that Glisan had lied when he testified against the Merrill defendants in this prosecution and claimed there was a guarantee. McMahon and Fastow had only agreed to use best efforts to remarket the barges as soon as possible.

Both of these crucial facts were confirmed by the yellow-highlighted notes that Stokes had given us. Even the raw notes of government agents' interviews with Fastow from 2004 corroborated what McMahon was telling us here at dinner in 2010. For McMahon and Fastow to agree on anything was an event that rivaled the perfect alignment of all the planets.

Even if McMahon were our only witness, he shot down the government's entire case and undermined every witness who only had hearsay testimony. McMahon was both the purported original guarantor and the one who heard what Fastow said on the phone call. Ruemmler was right—McMahon was "the key." Jeff McMahon was the key to Jim's vindication, exoneration, and freedom.

In addition, of great significance was the reality that the task force never prosecuted McMahon for making "the guarantee"—or anything else. The SEC had settled its civil complaint with him. The task force intensified its threats of indictment against him before and during the Barge trial to keep him from testifying for the defense. McMahon was shocked and appalled at what the prosecutors had claimed he said. It was all their lie.

The big question remained: Would he testify for Brown either at the retrial or at a hearing on a motion for new trial?

Dan and I inhaled and waited for the answer. We didn't have to wait long. McMahon had a simple answer. "If I am subpoenaed, I would have to testify truthfully."

That said it all. Dan and I relished the thought of putting him on the witness stand and getting Jim Brown the dismissal or acquittal that he deserved. We all wanted Jim's name cleared of any allegations of wrongdoing.

We also thought Werlein's eyes would be opened by the charts that we had filed with our motion to dismiss for prosecutorial misconduct. We showed what Ruemmler, Friedrich, and Hemann said at trial on the left side and the evidence they hid on the right side. It was beyond dispute that they hid every word from the key witnesses that contradicted what they told the jury. We were ready for the hearing Werlein had promised when he denied our Speedy Trial motion.

By this time, our trial date of August 2 was only a few months away, and we had firmly refused to waive any speedy trial issues. We had to force Stokes's hand. Every instinct I had told me that Stokes and his puppet master were taking perverse pleasure in dragging Jim through as much anxiety, turmoil, and expense as they could possibly inflict on him and his family. Stokes's voice just dripped with sarcasm or disdain any time he spoke to us. We had given him and his buddies on the task force hell. Stokes still refused even to agree to proceed to have Jim resentenced on the perjury and obstruction convictions. Anything we offered, he opposed, and he vehemently opposed a hearing on our motion for new trial.

Stokes filed the government's brief opposing our motion to dismiss for egregious prosecutorial misconduct without so much as a mention of the prosecutors' highlighting or the key words Ruemmler had left out of the *Brady* letter. Stokes just ignored all of it. He said the task force's pre-trial disclosures were "adequate," and anything recently produced wasn't "material" to Jim's defense; there was so much evidence of Jim's guilt.

We expected any day to receive a notice of the hearing on our motion. Instead of receiving a setting for a hearing, however, we were set for a pretrial conference to be held in Houston on June 24—less than six weeks before the scheduled trial date. A pretrial conference is where the attorneys and the judge usually discuss the plan for trying the case, submit jury instructions, and tend to the details to get ready for the trial itself. It's not a hearing with witnesses, testimony, evidence, or arguments.

June 24 was a blistering hot, muggy day in Houston—the kind where everyone sweats as soon as they step out of the air conditioning. We were meeting first in the beautiful offices of Porter Hedges, over-looking downtown Houston, before heading over to the courthouse together. Ironically the Porter Hedges offices had a fabulous view that included the skyscraper that was left as a shell when Enron imploded. As Jim, Nancy, Dan, Torrence, and I collected in the conference room, my BlackBerry buzzed. The Supreme Court had just handed down the *Skilling* decision. I had to scroll a bit to get the gist, even from the summary. Everyone huddled around.

Sure enough, the Supreme Court reversed the task force, Houston District Judge Sim Lake, and the Fifth Circuit yet again. Dan's legal assistant scurried to print out the lengthy opinions—one for each of us and Judge Werlein—and we began devouring them.

The Supreme Court reversed only the conspiracy count charging the "honest services" wire fraud, like the Fifth Circuit had reversed in Jim's case originally, but it remanded the rest of the case to the Fifth Circuit. The Supreme Court tasked the Fifth Circuit with sorting the extent and effect the honest services reversal would have on Skilling's convictions on eighteen other counts. The Supreme Court decision did finally make clear, however, that bribery and kickbacks were required to prove an "honest services" violation. The Supreme Court also issued its opinions in the *Black* and *Weyhrauch* cases, argued four months before *Skilling*. In *Black v. United States*, Conrad Black and other executives of Hollinger International had been convicted of mail fraud on alternative theories, including that they had deprived the company and its shareholders of the "intangible right to honest services." As a result of its decision in *Skilling* and consistent with the justices' questions and concerns at the oral arguments, the Supreme Court found that the honest services fraud instruction given to the jury in Black's case was incorrect. It therefore vacated and remanded the case. The third case, *Weyhrauch v. United States*, was also vacated and remanded in a one-sentence *per curiam* opinion based on the court's decision in *Skilling*. Weyhrauch, a former member of the Alaska legislature, had been prosecuted by Marsh and PIN in Operation Polar Pen.

I felt a quick glow of personal vindication in this decision. As I read Justice Ginsburg's majority opinion, I smiled as I recalled my meetings with other counsel in New York and DC. We had come a long way, and it had taken a ridiculously long time to get there. The Supreme Court had adopted the position that I had identified and argued for six years. Had it not been for my tenacity and relentless determination to brief the issue for *Brown*, the entire appeal could have been lost. We had made an important difference in the law that benefited all of these defendants who had been convicted on the department's bogus and continued "honest services" charges.

Torrence and Dan were buzzing with comments as they each read the decision as fast as they could. We had only a few minutes before we had to leave for the hearing.

As I snapped back to the crisis of the moment—preparation for the pretrial conference—I realized that this decision also torpedoed the government's newfangled theory that Jim was guilty on the same conspiracy and wire fraud indictment because "material economic information" was "property" within the meaning of a traditional wire fraud charge that requires the government to prove that a defendant schemed to defraud someone of their money or property. Once again, it didn't matter to the department that no case law supported that argument in the context of this case. And true to form, Werlein had already agreed with the government and denied our motion to dismiss the indictment for failure to state an offense. This decision made it even more obvious that Werlein was wrong. The Supreme Court had just gutted the prosecution even more.

We gathered up our briefcases and copies of the *Skilling* opinion—still warm from the printer—and made our way over to the federal courthouse for this pretrial conference. We took Houston's air-conditioned, shop-and-restaurant-lined underground tunnel walkways as much as we could to stay out of the sweltering heat. By the time we walked across the street to the federal court building, we were all soaked with perspiration.

Stokes and Stieglitz had an office in the building, so the two prosecutors appeared for the pretrial conference fresh as daisies.

Werlein hit the bench. He didn't even call the case. Stokes spoke first.

"Good morning, Your Honor. Patrick Stokes and Albert Stieglitz for the United States."

Judge Werlein responded, "Good morning, sir."

Dan Hedges was already standing and announced for us. "Dan Hedges, Sidney Powell, and Torrence Lewis for Defendant James Brown, and Mr. and Mrs. Brown are here."

Werlein's tone was icy. "All right. Well, we've got all kinds of motions pending. The government has sent me a paper suggesting how they would like to see this prioritized with respect to the motion for new trial. What's the defendant's position?"

Torrence and I cast a knowing sideways glance at each other. The government had gotten to him *ex parte* (without us) again. They hadn't even provided us a copy of the "paper."

Dan, the utmost professional, was trying to assume the best. "Your Honor, I know you've been on the bench this morning. I'm not sure if the court is aware that the Supreme Court issued its decision in the *Skilling* case this morning."

Werlein snapped, "Yes, I saw that."

"Would the court like a copy?" Dan inquired.

Werlein's reply gave himself away. "Well, I haven't printed it out. Yes. Thank you. Does it have any bearing on us?"

The conversation on that point went downhill from there. Stokes told Werlein it was "a nonissue."

That was all Werlein needed. "Well, let's put that on one side here. The government has urged that I give first attention to the defendant's motion for new trial on Counts Four and Five. What—how does the defendant wish to prioritize these things?"

Dan was perplexed. "Your Honor, really the issue here is what they meant by that somewhat vague motion that they filed. They said depending on how the court rules, the rest of their handling of the case is going to be affected. It's kind of hard for us to respond to that unless we know what they mean by that."

Werlein glowered at Dan. I hated it, but I was glad Dan was seeing it firsthand. It was hard to believe if you didn't see it.

"Have you all not had conversations still?" Werlein asked as if pain-stricken.

Dan was firm, but respectful. "We have."

Werlein responded, "Well, I guess they told you, then, all—"

"No, they didn't, Your Honor," Dan replied.

Werlein was furious—with us. "Well I don't know what you want to tell me, but what's your—tell me where we are, folks."

Stokes sucked right up. "Sure, Your Honor."

Werlein continued chastising us. "Seems like every time I'm with this group, it seems like the ships passing in the dark and it's sort of a case unlike any other, in terms of a lawyer's apparent inability to talk about their positions."

Dan took that one on. He and I had both reached out to Stokes several times. "Your Honor, I was the one who initiated the conversation. I called Mr. Stokes last week. We made a five-part proposal to them, Your Honor. And while they certainly did not agree to any of it, they only expressed specific objections to one of the parts. If we could resolve the other four parts and just let things go forward on that one part, it would greatly narrow the scope of the case and expedite the resolution of it."

"Does that require attention to a particular motion from your standpoint?"

Dan said, "The very motion that you just mentioned, Your Honor, the motion for new trial, Counts Four and Five."

"So both of you would feel that that would be something that I should give priority of attention to?"

We'd only been asking for a new trial for approximately three years—with mounting, shocking evidence of how bad the first trial and the prosecutorial misconduct were. And, not to mention, Werlein had denied our Speedy Trial Act dismissal because our motion for new trial required a hearing.

Dan stepped in quickly. "Yes, Your Honor. And if the court is inclined to grant the motion, we would join in their motion for an expedited ruling on it. If the court is still considering denying the motion, we would need some time to prepare for a hearing and present witnesses and, you know, make a full-blown record of it."

Werlein leaned forward and glared over his glasses at Dan.

"Well tell me what you mean by that? Whether—this—what kind of full-blown hearing do you contemplate? Because there are not always full-blown hearings on motions for new trial."

Dan responded, "No. I don't think it would be that lengthy a hearing, Your Honor, but what we have now is we've had access to witnesses and access to documents which we did not have at the time of the trial."

Even though Werlein claimed to be burdened by all our briefing, he queried, "Well, hasn't that been submitted in these voluminous papers?" If he had read our briefing, he would have known the answer.

Dan explained, "Some of it has and some of it has not. We have some witnesses that we still have not talked to but we are in process of arranging through their attorneys to talk to them. They're some of the people who were on the very call that Mr. Brown was convicted of misrepresenting to the grand jury. These are the people who were there and can say what really happened. And I would think that, you know, that belongs in the record."

Stokes was fidgeting and nervous. He was on the verge of going apoplectic at the thought of a hearing on any of the misconduct issues.

Stokes hastily interrupted. "In terms of a hearing, we think a hearing is absolutely unnecessary. . . . The Fifth Circuit has found that these factual issues are not matters that arise to the level of being a *Brady* violation, and quite the contrary, at times inculpatory or consistent with the government's theory. . . . We certainly don't see any need to bring in witnesses and, you know, have direct and cross-examination of folks on the very issues that everybody we think understands . . . Mr. McMahon, his lawyer, filed a—sent two letters: one to the Department of Justice, one to the SEC. The question is simply whether or not that letter, in and of itself, or those two letters, in and of themselves, should result in a new trial. . . . We intend to vigorously dispute the defense claims of government misconduct."

Dan stepped in before Stokes had heart failure. "Your Honor, if I can maybe take a little—the emotion out of this. Another way of looking at this motion for new trial is not necessarily just *Brady* violations, but sort of flip it over and say it's essentially newly discovered evidence. . . . And McMahon's supposedly the person who made the supposed guarantee. He will testify that he did not make any such guarantee. And I would think that is something that deserves to be on the record and heard and considered by the court."

Stokes was visibly terrified and anxious. "Your Honor, that is on the record. It was disclosed pretrial, and it's in the letters that his lawyer submitted to the Department of Justice and the SEC. . . . We'll stipulate that he would say that. From our perspective, we don't need to waste anymore of the court's time putting on evidence. We disclosed all this pretrial. This is just another effort by the defense to drag all of this out. This can be decided on the papers that have already been filed."

Stokes was fortunate a lightning bolt didn't come from the sky to strike him dead. I'd kept silent as long as I could. They had never disclosed the letters McMahon had written to the SEC and Department of Justice. I chimed in. "But what we also expect Mr. McMahon to say is that he would have been a witness for Brown in the first trial, except he was an unindicted coconspirator at the time and couldn't testify because of repeated threats of indictment by the government. Mr. McMahon was never indicted by the government. Mr. McMahon was supposedly the maker of the first guarantee and the participant in the Fastow phone call where that guarantee was allegedly ratified. He will testify affirmatively that there was no guarantee at either place. On top of that, he told the government those very facts long ago and they hid them from us."

Werlein tried to shut me up. "Well that was all argued to the jury at the first trial. There was no guarantee made."

I wasn't finished, and my tone was louder and angrier. "But without any evidence to support it."

Werlein tried again, "No, there was—"

I kept right on. "We weren't allowed to introduce even the evidence we did have from those witnesses at the first trial. And Brown's motion for new trial has not been addressed by the Fifth Circuit in any way, shape, or form."

Stokes cut in to argue our request was untimely, and there should not be a hearing because it was our fault we didn't raise this issue earlier. He was frantic: "This is more than three years after the trial; the defense for the first time today raised this issue."

"Not when it's just disclosed in violation of *Brady*, and the *Brady* material was withheld in the first trial," I retorted.

Dan chimed in too. "Yes. It's somewhat ironic for them to say that we waited too long to bring up information that they withheld from us all this time."

Stokes looked bewildered and was coming unglued. "Judge, Sidney indicated they got these notes from the witness—not from the government. Obviously that can't be *Brady*."

I had never heard him use my first name in any setting, and I didn't know where Stokes pulled that one from, but it was wrong on law and facts. The McMahon letters we finally did obtain—only from McMahon's counsel. But our source of any information had nothing to do with whether it was favorable to the defense or "*Brady*." The prosecutors violated *Brady* when they failed to disclose favorable evidence long ago—since 2002—and sent four men to prison while they hid it all. This argument sounded like Friedrich for sure.

I replied, "No. The McMahon notes we just received from the government on March 31 of this year."

Werlein looked puzzled and asked a question I still don't understand. "Which government?"

"This government," I all but shouted as I pointed to Patrick Stokes. "The production Mr. Stokes made on March 31 of this year included—"

Stokes suddenly became very pale and shaky. He looked like he might puke. "But I didn't—"

"Yes, you did," I countered. "It's in your letter of March 13 or so that we received on March 31."

Werlein suddenly realized, like Stokes, that Stokes had revealed something accidentally. "Well you've given it up now," the judge said.

Stokes tried to argue the original prosecutors had disclosed all of that, which was such a bald-faced lie it only made me angrier. Dan was trying to calm me down. Torrence was afraid I'd get held in contempt of court. I didn't care if I did.

Stokes accused us of wanting delay and was virtually begging. "We just don't—we're not interested in putting this off for a hearing to allow the defense to explore issues that are already well documented in the record. We think the record is perfectly sufficient for ruling on every one of these issues."

We had no intention of seeking delay. We'd been trying to end this for years. I wanted to make that clear.

"We're not asking for delay in the trial, Your Honor. We're perfectly prepared to go to trial on August 2 on the conspiracy and wire fraud counts. We're just asking for a full hearing at which we can make a record on all of the exculpatory evidence that the government withheld from us in the first trial or prohibited us from using by their ridiculous naming of one hundred people as unindicted coconspirators. Brown is entitled to a new trial on the perjury and obstruction counts. We didn't have access to any of these witnesses on the telephone call before the trial because the government was threatening to indict every one of them to keep them from testifying in our defense. And the same is true with respect to Fastow. And now we have information that Fastow was doped up on drugs when he testified in the Skilling trial. So there are questions about the veracity of his. . . ."

Werlein raised his eyebrows at the mention of Fastow being on drugs during the Skilling trial, and Stokes looked squeamish again.

I didn't even stop to breathe I was so fired up. "The court knows that we only recently received the raw notes of the government's thousands of hours of interviews of Fastow who supposedly used some kind of magic language and ratified the guarantee McMahon supposedly made. But the notes corroborate Jim Brown's defense and his grand jury testimony that there never was a guarantee—only an agreement to use best efforts to remarket the barges. So the Fastow raw notes— that we have now and that the government fought for years to hide from us—state that Fastow made no promise. He made a best-efforts representation, which was completely omitted from the government's *Brady* disclosure in Barge 1. Even Fastow's raw notes confirm what Mr. Brown told the grand jury was true."

I kept going. "The same is going to be true of the evidence from McMahon. . . . There's direct evidence now that what Jim Brown said was true, that was withheld from us by the government in the first trial. And we deserve a hearing at which we can present witnesses to make that record for reversal on Counts Four and Five—the perjury and obstruction counts."

Werlein was visibly uncomfortable. He managed to recall, "The defense called Katherine Zrike in the trial," as if that was supposed to solve the problem of all the evidence that the prosecutors had hidden as to Fastow, McMahon, and others.

"She did testify, Your Honor, but we didn't have the full information of what she knew, including that she had tried to negotiate the best-efforts agreement in the contract, and Vinson & Elkins [Werlein's former law firm] had kept it out because they did not even want that much risk retained by Enron."

Werlein was grasping for straws. "Well she's testified in this matter. There's no new evidence with respect to her."

"Yes, there is," I replied with increasing exasperation and ire. "The government held back significant evidence that kept the defense lawyers from having any idea of what they should ask her. And the law is that the defense is not required to call a witness 'blind' without knowing what she has to say."

Dan heard my rising anger and frustration with this attempted whitewash and chimed in to let me breathe and calm down. "Evidence was withheld from us. So it's now newly discovered by us. Of course, it's not newly discovered by the government. It's newly discovered by us because they withheld it from us. . . . We could not be held to 'we should have known it,' because it was specifically being withheld from us. So, Your Honor, they are two separate standards, for 'newly discovered evidence' and *Brady* violations, and we should be entitled to use both of them."

Werlein was clueless, another indication that he had not looked at anything we had filed—not even the few pages of simple charts in black, white, and yellow. "What does this evidence consist of?"

Dan and I both responded. "It consists of the raw notes of the FBI interviews of witnesses. It consists of what will be the testimony of those witnesses. They did not testify at trial because they were under threat of indictment if they testified to anything contrary to the government's position."

Werlein was arguing for Stokes now. "That's not so. Ms. Zrike testified at this—at the trial, I well remember. She was a very good witness for the defendants."

I blasted back. "There are a number of things that have come to light that Katherine Zrike had knowledge of that were not included in the first trial because the defense lawyers didn't know about them and the government had withheld them. We also have the testimony of Merrill counsel Dolan, who was even more involved in the negotiations than Katherine Zrike was. He was unavailable to us at the first trial because of the unindicted coconspirators and threats that Merrill Lynch was under at the time. And Alan Hoffman who wasn't even listed as a *Brady* witness by the government or as having any *Brady* material. There's substantial *Brady* material that we found from Alan Hoffman who was counsel for Merrill Lynch, outside counsel negotiating with Enron over the terms of the transaction. And all the lawyers for both sides knew about the best-efforts representation, but Vinson & Elkins—Enron's counsel—decided that it should not be included in the deal documents. They wanted to make sure that Enron did not retain any risk in the transaction. Everyone understood Enron was going to transfer its risk and Merrill was going to bear its risk of loss. Mr. Brown did not receive a fair trial the first time. And we need a hearing on the motion for new trial to put all this evidence in the record."

Werlein was really astute. "Well it does sound like you're just wanting to retry that issue."

I couldn't help myself. "That's the purpose of a motion for new trial. Mr. Brown is entitled to a new trial on the perjury and obstruction charges."

Stokes was enjoying having the judge argue the government's position for him—with even more preposterous and irrelevant assertions. "You're unable to distinguish what the new evidence is from what you claim a *Brady* violation is," the judge accused.

Dan tried again, beginning to sound frustrated now too. "Well, the evidence is the same, Your Honor, that evidence constitutes two different wrongs and two different bases for a motion for new trial. The evidence is the same, Your Honor. Everything they hid before the first trial that tells what really happened in this transaction."

I jumped in again with an example I hoped Werlein might grasp. "For example, Kelly Boots was going to testify for the defense in the first trial. She was with Fastow in his office when he supposedly ratified the McMahon guarantee. In opening statements, the prosecutors said they were going to call her as a witness. Then the defense said in its opening that we were glad they were, and that she would testify Fastow didn't say anything that anyone could think was a guarantee. Then all of a sudden, we learn that the prosecution dropped her as a witness and scared her to death. She comes to the courthouse, is terrified to get on the witness stand, and at the last minute told us she was going to take the Fifth Amendment. . . . We expect that she will testify that the task force left her with the clear impression that they would indict her for perjury if she testified for the defense in that trial."

I implored Werlein to realize what had happened here. "Everybody that was on the Fastow–Bayly call when Fastow supposedly ratified the McMahon guarantee and McMahon himself now, is willing to testify to what really happened on the phone call. And they're all consistent with what Mr. Brown told the grand jury. They all told the prosecutors that long before the first trial, and Weissmann, Ruemmler, Friedrich, and Hemann hid it from us. We need to make a record of that."

Stokes jumped in again to claim that the prosecutors provided all of this information in their *Brady* disclosures before the trial in 2004, and that "we just don't see the need to call these witnesses and have a hearing on the very issues where the facts are already before the court and we can discuss them and debate them today as to the meaning of those facts under the law." Stokes rebuked us for our "sensationalistic claims about what the government withheld" and our "conjecture there are *Brady* violations."

Completely exasperated, I turned to one last example. Werlein had sent Bill Fuhs to prison for three years, denying him bail pending appeal and denying two emergency motions to stay his reporting date, while the prosecutors claimed there was no substantial issue for appeal. Werlein agreed with them—refusing to consider any possibility that he had made any error in the trial. Finally, after Fuhs spent eight months in a maximum-security "hellhole" of a prison, the Fifth Circuit acquitted him completely. Fuhs never should have been indicted or tried—much less imprisoned.

The highlighted FBI interview form 302 we had finally been given regarding Merrill counsel Dolan was stunning in its revelations. The prosecutors had inserted language into their "disclosure" about Dolan's statements that minimized or altered anything that was exculpatory, and they made things sound inculpatory that were not. Even worse, they had highlighted but omitted from their "summary" the crucial fact that it was Merrill's in-house counsel Dolan—not Fuhs—who altered the engagement letter to make sure the transaction was lawful and was not a "parking transaction."

Dan also tried to explain how bad this was to this judge who had not looked at any of the material we submitted and didn't want to hear it. Dan explained that the statements the prosecutors carved out of their summary "just completely change the whole nature of the testimony. So I think the only fair thing to do. I think that the court needs to hear some of what was done in this case."

Reiterating his inattention to our briefs, Werlein asked, "Have you submitted those comparisons in writing between what you saw in the statement by Dolan and what you—"

I jumped in again, trying to impress upon him what they had all done to Bill Fuhs. "Yes, and Judge, it's something I think the court would benefit from by looking at visually. There are inserts that changed the nature of what Dolan actually said, and there are deletions. For example, if the court will recall from the first trial, when the government argued that Mr. Fuhs had edited the buyback language out of the engagement letter to hide it from the lawyers. That was the basis for their conviction of Bill Fuhs, whom the Fifth Circuit acquitted. It turns out that Merrill counsel Dolan made the changes to the engagement letter and instructed Jeff Wilson to make the changes to the engagement letter because that was not the deal."

Werlein actually paused for a moment—as if this point finally registered with him. I could see that he knew he had done wrong by Bill Fuhs even though he wouldn't admit it. He was a caring enough person that his determination to send Bill Fuhs to prison and deny four motions to stop it had to bother him to some extent. He looked at me and seemed to listen for the first time, so I continued.

The FBI 302 that Stokes finally produced—and the task force had yellow-highlighted—showed that "Attorney Dolan was aware of the ramification of a 'parking transaction.' He specifically referred to the need to avoid a 'parking transaction' . . . and the government deleted that from its disclosure to us before the Barge trial. They very carefully redacted and altered what Dolan actually said. . . . And Bill Fuhs spent eight months in a maximum-security prison because of testimony that the government misrepresented as to Dolan, and the misrepresentations that were made by the prosecution in the Barge 1 trial as to what had happened."

Just when we thought a little bit was sinking in, Werlein asked, "Fuhs asserts that the government was holding back things that it should have disclosed?"

Stokes quickly and nervously interjected, "Their claims about Mr. Fuhs are just simply completely immaterial to Mr. Brown." Stokes then obscured the truth by claiming that we already had this information, without acknowledging that the Dolan 302 itself, the McMahon raw notes, and the yellow highlighting had changed everything and altered the meaning of what little had been disclosed before the trial.

In his usual patronizing tone, Stokes repeatedly injected confusion, mischaracterizations, and outright lies. He was desperate to prevent a live hearing to flesh out this misconduct. "I don't think anybody could accuse Mr. Brown of not having taken his best shot. There are thousands of pages of 302s, transcripts, and other things for them to pluck statements out of and accuse the government of misconduct by simply taking things out of context, just what we think has happened here. But they've had months, even years, to do this. They're asking for more time to do more. Our position is that enough is enough. This record is what it is. It's very clear, the defense has had plenty of time to do this; nobody could accuse them of not having done a fulsome job of accusing the government of all sorts of misconduct and having pointed out in hundreds of thousands of pages of alleged misconduct. We have a record; we think the court can rule on that record. We just simply think it's time. . . . We clearly are reluctant to spend more time writing more briefs, arguing more over the same facts, putting on testimony on a factual record that is just simply as straightforward one as I've ever seen one in twelve years being a prosecutor." This was the longest sustained soliloquy that Stokes had ever made before Werlein. It was imperative that he foreclose any opportunity for us to subpoena the former Enron Task Force prosecutors from their new lofty perches.

Dan said once again that we did not want a delay of the trial date. "Of course, we're not asking for an extension of the trial date, Your Honor. So we're not asking for more time—we're simply asking for a two- or three-day hearing to hear motions."

I just had to add, "And just for the record, Your Honor, we have been asking for a hearing on the motion for new trial for more than two years. And there's even more that's come to light since our last briefing."

Werlein was aghast. "Well what do you mean there's more? What does it mean?"

"We received 141 pages of the raw notes of McMahon, and probably another fifty or sixty pages of raw notes of Tilney that have taken awhile to decipher. But we're in the process of doing that and obtaining significant information that wasn't disclosed before the 2004 trial. This motion is crucial. Mr. Brown served a year in prison for testimony that was true, that was literally true. And the government hid substantial amounts of evidence that showed that. At the same time Mr. Friedrich and Ms. Ruemmler were telling the court and the jury things based on hearsay-only evidence they presented to the jury, their assertions were directly refuted by firsthand evidence they withheld. And all we're asking for is a real hearing on our motion for new trial so that we can make a full record for appeal if necessary on those points."

This was really upsetting Werlein's plan. "How long will it take you to finish those notes and file a fifteen-page-limit brief?"

"Probably in two weeks. But that does not obviate the need for live testimony."

Werlein wasn't interested. "I understand your position, but it may, in evaluating whether I think I need live testimony."

I added, "I respectfully submit that the live hearing would be more helpful to the court than further briefing. I think it will be eye opening."

Werlein said, "Well I'm going to ask that you do that within fifteen pages, two weeks from now. I'll give the government two weeks from then, and you're limited to fifteen pages to respond."

I was beyond annoyed, and I spoke with great emphasis. "I assure you, I'm as tired of writing as you are of reading, but I'm still trying to give the court whatever it needs to get this case right. In terms of priorities, Judge, also I would encourage you to look at the motion to dismiss the indictment for facial invalidity, and the motions to reconsider that, because those motions are considerably shorter. They are correct legally, and particularly in light of *Skilling*, there is no kind of 'intangible right of shareholders to material economic information' that is going to survive as a valid crime to save this indictment again."

Stokes had just made up another "theory of a crime" that was even more lame than Friedrich and Ruemmler's original one that failed on appeal. He said the crime Brown committed—the "property" he took from Enron—was "material economic information." That concept wasn't defined in the wire fraud statute either, and like the allegation that Brown had committed wire fraud by depriving Enron of the "honest services of Andrew Fastow," all prior cases that found anyone guilty for stealing "material economic information" were cases in which the defendants had paid or received bribes or kickbacks.

As I began this argument, Werlein turned sideways in his chair, away from me, leaned back, picked up a document about fifteen pages long, and began flipping through it too fast to actually be reading it.

I kept talking regardless of whether he was listening. I was making a record for the court of appeals. "There's no new indictment. They simply took the old indictment, they whited out the reference to 'honest services,' and left in the bare-bones language of the statute that was necessarily recited to allege a wire fraud. Every case that the government cites that mentions 'material economic information' as any kind of property interest, rested on bribery and kickbacks. That is what the 'material economic information' was. Even *Wallach*, on which this court relied to rule against us, was a bribery and kickbacks case. There isn't a single precedent from any court or any circuit or any district that would support this court's prior decision on this point. I don't want the court to be misled about the law. This is an important issue—and the indictment should be dismissed for its failure to state an offense on its face. There's no allegation that Brown schemed to take anything that any court has recognized as 'money or property,' which is required to allege and prove a crime of wire fraud."

Werlein swung around in his chair and declared, "All right. Thank you. I looked back over this order that I did while you've been arguing, and I'm persuaded not to reconsider that ruling, and therefore that motion is denied."

Stokes caught on quickly. He could just go ahead right now, and the court would rule in his favor on each of the pending motions. "If the court wants to rule from the bench today, oral argument will permit the court to simply rule on all the pending motions."

Werlein didn't even look up as he said, "Thank you. I'm denying that motion for reconsideration at Document Number 1158."

That said it all. So much for taking any time to read any of the cases or actually thinking about the arguments or the law.

Then they turned to the motion we had filed contending that the Justice Department was treating Brown worse than his codefendants, punishing him for refusing to drop the misconduct charges against Ruemmler, Friedrich, Weissmann, and Hemann. This motion incensed Stokes and Werlein, and they both distorted its meaning and import. Werlein was outraged. "What about that? You're contending that they put a mole up there and got a plant into the Justice Department?"

"No, Your Honor," I replied calmly. "The motion simply states the facts that exist in the case, and that is that Mr. Lanny Breuer, who is the assistant attorney general in charge of the entire criminal division of the Department of Justice, did in fact previously represent Mr. Bayly. Mr. Bayly has been freely dismissed by the government. We don't know the terms or conditions of the dismissal. We can't find out who made the decision, how it was made, or anything else. We're entitled to that information itself under *Brady*. And there doesn't have to be impropriety on Mr. Breuer's part. There only has to be discrimination, facial discrimination in the way that the government has treated Mr. Bayly, versus the way the government has pursued Mr. Brown. Mr. Brown was consistently described by the government as less culpable than Mr. Bayly throughout the first prosecution." That was clear in the record.

I continued, "But here, Mr. Bayly has been dismissed without prejudice on Counts One, Two, and Three. And Mr. Brown can't even get an offer from the government to resolve this. Mr. Brown has been treated very differently by the government than Mr. Bayly has been because Mr. Brown is still alleging that the task force prosecutors suppressed evidence that was favorable to the defense. There was government misconduct here. It is a constitutional and ethical violation. Mr. Brown is entitled to raise that, and the government is just dragging him through all this litigation. Jim Brown wants his good name back. He spent a year in prison on an indictment that doesn't allege an offense, while the government hid the evidence that showed he was innocent."

Werlein tried again to pressure us into settling the case. He did not want to address these issues at all.

Dan asked to respond. "I made a very detailed, very fair offer, a week ago and have not received any response whatsoever."

Stokes lied again. "Mr. Hedges did, I responded at that time and repeated the offer that I had made to Ms. Powell. I don't know if Ms. Powell—"

I had to speak up. "I never heard an offer. I have not, to this day, heard an offer."

Werlein chastised us. "This is not good conduct."

Stokes whined and blamed us. "Your Honor, I would only submit that I think you've seen that with Mr. Furst and Mr. Bayly we have not had that issue at all."

Werlein asked, "Is there any precedent to dismiss an indictment for prosecutorial misconduct where the case has already been reversed and he's got a new trial coming up?"

Dan tried to focus him on the correct posture of this case. "He doesn't have a new trial coming up on Counts Four and Five, Your Honor. Jim Brown stands convicted of perjury and obstruction of justice. These two counts are what we are asking for a new trial on. He already gets a new trial on the conspiracy and wire fraud counts, but he stands wrongly convicted for perjury and obstruction because of the evidence the prosecution hid."

I was barely masking my disgust. If only we had Emmet Sullivan. What I would have given for that. I explained that in cases of egregious misconduct like here, "the government generally steps up to the plate and does what it should do and dismisses the indictment itself, particularly when it is in a court like Judge Sullivan's" who appointed a special prosecutor to investigate. In *Stevens,* "the government dismissed on its own, rather than face a hearing that exposes all of the misconduct and the resulting adverse publicity that comes from that."

Werlein shifted gears. "Is there any more *Brady* material to be supplied to the defendant in advance of this new trial?"

Stokes almost choked. "I'm sorry. Is there any more that has been or will be?"

Werlein repeated, "Is there any more to be produced?"

Stokes claimed, straight-faced, "We've provided additional documents to defense, and we maintained in our production to them that this is not *Brady* material. We're simply providing this to them." According to Stokes, every time he gave us anything, we filed a motion and accused the prosecution "of something." He protested. "We're just trying to put it all out on the table to make it clear to the court. There's nothing to hide here. . . . We just want to get these issues litigated. . . . So if the defense comes forward and requests something else, we'll certainly consider it. . . ."

As I was expecting Zeus's thunderbolt to strike Stokes any second, he quickly hedged. "Now we do have notes for 302s. We have not produced those."

Of course, we had specifically and repeatedly asked for those very notes.

Stokes still claimed they had done more than required. "We provided them with 302s, transcripts, and things that frankly under the rules of discovery they don't get but we provided them things. And, of course, they come back and say that we've violated discovery rules and we've held things too long, so on and so forth. We recognize that. We're prepared to argue those things. So we have provided the defense the entirety of what we believe is discoverable. If they ask for something specific, we'll certainly look at it and consider it and turn it over. If it relates to this case, we're going to turn it over."

I jumped on that one. "The government has just represented that it has nothing to hide. We can identify for them the names of the witnesses that we would like the raw notes of. One of those particularly being Katherine Zrike, and that shouldn't be too much of a burden."

Stokes backtracked immediately. "We do not intend to provide notes of 302s unless, of course, the court orders us to do so. We're being generous to the extent defense has in the past requested 302s or grand jury transcripts or the transcripts of witnesses. But turning over the notes of 302s, that's not the practice, is our position."

This sounded just like Friedrich and was the refrain in the Stevens prosecution too. They'd given us more than we were entitled to, and none of it was *Brady*. They had turned over what they "believed" was discoverable. That was the crux of the problem. They were still hiding whatever they wanted to because only Stokes defined what was discoverable.

"Judge," I argued, "it's especially important that we obtain the raw notes of their interviews of Zrike, Dolan, and the Merrill in-house attorneys who worked on the deal because of the differences we found between raw notes and what was disclosed by the government before. The attorneys were crucial because it turns out they did know about the best-efforts representation and tried to document it, contrary to what Mr. Friedrich told the court and jury at the first trial. I'm talking about Katherine Zrike, Dolan, Hoffman—our own attorneys who were part of the transaction."

"Attorneys on the transaction?" Werlein asked in disbelief, as if he had never heard of such a thing. He didn't know or remember that much of the hidden *Brady* evidence in *Stevens* was found in the notes of the prosecutors themselves, and the new prosecutors produced those voluntarily. Neither Stokes nor Werlein had learned anything from the *Stevens* debacle yet—nor did either of them intend to.

Stokes couldn't stand it, so he completely mischaracterized our request and misstated the law. "What they're requesting is that we scour the files and provide evidence of who in the Department of Justice had those documents and what files they're in and provided their files and the Department of Justice attorneys' notes on that, we think there's simply no basis to that. . . . We are well within circuit precedent in not providing raw notes, with providing 302s. . . . Their broad allegations of prosecutorial misconduct that have been made incessantly in this case are not sufficient to trigger some sort of requirement that we turn over raw notes. We, again, vigorously dispute any claim that there's been misconduct here."

Werlein had heard more than he wanted, and he turned to the topic of the length of trial. Stokes told him the government would need seven to eight days for its witnesses. We figured about the same. Werlein wasn't happy. He moved the trial date to September 18.

He limited us to a "supplemental submission not to exceed fifteen pages along with whatever relevant, pertinent, and important exhibits need to be attached so that we don't try to—so as to help me focus upon what I need to examine, rather than everything under the sun that counsel may have examined." Then he would decide if he needed a hearing. He added, "As for the additional materials the defense has requested from the government, it's such a long list that I'm not going to order any."

We were asking for notes of interviews of three Merrill attorneys. I wish I could say we were surprised. The "pretrial conference" was over, and we no longer harbored any illusion that we would get the hearing on our motion for new trial because of the *Brady* violations—even though he had refused to dismiss the indictment pursuant to our

Speedy Trial Act motion because a hearing was "required." The fifteen-page supplement was all we were going to get.

– 18 –

THE END OF THE BEGINNING

We began our fifteen-page brief with a reminder that Werlein had denied our Speedy Trial dismissal because our motion for new trial "required a hearing." We made him even more simple charts of the yellow-highlighted exculpatory statements withheld by Ruemmler, Friedrich, Weissmann, and Hemann right beside their contradictory representations to the court and jury. It was irrefutable.

We explained the yellow highlighting, its significance, and the careful, surgical omissions that were made to hide the crucial evidence from the defense for up to eight years. The most egregious examples were in the statements of McMahon, Zrike, and Dolan. We showed Judge Werlein that the scale and audacity of the deceit by the task force prosecutors rivaled or exceeded the prosecutorial abuse in Senator Stevens's prosecution, for which Judge Sullivan appointed a special prosecutor. We again requested discovery, an evidentiary hearing, and a dismissal of all pending charges. The government filed its reply two weeks later. It never mentioned the yellow highlighting.

On August 23, 2010, we received a sixty-three-page opinion from Judge Werlein, denying our motion for new trial or even a hearing on it. At times, he was scathing in his rebukes of us and what he referred to as our "prolix" or overly lengthy briefing that we had "unloaded" on him. At the same time, he applauded the prosecutor's briefing as "rather laudable."

On the merits, Werlein was equally contemptuous, repeatedly accusing us of "taking out of context" the exculpatory statements that we had found only in the handwritten notes of agents' interviews of Fastow, McMahon, and others, or in testimony the prosecutors had hidden. These were the notes that the government had refused to disclose for years and that Werlein never actually reviewed before the trial. It took a lot of work for us to read them; they took extensive time to decipher with care and accuracy. Ruemmler, Friedrich, and the rest of the team had given him fifteen hundred pages.

Instead of recognizing what Ruemmler and Friedrich had highlighted before the trial as *Brady* information—so designated by the prosecutors' own markings—or viewing the notes from the perspective of a reasonable juror or from the perspective of a capable defense attorney, Werlein went to great trouble and creativity to posit incriminating alternatives for what the notes "meant." We thought that was a jury's job in a fair trial.

In his sixty-three pages, Werlein—like the prosecutors—never mentioned the prosecutors' highlighting. He ignored our arguments. He said that we had all the "information" to proceed to trial back in 2004, so anything that was disclosed later was "cumulative." Our arguments simply had "no merit," and the "failures" at the first trial to gather evidence (if there were any) were solely the fault of Brown's (and the other defendants') attorneys at trial. His opinion was even worse than we could have imagined.

We got ready for trial and loaded for bear. McMahon would testify. We served subpoenas on key witnesses. Torrence was already on the ground in Houston. I was getting ready to fly there for the trial only a few days away. We had hotel reservations to stay for three weeks. We were in full-blown trial mode.

I was at my desk when into my e-mail popped a motion from the prosecutors for a continuance of the trial. Stokes was asking the judge to continue the trial on the conspiracy and wire fraud counts because if Brown were successful on appeal of Werlein's denial of his motion for new trial, the department would want to retry Jim on all of the original five counts. The government was trying to suggest that this continuance would "serve the public interest."

We had been asking for our motion for new trial to be heard for three years, so that there could be just one trial, and at the last minute, Stokes pulled this tactic. More stalling meant more agony for Jim and more expense on both sides.

The last six months had been pure torture for Jim. My instincts told me that Stokes had done nothing to prepare for this trial and had just used the threat of trial for Counts One, Two, and Three and the threat of return to prison for three years on Counts Four and Five as leverage to intimidate Jim into dropping our misconduct claims. By this time, our claims threatened the law licenses of very powerful and high-profile people. Ruemmler, Friedrich, Weissmann, and Hemann, and then Spencer and Stokes had long hidden evidence that was favorable to the defense. Sadly no one had the integrity to admit it and to dismiss these charges against Jim as Holder had done (actually been forced to do) against Senator Stevens. They were supremely confident that Judge Werlein bore no resemblance to Judge Emmet Sullivan and that Werlein would protect them from exposure and the truth. Werlein's order proved them right.

The Supreme Court had already taken three of the Enron cases to reverse the Fifth Circuit and the task force's tactics. The prosecutors knew it wasn't likely to take another one.

We were ready to get Jim Brown's case tried. We felt very strongly that we could get Jim acquitted of the legally and factually empty conspiracy and wire fraud charges with all of the evidence the government had finally produced. There was no way that the task force had "accidentally" omitted the very language they had highlighted in 2004 before the trial or any of the other discussions of the "best-efforts" agreement.

I called Mark Smith, a young associate with Porter Hedges, who had been a police officer before going to law school. He was fearless. Dan Hedges had asked him to help us with the case. I tasked Mark with finding Ben Glisan, the task force's original star witness who had already been released from prison and still lived in the Houston area. Mark was to ask him what he had heard from the government and what he had to say now. I dispatched Torrence to locate Tina Trinkle.

My phone rang. It was Mark Smith.

"You're gonna love what I just learned."

"Tell me quick," I implored.

"I had a nice chat with Ben Glisan. He said he hadn't heard from anyone with the government in years."

"Really! I do wonder how they plan to prove their case when McMahon will testify for us, we have the Fastow notes, and they haven't even contacted their star witness from the Barge trial?"

I picked up the phone and called the Bureau of Prisons where Andrew Fastow was incarcerated. We were just a few days from trial. The officer told me that Fastow had received no visitors, and there were no orders to transfer him to Houston or anywhere else.

It wasn't much longer before Torrence called—breathless. "They haven't talked to Tina Trinkle in years."

"Wow," I said. "That sounds familiar. Mark said they haven't spoken with Glisan, and I just confirmed they aren't doing anything with Fastow. Looks to me like we've caught Stokes filing a motion for continuance as a terror tactic when he never intended to take this case to trial. They've just been screwing Jim over every way they can—and with the taxpayers' money. We need to file an opposition to their motion that 'outs' this abuse of the entire process, and we've got to get it filed now. We also need to try again to get Jim resentenced on Counts Four and Five to keep that from hanging over his head."

At the same time I was speaking with Torrence, an e-mail popped up that the court was scheduling a phone conference. We had to hurry to get our opposition filed with these facts before Werlein granted the government's motion. We filed a searing opposition to the continuance on September 13, 2010. We began: "The government has requested this continuance—only a few days before the third trial setting—not in the interest of justice, but because it has not prepared for trial. Brown is entitled to this scheduled disposition of counts involving activities which occurred almost eleven years ago. The interests of Brown, due process, and the public demand it."

Sparing no one's feelings at this stage, we wrote, "In effect and at base, the government is attempting to enlist this court in its strategy to harass Brown and at the expense of Brown's constitutional and statutory rights." We outlined the work we had done in preparation for trial less than a week away and documented everything that the government had not done. It was time for Stokes to put up or shut up. This was a calculated abuse of prosecutorial power—not to mention the taxpayer dollars wasted.

The phone conference began promptly the next day at 5:00 p.m. on Thursday, September 14. Trial was scheduled for Monday, September 18.

Judge Werlein began by noting the government's motion to continue the trial date and ours for resentencing to time-served on Counts Four and Five. Stokes took over, claiming that Jim's "convictions are final," and stating that the only way for Jim to get a new sentence would be to file an entirely different proceeding. I was glad no one could see my face turning purple. Yet again, Stokes parroted the ridiculous argument that Arnold Spencer had made.

Werlein commented, "All right."

I went ballistic. "That's absurd, Your Honor. You recognized when you addressed this issue earlier that Brown's sentence was 'bundled' and that the Fifth Circuit's decision in *United States v. Bass* requires that Mr. Brown be resentenced."

Werlein's tone was condescending. "Well in *Bass* I think that the sentence had not been affirmed as it is here."

My tone was angry. "Oh it had. And the Fifth Circuit even said that it had said too much in its prior decision, and it changed its prior decision to make plain that Bass needed to be resentenced."

Stokes repeated his mantra that Jim's only relief would be to file a collateral suit.

This was at least the third time this issue had been discussed, and Werlein was still lost. "Well I can go back and look at *Bass* again. And so there's no question that, as I understand it, the rule is that when one or more counts are reversed on conviction and you have a bundled sentence, that the practice is that there should be then an unbundled sentencing upon remand. What makes this different is that the court did more than affirm the convictions here. It affirmed the sentences on Counts Four and Five as well. Now, the sentence—"

I interrupted, imploring understanding. "But, Your Honor, the sentences were not an issue in the appeal. . . . Nothing about the sentences was addressed. And the government agreed that Mr. Brown should be resentenced before rehearing petitions were even filed, so there was no issue for the court of appeals—the government had agreed to Brown's resentencing."

Werlein cut me off. "Yes. Well I said all along, I think, that until the Fifth Circuit gives me additional instruction, which I imagine it might have intended to do originally but did not, I would expect they will give some further guidance on it; but I have to try to live within the constraints that have been imposed upon me by the appellate court at the present time."

God, I thought, *what I would have given for Judge Sullivan to have had this case—or any judge with common sense, fortitude, and a moral compass for which true North was fundamental fairness.*

Werlein changed the subject. "Now, the other motion is for continuance. Mr. Stokes, you indicate that you want to wait until after the appeal with respect to denial of retrial on Counts Four and Five that have been affirmed by the Fifth Circuit and that you apparently—I'm a little surprised that you're quite as apprehensive about what the court of appeals is going to do on my order, but. . . ."

Stokes stumbled over himself to fawn again. "Well I certainly don't want it to be read as being apprehensive about that. But certainly that is, you know, our view is that should the Fifth Circuit reverse the court's order, we would want to be in a position, if there is going to be a new trial, of having all counts tried at once. . . ."

"But," he continued, "this is in large measure an issue of resources to the extent that we are going to be—if we have to try one of those cases, we should try it all together, we think that's best for the court and the government and the defense. The issue now is that if the convictions are upheld on Counts Four and Five, we, frankly, don't see much reason to go forward with a trial on the other counts because, in effect, we think the felony convictions are there. And so, you know, we think, therefore, that not trying the case until that issue is resolved makes the most sense, Your Honor."

We'd tried for at least three years to get them to drop Counts One through Three or retry all five together. We'd even offered months earlier to let it all be determined by our appeal of the misconduct issues, so that none of us would have to litigate any other issues. No, Stokes rejected our offer.

Dan cut in before I could say what I was thinking. "I think the government itself has given us the best way to preserve resources of any; and that is . . . 'a ruling in advance of September 20, so that if the court denies the government's motion to continue, the United States may assess in a timely manner whether it intends to proceed to trial on Counts One through Three.' So I think a dismissal of Counts One through Three would save the most resources."

Werlein responded with more equivocation. "All right. Well I'm coming to that, Mr. Hedges. But first, as I understand it, the government has said that if the court's order denying new trial on Four and Five is affirmed by the court of appeals, I gather it does not intend to prosecute again Counts One, Two, and Three if I grant this continuance. Is that the position of the government, Mr. Stokes?"

"Your Honor," Stokes replied, also equivocating, "I say that that is the likely position only because that is certainly our intention. But until that happens, I'm a bit reluctant to bind the government on that issue since I don't know who the decision makers will be at that time. But that is certainly the sense; that is certainly the opinion of the government at this time, that's what we would do."

Here we had yet another admission that some unnamed puppet master was calling the shots—and yet another indication that Judge Sullivan's words evaporated from Holder's and the department's memory as soon as they were spoken.

Werlein spoke again. "The other question is the one suggested by Mr. Hedges; and that is, if I deny this motion for continuance, is the government going to prosecute on Counts One, Two, and Three next week or not?"

Stokes was still waffling. "Your Honor, I think it is unlikely, but I need to, once the court rules—and if the court denies the motion to continue—I need to get confirmation of that from others." Calling it "a resource issue," Stokes said the continuance was "the lesser of two evils" and "the most appropriate resolution at present, so that if . . . the court's order is reversed, then we are able to try everything. But if not, if the court denies the motion to continue, we just think that our chances on appeal are very high, and so we are likely to dismiss."

I couldn't be quiet any longer. This was unmitigated bullshit. "Your Honor, if the government wanted things tried together, they should not have opposed the court deciding our motion for new trial for the past three years because we could have proceeded then to get it resolved, and it could have been retried with this trial setting. But to come in now—"

Stokes cut me off in his most condescending tone. "That, of course, is just silly, Your Honor."

I continued, "A week before trial when we have gone through extensive preparation to get ready for this and then ask for a continuance with absolutely no legal or factual basis is just appalling."

Werlein stepped in to argue for Stokes and make a completely irrelevant point. "Well, as I recall, some time ago the defendants made representations to me about how there was a whole new world of discovery and all sorts of things had to be done and there were millions of more papers and everything else. And as I recall, defendant's last filing in support of a motion for new trial was not long before I ruled on it here three or four weeks ago."

I couldn't hold back. Spencer and then Stokes had dribbled out statements, notes, transcripts, and 302s piecemeal—deliberately and even accidentally for three years—fighting all the way. At the same time, Werlein would never order them to produce anything and ignored our motions. "We're ready for trial, Judge, and my point is that the government has long opposed deciding the issue."

Werlein said, "Well—"

I kept going, "Which would have enabled us to resolve all this a few years ago instead of wasting the court's time this year, putting us to all this preparation, and running up to the eve of trial. They've obviously known for some time that they weren't going to try Brown again on these three baseless counts."

Werlein was still defending the government. "Well I allowed—"

I was livid. "Counsel now knows they're willing to dismiss," Werlein interjected.

Werlein and I were talking over each other. Werlein was blaming the defense. He said, "I allowed the defendant the time it wanted to go into all of that stuff, and the filings continued to come from the defendant. We don't need to go back to that. This is what—"

I was hopping mad. "That's because they dribbled out pieces of *Brady* material to us over a period of three years. We still don't have it all, and the very fact that they've expressed—"

Now Werlein was getting angry with me, and I didn't give a flip. "Ms. Powell!" he chastised.

Dan exclaimed to calm me down. "Sidney, Sidney, let the judge speak."

Werlein barked, "Just hold up. What I understand that you're saying, Mr. Stokes, is that the government does not represent that in the event this motion for continuance is denied that it is going to trial on Monday on Counts One, Two, and Three. Is that correct?"

Stokes replied, "That is right, Your Honor. But what I would say is that if the court denies the motion to continue, I will get back to the court and the defense shortly confirming what the government's position will be. But we are inclined not to go to trial on Monday if that's the case."

"All right," Werlein said calmly, as if he had long known this plan, and it was no concern at all that the government had dragged us all through the last seven months of litigation and trial preparation on three counts it had never intended to retry. Someone had to have conceived this plan at least by the time the department voluntarily dismissed Bayly in January.

Werlein continued as if there were nothing unusual. "Now the defendant has also said, based upon the investigation that they have been doing and preparations that they have undertaken, that they're unable to find that the government has sent out any witness subpoenas or has otherwise contacted persons that would probably be important witnesses to this prosecution. Is that correct?"

Stokes chose his words very carefully, claiming that "we have spoken to witnesses in this case previously. We have contacted counsel. We have not subpoenaed witnesses for the Monday trial, recognizing that if, well, we have Andrew Fastow coming in for trial, but other witnesses that are in the area we have not subpoenaed, recognizing that our position is we are seeking a continuance or that we are likely to dismiss."

He confirmed our worst suspicions. They had done nothing to prepare for trial because he always knew he could run us up to the eve of trial and dismiss it. To Stokes and his never-identified master manipulator, it was a big game of chicken.

Stokes ratified the indefensible abuse. "You know, without going into too much detail, I think that it is very likely that if the court would deny our motion to continue that we would not proceed to trial. I think we have also made that—despite Ms. Powell's continued claims the government has acted in bad faith, I think we have made it very clear all along; that the court's ruling on the new trial motion could have an impact on whether there would be a trial in this case, and we are proceeding exactly in that way, as we've alerted the defense and the court in the past."

Did I hear that correctly? Stokes certainly had not told us he would dismiss it, but he just admitted he had told Werlein "all along."

Sure enough, that's what he said. He even repeated it. "So, no, we have not subpoenaed any witnesses; but if we had to go to trial, I think that we could actually do this. But since our announced intent for some time is that we did not want to go to trial on those counts because we believe that the Counts Four and Five are sufficient. . . ."

"All right," Werlein replied as nonchalantly as if he had known this for years.

Stokes had never announced to us his intent not to go to trial on Counts One through Three, but he just admitted he had shared this little tidbit with Judge Werlein for "some time." To the contrary, he had repeatedly threatened us with the retrial on Counts One through Three, while also trying and threatening to send Jim back to prison to serve three more years on Counts Four and Five.

Stokes said, "And I should say that we disagree with the defense. We think that, of course, the ends of justice exception does provide means for the court to do this." Stokes opined that two trials "would be an extraordinary waste of resources" and if there were a trial, Jim should be "subjected to the full range of evidence and potential punishment in the indictment."

Werlein asked, "Does anyone have anything additional to say on these motions?"

Stokes said, "No, Your Honor."

Dan and I said nothing. Nothing we said mattered anyway. If Werlein granted the continuance after we found them totally unprepared and they admitted it—and they admitted they were prepared to dismiss Counts One, Two, and Three—I would say something that would no doubt qualify as contempt of court. It would be worth it.

Werlein had another script ready, confirming to me his foreknowledge. "All right. I think that under a certain scenario, and there are some cases that I have consulted on this, *United States v. Dusenberry*, 246 Fed Sup 2nd, 802, Northern District of Ohio case; *United States v. Levassure*, 635 Fed Sup 251, Eastern District of New York, and *United States v. Patton*, Eastern District of Louisiana case, 501 Fed Sup, 182 in 1980."

I couldn't help but wonder how long he had his law clerks digging to find those old district court cases, two not even in this circuit. *Where was he going with this?* It sounded like he was actually considering granting the continuance. Just the thought of it smacked of all abdication of any judicial responsibility.

Werlein continued reading, "Under the circumstances, however, where the government has, as Mr. Stokes has correctly recalled and stated, the government has suggested in the past that it may not wish to prosecute Counts One, Two, and Three in the event that the motion for new trial on Four and Five prevailed on that, and further, in view of the present position of the government that it's going to review this and in likelihood, I think the word was, 'will not prosecute on One, Two, and Three,' then I do not find a sufficient basis at this time to hold that ends of justice would warrant an excludable delay; and accordingly, I am going to deny the motion for continuance."

My heart stopped pounding long enough for me to hear that Werlein was finally forced to deny the government's motion for continuance. He did not mention it as a reason; he was still protecting the government. But our opposition to Stokes's motion for continuance, having caught them unprepared for this trial only four days away, and the fact that we had forced Stokes to admit no trial preparation, left him with no viable alternative. He had to deny the motion.

Stokes had been playing a game, and we had caught him. He had done nothing to prepare for this trial, and he never intended to do so.

Finally Jim would be free of the horrible stress and anxiety of a retrial on Counts One through Three—the conspiracy and wire fraud charges on which the Enron Task Force had made up both the law and the facts to charge and convict the Merrill defendants in 2004. Finally.

Werlein continued reading in monotone. He denied our motion for resentencing based upon his determination that he did "not have jurisdiction to resentence, given the order and mandate the way it was written and came out from the court of appeals." He said he would sign an order denying the motion for continuance. He told Stokes, "If the government proceeds or expects to proceed, as you've indicated it probably will or likely would, Mr. Stokes, I would appreciate your advising my case manager as early as possible and, of course, out of courtesy opposing counsel."

Stokes cheerily piped up, "Absolutely, Your Honor. I will endeavor to get an answer on my end as quickly as possible, and then I will let everybody know."

Werlein casually commented, "Very well."

I wanted something more concrete to tell Jim. "Do you have any idea when that might be?"

They all ignored me.

Werlein asked rotely, "Is there anything further in this now today?"

Stokes responded, "I don't believe so, Your Honor."

So the hearing was over.

Torrence and I called Jim and Nancy.

Nancy was tense. "Jim isn't home. Did he grant the continuance?"

"No," I replied. "We caught them with their pants down. Stokes had to admit they had not contacted witnesses. He said they were not going to trial on Counts One through Three. He told the judge they will be dismissing those 'to save resources.' Because Werlein denied our motion for new trial on Counts Four and Five, they have those convictions."

"So just what does that mean?" Nancy asked.

"Counts One, Two, and Three will be dismissed forever. The conspiracy and wire fraud charges are gone, dead, over. Jim can never be placed in jeopardy for those again. Stokes will be moving to dismiss them within the next day or two. He has to check with his higher-ups first. But the big thing is there will be no trial—you are finished with all of that. We should get a new trial on Counts Four and Five from the Fifth Circuit, but I'm sure now that the government would dismiss those counts rather than try them again either. The bottom line is that once we got the yellow-highlighted materials, they had no case and were at great risk if they put on any witnesses. We now know they knew they had no case, and they hid it all. It's their case that was a sham—not the Barge deal."

"I can't believe this. I'm afraid to tell anyone," Nancy replied.

I reassured her. "Werlein is going to enter an order denying the continuance. He's still refusing to resentence Jim, so that will still have to be sorted out. But I promise you, the worst is over. Stokes will let the court know tomorrow that he will be dismissing. There is no way he is going to try this case now—or ever. This part is over. I promise."

Late the next morning, Stokes contacted us for our position on the government's motion to dismiss and then filed it with the court. The Browns had suffered and endured through all of that time, terror, bluster, anxiety, stress, and ravages for eight years of persecution by the Enron Task Force, Spencer, then Stokes—as directed by their master. Then after dragging out the torture and threats as long as they possibly could, the government just walked away. There would be no trial—no chance to get the truth out. We would not have an opportunity to hold them to their burden to even try to prove his guilt—much less an opportunity for us to prove his innocence and their prosecutorial misconduct.

– 19 –

The Last Chance

We had filed a notice of appeal immediately based on Werlein's diatribe denying Jim a new trial on the perjury and obstruction convictions—and denying even a hearing on the issues. We briefed the appeal with no extensions of time and headed to the Fifth Circuit for the third time. The perjury and obstruction counts were still hanging over Jim's head—for four years now. And we were still waiting for Schuelke's report on the Stevens investigation.

Just a few weeks later, on September 26, 2010, the legal world reeled upon news of Nicholas Marsh's tragic suicide. Many saw it as an admission of guilt or shame for his role in hiding exculpatory evidence in the *Stevens* case. It was a painful demonstration of the stress that being investigated and the specter of prosecution has on someone. Regardless it was a needless tragedy, too great a price to pay, and we all felt for his family and their unfathomable pain. Newspaper and Internet headlines across the country broadcast: "Ted Stevens's Prosecutor Dead in Apparent Suicide." It brought the prosecutorial misconduct and the department's incompetence to the forefront again.

Marsh's suicide caused me to admire Jim and Nancy even more. I couldn't imagine how they had the strength to go through all that they had endured for so many years. The stress had to be incomprehensibly extreme. It was hard on all of us, but the strength of our personal convictions that Jim was innocent and that the prosecutors had corrupted the entire process compelled us to continue fighting.

There was considerable speculation that Schuelke's investigation was bearing down on Marsh and that it did not look good for the former PIN attorney. We expected Schuelke's report to be issued any time.

On the political front, on June 2, 2011, President Obama announced that Kathryn Ruemmler would move up to White House counsel—the primary legal advisor to the president. Obama praised Ruemmler as "an outstanding lawyer with impeccable judgment."

The *Huffington Post* reported that she had been the "youngest member of the ten-lawyer Enron Task Force." It noted that she had "made the closing arguments in a case that resulted in five [sic] convictions of investment bankers who helped the energy corporation manipulate its books," but the article did not mention the extraordinary reversal. The *Huffington Post* also described Ruemmler as "a fierce member of the legal team that brought down" Lay and Skilling and reported that she had received the Attorney General's Award for Exceptional Service for her work on the Enron investigation. Former administration official Jamie Gorelick touted Ruemmler for knowing "the traditions and values" of the administration. She had been principal associate deputy attorney general since January 2009 and then principal deputy White House counsel.

The Fifth Circuit scheduled oral argument on our new trial appeal for *Brady* violations for July 5, 2011, in New Orleans. I was ready and waiting for this one.

A week before our argument in the Fifth Circuit, we learned that our panel was Judge Jerry Smith from Houston, Judge Leslie Southwick from Mississippi, and newly appointed Judge James Graves from Mississippi. We knew that Jerry Smith, whom I had worked with and argued before many times, had ruled against Skilling, but the issues in *Brown* were different in important ways. Our case now was limited to the new evidence and prosecutorial misconduct; Skilling never got that far. The facts of both cases were different also. Smith had already seen some of this case in the civil suit *Regents of University of California v. Credit Suisse First Boston (USA) Inc.*, in which he had held that these Merrill bankers owed no duty to Enron or its shareholders. It was hard to imagine that he would impose criminal liability in the face of all of this new evidence the government had finally produced, when, without it, he did not see any civil liability.

Moreover Judge Smith was a stickler for rules. He had been the judge responsible for the circuit clerk's office for a long time. He had even issued an order striking one of my briefs years earlier because, according to him, it had too many footnotes under the rules. He expected all rules to be followed. Having known, worked, and taught with Smith for years, I expected him to have fair questions, be open-minded about these important issues of prosecutorial misconduct, and have no tolerance for federal prosecutors who didn't follow the rules.

Judge Southwick had been on several panels in other cases I had argued. He had asked polite and thoughtful questions in those, and he was known and liked as a person and a judge. We expected him to look at this carefully and to be troubled by what he saw. I did not know Judge Graves at all, other than as having an excellent reputation. I had no clue what to expect from him, but my firm conviction was that anyone looking at the yellow highlighting, juxtaposed against the prosecutors' case, would have to know there was a serious problem with the prosecutors' conduct here.

I anticipated—indeed, I had to believe—that they would be offended by what they saw. It seemed impossible to explain away information the prosecutors themselves had specifically identified as *Brady* before the trial and could only have deliberately hidden. And there was no reason to explain it away. Jim had already served a full prison sentence on those two counts. They could reverse the convictions, and the government would still have had its pound of flesh. At a minimum, we thought they would order Werlein to give us a full hearing on our motion for new trial. Faced with that prospect, we knew the government would dismiss the perjury and obstruction counts, and Jim would no longer have a conviction. These now politically powerful former prosecutors were not about to face possible perjury and obstruction charges themselves, which they would risk if they testified and lied. And they certainly couldn't get on a witness stand and tell the truth: they would face disbarment and their high-flying careers would end.

Federal circuit judges are only one notch below the United States Supreme Court. Many Supreme Court justices, including Chief Justice Roberts and Justices Breyer, Ginsburg, Kennedy, Scalia, and Sotomayor, first sat on a circuit court of appeals. Circuit judges are not appointed or even recommended by the president without being vetted by White House counsel and investigated thoroughly by the FBI. The Justice Department also plays a significant role. Typically White House counsel and senior department staff in the attorney general's office meet and work with federal circuit court nominees in the vetting and appointment process.

So at the same time that I held these judges in the highest regard, I had to wonder what, if any, role politics might play in this case.

Just as with *Brady* issues, I didn't know what I didn't know, and I still don't know.

I wondered if Graves, who was nominated by President Obama in June 2010 and confirmed in January 2011, might have some connection with Ruemmler. She, logically, would have been the person to advise the president on Graves's nomination and assist Graves in the confirmation process, preparing him for his senate hearings and doing dry runs of questioning. Ruemmler was White House counsel during his confirmation process.

Southwick, who was nominated by Bush in January 2007 and confirmed in October 2007, had served in the military in Operation Iraqi Freedom and had spent several years as deputy assistant attorney general in the civil division of the Department of Justice. With his own government experience, Southwick could be a staunch defender of the government in general—or his experience could weigh in favor of holding these prosecutors accountable. I wondered if Friedrich had been part of the confirmation process with Southwick. Friedrich's meteoric rise in the department placed him as chief of staff to Attorney General Gonzales when Southwick was nominated and confirmed.

The trial transcripts to which the judges should refer in deciding the case were replete with the names of Ruemmler and Friedrich. If they did their homework at all in the record itself, they would know who the prosecutors were, and we listed them in our brief as required so the judges could evaluate any need for recusal to take themselves off the case. Many Fifth Circuit judges could not hear Enron-related cases because of connections that required them to step back. Had these three judges noticed the names of the prosecutors before the argument? Would they deem it a relationship that required them to take themselves off the case?

In the first place, would any of these judges have the temerity to rule against the government, which rarely loses in a criminal case? The Fifth Circuit statistically affirms more than 95 percent of the criminal cases appealed.

Even more troubling to the judges could be the fact that their finding of a *Brady* violation not only would mean the reversal of the only two counts of conviction that survived at all from the government's ten-year persecution of the Merrill executives, but also would have serious personal and professional ramifications for Kathryn Ruemmler, current White House counsel; former Acting Attorney General Matthew Friedrich; Assistant US Attorney John Hemann; and the Jenner & Block partnership of Andrew Weissmann.

Upon a judicial finding of a *Brady* violation, each of these prosecutors would be in the same situation as was Stevens prosecutor Nicholas Marsh—amplified ten times because of their powerful positions. They could be investigated, prosecuted criminally, forced to resign, disbarred, or any combination thereof. Their misconduct couldn't be ignored or swept under the large Oriental rug in Attorney General Eric Holder's office any longer.

In fact, if, as Judge Sullivan had done, the Fifth Circuit found a *Brady* violation by Ruemmler, Weissmann, and Friedrich, it would ignite a legal, ethical, and political firestorm.

These judges had seen the fury in the press against the Stevens prosecutors. They had to know the effect of Judge Sullivan's order on the government and that Nicholas Marsh had committed suicide. Would these judges write an opinion that found a *Brady* violation and topple these rising superstars from their lofty, powerful political positions for the sake of getting the law right on one old prosecution? Did they even know who they were? Did they care—especially when Jim Brown was now out of prison and retired, and the case, from their perspective, was over?

If they wrongly affirmed the convictions, the judges could always distinguish their decision in *Brown* from the next case—if it mattered more what happened to the next defendant. The *Brown* defense had already beaten the wadding out of the government in this case anyway. We had already reversed twelve out of fourteen counts of conviction, obtained release for all the Merrill defendants, secured refunds of the fines and "restitution" they had been forced to pay, and had all the remaining charges dismissed in some fashion instead of a retrial.

Because of the significant ethical issues in this case, I had asked legal ethics expert Bill Hodes to review the case and make sure that we were right. Bill taught legal ethics for years as a law professor at Indiana, and coauthored the legal treatise known and used by lawyers and judges alike. *The Law of Lawyering,* by Bill and two coauthors, was the authority on legal ethical issues.

Bill was astonished at the outrageous misconduct he saw. He met Torrence and me in New Orleans the day before the argument to brainstorm and finish my preparation. We had heard that Stephan Oestreicher would argue for the government, and we were beyond ready. Jim and Nancy joined us for dinner. They had little hope of winning, but we knew that if the court followed the law properly, that was the only correct outcome.

July 5 in New Orleans was a typical sweltering, hot, humid day. We arrived at the courthouse early, got through security, checked in, and set up in the courtroom. Jim and Nancy sat behind the rail. Torrence, Bill, and I were at counsel table. I wore the same classic all-white summer suit I had worn to court in New Jersey four years earlier—the day we obtained Jim's release from prison. I was on a mission on both occasions, and it seemed symbolically fitting.

As the judges entered the courtroom and stood behind the bench, taking their seats at the conclusion of the usual "cry" from the courtroom deputy, Judges Southwick and Graves looked relaxed; Judge Smith looked tense and angry.

I stepped to the podium and began my argument. Smith was looking down, his jaw clenched. I knew something was wrong but had no clue as to what without a question from him.

I had not completed two sentences when Judge Southwick popped the first question. "Insofar as *Brady* is concerned, it seems to me the issue that we have is, how much did they know at the time, prior to trial; how much was there beyond that that was not in the summaries. You're not attacking use of summaries, are you? Are you seeing that as a fundamental error, structural error, that we have to reverse on, or are you making a different argument?"

I replied directly. "I'm not attacking summaries, per se. But this was a crime of actual words, where the words were the crime. Where words are the crime, *Brady* entitles the defendant to all of what the government knows the witnesses said the actual words were. And the government did not include in its summaries all the actual words that the call participants used. In fact, we had very little of that in any way, shape, or form. Brown was—"

Southwick interrupted. "I agree to some extent. It seems to me your argument is that the summaries, at least on two of the individuals, never indicated that they actually used the phrase along the lines of 'best efforts,' which is exactly what your fellow said."

"Correct," I injected.

"And that is fairly central," Southwick acknowledged. He continued, "But we still have to figure out the materiality, it seems to me, of these differences between the summaries and what they were actually told. Isn't that where this case turns, is just how material these differences were between what you were told and what was in the *Brady* material?"

I was fully loaded for that question and I had a lengthy explanation for why the statements the prosecutors had omitted from their pretrial disclosures were material to Jim's defense. Jim had specifically told the grand jury that he understood it to be a "best-efforts" representation, and that's precisely what the government edited out of the summaries it gave us. Meanwhile, the government actually told the jury, it's not a "best-efforts agreement."

The prosecutors had four separate witnesses testify "that there was no best-efforts agreement in this case, while they withheld from us the statements of McMahon, and Fastow, and our own counsel, saying that there was a best-efforts agreement, and Zrike tried to document it. They had even yellow-highlighted some of the best-efforts language for the district court and then did not give us that precise material that they had highlighted."

Judge Southwick was really on this. "What is in the record to show us exactly what the district judge was shown *in camera*?"

I explained that we had included the list in our brief and the most crucial yellow-highlighted statements were in our record excerpts and oral argument exhibits. The task force had actually yellow-highlighted "the *in camera* materials it gave the judge. And then certain of those, it did not even give us." I emphasized the importance of disclosing these materials to the defense—not the judge. "As the Supreme Court said in *Dennis*, it's enough to ask judges to judge; it's the advocate who's entitled to see this material and review it and decide how to use it in his preparation, from everything from deciding who to call as a witness; to how to prepare his opening statement; which witnesses to interview, if possible; which witnesses to cross-examine and how."

Southwick and Graves sat back and listened. Smith was still looking down, writing something or fidgeting. I kept pounding. "Brown went to trial with no 302, no grand jury transcript, no SEC transcript, and no quotes from any participant to the phone call that he was asked to testify about but wasn't even on. And he was questioned about a document written by an Enron employee. The indictment and the district court wrongly call it a 'Merrill Lynch document'; it wasn't. It was an Enron document that he didn't write, never saw, never had any communications with the person who wrote it. Without notes, 302s, or grand jury testimony, which is routinely recognized as *Brady* material by the Supreme Court in *Dennis* and this court in *Sype, Fisher,* and *Leka v. Portuondo,* we couldn't prepare for trial. None of the witnesses would talk to us. They were either indicted or threatened to be indicted, with frequent phone calls from prosecutors reminding them of the possibility of a pending indictment."

There was no innocent explanation for the task force's omission of the specific language they knew the defense needed, I explained. The court and the government knew no witness would speak with the defense. "That's why the court ordered the government to produce *Brady* material and summaries. But when the prosecutors even edited out of its summaries material they had highlighted to the district court, it seems inexcusable that that happened. It is particularly inexcusable when those edited out phrases included 'parking transaction' mentioned by our counsel, the 'best-efforts agreement' that Zrike tried to document. The 'parking transaction' mentioned by Dolan happens to be the one complete sentence they leave out of the highlighted material" from Dolan's 302.

I reminded them that Fuhs, whom they previously acquitted, had testified "that Brown continued to worry about the barges long after the deal had closed. Actually Brown left for vacation on December 23, shortly after the phone call. He had nothing to do with papering the transaction. He wasn't there to talk to Zrike further, who took it above his head and had it approved by his and Bayly's superior. She shepherded the deal through the process. And Zrike wouldn't talk to Brown or anyone else before the trial because the task force kept her under constant threat of indictment herself."

While I was on this roll, I looked directly at Judge Smith periodically, hoping he would ask a question. He kept looking down. I had had countless oral arguments before Judge Smith. He always participated in our annual Fifth Circuit seminar at my request—from the first year of his appointment to the bench. We had never interacted this way previously. Graves and Southwick were making eye contact with me, engaged, and asking questions. Had Smith's participation on the *Skilling* panel caused him to decide Brown's motion for new trial on entirely different facts?

I just kept going, trying to persuade the two whose attention I had and hoping Smith already "got it."

"Even without the *Brady* material we have now, over six thousand pages, this was a close case back then. The jury itself found that Brown did not substantially interfere with the administration of justice. Judge DeMoss, as you know, dissented and would have acquitted Brown, even without knowing everything that we know now. But it's the actual words of the individual call participants that were so important to Brown's defense. He had no way of knowing what they said since he wasn't on the call. There's no evidence he had talked to any of them directly. And he relied on counsel."

Judges Southwick and Graves were still listening, so I kept talking. "Not only did the prosecution have 'exclusive access to a storehouse of relevant facts,' they exploited it to their advantage. While the prosecutors told us before the trial that 'McMahon does not recall any guaranteed takeout at the end of the six-month remarketing period,' they elicited from Glisan and others testimony that 'Enron would sell the barges to Merrill Lynch based upon Jeff McMahon providing an oral guarantee that Merrill would be taken out of the transaction in six months for a set return.' They said Enron, in fact, made an oral guarantee. They repeated that theme in closing arguments and in rebuttal."

I was emphatic and specific. "Sixteen times they told the jury in closing arguments that 'McMahon made an oral guarantee,' and they referred to the testimony of Kopper and Glisan more than fifty times. Meanwhile they withheld the statements of McMahon made to six different government agents back in 2002 that contradict this testimony and the task force's arguments specifically. They withheld the statements that McMahon 'never made representation to Merrill Lynch that Enron would buy them out at a price or a set rate of return.' 'No, never guaranteed to take out Merrill Lynch with rate of return.' Specific, definitive, declarative statements directly opposite to what the government told the court, elicited testimony from its hearsay witnesses, and argued to the jury."

Meanwhile "they highlighted language like 'Andrew Fastow agreed that Enron would use its best efforts to help remarket the barges,' and didn't give us that. And then the icing on the cake, McMahon wrote a letter to the department shortly before Brown reported to prison in which he flat-out said that Glisan had lied in his testimony in this very case."

I directed them to the record excerpts in their hands. "Zrike's testimony, behind tab number two; we have three prosecutors arguing extensively that the 'written agreement between Enron and Merrill had no remarketing or best-efforts' provision.' They called it 'some suggestion from Ms. Zrike that Merrill Lynch defendants believed that all Enron had committed to do is remarket.' They said, 'You'll nowhere in these documents ever find a reference to a remarketing agreement or a best efforts' provision.' Friedrich said, 'If it's a remarketing agreement, there wouldn't have been a problem with that. If that's all it was, why wasn't it put in writing?' At the same time, they withheld testimony of Zrike, on pages 63 and 64 of her grand jury transcript, explaining the very answer to that question."

Those pages from "Katherine Zrike's grand jury testimony and her 302 explain very clearly that she tried to negotiate best efforts and remarketing in the documents but Enron's counsel said 'no that might amount to a buyback. We don't know what the remedy would be, you can't do that, and we're not going to agree to that.' And of course, the documents included an integration clause that the lawyers put in there to make sure that any prior oral representations would not be relied on by any party."

Judges Southwick and Graves were both looking concerned. Except for Judge Smith, this felt like it was going well. They were listening. Judge Smith had not said a word and still wouldn't look at me. Oestreicher was looking pained. He was the only prosecutor who had demonstrated any integrity in this case. I knew that he knew this wasn't right, but here he was forced to defend it by the "Justice Department."

I could sense that I was scoring points. "Anytime we tried to raise anything that would warrant a theory of defense instruction as to best efforts, the government objected and the district court sustained those objections. You'll nowhere in Zrike's trial testimony find even a reference to the words 'best efforts.' We didn't know what to ask her because the prosecutors hid it all."

My time to argue had flown by. My yellow light was on, indicating it was time for me to wrap up. I had saved five of my twenty minutes for rebuttal. I got in one more good swing. "Without this information, Brown was flying blind. The disclosure the Enron Task Force made as to Zrike does not even mention Jim Brown's name. Nor does it mention best efforts—much less her efforts to put it in writing and get it documented in the deal. There's example after example—"

Judge Smith looked up long enough to call, "Mr. Oestreicher?"

The appellate attorney for the department stepped to the podium and began.

"As Judge Southwick mentioned before, the issue in this case at this point is whether any difference between the government's disclosure letters and the underlying materials themselves was material. And we think the answer to that is no. And actually, we think there's very little daylight between the disclosure letters and the underlying materials when you look at the materiality issue in this case."

Sure enough, I thought. *Back to their song: it didn't matter. It was not material to the defense. They could only hope and pray the court would buy it, but it certainly shouldn't.*

Oestreicher continued, "Right now the issue is, did Mr. Brown perjure himself before the grand jury when he told the grand jury he didn't think there was a promise? The government's disclosure letters . . . disclosed that Fastow had told Merrill Lynch that 'Enron wouldn't buy back the barges, but represented instead that a third party would.' Then he went on to clarify—and we think this context is important, especially after the *Skilling* decision. The *Skilling* decision makes clear that the context of the notes is important. 'Third party' referred to LJM2, which Mr. Fastow himself controlled."

Judge Smith looked up at the mention of the *Skilling* decision, which he had helped decide. That was not a good sign. I was very concerned Smith was stuck there and did not tune in to the major factual and legal differences in the two cases.

Oestreicher continued. According to him, there were only "semantic" differences between the government's nine-page *Brady* letter signed by Ruemmler and the six thousand pages they withheld, including the yellow-highlighted material—which like Stokes and Judge Werlein, Oestreicher never even mentioned.

Judge Southwick started asking Oestreicher questions. "I can perhaps see your argument as to the Fastow notes, but what about McMahon and Zrike? It looks to me like there is more daylight between what you provided as *Brady* before trial and the more recently disclosed evidence?"

Oestreicher took full advantage of Judge Werlein's order and opinion and replied, "As to Ms. Zrike, in particular, we think the jury heard everything it was going to hear. And the district court made that clear, as well. That after having viewed all the witnesses and having seen all the testimony, it didn't see how anything would have been different as to Ms. Zrike. Now, as to Mr. McMahon, we would concede, I would think, that with the McMahon notes themselves, Mr. Brown could have attempted to impeach one declaration made to the jury through Ben Glisan."

From his tone, it sounded to me as if he were pushed, Oestreicher would confess error on the McMahon notes. *If we were only in the Ninth Circuit.*

Oestreicher continued, uninterrupted, "Mr. Glisan testified that he confronted Mr. McMahon, and McMahon confirmed that he had, in fact, made a guarantee. Mr. Brown could attempt to impeach that with Mr. McMahon's underlying notes. But it's not clear why he couldn't do the same thing with the disclosure that he already had, which is—the disclosure that he already had from the government was that 'Mr. McMahon doesn't recall there being any guarantee at the end of the six-month remarketing period.' So that is what essentially—as the district court—by the way, we think the district court's determination on materiality is due strong deference under this court's decision in *Sype*. We recognize the *Brady* inquiry is a *de novo inquiry*, but the district court found that this wouldn't have been material in the grand context of the government's evidence."

Judge Southwick had another question, indicating his serious concern. "You were talking about McMahon. Just to make sure I understand what was disclosed prior to trial, what's in the brief is three sentences perhaps. Is that the extent of what Brown would have known before trial?"

Oestreicher replied, "Four sentences in tab—yeah, it's—it's bare bones. We recognize that. And we recognize it in hindsight; it probably would have been better and safer for all involved for the government just to—for the prosecutors just to turn over the pertinent underlying documents."

This sounded even more like a confession of error—and it should be. *If the court would only press him. Oestreicher knew damn well the task force hid the ball regarding McMahon. Surely the court would not and could not ignore this.*

Judge Southwick again seemed as if he wanted to make sure Oestreicher knew the summaries should have been better. "They need to be good summaries. They need to be fair summaries."

Oestreicher nodded. "We think they were appropriate summaries. There's no question, they could have gone further. I think the McMahon letter, tab thirty where you'll see the full four-line disclosure—Mr. Brown calls 'meager.' We think it's short and to the point. And it's not as emphatic as Mr. McMahon was, but it's not clear again what difference that would have made in the grand context of this trial."

"Short and to the point"? I thought. *The summaries were completely misleading—not just useless, but a purposeful misdirection.* Then Judge Southwick took Oestreicher to the actual testimony for which Brown stood convicted of perjury and obstruction of justice and sought a new trial.

Judge Southwick continued, "Well let me look at what he allegedly perjured himself by saying. It seems to me that there are two, or perhaps three, phrases that have sent him where he is today. The question about 'whether there was a promise.' Brown said, 'It's inconsistent with my understanding of what the transaction was that there was a promise.' A little bit later maybe ellipses can hide a lot—but sometime later the short answer is, 'No, I didn't think it was a promise. I'm not aware of a promise. I'm aware of the discussions between the two companies, but I'm not—I don't think it was a promise.'"

After quoting Brown, Southwick shared his own thoughts. "I mean, this is—he didn't hedge as much as Fastow did, but he's hedging a bit, it seems to me, on what this really was. I mean, is this really—particularly based on what was not revealed that the jury, it seems to me we're at a very fine point here. I mean, Fastow was playing games with terminology and admitted it in the evidence that you have. I'm not saying that Mr. Brown was playing games, but he was saying there were promises and then there were not quite promises. Well, but how about the case on materiality and what a jury might have done with this elaboration?"

Oestreicher went to the government's favorite "evidence"—the e-mail Brown had written a year later, in an unrelated transaction, where he had said that "We had Bayly and the lawyers get on the phone with Fastow and promise to pay us back no matter what." Oestreicher harped on that for a while, arguing angrily that it proved Brown's guilt so clearly that nothing else mattered. Oestreicher elided the fact the e-mail was incorrect on its face and inadmissible multilevel hearsay, written regarding an entirely different transaction fifteen months after the barge deal.

Oestreicher argued emphatically, "He says in his own e-mail there was a promise. In so many words, he says there was a promise. And then to the grand jury he says there was no promise. So we think that viewing the entire evidence through that lens, it's difficult to see how the jury would have come to any different conclusion. We ask you to affirm the district court's thorough opinion denying Brown a new trial."

Judge Smith said, "Thank you. Ms. Powell, you saved time for rebuttal."

I practically bounded to the podium. These five minutes I'd saved would evaporate. I was hoping I didn't explode but wondering if I should.

"Mr. Oestreicher's entire argument assumes the existence of a conspiracy that the government has never proved because the original convictions were reversed, and the evidence was never tested against a valid indictment. The prosecutors walked away from all of these charges." As for materiality, I reminded the court again that "the government claimed not just once, but more than fifty times, that McMahon made a guarantee. Kopper and Glisan were the ones who testified about it. The call that is important to this appeal is the Bayly–Fastow call and all the evidence that the government hid with respect to the actual words used in that call."

They were listening, and I continued. "For example, with respect to Fastow, behind our record excerpt tab nine is a chart that puts in black, white, and red for you the pretrial *Brady* summary that we received regarding Fastow juxtaposed against the new evidence that was only found in the raw notes of Fastow. Whereas Brown testified it was 'inconsistent with his recollection, he wasn't aware of the promise,' Fastow said in the hidden material, 'the summary of the transaction was not consistent with his understanding because it included the word promise.' The Fastow notes said it was 'Enron's obligation to use best efforts to get third-party takeout. Best efforts would be to find third party to accomplish takeout.' With respect to the very Glisan e-mail on which opposing counsel relied, Fastow said he objected to the word 'obligate' in Glisan's e-mail; 'it's inconsistent with the transaction.' Every piece of evidence they withheld directly contradicted the testimony they elicited deliberately from multiple witnesses, at least Glisan, Kopper, Agent Bhatia, and one other." The hidden Fastow notes were almost identical to Brown's grand jury testimony.

It felt like I didn't even breathe so there was no opportunity to be interrupted with a question. "Everything they hid contradicted their entire theory of the case and supported Brown's theory of the defense. We couldn't even get a theory of defense instruction out of the district court because the prosecutors did such a good job of shutting down any mention of the 'best-efforts agreement' when we tried to use what little we did have with respect to Fastow to cross-examine on it."

I kept pounding. At least Judges Graves and Southwick were listening. "Nineteen pages of summary cannot fairly summarize 6,000-plus pages of testimony, 1,000 of which alone are attributable to Zrike, McMahon, and Fastow."

My voice became even more emphatic. "McMahon's testimony was the most important little bit of testimony ever. It's a big difference to say, 'I don't recall a guarantee,' than to say, 'No, never guaranteed takeout at specific rate of return. Never made a guarantee.' McMahon was definitive about that. And McMahon was never indicted. They threatened to indict him intensely before this trial, but they never indicted McMahon. When you look at the cumulative effect of all of this evidence, oh my gosh. We've got the two purported guarantors, Fastow and McMahon, who didn't even like each other, two years apart telling multiple government agents very clearly that there was a 'best-efforts' agreement in precisely the words Brown used to explain it to the grand jury."

And I didn't stop there. "The evidence they hid as to Zrike was just as bad. Our own in-house counsel had answered the precise question that the prosecutors threw on us, as if it was our burden to show why it wasn't in writing, while they hid the evidence that told us why it wasn't."

I reminded the panel, "The four witnesses who specifically testified about best efforts were Michael Kopper, Fastow's protégé who stole millions from Enron; government agent Henseler, who had interviewed McMahon and taken notes that said there was 'no guarantee,' but, of course, we didn't know that, so we couldn't ask him that; FBI lead case agent Bhatia, who would have known of all the hidden evidence; and Ben Glisan, Enron's former treasurer and the government's star witness. The government's misleading summaries, as the Supreme Court said in *Bagley*, 'wrongly represented to the defendant that the evidence does not exist and caused it to make pretrial and trial decisions on the basis of those erroneous assumptions.'"

I could see my red light was on which meant I was to sit down, and Judge Smith was now glaring at me, but I was in midsentence. "As to the Brown e-mail, even if it was admissible, it alone isn't sufficient to sustain a conviction, and *Brady* isn't a sufficiency inquiry. This was all for the jury to sort out. The e-mail, even if it was admissible, might have been some evidence of what Brown remembered a year later, but the jury should have heard all of the evidence—whether the task force agreed with it or not."

Judge Smith stopped me. He never asked a single question. He just said, "All right. Your time now has expired, Ms. Powell."

"Thank you, Your Honor."

"The case is under submission," he added.

Torrence and I hurried to pack up my argument materials as the court called the next case. Torrence, Bill Hodes, my good friend Don Richard, Jim and Nancy Brown, and I left the courtroom quickly and quietly. Oestreicher had simply disappeared. As we walked down the marble corridors of the second floor of the stately Fifth Circuit court-house, he was nowhere in sight.

All we could do now was wait. Judge Southwick was very troubled by the government's nondisclosures, especially as to McMahon and Zrike. Judge Graves seemed to have listened thoughtfully and was con-cerned. He had asked a couple of questions. Judge Smith was clearly not happy. Regardless of their wishes, I did not see how they could "write around" the law or the highlighting and the incontrovertible facts in this case.

Only six weeks later, on August 12, 2011, exactly five years since Jim's first day out of prison, the panel issued its decision. They denied our motion for new trial or even a hearing on it. Judge Smith authored the meager nine-page opinion, and Judges Southwick and Graves joined it. They applied a much more rigorous standard to review the issue than they should have. They deferred almost completely to Judge Werlein. Like the government and Judge Werlein, the opinion did not even mention the prosecutors' yellow highlighting in their own recognition of the statements as *Brady* evidence before trial. The court ignored the fact that the prosecutors had told the jury at least fifty times (sixteen in closing argument alone) that "McMahon made a guarantee," while they hid McMahon's statements that said "No—never guaranteed."

Even applying the wrong standard of review, the court held that the prosecutors "plainly suppressed" evidence "favorable to the defense." Defying logic, law, and fact, however, they said it "was not material" to Brown's defense.

I struggled to grasp how a court that I had respected so much for so long could issue an opinion as result-driven, tortured, and just plain bad as this one was. They simply refused to reverse the only two counts of conviction from this seven-year debacle of a prosecution or to hold the prosecutors accountable for their illegal, deceitful, and unethical conduct.

The prosecutors had built their entire case on their claim that "McMahon made a guarantee" and that the defendants had "hidden the truth from the lawyers." That was possible only because the prosecutors had hidden the precise, declaratory, contradictory evidence of McMahon, Fastow, and the lawyers at the same time the prosecutors kept those individuals in constant fear of being indicted so they would not and could not testify for the defense.

Judge Smith's opinion for the panel could "write around" that only by completely revising the case the government presented—as if the prosecutors had presented the case Judge Smith imagined. This meant ignoring the witnesses who actually testified, while at the same time ignoring the highlighting, just as Werlein had done, even though the highlighting was the prosecutors' own acknowledgment of these statements as *Brady* before the trial. The panel also had to ignore or work hard to distinguish the court's prior decisions.

We filed petitions for rehearing—both to the full court (*en banc*) and to the panel (of the three judges to whom we had argued). The opinion even conflicted with a recently issued opinion written by Judge Elrod in a case in which Judge Smith was also on the panel. Judge Elrod's decision came out about the time of our oral argument, and we had written the court a letter to bring it and its specific language to the panel's attention. When drafting our petition for rehearing *en banc*, Torrence went to check our favorite quote from Judge Elrod's opinion on the *Brady* point. He found that the *LaCaze* panel, including Judges Smith, Weiner, and Elrod, had revised the opinion to delete the very sentence we had wanted to cite in support of *en banc* rehearing by the full court on the *Brady* issue.

The Fifth Circuit denied our petitions for rehearing on September 19, 2011, without so much as a poll of the judges. For reasons unknown to us, Judge Elrod was recused from consideration of our *en banc* petition and could not participate.

Six weeks later, on October 26, 2011, FBI Director Robert Mueller announced that Andrew Weissmann would join the FBI as general counsel and deputy director, leaving his five-and-one-half-year partnership at Jenner & Block, in New York City. Friedrich, Ruemmler, and Weissmann had all rocketed to the top of the government from their task force launch pad of corrupted convictions with never a mention of their legacy of injustice.

We still awaited Schuelke's report and began our third petition for *writ of certiorari* to the United States Supreme Court.

– 20 –

INSIDE THE DEPARTMENT OF *IN*JUSTICE:
THE CALCULATED CORRUPTION OF JUSTICE

Judge Emmet Sullivan issued an order on November 21, 2011, amplified by all major national news outlets and providing a glimpse into a scathing report by Schuelke and Shields. Judge Sullivan quoted a few excoriating lines, declaring that the investigation and prosecution of Senator Stevens were "permeated by the systematic concealment of significant exculpatory evidence which would have independently corroborated his defense and his testimony, and seriously damaged the testimony and credibility of the government's key witness." Some of that concealment was both "willful" and "intentional." We still had to wait for the court to address issues with all of those mentioned in the report before the entire report would be available to the public, including us. The 500-plus-page report by Hank Schuelke and his law partner William Shields was released to the public as promised by Judge Sullivan on March 15, 2012.

On the same day, Alaska Senator Lisa Murkowski, Texas Senator Kay Hutchison, and four other senators in a bipartisan effort, introduced a bill that would clarify the *Brady* rule and give it some teeth. Senate Bill 2197, titled the "Fairness in Disclosure of Evidence Act," would create an enforceable law requiring the prosecution to give the defense all information that is favorable to the accused without being filtered by a prosecutor's view of what might be "material" or admissible. The act defines "covered information" to mean "any information, data, documents, evidence, or objects that may reasonably appear to be favorable to the defendant in a criminal prosecution brought by the United States."

In a massive show of support, more than a hundred former US attorneys, judges, and assistant US attorneys, including this author, signed a Call for Congress to Reform Federal Criminal Discovery, written by the nonprofit and bipartisan Constitution Project in support of this legislation, citing *Stevens* and other cases, and explaining the problems with the Department of Justice's practices. The Constitution Project letter was even signed by former Deputy Attorney General Larry Thompson, who had authored some of those department practices, had a hand in picking the Enron Task Force prosecutors, and presided over the destruction of Arthur Andersen. The American Bar Association also wrote a public letter in support of the legislation. The legislation had the support of virtually every major legal body in the country—except one.

The Department of Justice vehemently opposes this legislation.

Schuelke and Shield's 500-plus-page report is damning of the Department of Justice. The report and the responses from the attorneys investigated reveal that acting Attorney General Matthew Friedrich and his deputy, Rita Glavin, usurped the Stevens prosecution and directed use of the same tactics and gamesmanship that had worked so well for Friedrich, Ruemmler, Weissmann, and the Enron Task Force when they convicted Jim Brown and other targets.

Within a couple of weeks of being sworn in as acting attorney general in charge of the entire criminal division of the department, with Glavin at his side, Friedrich requested a memo asking for any "official acts" by Senator Stevens. He and Glavin began meeting with the PIN supervisors weekly, if not daily. The trial attorneys informed the new "front office" that most of the witnesses and the majority of the massive store of documents in the case were in Alaska. Friedrich and Glavin instructed PIN to get another thirty-day extension from the defense.

Friedrich and Glavin obtained all the charging documents, in addition to the plea agreements and transcripts of all the cooperating witnesses who had pleaded guilty in Alaska. Friedrich and Glavin met personally with the Williams & Connolly defense team.

Friedrich questioned the prosecution team as to whether the extremely broad "honest services" charge could be added to the indictment despite the recent reversal in *Brown* for its wrongful application. He and Glavin heavily edited the indictment. Then, whether for political or other reasons, Friedrich and Glavin rushed to get the case indicted—well before it was ready.

Only a few days before the indictment was filed, Friedrich upended the *Stevens* trial team. Over everyone's objections, Friedrich installed Brenda Morris as lead counsel. Friedrich overruled and circumvented PIN chief Bill Welch and put Morris in a direct line of reporting to himself and Glavin.

Within a day or two after the indictment, and long before the trial, Friedrich and Glavin met only with Morris and Welch. Friedrich wanted to know how discovery would be conducted.

Welch was shocked. In his twenty years in the department, he had never heard an assistant attorney general ask a question into that level of detail in a case or witnessed one intrude into the discovery process. Welch was even more shocked that Morris knew the question was coming, had prepared for it, and answered it without consulting Welch, her superior. Morris replied that she had "researched the law," and they would not disclose FBI 302s—the reports of witness interviews—to the defense. Welch said this was contrary to PIN's usual practices. In fact, PIN had another case in process in a nearby district where the FBI 302s had been given to the defense well in advance of the trial.

Friedrich said, "Good, possible obstruction issues."

Glavin said, "We'll have to play our cards close to the vest on this one . . . play hardball." Welch sat in stunned silence.

Welch later questioned Morris about her "research" and her position on discovery. He wanted to know who told her that "summaries" were appropriate. Morris would not tell him. She refused to give up her sources.

Not only was withholding 302s contrary to the standard practice in PIN, requiring prosecutors to create summaries was both far more dangerous and more time and labor intensive for this already rushed trial team than simply turning over the actual documents that contained the information that was favorable to the defense. It put an enormous burden on the prosecutors and created an enormous disadvantage for the defense. As Friedrich knew from the barge case, summaries left the defense with nothing it could use for cross-examination, and it allowed the prosecutors to filter, assess, eliminate, slant, and personally edit what might be important or "material" to the defense.

This extraordinary level of input from the "front office" only got worse. By August 22, 2008, before the trial began, the *Stevens* prosecutors knew that the Anchorage Police Department had begun a second investigation of key witness Bill Allen. Allen had been involved in possible human trafficking, prostitution with a minor, and obtaining a false sworn statement from that minor to protect himself. That is subornation of perjury. Welch told prosecutors Marsh and Sullivan to "get in front of the issue" and get the Anchorage Police Department file.

Somehow Friedrich and Glavin heard about it. They wanted more information. In a September 4 e-mail, Friedrich and Glavin asked if the prosecutors believed that the defense had the file yet or if there was reason to believe a subpoena had been issued for it. Welch then met with Friedrich and Glavin at 2:00 p.m. on September 5. Friedrich and Glavin told Welch "it made much more sense not to get it now because then it wouldn't be in our possession, and if Williams & Connolly never got it, well, then, we'd be in the best position possible."

Accordingly the prosecutors did not get the Anchorage file they all knew contained very damaging information about Bill Allen. This was directly contrary to the Supreme Court's constitutional mandate . . . and unethical gamesmanship, if not obstruction of justice, and they knew it.

Within an hour of Welch's meeting with Friedrich and Glavin, the trial team had a hearing by telephone conference with Judge Sullivan and the defense. It was 3:00 p.m. on September 5, 2008. The defense specifically asked for all information regarding Allen. PIN attorney Marsh had filed the government's carefully crafted opposition to any production, stating: "The government is presently not aware of any documents in its possession, custody, or control concerning any state or local investigation concerning Bill Allen."

Brenda Morris, Edward Sullivan, and Nicholas Marsh repeated those representations to the court and opposing counsel on the phone hearing—even though they all knew of the new investigation and that the Anchorage Police had offered them the 467-page file. PIN attorney Sullivan advised the court that the "department's view was that it did not have to obtain information from state authorities." Marsh even told the court that "it's not a federal matter, and we're not aware of anybody on this prosecution team working with state or local authorities in connection with this investigation."

Agent Kepner had arranged for the prosecutors to obtain the complete Anchorage file relevant to Bill Allen and the juvenile, but later that day, put a "hold" on it. Making matters worse, instead of disclosing what they knew to the defense, the prosecution disclosed the new investigation and possible additional crimes to Bill Allen himself—knowing full well that "he would come unglued." They were right; Allen was frantic. His extreme emotional condition put him right in the palm of the prosecutors' hands—desperate to make this too "go away," as the first charges had after he began "cooperating" with the Polar Pen team.

The prosecutors' last voluntary disclosure letter to the defense on September 9, just a few days later, cagily referenced the "recently closed or suspended investigation" of Allen's "sexual relationship with a juvenile," denied any role by the prosecutors in having that investigation suspended because of Allen's cooperation, and casually mentioned that Allen was the subject of a new investigation for statutory rape and had provided financial benefits to the victim.

As we had seen repeatedly in the barge case, the prosecutors added that the government was "providing additional information that was neither *Brady* nor *Giglio*." Instead of the truth, they misleadingly wrote: "In 2007, the government became aware of a suggestion that, a number of years ago, Allen asked the 'other female' to make a sworn, false statement concerning their relationship. . . . The government conducted a thorough investigation and was unable to find any evidence to support it." The *Brady* letter from Morris and Marsh added that the government was aware of "no evidence to support any suggestion" that Allen asked the other young woman "to make a false statement under oath."

Schuelke and Shields easily found just the evidence the prosecutors said did not exist. FBI Agent John Eckstein's 302 from his interview of the woman in 2004 was in the Anchorage Police file that Friedrich and Glavin told the prosecutors not to get. In addition, the government had made a sealed filing in a related case, where prosecutors had admitted that Allen had solicited a false sworn statement from the underage prostitute. These were astonishing revelations that contradicted prior representations made to the defense. Only after Bill Welch got his hands on the police file—midtrial—was this bombshell of information finally disclosed to the defense.

Putting it politely, the *Stevens* prosecutors' "*Brady* review" was "not a procedure calculated to be successful," as Marsh himself had admitted to Schuelke. Much of the alleged "*Brady* review" in *Stevens* was done by agents or lawyers not assigned to the case who didn't even know the important facts or the defense that would be presented or have reports to compare for inconsistencies. It was doomed to fail. No government lawyer, except for Assistant US Attorney Bottini, even reviewed his own handwritten notes for *Brady*. At a minimum, the procedure shows how callously and capriciously the prosecutors took their constitutional responsibilities at the same time they vehemently, repeatedly, self-righteously, and even indignantly told the federal court and the defense that they knew their *Brady* obligations and were complying with the law.

Friedrich-appointed lead counsel Morris claimed to Schuelke that she did not even know who was in charge of the *Brady* review and made no attempt to find out or to supervise it. This assertion strains credulity considering she signed the *Brady* letter, was deputy PIN chief, had been appointed lead counsel, and was being peppered with defense requests for *Brady* from day one. Despite her almost twenty years as a prosecutor in the Public Integrity Section and elsewhere, she claimed that it "didn't cross her mind to review any notes for *Brady*." Significantly, according to Morris, it was not unusual for agents to take a "first crack" at "highlight[ing]" *Brady* information, but that attorneys should always make "the final cut."

That was a news flash to this former assistant US attorney of ten years, and to Morris's own supervisor, Welch, with whom she had worked for three years. Welch, who as a practicing lawyer had only ever worked for the federal government, was "livid" when he found out that agents had reviewed evidence for *Brady*. He said that if "he had known agents were doing the *Brady–Giglio* review, he would have lost it." It was also not the practice of Alaska Assistant US Attorneys Bottini or Goeke.

The Brown team knew, however, that this was not Friedrich's first suppression of evidence favorable to the defense. As we had finally discovered, through Stokes's accidental production, Friedrich, Ruemmler, and the task force had highlighted *Brady* evidence (or had the agents do the initial highlighting), and then the prosecutors "cut" it extremely carefully. Only sophisticated, knowledgeable attorneys could have chosen the precise exculpatory words and sentences to omit—knowing exactly how valuable they would be to the defense. That is the only explanation for omissions of words like "parking transaction" and knowledge of the proposed buyback from Merrill counsel Zrike and Dolan. That is the only explanation for the task force prosecutors' determination to hide Merrill counsel's efforts to document the "best-efforts" transaction that they knew was the business deal, and their concealment of McMahon's and Fastow's statements that appeared only in raw notes, declaring there was "no guarantee" to Merrill—only an agreement to use "best efforts" to remarket the barges.

Morris's surprising revelation of the "highlighting" and "cutting" process and that attorneys "should always make the final cut" implicates Friedrich, Ruemmler, and Hemann—under Weissmann's supervision—in deleting the highlighted exculpatory language from the letter Ruemmler signed over all their names in *Brown*. Morris certainly did not learn that approach from Welch, who had supervised her for several years. She was taking her orders in *Stevens* directly from Friedrich and Glavin.

Schuelke found "evidence which compels the conclusion, and would prove beyond a reasonable doubt, that *Brady* information was intentionally withheld from the attorneys for Senator Stevens." Schuelke wrote: "The information withheld from the defense would have significantly corroborated the trial testimony of Senator Stevens and Catherine Stevens, his wife, on the central issue in the case." In addition, "it would have provided significant impeachment evidence against a key witness and challenged the very integrity of the prosecution."

Schuelke's findings of intentional concealment focused on Bottini and Goeke, and apparently on Nicholas Marsh too before his death. That appears to be because each of them clearly recognized that specific information was exculpatory, but they did not act to disclose it themselves. They deferred to their superiors instead of doing what they knew was right. Bottini was a highly respected and experienced assistant US attorney in Alaska. Goeke was much younger; to his credit, the team disclosed in full the only two grand jury transcripts Goeke was assigned to review because he had identified significant *Brady* information in both. Bottini and Goeke had both repeatedly flagged other information; however, that was never disclosed.

Surprisingly the report excused Morris.

One of the attorneys for a trial team member under investigation faulted Schuelke and Shields for accepting the "self-serving statements" of the supervisors despite their review, approval, and specific instructions at every turn. Unfortunately, however, Friedrich and Glavin were not within the purview of Schuelke's mandate from Judge Sullivan.

Schuelke merely interviewed them. They were not placed under oath, and they denied or "could not recall" any of the conversations that had so stunned Bill Welch.

From this author's perspective, anyone who had been sworn in to represent the United States of America and knew of the existence of evidence favorable to the defense in this case had a legal and ethical obligation to disclose it—on his own and in defiance of his superiors if necessary. That is certainly the standard to which the prosecutors held everyone they prosecuted for crimes—real or imagined—including Jim Brown, who they said was guilty of conspiracy and fraud because he was "silent on the Trinkle call."

Morris's excuses deserved no credit. From the moment she became lead counsel, she was responsible for the case. When Goeke again urged the disclosure to the defense of the problems with Bill Allen, she interrupted, shut him down, and snapped that the "necessary disclosure had occurred and he was 'covered.'" An excellent lawyer, she reduced herself to a pawn in Friedrich and Glavin's game with Senator Stevens's life. They deceived the defense and the court, corrupted justice, and defied the Constitution. She violated her legal and ethical obligations throughout the case.

More significantly for us, the Brown team, Schuelke's report exposed how Friedrich and Glavin usurped the entire prosecution of Stevens from the time they took office. They micromanaged even the smallest details of the presentation. They specifically ordered the withholding of exculpatory information. They strategized it all. Schuelke's report was a virtual road map of the tactics that Friedrich, Ruemmler, and their team had masterfully and corruptly employed to orchestrate the convictions of the Merrill defendants. This is also confirmed by statements filed and included in Schuelke's report by the attorneys for each of the *Stevens* prosecutors investigated.

In *Stevens*, Glavin reviewed the motions filed by Williams & Connolly and the prosecutors' responses to them. Although she and Friedrich denied any role in the discovery issues, their denials are belied by the sworn testimony of Welch, others, and some of the documents. Much of the litigation—indeed all of the important litigation—consisted of motions requesting *Brady* material and the government's oppositions to those motions. Glavin, if not Friedrich, reviewed those documents.

In addition to benching Nicholas Marsh at the last minute and assigning Brenda Morris as lead counsel to report directly to them, Friedrich and Glavin required advance submission of the scripts to be used by prosecutors in examination of witnesses and in arguments before the court. They reviewed and revised the opening statements and closing arguments of the prosecutors. They assigned each prosecutor to specific witnesses for direct and cross-examination.

When they heard that young PIN attorney Edward Sullivan sat at counsel table during Stevens's arraignment, they were "upset." They debated whether he should even remain on the pleadings. Thereafter they had "to grant Mr. Sullivan permission to sit inside the well of the court on the few occasions in which he attended the trial." Part of the carefully calculated corruption of justice was the appearance of a "bare-bones" trial team. Friedrich and Glavin told each prosecutor where he or she would sit in the courtroom and which hotel rooms each would stay in.

They took the cross-examination of Senator Stevens away from Marsh and dumped it on Bottini. They did the same with closing argument. Then they demanded a draft of Bottini's closing argument weeks before he was to give it—while he was trying to prepare Bill Allen for his trial testimony.

By October 5, Glavin had demanded that Morris "forward to her anything that came in from W & C." Morris admitted that the "front office" was "in the weeds on everything" and required her to send them letters and motions to review.

Friedrich and Glavin instructed Morris on the precise three questions she could ask General Colin Powell, a character witness for Senator Stevens.

Glavin was often present in the courtroom during the trial.

The "front office" input included the decision not to turn over 302s and not to obtain the Anchorage Police Department records that were so devastating for their witness Bill Allen. It also meant that instead of getting more than fifty-five typed 302s of interviews of Allen alone, the defense received only a "summary" a few lines long of his purported evidence. That strategic deception was quite familiar to the Brown team.

The *Stevens* trial team also drafted motions to exclude from evidence the "prior convictions of Allen, Anderson, and Williams . . . to keep out the sleazy stuff for Bill, Dave, and Rocky (sex and alcohol, and so on)." Bottini "omitted from the motion any disclosure of Mr. Allen's procurement of a false sworn statement from the minor expressly to 'smoke out how much Williams & Connolly knows'" as queried in the e-mail from Friedrich and Glavin. That motion also failed to disclose any of the *Brady* evidence they knew was in agent Eckstein's FBI 302 report of his interview or the information another assistant US attorney had filed under seal in a related case stating that the minor "signed a false affidavit at Mr. Allen's request."

Even the department's own investigation and report of the *Stevens* debacle, which finally came out four months after Schuelke's, on August 15, 2012, conceded that the prosecutors "violated the government's obligations under constitutional *Brady* principles and the Department of Justice policy."

Many similarities are now apparent between the Merrill prosecution orchestrated by Ruemmler, Friedrich, Hemann, and Weissmann, and the *Stevens* case orchestrated by Friedrich and Glavin following their extraordinary ascension to the top of the criminal division of the department.

In both cases, the prosecutors repeatedly assured the courts that they knew their obligations under *Brady* and would meet them—even when confronted with blatant failures to do so. They told the court in both cases that they had exceeded their *Brady* obligations and provided additional information only "out of an abundance of caution." They carefully crafted and edited "summaries" to create impressions far from the truth or to mislead completely.

Internal memoranda by the Stevens prosecutors before the trial showed that they had specifically identified the defense and arguments that would be made on behalf of Senator Stevens and then concealed the evidence that directly supported those defenses and arguments— and contradicted the government's own witnesses.

In Jim's case, it is equally obvious that Ruemmler, Friedrich, and Weissmann knew the precise defenses that would be raised. The Merrill defendants had all testified previously before Congress, the Enron Grand Jury, or the SEC, or had spoken to government agents. Brown personally had testified voluntarily three times. The Merrill defendants consistently testified that Merrill only agreed to accept Enron's best efforts to remarket the barges to a third party—a determinative fact that these prosecutors knew rendered the agreement lawful in every respect. So that is the very evidence that those prosecutors highlighted as *Brady* before the trial but withheld from the defense in Ruemmler's "summary" *Brady* letter ordered by Judge Werlein.

In *Brown*, Friedrich vehemently and successfully argued to Werlein that summaries were more than was required by *Brady*. Indeed, according to Friedrich in 2004, "we provided the court with what we believe that—is clear authority that providing those names is sufficient for *Brady* purposes."

So in *Stevens* and in *Brown,* the prosecutors provided the defense mere "summaries"—a few lines—of the extensive interviews, hundreds of pages of transcripts of prior testimony, and *Brady* evidence they held. Instead of quickly and easily producing usable documents, like grand jury testimony and FBI 302s, Friedrich had the *Stevens* prosecutors spend countless hours creating a short letter that was "misleading" and "inaccurate"—what most people would call false—just as they had done in *Brown.* The *Brady* letters in both cases worked to hide exculpatory information and testimony that directly contradicted the government's theory of each case, impeached their witnesses, rebutted their arguments, and supported the defense.

The department's own investigation of the *Stevens* case concedes that "the information should have been provided in the September 9, 2008, *Brady* letter; instead, that letter stated the opposite." The same was true in *Brown,* but the department refused to admit it when no federal judge would even scrutinize the facts or challenge the department at all. The Fifth Circuit recognized the *Brady* summary as to McMahon was contradicted by the truth. "'No' is not the same as 'I don't recall,'" but unlike Judge Sullivan, the Fifth Circuit did nothing about it. In both cases, the summaries the prosecution created were flat-out misleading and false.

In both cases, the most exculpatory evidence was buried in handwritten interview notes—most of which the Brown team never received. In both cases, "disclosures" by the prosecutors and even FBI 302s were written to give a misimpression of the substance of what the witness had actually said or only that portion that was helpful to the government.

In both cases, the prosecutors minimized or recharacterized evidence or information adverse to the government and rendered it useless to the defense by declaring it a "rumor" or a "suggestion," failed to disclose that a key witness shared the "same understanding" of the transaction as did the defendant, characterized documents or statements made by a defendant during the transaction and that supported his defense as being said or made "with a wink and a nod," claimed the defendant's prior words or notes were untrue and written at the time of the "crime" just to create an appearance of propriety or "CYA," and repeatedly said they would meet their *Brady* obligations, but while mouthing compliance, they actually resisted at every turn.

In both cases, even when court-ordered to produce information, they redacted too much and still concealed evidence. When they provided anything, it was with a denial that it was *Brady*. It was produced only "out of an abundance of caution," "in the spirit of cooperation," or because a portion "could arguably constitute *Brady* material." Without details, it was largely useless to the defense.

When caught hiding evidence that went to the heart of the defense and impeached key witnesses, all the department's prosecutors argued that the "substance" was disclosed in the summary or was cumulative and not *Brady*. That approach worked well for the government when Ewing Werlein was the district judge and the appeal was to the Fifth Circuit. Fortunately for Senator Stevens, Judge Sullivan was willing to work harder, dig deeper, look for the truth, and engage in some healthy skepticism. If Judge Sullivan had not held department lawyers in contempt, and then appointed Hank Schuelke, none of this would have surfaced.

And fortunately for Polar Pen defendants Kohring and Kott, they were convicted in the Ninth Circuit. Because of *Stevens*, the government was forced to admit that favorable evidence had been suppressed in both those cases because the Polar Pen prosecutors had concealed the same evidence about witness Bill Allen from those defendants also. Astonishingly Judge Sullivan's order and comments did not make a difference to the department on these cases. On remand to the district court, the government still argued that the *Brady* evidence it hid didn't matter; there was plenty of other evidence to convict Kott and Kohring, and the suppressed evidence that gutted their key witness wasn't material to the defendants. If it wasn't material, then the prosecutors didn't have to produce it, and the convictions should be affirmed.

Like Judge Werlein in *Brown*, Alaska District Judge John Sedwick bought the department's claim that the hidden evidence about Bill Allen was not material to the defense of Kott and Kohring. Sedwick denied the defendants' motions for new trial. Like Judge Werlein, Judge Sedwick went out of his way and ignored the law to find that the same evidence suppressed in *Stevens* and which warranted dismissal of all charges against the senator was not "material" to the defense of either Kott or Kohring.

Kott and Kohring each appealed to the Ninth Circuit. The Ninth Circuit vehemently disagreed with Judge Sedwick. The panel was appalled by the government's failure to learn anything from its misconduct in *Stevens*, and the panel said so. Indeed Ninth Circuit Judge Betty Fletcher was so outraged that she would have dismissed the prosecutions against Kohring and Kott also—for the same reasons as *Stevens* was dismissed. Judge Fletcher wrote that the prosecution's "reckless disregard" for the rights of the defendant and "unrepentant attitude indicates that no lesser remedial action will be effective." These "egregious violations of basic prosecutorial responsibilities" were "deeply troubling" to Judge Fletcher. She said that only the extreme remedy of dismissal was sufficient to "impress upon the government the reprehensible nature of its acts and omissions."

The release of the Schuelke report and all the press surrounding it was fortuitously timed, we hoped, to keep the overarching *Brady* issue in the forefront while the Supreme Court considered our petition for *certiorari* that we had filed on December 19, 2011. We asked the court to consider the issue of whether Brown was entitled to a new trial on perjury and obstruction because the evidence the prosecutors "plainly suppressed" really was material to his defense. The Fifth Circuit had deemed the evidence immaterial only by imagining that the task force had presented an entirely different case.

– 21 –

BOHICA? OR JUST OVER?

While we were waiting to hear from the Supreme Court on our petition for *certiorari*, supported by the *amicus* brief of significant national and state legal organizations and preeminent law professors, Brown's prosecutors surprised us with a new motion in the Fifth Circuit. Oestreicher filed a motion asking the Fifth Circuit to withdraw its mandate from the original 2006 decision. It was a novel event, and this was another way to drag it all out and make it more complicated when the government could have simply honored its agreement to Jim's resentencing years earlier. There was another kicker: the prosecutors again sought additional time in prison for Jim upon the remand to Judge Werlein.

The Fifth Circuit, through Judge Jolly (the author of the original opinion), granted the government's motion. The court also denied our request that the mandate make clear that Jim was to be resentenced to time served because of the government's original filing in the Fifth Circuit agreeing to Jim's release immediately.

Now clear that he could proceed after the five-and-one-half-year lapse, Werlein scheduled Jim's resentencing for April 19, 2012, and assigned a pretrial services officer to do an updated presentence report.

We had to make additional filings. It was another hullabaloo. The Brown household descended into a state of extreme stress and anxiety. Jim had been home and a productive member of society again for nearly six years. The government's position was wrong on the law. That was nothing new, but it would make absolutely no sense for Werlein to send Jim back to prison. Werlein obviously wanted us gone. By this time, he knew we weren't going to quit until the Supreme Court denied our last possible petition for rehearing or the proverbial "hell froze over"—whichever came last.

Sadly my confidence in the courts reaching the right result had been proved wrong so many times already that Jim and Nancy could not believe me when I assured them that Jim would not be sent back to prison. I knew that it was possible that Judge Werlein would give Stokes what he wanted again, so Jim steeled himself to go back to prison. This family, their friends, and some of their lawyers had lost all respect for and faith in the judicial system.

We prepared for sentencing and agreed Dan Hedges would speak—even that as little as necessary. According to the law, this should simply be a ministerial act of sentencing Jim to time served. I viewed it as that and wanted Jim to do the same. We had decided not to have Nancy and Jim's children come in order to reduce their anxiety and to make clear that we saw this as a routine resentencing to time served—basically an administrative act of housekeeping unworthy of any significant attention. We had also told Jim's many friends that they did not need to be there. So much had gone wrong for so long that the Browns had to prepare for the very worst yet.

Werlein was poker-faced as he came on the bench. "Please be seated. The court calls for sentencing—resentencing, technically—No. 03-363, *United States v. James A. Brown*. For the United States?"

We announced ourselves and he called us to come forward, adding, "Mr. Stokes, if you wish, take a place at the podium in case you are called on to speak."

Werlein continued, "It's correct, is it not, that the defendant was adjudged guilty of Counts Four and Five of the third superseding indictment in the matter, and the case has been remanded by the court of the appeals to resentence on those two counts?"

Dan said, "That is correct, Your Honor."

Werlein inquired, "And have you received the supplemental report, third addendum and fourth addendum, and had an opportunity for your client to read them and discuss them with you?"

Dan said, "We have read them, and we have filed with the court documents responsive to them."

Werlein was cold and formal. "I've considered both presentations, both developments, both points of view on that. I sustain the government's objection on all four points, and I deny all of the defendant's objections to the fourth addendum. The remaining objection of the defendant was a statement that the court had no discretion to sentence the defendant to other than time served. That's denied. Have I ruled on all of the objections now?"

We all agreed he had.

I had predicted that Werlein would rule against us on everything he possibly could, and I had warned Jim accordingly. Still I had a strong feeling that wouldn't make any difference this time. One thing I was sure of: Werlein wanted this litigation over and me out of his courtroom—never to return if at all possible. Sending Jim back to prison would not accomplish that objective.

We had also all decided that we would argue nothing, and Jim would not make a statement. Instead he simply wrote Werlein a short letter about how he had resumed his life, strengthened his family bonds, and was a contributing member of society. In fact, Jim had been on probation for two years longer than his entire sentence would have been. The government had supervised him, controlled his life, and jerked him around at will for almost eight years—about a deal he warned Merrill not to do. The irony would be laughable if he hadn't been through hell.

But here we were, standing in front of Judge Werlein once again, waiting to be sentenced. The entire fate of the Brown family rested on the hands of a man who was personally likable but for whom we had lost all professional regard, and the department of injustice was on its third or fourth effort to send Jim back to prison.

Werlein had another script. Most any judge would read one to impose a sentence under the inordinately complicated federal sentencing guidelines. He went through the required calculations of the sentencing guidelines and came up with "an offense level of fifteen, custody range of eighteen to twenty-four months, and a recommended fine of up to $75,000." That put Jim in a category for which he could easily be required to return to prison.

"Very well. Mr. Hedges, do you wish to make a statement on behalf of the defendant?"

"I do, Your Honor," Dan responded and kept it short. He reminded the court of Jim's "exemplary conduct the year that he was in prison" and during his highly unusual term now of almost six years on probation "with the burdens that probation entails."

Dan added, "In terms of comparable sentencing, Mr. Brown has served twelve months. Mr. Bayly served ten months and twenty-two days, and Mr. Furst served eight months and fourteen days. The government has always taken the position that Mr. Bayly and Mr. Furst had more culpability than Mr. Brown. So, looking at comparable sentences, it would appear that Mr. Brown has certainly served an appropriate time compared to some of the other defendants in the case."

Werlein looked at me. "Ms. Powell?"

"I have nothing, Your Honor."

Werlein's relief was visible. "All right. Thank you. Mr. Brown, do you wish to make a statement on your own behalf, sir?"

"No, thank you, Your Honor," Jim replied as politely as he could muster.

"All right. Thank you. Mr. Stokes, do you wish to make a statement for the government?"

Suddenly Stokes's tune had changed. "Your Honor, we'll submit on the papers we submitted to the court. We defer to the court on the specific sentence."

Werlein began again in sentencing guidelines mumbo-jumbo. "Very well. The court has considered the guidelines. Under these circumstances, where the court is entitled to give appropriate weight to the defendant's postsentencing rehabilitation, that is, after the first sentence that was imposed some years ago, and finds that a further downward departure would be reasonable in the—for at least three offense levels, to an offense level twelve, a criminal history category I and will sentence within that range. I find that this would provide a sentence that would be sufficient but not greater than necessary to achieve the sentencing objectives of 18 USC Section 3553 (a)."

Adding to the tension, Werlein seemed to be just dragging this out with us still standing there and Jim barely breathing.

"I'll state the sentence. I'll give final opportunity for any legal objection, if there are any, before it is finally imposed pursuant to the Sentencing Reform Act of 1984. It's the judgment of the court that the defendant, James Brown, is hereby committed to the custody of the Bureau of Prisons to be imprisoned for a term of time served as to each of Counts Four and Five of the third superseding indictment, such terms to run concurrently for a time-served sentence."

Werlein pronounced sentence in such a drone that we weren't sure we heard it right. Did he say "time-served"? Yes, he did.

I whispered to Jim, "It's over," and I gave Nancy a thumbs-up behind my back. Werlein was still assessing the sentence—on and on and on.

He finally set "a fine in the amount of $40,000 on each of Counts Four and Five of the third superseding indictment, to run concurrently for a total of $40,000." Jim had been required to pay a fine of $250,000 in 2005, so now the government owed Jim a refund of $210,000. Of course, the government didn't have to pay him any interest.

Judge Werlein then recognized that "Defendant Brown has effectively been on supervised release since his release from prison without any adverse incident," and he terminated Jim's probation.

It really was over. Werlein was done with us, we were done with him, and he was covering all his bases.

Werlein continued, "Is there any legal reason why the sentence should not be imposed as stated?"

Stokes wanted more assurance from the judge. "Your Honor, I would just ask—I don't believe the government intends any additional litigation here at all, I don't know about the defense, so I would ask that the court just for purposes of the record could provide some further specifics on the downward departure, which may affect the guidelines, the fine calculation as well, and I would just ask the court to just put that on the record, so if there is any appeal by the defense we have it on the record and we're able to address it at that time."

Stokes should have read the original sentencing transcript where Friedrich put his foot in it and asked Werlein for clarification. Werlein was peeved. He doesn't like to be asked questions, and he wasn't sure what Stokes was asking. "Well, I think I have fully stated what my—"

Stokes backed up. "That's right."

But Werlein took the cue in case he had missed something and rambled on. "And I adjusted seven levels, as I had in the original sentence based upon the disparity between the 2000 and 2001 guidelines. I made a further departure of three levels based upon the postsentencing conduct, which I felt deserved that type—"

Stokes interrupted again with a "Thank you."

Werlein continued, "—of adjustment in order adequately to give appropriate weight to his postsentencing rehabilitation over now a period of some years under supervision by the probation office. And I would find further that this would take—the circumstances here would fall outside of the heartland of the guidelines such as to enable such a further departure. I further, however, in the event I'm wrong in the analysis of the advisory guidelines, then I would impose the same sentence as a variant sentence, believing that it is the appropriate sentence to achieve the objectives of Section 3553(a) and constitutes a sentence that is sufficient but not greater than necessary to achieve the sentencing objectives under Section 3553 (a)."

Werlein had covered all the bases, but Stokes still wouldn't shut up and got even more ridiculous while we were still standing there. "I appreciate that, Your Honor. And solely for the purpose if the defense were to appeal this, we just simply note our objection simply for cross-appeal. Your Honor, if I may, just for the record, the court—the court may very well be aware of this, Mr. Bayly and Mr. Furst both paid a $300,000 penalty in the SEC resolution. It related to the barge case, and I don't know if that also plays in the court's consideration."

Werlein asked, "Did Mr. Brown pay?"

Stokes was stuck. He now had to make an admission that we had repeatedly argued was important. "Mr. Brown was not charged in the SEC. My point being that Mr. Furst and Mr. Bayly from the same conduct, albeit with a different agency, paid more than the fine amount the court has ordered here."

Stokes couldn't stand the fact that the government was going to have to refund $210,000 to Jim because of the wrongful fine he had paid in 2005. I was shaking my head in disgust. Jim was shuffling to keep his knees from locking and still wondering how all this was coming out. Dan was poker-faced.

Happily for us, Werlein caught Stokes's sleight of hand and showed minor irritation. "I understand, but I am now sentencing only on Counts Four and Five—which I've been ordered to do by the Court of Appeals, and I believe that this is the fine amount that's warranted with respect to those crimes."

Stokes finally stopped.

Werlein capped it off. "All right. Then pursuant to the Sentencing Reform Act of 1984, it's the judgment of the court that the sentence as stated is imposed upon James A. Brown."

With a note of sarcasm in his voice, he read the required notice. "Now, Mr. Brown, you have a right to appeal this matter. If you cannot afford a lawyer to represent you on appeal and can satisfy the court that you meet the criteria for the appointment of counsel, I will appoint a lawyer for you. Your counsel, Mr. Hedges and Ms. Powell, will advise you of your appeal rights, I'm sure. I'll give you this written notice of your appeal rights that you may take with you."

Then Werlein softened a bit. He had a personal word for Jim that, in his own way, sounded slightly apologetic. "I trust that this should bring, however, to an end this saga. And I do want to commend you, Mr. Brown, on the good things that you've indicated that you have done since the time of the original—since the time of the trial. And I'm also very happy for you and your family that your son had a good recovery and apparently is going on to do good things, so. And I wish you well and your family in that regard."

Jim thanked him, and we left the courthouse as quickly as we possibly could.

It was over. No more threat of prison.

Even if the Supreme Court granted our petition, reversed the Fifth Circuit, and sent Counts Four and Five back to Werlein for a new trial, we knew now the government would drop the case and not try it again. The perjury and obstruction charges were more lame and spurious than the conspiracy and wire fraud charges the government had no evidence to prove.

Finally after nine long years—the entire teenage years of his children's lives and one-fifth of his own, the 800-pound gorilla was off Jim's back—and Nancy's too. Sadly Jim was still a convicted felon. Their lives had been fractured forever and irreparably changed.

Our *certiorari* petition was still pending before the Supreme Court with the impressive support of multiple groups and noted law professors who had filed an *amici* brief in our behalf. The focus and additional briefing by these groups as "friends of the court" brought significant attention to the case nationally and in the Supreme Court. It is rare to have a brief by others filed in support of a petition for *certiorari*—to join in asking the court to accept the case in the first place. Briefs by others in support of a position of a particular party are far more often filed after the court has agreed to take the case.

The *amici* brief was written independently by Lucas Walker, Steven Molo, and Jeff Lamken at the superstar MoloLamken firm, with collaboration from prominent attorneys who were members of the groups who joined the brief. This brilliant brief was written initially on behalf of the New York Council of Defense Lawyers, but upon reading it, others rapidly joined, including the Texas Criminal Defense Lawyers Association, the National Association of Criminal Defense Lawyers, and prominent law school professors. The brief urged the Supreme Court to grant our petition and take the opportunity to end the use of summaries by prosecutors.

On April 13, 2012, we made the SCOTUSblog for cert petitions to watch. This blog is the leading publicly available source of information on all things Supreme Court related and run by prominent and knowledgeable lawyers who are former Supreme Court clerks. Being on the list of "petitions to watch" meant that these attorneys who focused exclusively on the Supreme Court thought our petition was "cert-worthy" and we had a good chance of having it granted.

Criminal defense attorneys who knew about the case at all wanted the Supreme Court to take this case. We desperately need a clear statement for all prosecutors that their view of materiality has no place in their determination to provide the defense with all favorable information. If the information is favorable to the defense in any way, the government should produce it. Moreover when the prosecutors take advantage of what they have hidden, specifically telling the jury the opposite, it should be deemed material and reversal of the conviction required as a clear rule of law—automatically.

From some of the questions the justices had asked in the recent oral argument of the New Orleans case of *Smith v. Cain,* it seemed they also viewed the *Brady* rule as requiring production of all information favorable to the defense. However the Supreme Court justices didn't seem to realize the reality and pervasiveness of the department's determination to allow prosecutors to filter all disclosures through the prosecutors' own biases, self-interest, or uninformed perspective of what was material to the defense. Allowing a prosecutor to filter disclosures through his view of materiality usurps the role of the defense attorney and puts the prosecutor on the bench and in the jury box too.

On April 23, 2012, only a month after the uproar caused by publication of the Schuelke report, the contemporaneous national outcry for action, and a few days after Jim's resentencing, the Supreme Court denied our *cert* petition. They were not going to take the case. All hope I had that the judicial system would render justice in this case was gone.

I hated to call Jim and Nancy, but with grace and kindness, they took the news better than I did. I don't know which is worse: that they no longer had any hope or expectation of the judicial system working or that I did—at least until then.

The courts and system of justice to which I had devoted my entire professional life—and had wanted to be a part of since I was five years old—had failed to rectify the most egregious legal wrong that I had ever personally witnessed. The only remaining possibility was that the state bar associations for each prosecutor would investigate based on the Fifth Circuit's determination that they had "plainly suppressed" evidence favorable to the defense. That alone was a finding of the violation of the plain text of the ethical rule governing prosecutors.

– 22 –

THE BAR AT ITS LOWEST

Neither the government, District Judge Werlein, nor Fifth Circuit Judges Smith, Southwick, and Graves ever acknowledged—much less discussed—the prosecutors' own highlighting of the crucial statements in recognition that the prosecutors knew this information was *Brady* before the Barge trial.

No court ever required the politically powerful former prosecutors to answer for their conduct. No court cared that they capitalized on their misconduct repeatedly. It didn't matter that they had told the contrary a hundred times to the jury and multiple courts, solicited testimony from multiple witnesses that the hidden evidence contradicted, and took advantage of having hidden the evidence even more than did the prosecutors in *Stevens*. While they contrived a crime and concealed the truth to obtain these wrongful convictions, four Merrill executives went to prison.

Upon the failure of the justice system at every level, the ethics rules required that we report the conduct of these prosecutors. The rule states, "A lawyer who knows that another lawyer has committed a violation of the Rules of Professional Conduct that raises a substantial question as to that lawyer's honesty, trustworthiness or fitness as a lawyer in other respects, shall inform the appropriate professional authority." Our cocounsel Bill Hodes, a former law professor and widely regarded legal ethics expert, was adamant that we report these violations, and he took the lead in doing so. Bill said that not only was it our legal and ethical duty to file charges, but also that we had a moral obligation as lawyer-citizens not to just sit back—silent and content—because we had at least kept Jim from going back to jail.

Because Kathryn Ruemmler was White House counsel and held a position of extreme trust, power, and influence, we filed first against her on July 24, 2012, with the Office of Bar Counsel, Board on Professional Responsibility, DC Court of Appeals. We filed shortly thereafter against Friedrich with the Texas Bar and against Weissmann with the New York Bar. We wrote a similar letter to the Justice Department's Office of Professional Responsibility against Hemann because he had returned to being an assistant US attorney in San Francisco. Bill was clear that we would be violating the ethics rules ourselves if we did not report their violations. The complaints against Ruemmler, Friedrich, and Weissmann cited the key ethics rules that each violated and attached key exhibits.

In fact, the primary ethics rule for prosecutors was even clearer than *Brady*:

Rule 3.8. Special Responsibilities of a Prosecutor.

The prosecutor in a criminal case shall

(d) make timely disclosure to the defense of all evidence or information known to the prosecutor that tends to negate the guilt of the accused or mitigates the offense, and, in connection with sentencing, disclose to the defense and to the tribunal all unprivileged mitigating information known to the prosecutor. . . .

This is the disciplinary version of the *Brady* rule. Obviously it contains no requirement that the favorable evidence be material. All evidence that tends to negate guilt or mitigate the offense must be disclosed.

Bill Hodes told the DC Bar that "Kathryn Ruemmler and her Enron Task Force colleagues carefully identified but then, deliberately and systematically, kept critical information about the most crucial first-hand witnesses from the defense and from the jury. Even if Ruemmler did not herself credit the statements of these witnesses, it was her ethical obligation and her duty under the District Court's Order to disclose the evidence so that the defense could evaluate it, and then the jury could consider it in reaching its verdict."

Bill explained that "instead of fairly summarizing 'the exculpatory information' that they possessed with respect to these witnesses and had yellow-highlighted, the prosecutors created 'summaries' that were a calculated and deceitful exercise in selective inclusion and misdirection. Indeed . . . the bogus 'summaries' put the defendants in a worse position than they were before the court's order, because the defense had to assume that exculpatory information not produced in response to a court order simply did not exist." Ruemmler not only violated several Rules of Professional Conduct governing lawyers generally and prosecutors in particular, but "she acted in defiance of a specific court order as well."

Bill informed the DC Bar of the Fifth Circuit's recent decision of August 12, 2011, holding that the Enron Task Force prosecutors "plainly suppressed" favorable information. That alone was a finding by a federal court of a violation of the plain language of Rule 3.8—the special responsibilities of a prosecutor.

We asked the state bar grievance committees to investigate these prosecutors. We cited a host of other ethics rules and violations also.

First, Ruemmler signed the *Brady* letter and falsified evidence through use of the same misleading and false summaries that misled the defense into thinking that favorable evidence was either unfavorable or nonexistent. She knowingly disobeyed "a ruling of a tribunal" when she deliberately failed to provide genuine and accurate summaries of the exculpatory evidence known to the prosecution, but instead provided bogus and actively misleading summaries that concealed rather than disclosed what the trial court ordered to be disclosed. Finally, her use of the false and misleading summaries, made worse by capitalizing on the defense team's resulting ignorance of the actual facts, is quintessentially "conduct involving dishonesty, fraud, deceit, or misrepresentation." All of this conduct violates other rules as well as 3.8.

These ethics charges are serious. In other cases, including *Stevens*, equivalent conduct by other prosecutors warranted extensive investigation. Although far too rare, other prosecutors have been fired, suspended from the practice of law, or disbarred. For example, in North Carolina several years ago, Durham County prosecutor Michael Nifong, who concealed evidence in the highly publicized Duke Lacrosse case, was disbarred, even though the case against the lacrosse players never went as far as a trial.

In 2012, Texas State District Judge Ken Anderson faced a rare "Court of Inquiry" in Texas for his misconduct as a prosecutor twenty-five years earlier. As a state district attorney, Anderson concealed evidence that caused Michael Morton's wrongful conviction and imprisonment for twenty-five years for a murder Morton did not commit. Meanwhile the real murderer was free and killed another woman. Anderson used the conviction of Morton to promote himself in his campaign for a state judgeship. Judge Anderson was arrested in May 2013. He was forced to resign from the bench, and he surrendered his law license. Found in contempt of court, Anderson was sentenced to a farcical term of imprisonment of ten days, a $500 fine, and five hundred hours of community service. He served five days.

When anyone other than a prosecutor hides evidence or makes false statements in court or to a government agent, it is a federal crime or crimes: perjury, obstruction of justice, false statements to a federal agent, subornation of perjury, witness tampering, and so on. It is beyond ironic that Jim Brown is still a felon convicted of perjury and obstruction of justice while the prosecutors hid evidence of the truth; Jeff McMahon said that it was Ben Glisan who had lied, and these prosecutors likely suborned perjury.

Bill Hodes filed essentially the same grievance against Matthew Friedrich for his statements and actions in the Barge prosecution, on July 30, 2012, with the Texas Bar. Friedrich is an honors graduate of the University of Texas School of Law. He clerked for Dallas federal Judge Royal Furgeson. He is a high-profile, well-heeled lawyer with significant connections. Especially in view of the Morton Court of Inquiry, we expected the Texas Bar to take the complaint seriously. Our mistake.

The thirty-five-page grievance against Friedrich bounced like a Super Ball. Almost by return mail, the Texas Bar sent a form letter of rejection, stating that "this office has determined that the information alleged does not demonstrate professional misconduct or an attorney disability. Accordingly this grievance has been classified as an Inquiry and has been dismissed."

Loosely translated, the letter means that the bar simply tossed the complaint in the trash can. Bill Hodes replied, citing what he called "a disturbing breakdown in the disciplinary system at the Office of Chief Disciplinary Counsel and the Board of Disciplinary Appeals." He had cited all of the rules and provided evidence including the recent Fifth

Circuit decision finding a *per se* violation of the text of Rule 3.8. We asked the bar to do its job by investigating.

Bill explained again how the prosecutors "repeatedly capitalized on having both sanitized the information produced to the defense and lied about the evidence key witnesses had given the government before trial. The prosecutors presented phony hearsay evidence directly contradicted by first-hand evidence they knew existed (and had carefully suppressed), without fear of impeachment or contradiction."

Bill was adamant. "Remarkably, in its form rejection letter, the Office of Chief Disciplinary Counsel has stated that the facts laid out in the grievance and exhibits—even if true—do not violate any disciplinary rules in Texas. And the Board of Disciplinary Appeals is of the view that the same facts on their face do not even 'allege' professional misconduct. These bald conclusions are flatly incorrect under the Rules."

This entire scenario bore no resemblance to justice. Bill repeatedly tried to get the bar's attention. "Serious prosecutorial misconduct and abuse of power eat at the heart of the justice system and undermine the rule of law. But courts are often loath to overturn convictions, and prosecutors like Matthew Friedrich have absolute immunity from suit by a wronged citizen. A stern but fairly administered disciplinary system is society's best hope. Here, it is the only hope—to curb these abuses, but so far the Texas system has failed at every turn."

All we received was silence. The Texas State Bar did not have the integrity, the fortitude, or the conscience to do what was required by the ethical rules. No one was willing to take on these powerful people or do the work needed to uncover what really happened. It was far easier to pretend it was nothing.

On August 8, 2012, we received an equally vapid response from the DC board regarding our complaint against White House Counsel Ruemmler. The DC board said nothing new had happened since 2008 when it immediately rejected a complaint filed by Jim Brown. Jim had filed that after we received the Fastow notes, but two years before we discovered the yellow highlighting and the corroborating exculpatory statements by McMahon and others. The DC board pointed to Judge Werlein's tortured opinion, ignored the Fifth Circuit's reversal of key points, and proclaimed:

> It is sufficient to state that the court did not find that the government had an obligation to disclose the documents or information described in your complaint and that the government did not deny you access to witnesses. The decision of the court of appeals, *United States v. Brown*, 650 F.3d 581 (5th Cir. 2011) also failed to find *Brady* violations.

As had the department and all the judges, the DC board ignored the prosecutor's yellow highlighting of evidence pretrial as *Brady*. The DC Bar ignored the Fifth Circuit's finding that Ruemmler and team had "plainly suppressed" evidence favorable to the defense, and that the circuit had found some of Werlein's findings clearly erroneous. Hodes appealed that rejection, but the matter is lost in political airspace in DC.

So the bar says it's up to the courts to find a *Brady* violation—which requires reversal of a criminal conviction—while the courts apply the wrong legal standard and are loath to reverse convictions, the department claims nothing is material unless the department says so, and corrupt prosecutors run rampant.

The charges against Andrew Weissmann were pending investigation by the New York Bar authorities for over a year until, unbeknownst to us, they were "referred" for further investigation to the Office of Professional Responsibility within the Department of Justice in September 2013. This was both odd and disturbing because the Department of Justice itself was defending Weissmann on the New York charges because he was deputy director/general counsel of the FBI. His defense, advanced by the department, was that the ethical rule does have a materiality requirement and must be read coextensive with the *Brady* rule. This position cannot be squared with the text of the ethical rule itself, and it would be a news flash to at least forty-seven jurisdictions, yet that is what the Department of Justice argued in Weissmann's defense in New York.

In fact, the Department of Justice now seeks to impose that rule nationwide. That is the reason for its opposition to the new legislation to codify *Brady* that has languished in Congress for two years. The Department of "Justice" wants the sole discretion to withhold whatever evidence it wants to withhold. It wants to be the sole arbiter of what is material to the defense. It wants an unlimited and unchecked License to Lie.

This is the same Office of Professional Responsibility that refused to take any action on Jim Brown's complaints about Matthew Friedrich when he was in the department, or on the grievance Bill Hodes filed against San Francisco Assistant US Attorney John Hemann. This is the same Office of Professional Responsibility that ignored our multiple letters to it and to Attorney General Holder—sent by this author and Dan Hedges. This is the same Department of Justice office that could not be trusted to investigate itself in the *Stevens* debacle, and the same department that was already defending Weissmann on the New York Bar grievance. The New York Bar just amplified the farce. The department was supposed to defend and investigate Weissmann on the New York charges?

The punt from New York to the department's Office of Professional Responsibility worked well—for Weissmann. On October 22, 2013, we received a dismissal signed by Robin Ashton in the department before we even knew New York had punted it to her.

In early 2014, we learned that Weissmann quietly left the FBI in October 2013 and joined the faculty at NYU. The department's dismissal cleared his way. Bill Hodes wrote again to Jorge Dopico, chief counsel for the first judicial department disciplinary committee, urging that New York investigate Weissmann. They did not.

As Ninth Circuit Chief Judge Alex Kozinski wrote recently in what, unfortunately, was a dissent from a denial of rehearing *en banc* on an egregious *Brady* violation: "There is an epidemic of *Brady* violations abroad in the land. Only judges can put a stop to it." Ninth Circuit Judges Pregerson, Reinhardt, Thomas, and Watford joined Kozinski's dissent, but they did not have enough votes to get the court to look at the case again and reverse it.

Our system of justice is crying for a culture change. We must return to a system in which prosecutors seek justice more than headlines and in which judges are willing to judge. Our Founding Fathers created three separate but equal branches of government. They intended the federal courts to serve as a check and balance on the executive branch, which runs the prosecutions, and on the legislative branch, which makes the laws. Judges are the only immediate and most meaningful check on wrongful prosecutions and the misconduct of prosecutors. Judges are the only ones who can spare a defendant the stress and anxiety of a trial on bogus charges or concocted facts. When judges hold prosecutors to the highest standards and provide a fair trial, they do justice.

As Judge Sullivan said, more federal judges need a "healthy dose of skepticism" when the Department of Justice attorneys rotely recite their mantra: "We're aware of our *Brady* obligations, and we will meet them." Summaries of documents crafted by prosecutors should almost never be allowed, and certainly not without painstaking judicial review and only in rare circumstances. The defense should be given the actual source documents—the grand jury testimony, the FBI 302s, and the notes that contain evidence favorable to the defense. "Summaries" are useless to the defense. They are more work for the government than providing the actual documents, and they provide far too great an opportunity for "mistakes or mischief."

One court remains over which the government, the Department of Justice, and the current and former prosecutors still have no control—the court of public opinion.

The games and tactics of Friedrich, Ruemmler, Weissmann, Caldwell, and others on the Enron Task Force should never have been tolerated by the Houston federal judiciary or by the Fifth Circuit—much less reinvigorated by Friedrich and Glavin as heads of the Criminal Division of the Department of Justice to pervert the trial of a United States Senator. There is no telling how many others have been or will be wrongly convicted as this cabal of corrupt cronies ambitiously climbs and weaves through the highest ranks of the Department of Justice, the FBI, and the White House—in between their powerful partnerships in some of our country's most prestigious and influential law firms.

What happened to the defendants in this book can happen to anyone. Judges blind to prosecutorial misconduct and abusive tactics cannot render justice.

If it were your husband, your sister, your child on trial, what should the rules be? Should the prosecutor be required to disclose everything that only he possesses that is favorable to the defense? Should those who are supposed to enforce the laws be required to abide by them?

Senate Bill 2197, the Fairness in Disclosure of Evidence Act, is still sitting in Congress. It would create a clear rule that federal prosecutors must produce all evidence favorable to the defense. Neither a prosecutor nor a judge is in a position to determine what is material to the defense. That is the defense attorney's job. Senators and congressmen respond to voter pressure. Citizens, judges, lawyers, and taxpayers need to make their voices heard on this issue.

Nicholas Marsh paid far too high a price, and so did Senator Stevens, Dan Bayly, Jim Brown, Rob Furst, Bill Fuhs, Scott Yeager, and all their families, as well as many others. Meanwhile the prosecutors truly responsible for these injustices are not only unscathed but flourishing. As long as they are free from accountability, the innocent are at risk and the public can have no confidence in our legal system. The rule of law has to apply to everyone. Unless and until these prosecutors are convicted in the court of public opinion, or disbarred, these very powerful and politically connected lawyers are still licensed to lie.

Look for yourself, the evidence is all there—in black, white, and yellow.

ETF STATEMENTS AND ARGUMENTS DIRECTLY CONTRADICTED BY EVIDENCE THE ETF PLAINLY SUPPRESSED

ETF Statements and Arguments	Evidence Concealed by ETF
Matthew Friedrich: "If it's just 'best efforts,' then it would have been okay." Tr. 4528, 4520. "There is nothing wrong with remarketing. There's nothing wrong with that. They could have gotten sale and a gain treatment on this. If it was a remarketing agreement, there wouldn't have been a problem with that." Tr. 6486.	**Andrew Fastow:** "It was [Enron's] obligation to use 'best efforts' to find 3rd Party takeout. Fastow went on to detail his sophisticated knowledge of a best efforts agreement: 'Best Efforts' - must do everything possible that a reasonable businessman would do to achieve result. . . . Best effort would be to find a 3rd Party to accomplish buy out." Dkt.1168, Raw Notes, Ex. C, at Bates 000263.

ETF Statements and Arguments	Evidence Concealed by ETF
John Hemann: "McMahon called Merrill Lynch and he cut a deal . . . and what was the deal? . . . that was the guarantee that Merrill Lynch got from [] McMahon." Tr.402-404.	**Jeffrey McMahon:** "Disc[ussion] between Andy [Fastow] & ML [Merrill Lynch]. Agreed E[nron] would use best efforts to help them sell assets." Ex. B, Raw Notes, DOJ-ENRONBARGE 000447.
Kathryn Ruemmler: "You know that Enron, through its treasurer [McMahon] and chief financial officer [Fastow], made an oral guarantee to these Merrill Lynch defendants, that they would be taken out of the barge deal by June 30th, 2000, at a guaranteed rate of return." Tr.6144.	"NO - never guaranteed to take out [Merrill Lynch] w/rate of return." *Id.* at 000493.
	000494: "Andy agreed E[nron] would help remarket [the] equity w/in next 6 months—no further commitment"
Hemann: "The purpose of the handshake . . . was to confirm the deal that had been cut by Mr. McMahon." Tr. 404. *See* Tr. 6527-28 (Friedrich: same).	**000513:** "Enron would use best efforts to help remarket the equity."
Ruemmler: "And during that conversation [between Glisan and McMahon], Mr. McMahon confirmed to Mr. Glisan that he had, in fact, given an oral guarantee to Merrill Lynch." Tr. 6159. *See* Tr.6157-58 (same).	"[A]t no time during the call [with Merrill Lynch] did Mr. Fastow ever suggest that Enron would 'repurchase' the interest from Merrill Lynch or 'guarantee' that Merrill Lynch would not incur risk of loss associated with the [Barge equity] investment." Dkt.1168, McMahon Memorandum to the SEC, Ex. D, at pp. 4-6.
Ruemmler: "So the key, . . . was Jeff McMahon. . . . Trinkle told you . . . and Glisan told you that Jeff McMahon confirmed to him that he gave that exact guarantee." Tr. 6159-60. *See* Tr. 6218-19 (same).	Mr. McMahon "reviewed the transcript of Mr. Fastow and former Enron treasurer Ben Glisan's testimony in the Lay-Skilling trial, Mr. Glisan's testimony in the trial of the Nigerian Barge case and
Ruemmler: "It was [Bayly's] job . . . to get on the phone with Mr. Fastow . . . and make sure that Mr. Fastow ratified the oral guarantee that Mr. McMahon had already given to Mr. Furst." Tr. 6168.	the FBI's Form 302 of Mr. Fastow's statements regarding the transaction. Based on that review and his knowledge of what actually occurred, [he] concluded that both men testified falsely. . . ."

EPILOGUE

Judge Sullivan's excoriation of the Stevens prosecutors and the department and his appointment of a special prosecutor were legal watersheds, but apparently water under the bridge for the department. We have a long way to go. The collateral damage from a wrongful prosecution is beyond measure. Marriages are shattered, children left parentless, careers ended, families devastated, finances ruined—all for what? To advance the career of a headline-grabbing, ethically, morally, and legally corrupt prosecutor? An indictment and corrupt criminal prosecution fracture lives forever. Minutes turn into hours, then days, months, and years—stolen and destroyed in the calculated corruption of justice by the very people who are sworn and empowered to protect us. When an innocent person is imprisoned, either the guilty person is still free or there is no guilty party at all because no actual crime has been committed. The administration of justice is robbed of any validity, and society loses from all sides. The majority of the public—and now even good lawyers—have no faith in the fairness of our system.

As for the many prosecutors discussed in this book—

Bill Welch left PIN and became senior litigation counsel with the US Attorney's Office in Massachusetts where he also prosecuted one of the Obama administration's controversial "leak" cases.

Brenda Morris left PIN, became a senior litigation counsel with the US Attorney's Office in Atlanta, then went to the private sector as deputy general counsel at Booz Allen Hamilton, the leading provider of management and technology consulting services to the government in defense, intelligence, and in civil markets.

Edward Sullivan, the youngest and least experienced of the Stevens trial team members, continued to prosecute cases for the Department's Public Integrity Section.

Alaska Assistant US Attorney James Goeke became an assistant US attorney in the state of Washington.

Veteran Alaska Assistant US Attorney Joseph Bottini remained an assistant US attorney in Alaska.

In the wake of the Schuelke report and its own investigation, the department's Office of Professional Responsibility recommended only that Bottini and Goeke be suspended without pay for forty and fifteen days respectively. Those suspensions were overturned by an administrative law judge on April 8, 2013. The department ultimately appealed that ruling and it's still pending.

Matthew Friedrich joined the prestigious Boies, Schiller & Flexner firm after leaving the department. He left Boies to practice with Freshfields Bruckhaus Deringer, an international law firm.

Rita Glavin left the department shortly after our prickly meeting with her on *Brown*. She returned briefly to the US Attorney's Office for the Southern District of New York, ironically, to teach young prosecutors. Shortly thereafter, she joined Vinson & Elkins's New York office to build its white-collar crime section, then moved to Seward & Kissel.

No one seems to have followed up on the evidence Schuelke uncovered of the involvement of Friedrich and Glavin in the *Stevens* injustice and corruption.

Patrick Stokes remains with the department and was promoted in January 2014 to head the Foreign Corrupt Practices Act Unit.

Meanwhile former Enron Task Force prosecutors were promoted into virtually every significant law enforcement division of the executive branch of our national government.

Kathryn Ruemmler, who "plainly suppressed" evidence favorable to the defense in the Barge case and prosecuted Lay–Skilling, moved between a Latham & Watkins partnership, the Department of Justice, and the White House as the president's counsel.

At the same time **Attorney General Eric Holder** claimed he wanted any *Brady* violation brought to his attention, he ignored our multiple letters regarding *Brown*—just as the department did in *Stevens*. Meanwhile, the department now seeks to include "materiality" in the applicable ethics rule nationwide, rendering *Brady* meaningless—with no counterweight or means for review.

The government's recent "deal" with **Jeff Skilling** required that Skilling drop his misconduct claims in exchange for reducing his sentence from twenty-four years to a total of fourteen years. Those misconduct claims would have shined a spotlight on Ruemmler's and possibly Sean Berkowitz's failure to give crucial exculpatory evidence to Skilling's defense counsel—a situation the Fifth Circuit had already, and repeatedly, called "troubling." Indeed the Fifth Circuit invited Skilling to file a motion for new trial to raise the prosecutors' suppression of evidence, which included a handwritten note that never made it into the FBI 302—much like that found in *Stevens*—that undercut Fastow's trial testimony. The department's deal with Skilling protects White House counsel from a hearing and scrutiny on this very problematic issue.

Lisa Monaco, who prosecuted the Enron Broadband case that was plagued with misconduct allegations and resulted in acquittals, deadlocks, and two Supreme Court reversals, became assistant White House counsel. Monaco is the president's primary legal advisor on homeland security and counterterrorism. A former advisor to FBI Director Robert Mueller, Monaco was widely rumored a frontrunner to be the first woman to head the FBI. Instead, she was President Obama's counterterrorism advisor.

Andrew Weissmann, who with Leslie Caldwell and Matthew Friedrich destroyed Arthur Andersen and oversaw the prosecution of the Merrill and Broadband defendants, became deputy director/general counsel of the FBI with Director Robert Mueller. He quietly slipped from the FBI to NYU in late 2013 without his deparure being reported by any major newspaper.

The original task force director, **Leslie Caldwell**—the "terror of a prosecutor" who destroyed Andersen—was nominated to head the Criminal Division of the Department of Justice after a partnership at Morgan Lewis. Upon Caldwell's confirmation, Enron Task Force prosecutors will have been in positions to inform, if not decide, all legal matters in the White House, the FBI, and the Criminal Division of the Department of Justice throughout the Obama administrations.

This cabal of prosecutors, who came together in early 2002, emboldened and fed each other's worst traits. In their distorted pursuit of convictions and power, they sought to win at any cost. Only they know all of the evidence they withheld and all of the laws they broke to achieve their self-defined ends. They have continued through the years to protect and encourage each other, and they have been promoted by Obama to positions of enormous power and influence despite their legacy of injustice.

Of the cases the Enron Task Force actually took to trial, all were reversed in whole or in part: *Arthur Andersen LLP v. United States*, 544 U.S. 696 (2005); *United States v. Brown*, 459 F.3d 509 (5th Cir.

2006); *United States v. Howard*, 517 F.3d 731 (5th Cir. 2008); *Yeager v. United States*, 129 S. Ct. 2360 (2009); *Hirko v. United States*, (remanded in light of *Yeager*); and *Skilling v. United States*, 130 S. Ct. 2896 (2010).

It took Broadband defendant **Scott Yeager** seven years to clear his name. He was repeatedly prosecuted even after the jury acquitted him on six counts and hung on others. Finally the Supreme Court found a double jeopardy violation, and the Fifth Circuit ordered Yeager's acquittal when the case came back to it.

The Enron Task Force prosecutors dragged Broadband defendant **Kevin Howard** through two trials. The second was reversed by District Judge Gilmore herself because their "honest services" charges failed after *Brown*. Nonetheless the prosecutors appealed that decision to the Fifth Circuit. Wisely the Fifth Circuit affirmed Judge Gilmore on that in 2008. The prosecutors then continued charging Howard by taking the Fifth Superseding Indictment against Howard, scratching out the lines about "honest services," and calling it the Sixth Superseding Indictment. They were putting him on trial a third time, using the same tactics they had against Brown. Howard couldn't take it anymore—financially, physically, or emotionally. After eight years of fighting, he pleaded guilty to one count of falsifying books and records. Judge Gilmore sentenced Howard to one year of probation and nine months of home confinement in November 2009.

Broadband defendant **Michael Krautz** was acquitted in his second trial, while another Broadband defendant, **Joe Hirko**, finally entered a guilty plea and was sentenced to sixteen months in prison.

Rex Shelby was the last to give up in the face of ten years of prosecution. He pleaded guilty to one count of insider trading in 2011 and received a sentence that included three months in a halfway house, home confinement, community service, probation, and forfeiture of

$2.6 million.

Even some of the guilty pleas the Enron Task Force prosecutors extorted had to be undone. Former Arthur Andersen partner **David Duncan**, who testified for the government to obtain the wrongful conviction of the partnership, withdrew his guilty plea on November 23, 2005. The conduct Caldwell and Weissmann told him was "criminal" actually was not.

Christopher Calger, an Enron accountant, was allowed to withdraw his guilty plea after we obtained the reversal of the honest services convictions in *Brown* because the conduct the task force alleged was not criminal.

Andrew Fastow, the true architect of the fraud within Enron, who stole millions from the company but sang for the task force chorus, served only fifty-five months in prison after Ruemmler told Judge Werlein repeatedly that Fastow "must serve ten years."

Michael Kopper, Fastow's corrupt protégé, served twenty-three months of a thirty-seven-month term in a low-security prison, while his domestic partner kept millions from Kopper's fraud.

Former Enron Treasurer **Ben Glisan** also testified for the government in the Lay–Skilling trial. He served approximately three years of a five-year term in prison, having cut more than twenty months from his sentence through good behavior and completion of a prison alcohol program with the government's agreement after he began "cooperating."

Former Barge defendants **Dan Bayly, Jim Brown, Rob Furst, Bill Fuhs**, and their families have put their lives back together as best they can following their release from prison and the belated terminations of their prosecutions. The Fifth Circuit completely acquitted Bill Fuhs.

Alaska legend and World War II hero **Ted Stevens** died in the crash of a private plane after the jury verdict was thrown out, his senate seat lost in the election, and the balance of power changed in the senate. The senator never had a chance to see the Schuelke report or to introduce the legislation he sought in his desire to make sure this did not happen to others. Alaska Senator **Lisa Murkowski** picked up that torch and introduced the Fairness in Disclosure of Evidence Act.

New York Times reporter **Kurt Eichenwald** wrote *Conspiracy of Fools*, which became a best-seller and a movie. *Wall Street Journal* reporters **John Emshwiller** and **Rebecca Smith** wrote *24 Days*, a best-seller, revealing the events that led to Enron's implosion. *Fortune* magazine writer **Bethany McLean**, who first dared question and shine a light on Enron's black box, coauthored with **Peter Elkind** *The Smartest Guys in the Room*—also a best-seller. It was made into a documentary of the prosecution's view of the case, called *Enron: The Smartest Guys in the Room*. McLean married former task force Director **Sean Berkowitz**, who became a partner at Latham & Watkins.

Not only did the Supreme Court reverse four task force cases, it also reversed a key Polar Pen conviction in *United States v. Weyhrauch*, the Alaska legislator wrongly convicted of an honest services violation, prosecuted by Bottini, Goeke, Marsh, and Sullivan.

The Ninth Circuit reversed the Polar Pen prosecutions of **Kohring** and **Kott**. In *United States v. Kohring*, 637 F.3d 895, 901 (9th Cir. 2011), Ninth Circuit Judge Sidney Thomas authored the strong decision, joined by Judge Wallace Tashima. Unlike the Fifth Circuit in Brown, they rejected the department's argument that the suppressed evidence favorable to Kohring was not "material" and reversed the district judge's denial of a new trial. Judge Betty Fletcher concurred in the reversal but said the court should have done more. Mere reversal of the conviction in light of the government's "flagrant" misconduct and "unrepentant attitude" was not enough. The prosecutors' conduct was an "affront to the integrity of our system of justice."

The Ninth Circuit has tuned into *Brady* violations and prosecutorial misconduct more than any other circuit court to date. It reversed *Milke v. Ryan, Aguilar v. Woodford, Dow v. Virga,* and in an *en banc,* forced the government to confess error in *United States v. Maloney.* It seems to be the only circuit that is willing to address prosecutorial misconduct in a meaningful way, but as Kozinski's seething dissent from the denial of rehearing *en banc* in *Olsen* makes plain, even that court is falling short. See www.Seeking-Justice.org.

FBI Agent **Chad Joy**, who blew the whistle on the *Stevens* prosecution, left the FBI shortly thereafter. FBI Agent **Mary Beth Kepner**, whose conduct in Polar Pen was highly questionable, and FBI Agent **Raju Bhatia**, who testified wrongly or falsely in the Barge case and had to have assisted in hiding the yellow-highlighted evidence, remained FBI agents.

The bipartisan, nonprofit Constitution Project periodically provides the senate committee an update on *Brady* problems, but there is still no progress with the legislation, which the Department of Justice steadfastly opposes.

The *Wall Street Journal,* the *New York Times,* the *Washington Post,* and the *LA Times* are beginning to notice and write about the *Brady* problems, but more needs to be done. *USA Today* did a feature series on prosecutorial misconduct. *Pro Publica* has done a study of wrongful convictions in New York that are attributable to prosecutorial misconduct. The *Wall Street Journal* published an editorial titled "The Department of Injustice" and others. See www.Seeking-Justice.org and www.LicensedToLie.com.

As for me, I question deeply whether I can continue to practice law. I have lost trust and faith that most of the Fifth Circuit judges will do the tedious work, keep an open mind, put ideology aside, rule based solely on the law, and ferret out the true facts in the most difficult cases if it means ruling against the government. If one can be heartbroken by a court, I am.

The various bar associations have abdicated all responsibility regarding the violations by these high-profile lawyers and prosecutors in general. If these facts are not enough to warrant a real investigation, our rules of ethics are meaningless. The Texas Bar, like the Department of Justice, has learned nothing from its prior mistakes. The only "change" in the Department of Justice has been for the worse.

Meanwhile misguided, ignorant, overzealous, ambitious, narcissistic, or dishonest current and former prosecutors, some of whom destroyed innocent people while they deliberately withheld evidence they knew contradicted their cases, are making daily decisions that affect all of our lives and the very future of this country. Their conduct stands in sharp contrast to the oath by which they swore to "uphold and defend the Constitution of the United States of America."

Much more must be required of those who have the honor, privilege, and responsibility of representing us in our courts. They hold in their hands the very lives of our citizens while they are entrusted with and wield the fearsome might and unbridled power of the Sovereign to seek Justice or deal egregious Injustice. We can make the system work better. What will it take for us to do that?

Acknowledgments

Virtually everyone I call a friend has contributed in some way to this book—from listening to my increasingly mounting concerns with the horrific failures of our justice system over the last decade to pushing and encouraging me to get this written. They all know who they are, and they have my deepest thanks.

A few must be mentioned by name for their long and invaluable assistance. Hellen Goldfarb and Torrence Lewis fought the fight with me, virtually day in and day out for more than six years of the Brown defense, countless motions, and numerous court appearances. They also assisted with the manuscript and moral support. Hellen managed to read both my hieroglyphics and my mind. Torrence was a resource in his own right, assisting with technical details, with various arguments and briefs, and with his ability to find quotes, sources, and numerous citations that are included in the book and on the website. Indiana University Mauer School of Law Professor Aviva Orenstein helped with various briefs throughout the defense, adding her brilliant command of the language to make them better. Ethics expert Bill Hodes joined us in the Brown defense, worked pro bono to file the grievances discussed in the book, and reviewed the manuscript.

I will always be grateful to my good friend Patricia Falvey, a brilliant accountant turned amazing author. She read my first outline and enthusiastically pushed me into the deep end of the literary world. She encouraged and shepherded me through the writing and publication process with priceless tips and support.

Of course, my erudite editor Dr. Janet Harris made this book better in every way and was a delightful collegue in the writing process.

Recognition of my abiding gratitude is also due my friends who are on the bench and "get it," especially Judge Alex Kozinski for writing the compelling foreword; my brother Ike for his unwavering support and various areas of expertise; my aunt Becky who was my biggest cheerleader after the loss of my parents; and my good friends Tricia Berk Dale, Ron Dale, Bernadette Schaeffler, Karen Watson, Tanya Roberts, Sharall Grissen, Teresa Cantrell, Sue Peterson, Jane Davis, Michael Adams, Don Richard, Morgan Hare, Andrew Bachenheimer, Lynn Surls, and all others who recognized the significance of this information, even read or edited drafts, and kept after me to share it with anyone who would read it.

I remain convinced that together we can make a difference. Share this book with all of your friends, talk about these issues, remember the presumption of innocence, and please continue to follow my work at www.sidneypowell.com.

SOURCES

The details in this book have been gleaned from extensive research, myriad news articles and public sources, official reports and transcripts of trials, published and unpublished decisions of various courts, transcripts of hearings and appellate arguments, and personal knowledge and experience of the author. For the actual documents and far more sources, go to LicensedToLie.com.

Foreword

Arthur Andersen LLP v. United States, 544 U.S. 696 (2005).

Berger v. United States, 295 U.S. 78 (1935).

Brady v. Maryland, 373 U.S. 83 (1963).

Bresnahan, John. "FBI Whistleblower: Violations Occurred During Ted Stevens' Probe and Trial." *Politico*, Dec. 22, 2008. http://goo.gl/VHUsfU.

"Election Results 2008." *New York Times*, Dec. 9, 2008. http://goo.gl/yt9Tyq.

An Epidemic of Prosecutor Misconduct. Center for Prosecutor Integrity (Dec. 2013).

Giglio v. United States, 405 U.S. 150 (1972).

Kyles v. Whitley, 514 U.S. 419 (1995).

Lewis, Neil A. "Tables Turned on Prosecution in Stevens Case." *New York Times*, Apr. 8, 2009, A1.

Markham, Jerry W. *A Financial History of Modern U.S. Corporate Scandals: From Enron to Reform.* Armonk: M. E. Sharpe, Inc., 2005.

Report of Henry F. Schuelke III to Hon. Emmet G. Sullivan of Investigation Conducted Pursuant to the Court's Order, dated April 7, 2009, *United States v. Theodore F. Stevens*, Crim. No. 1:08-cr-00231-EGS (D.D.C. 2009), March 15, 2012.

Smith v. Cain, 132 S. Ct. 627 (2012).

United States v. Olsen, 737 F.3d 625, 631–33 (9th Cir. 2013) (Kozinski, C.J., dissenting from denial of rehearing *en banc*).

United States v. Theodore F. Stevens, Crim. No. 1:08-cr-00231-EGS (D.D.C. 2009) [all filings, transcripts, orders, etc.].

Chapter 1: The Ultimate Toll

Department of Justice, Office of Professional Responsibility. Report. Investigation of Allegations of Prosecutorial Misconduct in *United States v. Theodore F. Stevens*, Crim. No. 08-231 (D.D.C. 2009) (EGS), August 15, 2011.

Huffington Post. "Ted Stevens Plane Crash: NTSB Issues Report on Cause of Crash that Killed Alaska Senator," July 24, 2011.

Johnson, Carrie. Interview. "Prosecutor Buckled under Pressure of Stevens Trial." *NPR*, October 1, 2010.

NTSB. Aircraft Accident Report. "August 9, 2010-Collision into Mountainous Terrain GCI Communication Corp. de Havilland DHC-3T, N455A, Aleknagik, Alaska." Report date: May 24, 2011.

Reilly, Ryan. "Ted Stevens Prosecutor Felt 'Scapegoated' during Misconduct Investigation." *TPM*, September 28, 2010.

Report of Henry F. Schuelke III to Hon. Emmet G. Sullivan of Investigation Conducted Pursuant to the Court's Order, dated April 7, 2009, *United States v. Theodore F. Stevens*, Crim. No. 1:08-cr-00231-EGS (D.D.C. 2009), March 15, 2012.

United States v. Theodore F. Stevens, Crim. No. 1:08-cr-00231-EGS (D.D.C. 2009) [all filings, transcripts, orders, etc.].

Washington, DC Metropolitan Police Department, Death Report on the Suicide of Nicholas Marsh, September 26, 2010.

———. Incident Based Event Report on the Suicide of Nicholas Marsh, September 26, 2010.

———. Investigative Supplement Report on the Suicide of Nicholas Marsh, September 27, 2010.

Yardley, William. "Former Senator Ted Stevens Killed in Plane Crash." *New York Times*, August 10, 2010.

Yost, Pete. "Nicholas Marsh, Ted Stevens Prosecutor, Dead in Apparent Suicide." *Huffington Post*, September 27, 2010.

Chapter 2: The Dangerous Fuel of Public Outrage

AIM. "AIM Report: Was Cliff Baxter Out of His Mind." July 25, 2002. Last accessed December 19, 2013. http://www.aim.org.

Banham, Russ. "Andrew Fastow Profile: How Enron Financed Its Amazing Transformation from Pipelines to Piping Hot." *CFO*, October 1, 1999. Last accessed December 19, 2013. http://www.cfo.com.

Davis, Marc. "How September 11 Affected the US Stock Market." *Investopedia*, September 9, 2011. Last accessed December 20, 2013. http://www.investopedia.com.

Dolan, William, Counsel for Jeffrey McMahon. Letter to the Department of Justice, April 25, 2005.

Eichenwald, Kurt. "Justice Department to Form Task Force to Investigate Collapse of Enron." *New York Times*, January 10, 2002.

Emshwiller, John, "Enron Transaction with Entity Run by Executive Raises Questions." *Wall Street Journal*, November 5, 2001.

———. "Enron's Skilling Cites Stock-Price Plunge as Main Reason for Leaving CEO Post." *Wall Street Journal*, August 16, 2001.

———. "Enron's Stock, Bonds Take a Beating Following Release of Financial Filing." *Wall Street Journal*, November 21, 2001.

Emshwiller, John, and Rebecca Smith. "Behind Enron's Fall: A Culture of Secrecy Which Cost the Firm Its Investors' Trust." *Wall Street Journal*, December 5, 2001.

———. "Enron Posts Surprise 3rd-Quarter Loss after Investment, Asset Write-Downs." *Wall Street Journal*, October 17, 2001.

———. "SEC Elevates Enron Financial Inquiry to the Level of Formal Investigation." *Wall Street Journal*, November 1, 2001.

Federal Bureau of Investigation. "Crime in the Suites: A Look Back at the Enron Case." December 13, 2006. Last accessed December 31, 2013. http://www.fbi.gov.

———. Press Release. "Assistant Director Press Conference with Attorney General." September 17, 2003. Last accessed December 20, 2013. http://www.fbi.gov.

Flood, Mary. "Changing of Guard for Enron Task Force." *Houston Chronicle*, March 2, 2004.

Hamburger, Tom. "Ex-Andersen Official Says He May Take Fifth To Avoid Testifying at Congressional Hearing." *Wall Street Journal*, January 23, 2002.

Kirkendall, Tom, Counsel for Jeffrey McMahon. Confidential Memorandum to the SEC dated July 28, 2006.

McLean, Bethany. "Is Enron Overpriced?" *Fortune*, March 5, 2001.

McLean, Bethany, and Peter Elkin. *The Smartest Guys in the Room*. New York: Portfolio Trade, 2004.

Office of the Medical Examiner of Harris County, Texas. Autopsy Report of John C. Baxter, January 25, 2002.

Oppel Jr., Richard A., and Kurt Eichenwald. "Enron Paid Out 'Retention' Bonuses before Bankruptcy Filing." *New York Times*, December 6, 2013.

Oppel Jr., Richard A., and Andrew Ross Sorkin. "Enron's Collapse: The Overview: Enron Corporation Files Largest U.S. Claim for Bankruptcy." *New York Times*, December 3, 2001.

Pelligrini, Frank. "Bush's Enron Problem." *Time*, January 10, 2002. Last accessed December 19, 2013. http://www.time.com.

Skilling's Renewed Motion for Change of Venue, *United States v. Skilling*, Crim. No. H-04-25 (S.D. Tex. January 4, 2006).

Smith, Rebecca, and John Emshwiller. *24 Days: How Two* Wall Street Journal *Reporters Uncovered the Lies that Destroyed Faith in Corporate America*. New York: Harper-Collins, 2003.

——. "Combination of Brilliance, Overconfidence Helped Enron Fly High and Plummet Fast." *Wall Street Journal*, November 8, 2001.

——. "Enron Aims to Be Easier Read in Order to Refuel Enthusiasm." *Wall Street Journal*, August 28, 2001.

——. "Enron CFO's Tie to a Partnership Resulted in Big Profits for the Firm." *Wall Street Journal*, October 19, 2001.

——. "Enron Faces Collapse as Dynegy Bolts and Stock Price, Credit Standing Dive." *Wall Street Journal*, November 29, 2001.

——. "Enron Replaces Fastow as Finance Chief; Move Follows Concerns over Partnership Deals." *Wall Street Journal*, October 25, 2001.

——. "Enron Says Its Links to a Partnership Led to $1.2 Billion Equity Reduction." *Wall Street Journal*, October 18, 2001.

Third Interim Report of Neil Batson, Court Appointed [Enron Bankruptcy] Examiner, *In re Enron Corp.*, Civil No. 01-16034 (S.D.N.Y. June 30, 2003) (AJG).

Wilke, John. "Michael Chertoff Cut His Teeth Facing Down New York Mob Bosses." *Wall Street Journal,* March 15, 2002.

Chapter 3: The Task Force Annihilates Arthur Andersen

AIM. "AIM Report: Was Cliff Baxter Out of His Mind." July 25, 2002. Last accessed December 19, 2013. http://www.aim.org.

Ainslie, Elizabeth K. *Indicting Corporations Revisited: Lessons of the Arthur Andersen Prosecution*, 43 American Criminal Law Review 107 (2006).

Brown, Ken. "Called to Account: Indictment of Andersen in Shredding Case Puts Its Future in Question." *Wall Street Journal,* March 15, 2002.

Department of Justice. Press Release. "Enron Task Force Director Leslie Caldwell to Step Down, Andrew Weissmann Named Director." March 1, 2004. Last accessed December 31, 2013. http://www.justice.gov.

Eichenwald, Kurt. "Four at Merrill Accused of an Enron Fraud." *New York Times*, March 18, 2003.

Federal Bureau of Investigation. Press Release. "Three Top Former Merrill Lynch Executives Charged with Conspiracy, Obstruction of Justice, Perjury in Enron Investigation." September 17, 2003. Last accessed December 19, 2013. http://www.fbi.

Jacoby, Mary. "Enron Task Force Is Glue That Binds As Ex-Prosecutors Rise through the DOJ Ranks." *Main Justice*, August 21, 2013. Last accessed December 19, 2013. http://www.mainjustice.com.

Office of the Medical Examiner of Harris County, Texas. Autopsy Report of John C. Baxter, January 25, 2002.

Oregan, Chris. "The Mysterious Death of an Enron Executive." *CBS News*, April 10, 2010. Last accessed December 19, 2013. http://www.cbsnews.com.

Press Conference Announcing Arthur Andersen Indictment, March 14, 2002. Last accessed December 19, 2013. http://www.justice. gov and http://www.c-spanvideo.org.

Press Conference Transcript. "Accounting Firm Arthur Andersen Found Guilty of Obstruction." CNN.com, June 15, 2002. Last accessed December 20, 2013. http://transcripts.cnn.com.

S.E.C. v. Merrill Lynch & Co., Inc., Daniel H. Bayly, et.al., Civil Action No. H-03-0946 (S.D. Tex. February 12, 2003).

United States Court of Appeals for the Fifth Federal Circuit Judicial Workload Statistics, 2011-2013. Last accessed December 19, 2013. http://www.ca5.uscourts.gov.

United States v. Arthur Andersen, Dockets [including all publicly available filings, transcripts, orders, opinions, etc.] in S.D. Tex., Fifth Circuit, and Supreme Court.

United States v. James A. Brown, Dockets [including all filings, transcripts, orders, opinions, etc.] in S.D. Tex., Fifth Circuit, and Supreme Court.

USA Today. "Prosecutors Far from Finished." October 3, 2002.

Weil, Jonathan, and Alexi Barrionuevo. "Arthur Andersen Is Convicted on Obstruction-of-Justice Count." Wall Street Journal, June 16, 2002.

Chapter 4: Wanna Buy a Barge?

Flood, Mary. "All-Star Team of Federal Prosecutors Says Merits of Cases Outweighs Hardships." Houston Chronicle, December 19, 2004.

———. "Changing of Guard for Enron Task Force." Houston Chronicle, March 2, 2004.

———. "For 114, A Time to Watch and Wait." Houston Chronicle, December 2, 2004.

———. "Prosecution Beefs up Its Team." Houston Chronicle, September 26, 2003.

Johnson, Carrie. "Taking Enron to Task." *Washington Post*, January 18, 2006.

United States v. Arthur Andersen, Dockets [including all publicly available filings, transcripts, orders, opinions, etc.] in S.D. Tex., Fifth Circuit, and Supreme Court.

United States v. James A. Brown, Dockets [including all filings, transcripts, orders, opinions, etc.] in S.D. Tex., Fifth Circuit, and Supreme Court.

Chapter 5: Nailing the Coffins

Cohen, Laurie P. "In the Crossfire: Prosecutors' Tough New Tactics Turn Firms Against Employees." *Wall Street Journal*, June 4, 2004.

Fowler, Tom. "Verdict from Houston Residents Polled: Guilty." *Houston Chronicle*, July 19, 2004.

Glater, Jonathan D. "Deterrence Strategy Prosecutors Send a Message: Are Executives Listening?" *New York Times*, March 14, 2004.

Thomsen, Linda Chatman, Deputy Director, Division of Enforcement US Securities and Exchange Commission. Statement. July 8, 2004. Last accessed December 20, 2013. http://www.sec.gov.

United States v. Arthur Andersen, Dockets [including all publicly available filings, transcripts, orders, opinions, etc.] in S.D. Tex., Fifth Circuit, and Supreme Court.

United States v. James A. Brown, Dockets [including all filings, transcripts, orders, opinions, etc.] in S.D. Tex., Fifth Circuit, and Supreme Court.

Chapter 6: Facing the Firing Squad

Thomas, Landon. "A Banker's 'Nightmare' after Enron Deal." *New York Times*, November 21, 2005.

United States v. James A. Brown, Dockets [including all filings, transcripts, orders, opinions, etc.] in S.D. Tex., Fifth Circuit, and Supreme Court.

Chapter 7: Supreme Reversals

Ainslie, Elizabeth K. "Indicting Corporations Revisited: Lessons of the Arthur Andersen Prosecution." 43 American Criminal Law Review. 107 (2006).

Bass, Jack. *Unlikely Heroes.* New York: Simon & Schuster, 1981.

Lane, Charles. "Justices Overturn Andersen Conviction." *Washington Post*, June 1, 2005.

United States v. Arthur Andersen, Dockets [including all publicly available filings, transcripts, orders, opinions, etc.] in S.D. Tex., Fifth Circuit, and Supreme Court.

Chapter 8: The Longest Year

Barrionuevo, Alexi. "Enron Chiefs Guilty of Fraud and Conspiracy." *New York Times*, May 25, 2006.

Barrionuevo, Alexi, and Simon Romero. "US Levels a Final Blast at Enron Chiefs." *New York Times*, May 16, 2006.

Department of Justice. Enron Trial Exhibits and Press Releases. Last accessed December 31, 2013. http://www.justice.gov.

———. Press Release. July 18, 2005. Last accessed December 31, 2013. http://www.justice.gov.

———. Press Release. "Attorney General Alberto R. Gonzales Honors Employees and Others at the Department of Justice's Annual Awards Ceremony." September 12, 2006. Last accessed December 20, 2013. http://www.justice.gov.

Emshwiller, John. "'Benron' behind Bars." *Wall Street Journal*, April 21, 2007.

Flood, Mary. "Enron Prosecutors Showed Jurors Wrong Tape." *Houston Chronicle*, May 2, 2005.

———. "Enron Task Force Receives Top Award." *Houston Chronicle*, September 17, 2006.

———. "Task Force Gets New Chief." *Houston Chronicle*, July 19, 2005.

———. "Witness Takes Stand Despite Being Target." *Houston Chronicle*, June 9, 2005.

Hays, Kristen. "Task Force Prosecutors Prosper after Enron Case." *Houston Chronicle*, November 2, 2006.

Johnson, Carrie. "Enron Trial Prosecutor Joins Latham." *Washington Post*, February 5, 2007.

———. "Enron's Lay Dies of Heart Attack." *Washington Post*, July 6, 2006.

———. "US Ends Prosecution of Arthur Andersen." *Washington Post*, November 23, 2005.

Kirkendall, Tom. "A Crushing Defeat for the Enron Task Force." *Houston's Clear Thinkers*, July 21, 2005.

———. "The Enron Broadband Trial." *Houston's Clear Thinkers*, April 16, 2005.

———. "The Fifth Circuit Rules in the Skilling Appeal." *Houston's Clear Thinkers*, January 7, 2009.

———. "Finessing Witness Intimidation." *Houston's Clear Thinkers*, October 17, 2005.

———. "More Misconduct by the Enron Task Force?" *Houston's Clear Thinkers*, July 9, 2005.

———. "More on the Enron Broadband Trial Closing Arguments." *Houston's Clear Thinkers*, July 15, 2005.

———. "The Stench of Prosecutorial Abuse." *Houston's Clear Thinkers*, March 14, 2008.

Lattman, Peter. "Enron: Ruemmler's Ramble and Petrocelli's Passion." *Wall Street Journal* (blog), May 16, 2006. Last accessed January 8, 2014. http://blogs.wsj.com.

Pincus, Walter. "Silence Angers Judiciary Panel." *Washington Post*, June 7, 2006. Last accessed December 20, 2013. http://www.washingtonpost.com.

United States v. Jeffrey K. Skilling, Dockets [including all publicly available filings, transcripts, orders, opinions, etc.] in S.D. Tex., Fifth Circuit, and Supreme Court.

Wall Street Journal. "Status of Enron Cases," January 28, 2006. Last accessed January 9, 2014. http://online.wsj.com.

Weissmann, Andrew. "Heading to Jenner, Not Looking Back at Enron." *20 Corporate Crime Reporter* 9, no. 10 (2006). Last accessed December 20, 2013. http://www.corporatecrimereporter.com.

Chapter 9: BOHICA

Hays, Kristen. "Task Force Prosecutors Prosper after Enron Case." *Houston Chronicle*, November 2, 2006.

Johnson, Carrie. "Enron Trial Prosecutor Joins Latham." *Washington Post*, February 5, 2007.

Regents of University of California v. Credit Suisse First Boston (USA), Inc., 482 F.3d 372 (5th Cir. 2007), *cert. denied*, 552 U.S. 1170 (2008).

United States v. James A. Brown, Dockets [including all filings, transcripts, orders, opinions, etc.] in S.D. Tex., Fifth Circuit, and Supreme Court.

Chapter 10: More Surprises

Berger v. United States, 295 U.S. 78 (1935).

Dolan, William, Counsel for Jeffrey McMahon, Letter to the Department of Justice, April 25, 2005.

Gutierrez, Pedro Ruz. "Matthew Friedrich Named New DOJ Criminal Division Chief." *Legal Times* (blog), May 22, 2008. Last accessed January 8, 2014. http://legaltimes.typepad.com.

Jordan, Lara Jakes, "Ted Stevens Indicted On 7 Criminal Charges." *Huffington Post*, July 29, 2008.

Kirkendall, Tom, Counsel for Jeffrey McMahon. Confidential Memorandum to the SEC, July 28, 2006.

Report of Henry F. Schuelke III to Hon. Emmet G. Sullivan of Investigation Conducted Pursuant to the Court's Order, dated April 7, 2009, *United States v. Theodore F. Stevens*, Crim. No. 1:08-cr-00231-EGS (D.D.C. 2009), March 15, 2012.

Senator Ted Stevens Indictment Press Conference, July 27, 2008. Last accessed December 20, 2013. http://www.c-spanvideo.org.

Senator Ted Stevens Verdict News Conference, October 27, 2008. Last accessed December 20, 2013. http://www.c-spanvideo.org.

Transcript of Senator Ted Stevens Indictment Press Conference, July 27, 2008. Last accessed December 27, 2013. http://www.justice.gov.

United States v. James A. Brown, Dockets [including all filings, transcripts, orders, opinions, etc.] in S.D. Tex., Fifth Circuit, and Supreme Court.

United States v. Jeffrey K. Skilling, Dockets [including all publicly available filings, transcripts, orders, opinions, etc.] in S.D. Tex., Fifth Circuit, and Supreme Court.

United States v. Theodore F. Stevens, Crim. No. 1:08-cr-00231-EGS (D.D.C. 2009) [all filings, transcripts, orders, etc.].

Chapter 11: The Department of *In*justice: Polar Pen Melts

Barret, Devlin, and Nedra Pickler. "Ted Stevens Conviction to Be Voided." *Huffington Post*, April 1, 2009.

Department of Justice. Press Release. "Statement of Attorney General Eric Holder Regarding *United States v. Theodore F. Stevens*," April 1, 2009. Last accessed December 21, 2013. http://www.justice.gov.

Editorial Opinion. "The Ted Stevens Scandal." *Wall Street Journal*, April 2, 2009.

Press Release. "Statement of Williams & Connolly LLP, Brendan V. Sullivan and Robert M. Cary, Counsel to Senator Ted Stevens," April 1, 2009.

Report of Henry F. Schuelke III to Hon. Emmet G. Sullivan of Investigation Conducted Pursuant to the Court's Order, dated April 7, 2009, *United States v. Theodore F. Stevens*, Crim. No. 1:08-cr-00231-EGS (D.D.C. 2009), March 15, 2012.

Totenberg, Nina. Audio. "Justice Dept. Seeks to Void Stevens' Conviction." *NPR*, April 1, 2009. Last accessed December 20, 2013. http://www.npr.org.

United States v. Theodore F. Stevens, Crim. No. 1:08-cr-00231-EGS (D.D.C. 2009) [all filings, transcripts, orders, etc.].

Chapter 12: The Mother of All Hearings

Report of Henry F. Schuelke III to Hon. Emmet G. Sullivan of Investigation Conducted Pursuant to the Court's Order, dated April 7, 2009, *United States v. Theodore F. Stevens*, Crim. No. 1:08-cr-00231-EGS (D.D.C. 2009), March 15, 2012.

United States v. Theodore F. Stevens, Crim. No. 1:08-cr-00231-EGS (D.D.C. 2009) [all filings, transcripts, orders, etc.].

Chapter 13: Move Over, DOJ: There's a New Sheriff in Town

Jacoby, Mary. "Stevens Prosecutors Select All-Star Cast of Criminal Defense Lawyers." *Main Justice*, April 22, 2009. Last accessed December 20, 2013. http://www.mainjustice.com.

Palazzolo, Joe. "Help Wanted: Public Integrity Chief." *Main Justice*, November 5, 2009. Last accessed December 27, 2013. http://www.mainjustice.com.

——. "Life after Stevens." *Main Justice*, April 15, 2010. Last accessed December 27, 2013. http://www.mainjustice.com.

——. "A Long Career near the Spotlight but Rarely in It." *Main Justice*, July 17, 2009. Last accessed December 20, 2013. http://www.mainjustice.com.

———. "Stevens Prosecutor Exits DC." *Main Justice,* September 25, 2009. Last accessed December 27, 2013. http://www.mainjustice.com.

———. "Sullivan Grants Subpoena Power in Probe of Stevens Prosecutors." *Main Justice,* July 28, 2009. Last accessed December 27, 2013. http://www.mainjustice.com.

Powell, Sidney, Counsel for James A. Brown. Letter to Attorney General Eric Holder, July 20, 2010.

Report of Henry F. Schuelke III to Hon. Emmet G. Sullivan of Investigation Conducted Pursuant to the Court's Order, dated April 7, 2009, *United States v. Theodore F. Stevens,* Crim. No. 1:08-cr-00231-EGS (D.D.C. 2009), March 15, 2012.

Savage, Charles. "Prosecutor Who Pursued Stevens Case Kills Himself." *New York Times,* September 28, 2010.

Scarcella, Mike. "Vinson & Elkins Picks up DOJ's Rita Glavin." *Legal Times* (blog), March 1, 2010. Last accessed January 8, 2014. http://legaltimes.typepad.com.

Supreme Court Oral Argument Transcript, *Black v. United States,* No. 08-876 (Deccember 8, 2009). Last accessed December 27, 2013. http://www.oyez.org.

Supreme Court Oral Argument Transcript, *Weyhrauch v. United States,* No. 08-1196 (Deccember 8, 2009). Last accessed December 27, 2013. http://www.oyez.org.

United States v. Jeffrey K. Skilling, Dockets [including all publicly available filings, transcripts, orders, opinions, etc.] in S.D. Tex., Fifth Circuit, and Supreme Court.

United States v. Theodore F. Stevens, Crim. No. 1:08-cr-00231-EGS (D.D.C. 2009) [all filings, transcripts, orders, etc.].

Yeager v. United States, 557 U.S. 110 (2009).

Chapter 14: Another Try

Huffington Post. "Kathryn Ruemmler: Meet Obama's New White House Counsel," June 2, 2011.

Ogden, David. "Guidance for Prosecutors Regarding Criminal Discovery," January 4, 2010. Last accessed December 26, 2013. http://www.justice.gov.

Report of Henry F. Schuelke III to Hon. Emmet G. Sullivan of Investigation Conducted Pursuant to the Court's Order, dated April 7, 2009, *United States v. Theodore F. Stevens*, Crim. No. 08-231 (D.D.C. 2009) (EGS), March 15, 2012.

United States v. James A. Brown, Dockets [including all filings, transcripts, orders, opinions, etc.] in S.D. Tex., Fifth Circuit, and Supreme Court.

United States v. Jeffrey K. Skilling, Dockets [including all publicly available filings, transcripts, orders, opinions, etc.] in S.D. Tex., Fifth Circuit, and Supreme Court.

Chapter 15: The Big Oops

United States v. James A. Brown, Dockets [including all filings, transcripts, orders, opinions, etc.] in S.D. Tex., Fifth Circuit, and Supreme Court.

Chapter 16: Truth Be Told

United States v. James A. Brown, Dockets [including all filings, transcripts, orders, opinions, etc.] in S.D. Tex., Fifth Circuit, and Supreme Court.

Chapter 17: The Beginning of the End

Black v. United States, 561 U.S. 465 (2010).

Flood, Mary. "For 114, A Time to Watch and Wait." *Houston Chronicle*, December 2, 2004.

United States v. James A. Brown, Dockets [including all filings, transcripts, orders, opinions, etc.] in S.D. Tex., Fifth Circuit, and Supreme Court.

United States v. Jeffrey K. Skilling, Dockets [including all publicly available filings, transcripts, orders, opinions, etc.] in S.D. Tex., Fifth Circuit, and Supreme Court.

Weyhrauch v. United States, 561 U.S. 476 (2010).

Chapter 18: The End of the Beginning

United States v. James A. Brown, Dockets [including all filings, transcripts, orders, opinions, etc.] in S.D. Tex., Fifth Circuit, and Supreme Court.

Chapter 19: The Last Chance

Federal Bureau of Investigation. Press Release. "Andrew Weissmann Appointed as FBI's General Counsel." October 26, 2011. Last accessed December 26, 2013. http://www.fbi.gov.

Huffington Post. "Kathryn Ruemmler: Meet Obama's New White House Counsel," June 2, 2011.

Johnson, Carrie. Interview. "Prosecutor Buckled under Pressure of Stevens Trial." *NPR*, October 1, 2010.

LaCaze v. Warden, 645 F.3d 728 (5th Cir.), opinion amended on denial of rehearing *en banc* 647 F.3d 1175 (5th Cir. 2011).

Reilly, Ryan. "Ted Stevens Prosecutor Felt 'Scapegoated' during Misconduct Investigation." *TPM*, September 28, 2010.

Savage, Charles. "Prosecutor Who Pursued Stevens Case Kills Himself." *New York Times*, September 28, 2010.

Southwick, Leslie. *The Nominee: A Political and Spiritual Journey.* Jackson: UP Mississippi, 2013.

United States v. James A. Brown, Dockets [including all filings, transcripts, orders, opinions, etc.] in S.D. Tex., Fifth Circuit, and Supreme Court.

United States v. Theodore F. Stevens, Crim. No. 1:08-cr-00231-EGS (D.D.C. 2009) [all filings, transcripts, orders, etc.].

Yost, Pete. "Nicholas Marsh, Ted Stevens Prosecutor, Dead in Apparent Suicide." *Huffington Post,* September 27, 2010.

Chapter 20: Inside the Department of *In*justice: The Calculated Corruption of Justice

Department of Justice, Office of Professional Responsibility. Report. "Investigation of Allegations of Prosecutorial Misconduct in *United States v. Theodore F. Stevens.*" Crim. No. 08-231 (D.D.C. 2009) (EGS), August 15, 2011.

Fairness in Disclosure of Evidence Act of 2012, S. 2197, 112th Cong. (2012).

Johnson, Carrie. "Report: Prosecutors Hid Evidence In Ted Stevens Case." *NPR,* March 15, 2012. Last accessed December 27, 2013. http://www.npr.org.

Letter to the Judiciary Committee of the U.S. Senate, June 5, 2012, on behalf of the Constitution Project et al.

Report of Henry F. Schuelke III to Hon. Emmet G. Sullivan of Investigation Conducted Pursuant to the Court's Order, dated April 7, 2009, *United States v. Theodore F. Stevens*, Crim. No. 1:08-cr-00231-EGS (D.D.C. 2009), March 15, 2012.

United States v. James A. Brown, Dockets [including all filings, transcripts, orders, opinions, etc.] in S.D. Tex., Fifth Circuit, and Supreme Court.

United States v. Kohring, 637 F.3d 895 (9th Cir. 2011).

United States v. Kott, 423 Fed.Appx. 736 (9th Cir. March 24, 2011).

United States v. Theodore F. Stevens, Crim. No. 1:08-cr-00231-EGS (D.D.C. 2009) [all filings, transcripts, orders, etc.].

Wall Street Journal. "Department of Injustice," March 16, 2012.

Chapter 21: BOHICA? Or Just Over?

Bush, Matthew. "Petitions to Watch: Conference of April 20, 2012." *SCOTUS* (blog), April 13, 2012, 10:55 p.m. Last accessed December 27, 2013. http://www.scotusblog.com.

Supreme Court Oral Argument Transcript, *Smith v. Cain*, No. 10-8145 (November 8, 2011). Last accessed December 27, 2013. http://www.oyez.org.

United States v. James A. Brown, Dockets [including all filings, transcripts, orders, opinions, etc.] in S.D. Tex., Fifth Circuit, and Supreme Court.

Chapter 22: The Bar at Its Lowest and Epilogue

Bloomberg News. "Enron Exec Who Pleaded Guilty Is Freed," January 3, 2009.

Brubaker Calkin, Laurel. "Ex-Enron Broadband Executive Rex Shelby Sentenced for Insider Trading." *Bloomberg News,* March 28, 2011.

Department of Justice. Press Release. *"United States v. Howard,"* June 1, 2009. Last accessed December 27, 2013. http://www.justice.gov.

Emshwiller, John. "'Benron' Behind Bars." *Wall Street Journal*, April 21, 2007.

———. "Deal to Cut Ex-Enron CEO's Sentence." *Wall Street Journal*, May 8, 2013.

Flood, Mary. "Ex-Enron Broadband Figure Given Home Confinement." *Houston Chronicle*, November 2, 2009.

Fowler, Tom. "Legal Cloud Beginning to Lift for Fastow." *Houston Chronicle*, November 25, 2011.

Hays, Kristen. "Judge Allows Withdrawal of Guilty Plea in Enron Case." *Houston Chronicle*, April 3, 2007.

——. "Prosecutors File for Dismissal against Former Enron Executive." *Houston Chronicle*, March 31, 2007.

Hodes, William. Letter to The State Bar of Texas in regard to Complaint of Matthew Friedrich, November 29, 2012.

Hodes, William, and Sidney Powell. Complaint of Andrew Weissmann to the Office of the New York State Bar, July 31, 2012.

——. Complaint of John Hemann to the Office of Professional Responsibility, Department of Justice, August 29, 2012.

——. Complaint of Kathryn Ruemmler to the Office of the District of Columbia Bar, July 24, 2012.

——. Complaint of Matthew Friedrich to the Office of the Texas State Bar, July 30, 2012.

Jacoby, Mary. "Enron Task Force Is Glue That Binds As Ex-Prosecutors Rise Through the DOJ Ranks." *Main Justice*, August 21, 2013. Last accessed December 19, 2013. http://www.mainjustice.com.

Kapos, Shia. "Enron Tale Author Bethany McLean Has a New Book She Wrote from Her Chicago Home." *Crain's Chicago Business*, November 15, 2010.

Koons, Jennifer. "DOJ Appeal Says Judge Erred in Reversing Stevens Prosecutors' Discipline." *Main Justice,* September 17, 2013. Last accessed December 27, 2013. http://www.mainjustice.com.

——. "Former Enron Prosecutor Tapped to Head Criminal Division." *Main Justice,* September 17, 2013. Last accessed December 27, 2013. http://www.mainjustice.com.

Morris, Brenda. Profile. *LinkedIn.* Last accessed December 27, 2013. http://www.linkedin.com.

Oxfeld, Jesse. "The Happiest Gal in the Courtroom." *New York Magazine*, August 7, 2006.

Palazzolo, Joe. "Life after Stevens. "*Main Justice,* April 15, 2010. Last accessed December 27, 2013. http://www.mainjustice.com.

Pickler, Nedra. "Kathryn Ruemmler, Obama's Top Lawyer, Is Sticking around a Little Longer than Expected." *Huffington Post,* December 4, 2013.

Reilly, Ryan. "Leslie Caldwell Is Obama's Nominee to Head DOJ's Criminal Division." *Huffington Post,* September 17, 2013.

Savage, Charlie. "Judge Reverses Suspensions of Prosecutors in Stevens Case." *New York Times,* April 7, 2013.

Seward & Kissel. Press Release. "Prominent Former Federal Prosecutors Rita Glavin and Michael Considine Join Seward & Kissel to Head New Practice Group," February 12, 2011. Last accessed December 27, 2013. http://www.reuters.com.

United States v. Howard, 517 F.3d 731 (5th Cir. 2008).

United States v. Olsen, 737 F.3d 625, 631–33 (9th Cir. 2013) (Kozinski, C.J., dissenting from denial of rehearing *en banc*).

United States v. Jeffrey K. Skilling, Dockets [including all publicly available filings, transcripts, orders, opinions, etc.] in S.D. Tex., Fifth Circuit, and Supreme Court.

"This book is a testament to the human will to struggle against overwhelming odds to fight a wrong and a cautionary tale to all—that true justice doesn't just exist as an abstraction apart from us. True justice *is* us, making it real through our own actions and our own vigilance against the powerful who cavalierly threaten to take it away."

—Michael Adams, PhD
University Distinguished Teaching Associate Professor of English
Associate Director, James A. Michener Center for Writers,
University of Texas–Austin

"I have covered hundreds of court cases over the years and have witnessed far too often the kind of duplicity and governmental heavy-handedness Ms. Powell describes in her well-written book, *Licensed to Lie*."

—Hugh Aynesworth
journalist, historian, four-time Pulitzer Prize finalist
author, *November 22, 1963: Witness to History*

"*Licensed to Lie* reads like a cross between investigative journalism and court-room drama. The takeaway is that both Bushies and Obamaites should be very afraid. Over the last few years, a coterie of vicious and unethical prosecutors who are unfit to practice law has been harbored within and enabled by the now ironically named Department of Justice."

—William Hodes
Professor of Law Emeritus, Indiana University
coauthor, *The Law of Lawyering*

"Sidney Powell brings a subject to light which is often overlooked or even purposely hidden: the unfair tactic that some prosecutors have used to secure a conviction. As a prosecutor for over twenty-nine years in the state courts of Texas, I am aware of both the possibilities for unfairness to the accused and of the pressures on some prosecutors to win cases. Sidney is able to articulate these issues in telling the stories within *Licensed to Lie*, and she holds up a clear moral and legal compass to point us all toward prosecution according to law and the facts."

—Jane Davis
former lead prosecutor, District Courts, Bexar County, Texas
First Assistant to the Guadalupe County Attorney

INDEX
LICENSED TO LIE